NETWORK POWER

NETWORK POWER

JAPAN AND ASIA

. . . .

EDITED BY

Peter J. Katzenstein

and **Takashi Shiraishi**

Cornell University Press   ITHACA AND LONDON

The costs of publishing this book have been defrayed in part by the 1996 Hiromi Arisawa Memorial Awards from the Books on Japan Fund with respect to *Edo and Paris: Urban Life and the State in the Early Modern Era* and *"Rich Nation, Strong Army": National Security and the Technological Transformation of Japan* published by Cornell University Press. The Awards are financed by The Japan Foundation from generous donations contributed by Japanese individuals and companies.

First published 1997 by Cornell University Press
First printing, Cornell Paperbacks, 1997

Printed in the United States of America

Library of Congress Cataloging-in-Publication Data

Network power : Japan and Asia / Peter J. Katzenstein and Takashi Shiraishi, eds.
    p. cm.
  Includes indexes.
  ISBN 0-8014-3314-2 (alk. paper). — ISBN 0-8014-8373-5 (pbk. : alk. paper)
  1. Asia—Relations—Japan. 2. Japan—Relations—ASIA. I. Katzenstein, Peter J. II. Shiraishi, Takashi, 1950– .
DS33.4.J3N47 1996
303.48'25'052—DC20   96-38802

Cloth printing: 10 9 8 7 6 5 4 3 2 1

Paperback printing: 10 9 8 7 6 5 4 3 2

TO OUR STUDENTS

Contents

Preface

The end of the cold war has reshaped the dynamics of Asian regionalism. This is one of two volumes. *Tamed Power: Germany in Europe* is a companion to *Network Power: Japan and Asia* that also explores the role of regions in world politics.

This book is the outgrowth of the contributors' attempts to explain to their students and themselves the effects of a global system in flux. When Takeshi Hamashita visited Cornell University in the fall semester of 1991, Victor Koschmann and Takashi Shiraishi prevailed on him to join them in teaching a new undergraduate seminar on Asian regionalism. Intrigued by the seminar's approach and reading list, Peter Katzenstein audited the class. Based on discussion about what was, and what was not, natural or problematic about Asian regionalism, Katzenstein, Koschmann, and Shiraishi offered in the spring of 1993 a large undergraduate lecture course that compared Japan's position in Asia with Germany's in Europe. And Katzenstein attended a new and challenging graduate seminar that Mark Selden had developed on Asian regionalism at SUNY Binghamton in the spring of 1994. Through their teaching interests this project thus attracted several participants.

It was easy to recruit others. T. J. Pempel had been a colleague at Cornell for many years, and he and Katzenstein had co-taught courses on Japanese and German public policy. In the 1980s Bruce Cumings and Peter Evans had discussed with Katzenstein a coauthored volume on regionalism; Saya Shiraishi's exciting research on mass culture in Asia made her another ideal candidate for empirical analyses. Susumu Yamakage had been a colleague of Takashi Shiraishi at the University of Tokyo and had met Katzenstein in Cambridge, Massachusetts, in 1988–89.

The Global Transistions Program of Cornell's Center for International Studies, the Walter S. Carpenter, Jr., Chair of International Studies, and the Suntory Foundation provided necessary funds for two workshops, which Cornell's Southeast Asia Program hosted in May 1994 and March 1995 for graduate students and faculty at Cornell and SUNY Binghamton. This book contains papers rewritten after they had been presented at these two workshops.

We thank Cornell University and the Suntory Foundation for their financial support, and our colleagues and students at Cornell and SUNY Binghamton as well as other workshop participants for their spirited debate and constructive criticism. Peter Katzenstein thanks the Wissenschaftskolleg Berlin for providing the support and quiet that made it possible to complete the final revisions of this manuscript in the early fall of 1996.

Political and professorial grumbling to the contrary notwithstanding, this book illustrates, we believe, one of the greatest strengths of American universities: the close connection between research interests and classroom teaching. Hence we dedicate this book to our undergraduate students at Cornell.

P.J.K.
T.S.

Ithaca, New York

Contributors

BRUCE CUMINGS is the John Evans Professor of International History and Politics and the Director of the Center for International and Comparative Studies at Northwestern University.

RICHARD F. DONER is Professor of Political Science at Emory University.

TAKESHI HAMASHITA is Professor of history and Director of the Institute of Oriental Studies at the University of Tokyo.

PETER J. KATZENSTEIN is the Walter S. Carpenter, Jr., Professor of International Studies at Cornell.

J. VICTOR KOSCHMANN is Professor of History at Cornell University.

T. J. PEMPEL is the Boeing Professor of International Studies in the Henry M. Jackson School of International Studies at the University of Washington, Seattle.

MARK SELDEN is Professor of Sociology at the State University of New York, Binghamton.

SAYA S. SHIRAISHI is Professor of Anthropology at Kyoto Bunkyo University.

TAKASHI SHIRAISHI is Professor at the Center for Southeast Asian Studies, Kyoto University.

SUSUMU YAMAKAGE is Professor of International Relations at the University of Tokyo.

NETWORK POWER

Introduction: Asian Regionalism in Comparative Perspective

PETER J. KATZENSTEIN

The end of the cold war and the breakup of the Soviet Union have reduced the impact of global factors in world politics and increased the weight of regional forces, which were operating all along under the surface of superpower confrontation. In Asia, as elsewhere, international and national developments are increasingly shaped by regional dynamics. This book explores how these regional dynamics affect, and are affected by, Japan's changing position in Asia. Asia refers here to Northeast and Southeast Asia, in national terms Japan, China, South Korea, Hong Kong, Taiwan, Singapore, Thailand, Malaysia, Indonesia, the Philippines, Vietnam, Laos, Kampuchea, and Burma. In this introduction I place Asian regionalism in a broader comparative perspective. In subsequent chapters the other contributors analyze how two hegemonic systems—one centered on China, the other on the United States and Britain—have shaped Japan and Asia historically and continue to do so today.

Will Asia tend toward openness or closure? I believe that Asian regionalism, which is not well institutionalized, tends toward openness. Because

For comments and suggestions on previous drafts I thank Richard Doner, Peter Gourevitch, Stephan Haggard, Natasha Hamilton-Hart, Kozo Kato, Mary F. Katzenstein, Jonathan Kirshner, Mark Selden, Takashi Shiraishi, Steve Webber, an anonymous reviewer for Cornell University Press, and especially Andrew MacIntyre. For their critical comments I am also indebted to the participants in the May 19–20, 1994, and March 31–April 1, 1995, meetings of the Cornell workshop "Japan in Asia" and the participants in the Cornell Government Department Political Economy Research Colloquium.

Two different versions of this chapter have been published under the title "Regionalism in Comparative Perspective," in *Cooperation and Conflict* 31.(2): 123–59, and as ARENA Working Paper no.1 (Oslo, January 1996).

1

Figure I-1. The Asia-Pacific region

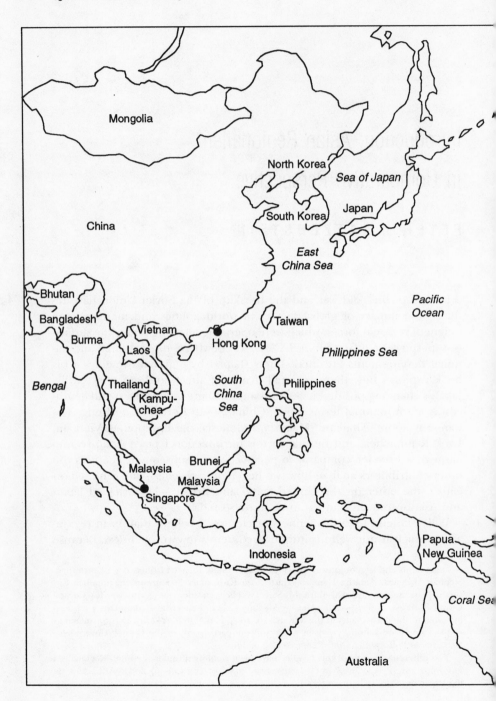

Asian states operate by consensus rather than by majority vote in regional organizations, each individual Asian state exercises effective veto power over all collective actions. Indeed, the history of formal regional institutions in Asia is a history of failures so conspicuous, in comparison to Europe, that they beg for explanation.[1] It would, however, be a great mistake to compare European "success" with Asian "failure." Such a Eurocentric view invites the unwarranted assumption that the European experience sets the standard by which Asian regionalism should be measured. It is better to acknowledge instead that the scope, depth, and character of regional integration processes vary across numerous dimensions and among world regions. Comparative analysis thus highlights the inclusive character of Asia's network-style integration in contrast to the exclusive character of Europe's emphasis on formal institutions.

Will Asia be dominated by Japan, China, or the United States? Will it be divided by ethnically based coalitions that express Chinese and non-Chinese identities? Will it be transformed by globalization? Or will Asia be shaped by multiple centers of influence? The future of Asian regionalism is open. A neomercantilist perspective, for example, emphasizes that the world is moving toward relatively closed regional blocs. In this view, since 1990 often associated with the Malaysian prime minister Mahathir Mohamad, Japan is at the brink of reestablishing a new version of the Co-Prosperity Sphere. The opposing, liberal view holds instead that global markets are creating convergent pressures across all national boundaries and regional divides. This book takes a middle position between these perspectives. Distinctive world regions are shaping national polities and policies, but these regions are indelibly linked to both the larger international system of which they are a part and to the different national systems that constitute them. On balance the essays collected here highlight the factors that are creating an Asia that is marked by multiple networks and centers of influence, including Japan, China, and the United States.

Asia illustrates the growth of regional forces in world affairs. Intra-Asian trade, for example, has increased greatly in the 1980s and 1990s.[2] Al-

---

[1] Ernst Haas was the first to compare integration processes across different world regions. An article initially published in 1961 compares Europe with the Soviet bloc, the Arab world, and the western hemisphere. Asia is barely mentioned. See Haas, "International Integration: The European and the Universal Process," in *International Political Communities: An Anthology* (Garden City, N.Y.: Doubleday, Anchor Books, 1966), pp. 93–129.

[2] Walter Hatch and Kozo Yamamura, *Asia in Japan's Embrace: Building a Regional Production Alliance* (New York: Cambridge University Press, 1996). Kenichi Ohmae, "The Rise of the Region State," *Foreign Affairs* 72 (Spring 1993): 78–88, and *The End of the Nation State: The Rise of Regional Economics* (New York: Free Press, 1995); James Fallows, *Looking at the Sun: The Rise of the New Asian Economic and Political System* (New York: Pantheon, 1994), pp. 241–406; Masato Hayashida, Masatoshi Inouchi, Hisahiro Kanayama, and Eimon Ueda, "East Asia and Japan:

though the United States still buys nearly a quarter of total Asian exports, more than two-fifths of Asian trade now occurs within the region. And intra-Asian trade is growing four times faster than Asian exports to the United States.[3] Political developments also point to the growing importance of regional factors. Japan's backing of South Korean trade minister Kim Chul Su as the "Asian" candidate, running against a "European" and a "North American" candidate, has helped make the selection of the first director general of the new World Trade Organization (WTO) an exercise in regional international politics.[4] And well-placed, senior individuals in government and business are seriously considering endorsing Japan's admission to the East Asian Economic Caucus (EAEC) as long as Australia and New Zealand are also permitted to participate. Thus they hope to dilute the "Asian" character of the caucus while also creating a diplomatic instrument perhaps capable of opposing, if necessary, some of the political objectives of the United States in Asia.[5] Moreover, Asians tend to feel at home with Japan and the Japanese. A Taiwanese businessman expressed this feeling well: "You see how much more natural it is for us to work with the Japanese. We both write with characters. We're in the same time zone. Their service technicians can come over in an hour if there is a problem. It feels more natural [working] with them."[6]

Such real-world developments, Joseph Nye noted, had already begun to

---

Japan's Diplomatic Strategy for Seeking Common Interests," IIPS Policy Paper 134E, Tokyo, September 1994; Ross Garnaut and Peter Drysdale, with John Kunkel, eds., *Asia Pacific Regionalism: Readings in International Economic Relations* (New York: Harper Educational, 1994); Vera Simone and Anne Thompson Feraru, *The Asian Pacific: Political and Economic Development in a Global Context* (White Plains, N.Y.: Longman, 1995), pp. 263–366; Mark Borthwick, *Pacific Century: The Emergence of Modern Pacific Asia* (Boulder, Colo.: Westview Press, 1992), pp. 507–46; C. Fred Bergsten and Marcus Noland, eds., *Pacific Dynamism and the International Economic System* (Washington D.C.: Institute for International Economics, 1993); Jeffrey A. Frankel and Miles Kahler, eds., *Regionalism and Rivalry: Japan and the United States in Pacific Asia* (Chicago: University of Chicago Press, 1993); Davis B. Bobrow, Steve Chan and Simon Reich, "Southeast Asian Prospects and Realities: American Hopes and Fears" (Graduate School of International Affairs, University of Pittsburgh, 1995); and Suisheng Zhao, "Soft versus Structured Realism: Organizational Forms of Cooperation in Asia Pacific" (paper presented at the APSA annual meeting, Chicago, September 2, 1995).

[3] Carnegie Endowment Study Group, *Defining a Pacific Community* (New York: Carnegie Endowment for International Peace, 1994), pp. 17–19.

[4] David P. Hamilton, "Japan Supports Korean to Lead Trade Council," *Wall Street Journal,* October 7, 1994, A8; David E. Sanger, "For Clinton Administration, An Exercise in Diplomacy," *New York Times*, February 26, 1995, A8.

[5] Edward J. Lincoln, "Japan's Rapidly Emerging Strategy toward Asia" (Paris: OECD, Research Program on Globalisation and Regionalisation, 1992), p. 19; "Keidanren Mulls Asia Caucus Stand," *International Herald Tribune*, December 8, 1994, p. 19.

[6] Quoted in Fallows, *Looking at the Sun*, p. 250.

outpace the grasp of both policymakers and scholars.[7] For policymakers the attraction of regionalism then was the same as it is now. Regionalism offers a stepping-stone for international cooperation between unsatisfactory national approaches on the one hand and unworkable universal schemes on the other. For scholars regionalism brings into clearer focus an important intersection of the international and domestic factors that shape the economic fortunes, security interests, and cultural identities of political actors.

Theories based on Western, and especially West European experience, have been of little use in making sense of Asian regionalism. Functionalist integration theories, for example, underline the importance of institutional learning on the changing attitudes and behavior of political elites.[8] A core proposition of functionalist theory stipulates a spillover effect that ineluctably transforms economic unions to political ones. The history of Asian regionalism in the 1980s and 1990s appears to contradict that expectation.[9]

Rationalist theories of cooperation, typically based on the analytical imagery of economics, seek to specify how the conflicting interests of different actors can reach a dynamic, cooperative equilibrium. Such theories underline how institutions can promote cooperation by reducing transaction costs, enhancing transparency, assuring verification, and diminishing uncertainty. Richard Doner illustrates some aspects of this style of analysis in Chapter 6.

Despite its power, this perspective gives only partial insight into the network style of Asian regionalism, as Victor Koschmann argues in Chapter 2. Asian regionalism is often also characterized by overlapping identities of economic and political actors. Strategic interactions in or through economic institutions can alter the views actors hold of what each can do separately and what both can accomplish jointly. Distinct identities thus can become blurred, leading to subsequent redefinitions of interests as actors discuss joint possibilities that may reflect a redefinition of identities, objectives, and strategies.[10]

---

[7] Joseph S. Nye, Jr., Introduction to *International Regionalism*, ed. Nye (Boston: Little, Brown, 1968), pp. v–vi. See also *International Political Communities*.

[8] Haas, "International Integration," pp. 93–129.

[9] Even in Europe, however, the primary impetus to move from the 1992 program toward the Maastricht Treaty was not a functional spillover from "low" issues of the economy to "high" issues of diplomacy. Instead the political effects of German unification proved decisive for another attempt at furthering European integration.

[10] Charles Sabel, John Griffin, and Richard E. Deeg, "Making Money Talk: Toward a New Debtor-Creditor Relation in German Banking" (paper presented at the Conference on Relational Investing, Center for Law and Economic Studies, Columbia University School of Law,

For different reasons the analytical perspectives of specialists in the fields of international relations and Asian politics do not fully grasp regional developments. International relations scholars favor sparse structural models. Realists, for example, seek to derive from the bipolar or multipolar structure of the international system certain outcomes that either constrain or determine the foreign policy of states. Liberals focus on the effect international institutions have on reducing uncertainty and transaction costs and thus influencing the foreign policy of states. Such international perspectives largely ignore local, national, or regional political contexts central to those writing on Asian regionalism. Asian specialists typically err in the opposite direction. They rarely take into account the broader comparative and international perspective in which regional developments are taking place.

In this book we seek to avoid these analytical biases in two ways. First, we eschew the self-consciously sparse theories of international relations. The contributors offer instead an interdisciplinary approach that situates the subject of Japan and Asia in terms of political economy and culture (Chapters 1 and 2), and then combines a historical approach (Chapters 3 through 5) with an institutional analysis applied to issues of political economy (Chapters 6 and 9), culture (Chapter 7), and security (Chapter 8).

Second, in the two framing chapters we place the analysis of Asian regionalism and Japan's changing role in Asia in a comparative perspective by focusing, in this Introduction, on a comparison of Asian and European integration and in the Conclusion, on a comparison of Japan's position in Asia with Germany's position in Europe. Our intent in the two chapters is to highlight what is distinctive about these topics. Thus, we seek to avoid both the international relations scholar's perception of the alleged "im-

---

New York, May 6–7, 1993). The insurmountable problems that purely functional or rationalist explanations have with Asian regionalism have both theoretical and empirical roots. For the former, see Stephan Haggard, "Thinking about Regionalism: The Politics of Minilateralism in Asia and the Americas" (paper presented at the annual meeting of the American Political Science Association, New York, September 1–4, 1994), pp. 12–18, 22–24, 35–38. For the latter, see Joseph M. Grieco, "Variation in Regional Economic Institutions in Western Europe, East Asia and the Americas: Magnitude and Sources" (Political Science Department, Duke University, 1994), pp. 15–20. Analytically and empirically comprehensive overviews are offered in Richard Higgott, "Introduction: Ideas, Interests and Identity in the Asia-Pacific," *Pacific Review* 7.4 (1994): 361–83, and Peter F. Cowhey, "Pacific Trade Relations after the Cold War: GATT, NAFTA, ASEAN and APEC," in *U.S.–Japan Relations and International Institutions after the Cold War*, ed. Peter Gourevitch, Takashi Inoguchi, and Courtney Purrington (forthcoming). For a particularly interesting application of role theory to Japan and Asian regionalism, see Martin W. Sampson III and Stephen G. Walker, "Cultural Norms and National Roles: A Comparison of Japan and France," in *Role Theory and Foreign Policy Analysis*, ed. Stephen G. Walker (Durham, N.C.: Duke University Press, 1987), pp. 105–22.

maturity" of Asian integration and the Asian specialist's view of Japan's as a potentially threatening regional hegemon. By taking a comparative perspective we can acknowledge the distinctiveness of Asian regionalism and Japan's changing role within it but rejects equally appeals to universality or uniqueness.

Here I explore what we mean by "Asia" and articulate the rationale for the historical and institutional approach that this book takes. Then I argue that Asian regionalism is characterized by dynamic developments in markets rather than by formal political institutions. I explain the weak formal institutionalization of Asian regionalism in terms of international power and norms and in terms of domestic state structures and illustrate these two determinants of Asian regionalism with specific reference to the Association of South-East Asian Nations (ASEAN) on the one hand and Japanese corporate structures and the networks of overseas Chinese on the other. I conclude by outlining some of the implications of my argumet and by summarizing the chapters that follow.

Japan and Asia

Situating the subject matter of this book is easy geographically and difficult analytically. Geographically, "Japan" refers to the four home islands as well as Okinawa; "Asia," to Northeast and Southeast Asia including China. But analytically, one is forced to admit that geographic designations are not "real," "natural," or "essential." They are socially constructed and politically contested and are thus open to change and vulnerable to the twin risks of reification and relativization. This book's historical and institutional approach is designed to avoid those risks.

Geography is not destiny. In the 1990s the "West" encompasses, among others, Western Europe and the United States as well as Canada, New Zealand, and Australia—and Japan. The "Islamic world" describes, not a precise geographic location in the Middle East, but refers to an area that stretches from Indonesia to Nigeria and North Africa. As products of culture and economics, history and politics, geographically defined regions change over time.

This is true also of Asia, which is too heterogeneous to permit the invocation of a "real," "natural," or "essential" Asian identity. Southeast Asia, for example, is divided deeply along ethnic, linguistic, and religious lines; and in Northeast Asia the effects of Japanese colonialism and imperialism have left sharply diverging historical memories and interpretations. Such divisions inhibit the emergence of a common Asian identity. Outside Asia such an Asian identity is easier to define, for example, in East

Africa (where it designates primarily Pakistanis and Indians), in global political contexts (such as China's rallying of the Third World in the 1957 Afro-Asian People's Solidarity Conference held in Cairo), and in the United States (where it may become a powerful symbol of collective identity for a growing Asian American community).

The changeable nature of regional designations makes intelligible the numerous definitional ambiguities that characterize the writings of international relations specialists on the subject of regionalism. Louis Cantori and Steven Spiegel's inclusive definition emphasizes geographic proximity, international interaction, common bonds (ethnic, linguistic, cultural, social, and historical), and a sense of identity that is sometimes heightened by the actions and attitudes of states external to the region.[11] They admit that this list does not lend itself easily to the clear-cut identification of regional subsystems. Similarly, Bruce Russett's five criteria (social and cultural homogeneity, political attitudes or external behavior, political institutions, economic interdependence, and geographical proximity) also illustrate the ambiguity of region as an organizing concept.[12] Based on the work of twenty-two scholars, William Thompson's composite definition[13] lists twenty-one commonly cited attributes, which he condenses to a list of three necessary and sufficient conditions for defining a regional subsystem: general geographic proximity, regularity and intensity of interactions, and shared perceptions of the regional subsystem as a distinctive theater of operations. These three conditions overlap with those Cantori and Spiegel and Russett have identified; however, they contain some serious analytical ambiguities: "general geographic proximity" is a stretchable term; "particular degrees of regularity of interactions" are difficult to identify or measure; and the "perception of the regional system" often contradicts the "objective" facts of geography.[14]

This may explain why the international relations literature reports so little progress in the analysis of regionalism. There are several in-depth studies of particular regional systems. During the cold war, for example, some students of regional systems argued against the decisive effects of

[11] Louis J. Cantori and Steven L. Spiegel, eds., *The International Politics of Regions: A Comparative Approach* (Englewood Cliffs, N.J.: Prentice-Hall, 1970), pp. 6–7.

[12] Bruce M. Russett, *International Regions and the International System: A Study in Political Ecology* (Chicago: Rand McNally, 1967), p. 11, and "Delineating International Regions," in *Quantitative International Politics: Insights and Evidence*, ed. J. David Singer (New York: Free Press, 1968), pp. 317–52.

[13] William R. Thompson, "The Regional Subsystem: A Conceptual Explication and a Propositional Inventory," *International Studies Quarterly* 17 (March 1973): 89–117.

[14] Paul Doremus, "Regionalism: A Review of the Literature" (Government Department, Cornell University, July 1988), p. 24.

the bipolar international system on all important facets of regional politics.[15] Others rejected both the prevailing theory of systemic polarity and the inductive critiques it had generated. Such studies emphasized instead regional theory with no more than a smattering of illustrative data.[16] Cantori and Spiegel extended this line of research.[17] They created an empirically grounded theoretical framework that focused on the comparison between different regional systems; however, their ambitious scheme was marred by a proliferation of variables.[18] Their scheme may be considered, at best, a comprehensive taxonomy.[19]

Yet despite its weaknesses, international relations scholarship on regionalism is correct in its central insight. Politicians frequently invoke collective identities designating particular regions. Malaysia's prime minister Mahathir Mohamad and Singapore's elder statesman Lee Kuan Yew are outspoken advocates of an Asian identity. Typically, they use the identity argument to celebrate strong group and family affiliations as the foundation for Asian capitalism and Asian human rights.[20] Political leaders use such arguments for intrinsic and instrumental reasons. But in terms of identity, Asian regionalism is contested with a large APEC (Asia-Pacific Economic Cooperation) and a small East Asian Economic Caucus (EAEC) representing two different visions. The EAEC expresses more clearly ideas

[15] Leonard Binder, "The Middle East as a Subordinate International System," *World Politics* 10 (April 1958): 415; Michael Brecher, "International Relations and Asian Studies: The Subordinate State System of Southern Asia," *World Politics* 15 (January 1963): 213–35.

[16] Doremus, "Regionalism," p. 14; Oran Young, "Political Discontinuities in the International System," *World Politics* 20 (April 1968): 369; William Zimmermann, "Hierarchical Regional Systems and the Politics of System Boundaries," *International Organization* 26 (Winter 1972): 18–36.

[17] Cantori and Spiegel, *International Politics of Regions;* Louis J. Cantori and Steven L. Spiegel, "The Analysis of Regional International Politics: The Integration versus the Empirical Systems Approach," *International Organization* 27 (Fall 1973): 465–94.

[18] Cantori and Spiegel distinguish seven types of states, fourteen types of regional systems (each of which contains a core, a periphery, and an "intrusive system"), and four pattern variables.

[19] For an earlier application of this approach to East Asia, see Donald C. Hellmann, *Japan and East Asia: The New International Order* (New York: Praeger, 1972).

[20] See, for example, Mahathir Mohamad, "Regional Groupings in the Pacific Rim: An East Asian Perspective," in *The Future of the Pacific Rim: Scenarios for Regional Cooperation*, ed. Barbara K. Bundy, Stephen D. Burns, and Kimberly V. Weichel (Westport, Conn.: Praeger, 1994), pp. 94–99, and Kit G. Machado, "Malaysian Cultural Relations with Japan and South Korea in the 1980s," *Asian Survey* 27 (June 1987): 638–60. For a strong argument contesting the authoritarianism of the "Asian way" from the perspective of human rights, see Edward Friedman, "The Subtext of Asian Authoritarian Discourse: Can East and Southeast Asia Join to Build an International Human Rights Regime?" (paper presented at the Conference on the Politics and Economics of Regional Cooperation in East and Southeast Asia, University of Wisconsin, Milwaukee, April 28–29, 1995).

about inherent cultural conflicts between "East" and "West" than does APEC, which gives expression to a regional identity that is more open to global influences.[21]

Hence it is not so surprising that new champions of a growing Asian identity emphasize two cultural components that are often in tension with each other: the effect of a common culture on Asian identity[22] on the one hand and the effect of Asian identity on a common culture of "middle-class globalism on the other."[23] With specific reference to Japan and Asia it thus makes a great deal of difference whether we refer to Japan *and* Asia or Japan *in* Asia.[24] For, as Carol Gluck argues, Japan's rhetoric of relations with the outside world over the last century has encompassed triangulation (among Japan, Asia, and the United States), separation from Asia (through escape or leadership causing imperialist domination), and identification with Asia (through an affirmative identity of common culture as well as a defensive identity of a common race). In the nineteenth and twentieth centuries, and especially since 1945, Asian politics has been defined primarily by the relations between different states. The Western, Westphalian state system, not Asian empires, define the relations between distinct actors, Japan *and* Asia.[25]

Apparently "Asia" lacks an unambiguous, concrete referent.[26] Victor Koschmann argues in Chapter 2 that the concept of Asia is relational, not intrinsic. The East, or "Orient," is, he contends, necessarily linked conceptually to the West, or "Occident." This link underlines the constructed and contested nature of the concept "Asia." Hierarchical political and economic relations proved more stable than shifting modes of rhetoric in the 1930s, when Japan took a rhetorical turn from an escape from Asia

---

[21] Richard Higgott and Richard Stubbs, "Competing Conceptions of Economic Regionalism: APEC versus EAEC in the Asia Pacific," *Review of International Political Economy* 2 (Summer 1995): 549–68.

[22] Kazuo Ogura, "A Call for a New Concept of Asia," *Japan Echo* 20 (Autumn 1993): 37–44; Kishore Mahbubani, "The Pacific Way," *Foreign Affairs* 74 (January/February 1995): 100–111.

[23] Yoichi Funabashi, "The Asianization of Asia," *Foreign Affairs* 72 (November/December 1993): 78.

[24] Carol Gluck, "The Call for a New Asian Identity: An Examination of the Cultural Arguments and Their Implications," in *Japan Programs Occasional Papers*, no.5 (New York: Carnegie Council on Ethics and International Affairs, 1994), p. 5.

[25] On this central point the situation in Europe differs. See Peter J. Katzenstein, ed., *Tamed Power: Germany in Europe* (Ithaca: Cornell University Press, 1997).

[26] On the evolving meaning of Southeast Asia, see Hajime Shimizu, "Southeast Asia as a Regional Concept in Modern Japan: An Analysis of Geography Textbooks," in *The Japanese in Colonial Southeast Asia*, ed. Saya Shiraishi and Takashi Shiraishi (Ithaca: Cornell University, Southeast Asia Program, 1993), pp. 21–61. See also Kanishka Jayasuriya, "Singapore: The Politics of Regional Definition," *The Pacific Review* 7.4 (1994): 411–20, and David Camroux, "The Asia-Pacific Policy Community in Malaysia," ibid., pp. 421–33.

to leadership of Asia. But despite notable differences in the ideological construction of a traditional "exoteric" and that of a modernist "esoteric" conception of Asia, both were an integral part of the war-prone 1930s and 1940s. Koschmann thus concludes that "liberal, ostensibly internationalist discourse remains capable of accommodating, and even promoting, imperialism"—then and now.[27]

Granting that collective identities are socially constructed and politically contested in no way denies their objective existence. Changing definitions of Asia are reflected in the real world. In its organizational structure the British Foreign Office, for example, continues to label Asia today as it did at the beginning of the century, as the "Far East." Australia, by way of contrast, has gone through a conceptual revolution in the last two decades.[28] It now recognizes itself to be an integral part of Asia-Pacific. And since the late 1980s India, long a westward-looking "jewel in the Crown," has begun to reorient itself toward a dynamically growing Pacific community in the East. Definitions of collective regional identity do not exist to be discovered. They are political constructs that actors contest and which evolve over time.

To escape the twin dangers of reification (typical of much of the behavioralist international relations literature and the analysis of economists) and relativization (characteristic of many postmodern cultural styles of analysis) an analysis of Japan's role in Asia must be grounded in a proper understanding of the concept "region." Although the contributors to this book subscribe to views that are inevitably somewhat different, they tend to agree with Karl Deutsch, who defines a region as a group of countries markedly interdependent over a wide range of different dimensions. This interdependence is often, but not always, indicated by a pattern of socioeconomic and political transactions and communications that differentiates the group of countries under investigation from other, comparable

---

[27] Koschmann, this volume, p. 110. See also Miwa Kimitada, "Japan in Asia Past and Present: How the Southeast Asians View the Japanese and How the Japanese Ought to Implement Their Newly Emergent Pacific Basin Cooperation Concept" (Institute of International Relations, Sophia University, A-42, 1981), pp. 12–13.

[28] Andrew Mack and John Ravenhill, eds., *Pacific Cooperation: Building Economic and Security Regimes in the Asia-Pacific Region* (Boulder, Colo.: Westview Press, 1995); Richard Higgott, Richard Leaver, and John Ravenhill, eds., *Pacific Economic Relations in the 1990s: Cooperation or Conflict?* (Boulder, Colo.: Lynne Rienner, 1993); Gavan McCormack, "Austral-Asia: A Regional Future?" in *Occasional Papers*, no.2 (Nedlands: University of Western Australia, Centre for Asian Studies, 1991); Tatsuo Akaneya, "The Development of Postwar Japan-Australia Relations and the Impact of Declining American Hegemony," Pacific Economic Paper No. 153, Australia-Japan Research Centre, Australian National University, Canberra, 1987; Alan Rix, *Coming to Terms: The Politics of Australia's Trade with Japan, 1945–47* (London: Allen & Unwin, 1986). Anthony Milner at the Australian National University is coordinating the Australian-Asian Perception Project. Its results are to be published in three volumes.

groups.[29] This view supports an approach that reflects change not stasis and thus uncovers the constructed character of essentialist arguments, yet avoids portraying the world as a totally fluid agglomeration of continuously shifting, relationally defined identities. A historically informed, institutional analysis offers a sufficiently stable, yet contextualized, ground for empirical analysis of the interplay of two worlds, Sinocentric and Anglo-American, that has shaped Japan and Asia.

Asian Regionalism in Markets Rather Than Through Formal Institutions

Regional integration in Asia occurs in markets that are changing rapidly under the confluence of globalization and growing links between national economies.[30] By contrast, Asian integration is unimpressive in terms of the formal international institutions that students of European or North American regional integration normally have in mind.

T. J. Pempel reviews in Chapter 1 the political economy of Asian regionalism. A generation ago, in 1960, Japan and Northeast Asia accounted for only 4 percent of world GNP, compared to 37 percent for the United States, Canada, and Mexico. In 1992 the combined economies of Japan, the Newly Industrializing Economies (NIEs), the ASEAN states, and Greater China nearly matched that of either North America or Western Europe, each of which account for about 30 percent of the world's GDP. Furthermore, because Asia accounts for more than half of the world's total economic growth, it is expected to take the lead in the near future.[31]

The stunning growth of the economy of "Greater China" since the mid-1980s has reinforced the process of regional economic integration in Asia. Three-quarters of the 28,000 Chinese firms with significant foreign equity

[29] Karl W. Deutsch, "On Nationalism, World Regions, and the Nature of the West," in *Mobilization, Center-Periphery Structures and Nation-Building: A Volume in Commemoration of Stein Rokkan.* Per Torsvik (Bergen: Universitetsforlaget, 1981), p. 54.

[30] Higgott, Leaver, and Ravenhill, *Pacific Economic Relations*; Mack and Ravenhill, eds., *Pacific Cooperation,* chapter 11, which discusses further the relationship between globalization and regionalism.

[31] World Bank, *World Development Report 1994: Infrastructure for Development* (Oxford: Oxford University Press, 1994), pp. 166–67. China's GDP is multiplied in this report by a factor of three as explained in note 33. See also Mahbubani, "The Pacific Way," pp. 100–101; U.S. International Trade Commission, *East Asia: Regional Economic Integration and the Implications for the United States* (Washington, D.C.: USITC Publication 2621, May 1993); Paul Krugman, "The Myth of Asia's Miracle," *Foreign Affairs* 73 (November/December 1994): 62–78. For a critical discussion of Krugman, see Don Russell, "APEC and the Anti-Asia Brigade," *Analysis* 6 (April 1995): 19–23.

are financed by ethnic Chinese not living in the People's Republic of China (PRC). That financing accounts for up to four-fifths of direct foreign investment in the PRC.[32] One estimate puts the Chinese diaspora at only 4 percent of the Chinese population. But its hypothetical "national" income is estimated to run perhaps as high as two-thirds of the Chinese GDP.[33] Worldwide, overseas Chinese hold an estimated $2 trillion of liquid assets, excluding securities, compared to an estimated $3 trillion that are deposited in Japanese bank accounts.[34] Fueled by Japanese and overseas

[32] Andrew B. Brick, "The Emergence of Greater China: The Diaspora Ascendant," *The Heritage Lectures* 411 (Washington, D.C.: Heritage Foundation, 1992), pp. 1–2. In "The Myth of Asia's Miracle," p. 75, Krugman reports that official statistics on foreign investment may overstate real figures by as much as a factor of six because provincial governments offer tax rebates and regulatory incentives to attract foreign investments, which encourages domestic entrepreneurs to invent fictitious foreign partners or to work through foreign front operations. "Round tripping" apparently is very common. Domestic entrepreneurs channel their investments through foreign intermediaries, normally located in Hong Kong, to take advantage of preferential government policies for foreign investors. This practice casts a shadow on official foreign investment figures of about $4 billion in 1991, $11 billion in 1992, $27 billion in 1993, and $34 billion in 1994. See Edward M. Graham, "Toward an Asia Pacific Investment Code," *Transnational Corporations* 3 (August 1994): 2–9; Fred R. Bleakley, "Foreign Investment in U.S. Surged in 1994," *Wall Street Journal,* March 15, 1995, A2. Guandong province reportedly signed 13,000 contracts worth $23.5 billion in first eight months of 1993 alone. *China Daily,* September 20, 1993, p. 5. Before the great investment surge of the early 1990s, three-way cumulative investment between the PRC, Hong Kong, and Taiwan stood at $36 billion in 1991. David M. Lampton et al., *The Emergence of "Greater China": Implications for the United States* (New York: National Committee on United States–China Relations, 1992), p. 1. Because long-term economic comparison is not yet possible, Philip Bowring is skeptical about the growth potential of trade and investment flows in Greater China. See his article "In Fact, Greater China May Be Mostly in the Mind," *International Herald Tribune,* May 27, 1994, 6.
[33] Brick, "Emergence of Greater China," p. 5; "China's Diaspora Turns Homeward," *Economist,* November 27, 1993, p. 33. Estimates of Chinese GDP differ by as much as a factor of ten. The statistic given in the text is based on a low-end World Bank figure of $375 billion based on official exchange rates. Brick, "Emergence of Greater China," p. 5. Some estimates are almost ten times as large, or $2.90 trillion. Alan Siaroff, "Interdependence versus Asymmetry? A Comparison of the European and Asia-Pacific Economic Regions" (paper presented at the ISA-West Meetings, Seattle, Wash., October 14–15, 1994), p. 23. Based on purchasing power parity indexes that take into account data on food consumption, infant mortality, and life expectancy, a widely accepted estimate puts the PRC's GDP at about $1.25 trillion. See Nicholas Lardy, *China in the World Economy* (Washington, D.C.: Institute for International Economics, 1994), pp. 14–18. This estimate is three times as high as the World Bank figures. It makes the economic size of China comparable to Italy's ($1.2 trillion) and France's ($1.3 trillion) while still ranking significantly behind that of Germany ($ 1.8 trillion). World Bank, *World Development Report, 1994,* pp. 166–67. China's economy, by this estimate, is still only one-third the size of Japan's. In terms of per capita income the ratio was about 1:25 in 1990, $1,100 for China and $26,930 for Japan. See also Chapter 9 in this volume, pp. 314–16, 333–34.
[34] There are, however, twice as many Japanese as Overseas Chinese. Brick, "Emergence of Greater China," p. 5.

Chinese investors, during the last decade the economic dynamism of Asia's regional economy has become one of the central features of the international economy.

Asian regionalism is defined foremost in market terms; however, Asian markets do not consist of myriads of private individual transactions, but express instead institutional and political relationships that in their operations implicate deeply both business and government. Following the growth of direct foreign investment, multinational corporations now control to an unprecedented degree the bilateral trade in the region. In the case of Japan, for example, intracompany trade accounts for about four-fifths of total Japanese exports and half of Japanese imports.[35] Foreign investment has also encouraged the expansion of vertical keiretsu structures from Japan into foreign markets, as Japanese corporations have enticed their suppliers to follow them abroad.[36]

Furthermore, public policies encourage the emergence of subregional groupings, including the links between Singapore and Malaysia's Johor and Indonesia's Riau provinces, between Taiwan, Hong Kong, and Guangdong and Fujian provinces in China, and between China's Dalian export zone and Japan and South Korea. Four additional subregional groupings are now being planned.[37] Michael Borrus thus writes that we are witnessing "the apparent emergence of coherent sub-regional trade and investment patterns that lie 'below' the aggregate regional picture but 'above' the interactions between states—a kind of parallel in the productive sphere to the region's noted 'investment corridors.' "[38]

[35] Dennis J. Encarnation, "The Regional Evolution of Japanese Multinationals in East Asia: A Comparative Study" (MIT Japan Program and Pacific Basin Research Program, Kennedy School of Government, Harvard University, November 1, 1994), p. 2.
[36] In manufacturing, Japanese affiliates in East Asian markets obtain a smaller share of inputs on an intrafirm basis than do U.S. affiliates. See Wendy Dobson, "FDI and Intra-Regional Trade in East Asia" (paper presented at the Workshop on Multinationals and East Asia Integration," Cambridge, Mass., November 18–19, 1994), p. 2.
[37] Chia Siow Yue and Lee Tsao Yuan, "Subregional Economic Zones: A New Motive Force in Asia-Pacific Development," in *Pacific Dynamism and the International Economic System*, ed. C. Fred Bergsten and Marcus Noland (Washington, D.C.: Institute for International Economics, 1993), pp. 225–72; Mitsuhiro Seki, *Beyond the Full-Set Industrial Structure: Japanese Industry in the New Age of East Asia* (Tokyo: LTCB International Library Foundation, 1994); Encarnation, "Regional Evolution of Japanese Multinationals," pp. 2–3; Brantly Womack and Guangzhi Zhao, "The Many Worlds of China's Provinces: Foreign Trade and Diversification," in *China Deconstructs: Politics, Trade and Regionalism*, ed. David S. G. Goodman and Gerald Segal (New York: Routledge, 1994), pp. 131–76; Lee Tsao Yuan, ed., *Growth Triangle: The Johor-Singapore-Riau Experience* (Singapore: Institute of Southeast Asian Studies, 1991); Ohmae, *End of the Nation State*.
[38] Michael Borrus, "MNC Production Networks and East Asian Integration: A Research Note" (Berkeley Roundtable on the International Economy, University of California, Berkeley, 1994), p. 5.

Table I-1. Main Regional Organizations in the Asian-Pacific Region

Nation[a]	ASEAN 1967	PAFTAD 1968	PBEC 1968	PECC 1980	APEC 1989	AFTA 1992	EAEC 1993
Japan	○	●	●	●	●		□
South Korea	○	●	●	●	●		□
North Korea							b
Taiwan		●	●	●	●		□
China				●	●		□
Hong Kong			●	●	●		□
United States	○	●	●	●	●		
Canada	○	●	●	●	●		
Mexico			●	●			
Peru			●	●			
Chile			●	●			
Thailand	●	●		●	●	●	□
Indonesia	●	●		●	●	●	□
Philippines	●	●	●	●	●	●	□
Malaysia	●	●	●	●	●	●	□
Brunei	●	●		●	●	●	□
Singapore	●	●		●	●	●	□
Vietnam							□
Laos							□
Cambodia							□
Myanmar							□
Australia	○	●	●	●	●		
New Zealand	○	●	●	●	●		
Pacific Is.							
Russia				⊙			
EC	○			⊙			

Source: Shinichi Ichimata, "Regional Integration Issues in Asia," in Korea Economic Institute of America, *Joint Korea-U.S. Academic Symposium,* vol. 4 (Washington, D.C.: Korea Economic Institute of America, 1994), p. 106.
[a] ●, Members; ○, Attend ASEAN Post-Ministerial Conference; ⊙, Observers; □, Expected initial members. ASEAN, Association of Southeast Asian Nations; PAFTAD, Pacific Trade and Development Conference; PBEC, Pacific Basin Economic Council; PECC, Pacific Economic Cooperation Council; APEC, Asia-Pacific Economic Cooperation; AFTA, ASEAN Free Trade Area; EAEC, East Asian Economic Caucus.
[b] Unknown.

Compared to the dynamic integration in markets, the relative weakness of formal regional institutions is very notable. Membership in the most important Asian regional organizations is summarized in Table I-1.
Neither Asia nor any of its subregions have any true equivalent to the panoply of European-wide institutions, foremost the European Union (EU). In the establishment of formal institutions Asian regionalism during the last decades has experienced a series of false starts. Only the fringes of the wider Pacific Community—the North American Free Trade Asso-

ciation between the United States, Canada, and Mexico (NAFTA) and the Closer Economic Relations Treaty (ANCERT) signed by Australia and New Zealand—aim at the total elimination of tariffs. Even the arguably most successful institution of Asian regional economic integration, ASEAN, eschews the elimination of tariffs. Until recently it was committed only to negotiating some preferential tariff margins for member states on selected goods. Per Magnus Wijkman and Eva Sundkvist Lindstroem thus argue that in Asia "only the more developed countries appear prepared to accept deeper forms of integration."[39]

The history of regional institutions in Asia dates back a generation.[40] In the early 1960s the Japan Economic Research Center (JERC) served as a meeting ground for a discussion of regional integration that brought together Japanese scholars and officials as well as representatives from the United States, Canada, Australia, and New Zealand. Subsequently, Saburo Okita, later Japan's foreign minister, articulated the concept of Pacific Economic Cooperation (PEC). Okita proposed annual meetings of representatives of these five countries for discussion of economic, cultural, and other issues of common concern. This Japanese initiative never went anywhere.

In 1966 the Japanese government took the lead in setting up the Asian Development Bank (ADB) in the United Nations Economic Commission for Asia and the Far East (ECAFE). Although Japan's financial contribution equaled that of the United States, at the behest of the Bank's members, and to the consternation of the Japanese government, the headquarters of the ADB were located in Manila, not Tokyo.[41] In the same year, in an attempt at regional burden-sharing with the United States, the Japanese government convened the Ministerial Conference on Economic Development in Southeast Asia (MCEDSEA). This organization was designed to help disburse Japanese aid, in exchange for general political support for Japanese foreign policy by its Southeast Asian neighbors. But

---

[39] Per Magnus Wijkman and Eva Sundkvist Lindstroem, "Pacific Basin Integration as a Step toward Freer Trade," in *Toward Freer Trade between Nations*, ed. John Nieuwenhuysen (Melbourne: Oxford University Press, 1989), p. 145.

[40] Hadi Soesastro and Sung-joo Han, eds., *Pacific Economic Cooperation: The Next Phase* (Jarkata: Centre for Strategic and International Studies, 1983); Higgott, Leaver, and Ravenhill, *Pacific Economic Relations*; Michael Haas, *The Asian Way to Peace: A Story of Regional Cooperation* (New York: Praeger, 1989); Stuart Harris, "Policynetworks and Economic Cooperation: Policy Coordination in the Asia-Pacific Region," *Pacific Review* 7.4 (1994): 381–95; T. Keisei Tanahashi, *Asian Alternative for Regional Cooperation: A Quest of Asian Strategy for Globalization* (Bangkok, Thailand: Chulalongkorn University, Institute of Asian Studies, 1992).

[41] Japanese citizens have acted as the bank's presidents since its inception; and Japan's construction and heavy industries have gained substantial contracts with the bank's assistance.

the Southeast Asian states did not like dealing directly with Japan through MCEDSEA. By 1975, MCEDSEA had ceased meeting.[42] In 1967 Japan proposed the establishment of an "Asian-Pacific Sphere of Cooperation." Nothing came of this political initiative either. Finally, following a proposal of South Korean president Chung Hee Park, and intimately linked to the war in Vietnam, the Asian and Pacific Council (ASPAC) was set up in 1966. Because of its anti-Chinese character the U.S.-Sino rapprochement of 1971 led to ASPAC's quiet demise. By 1974 it had effectively ceased to operate.[43]

Thus, the 1960s were inauspicious for a number of Japanese attempts to advance the cause of Asian regional integration. Political suspicion of Japanese motives was a major reason. Henceforth the Japanese government supported looser, nongovernmental institutions that either diffused Japanese influence through broad membership or operated without Japanese participation altogether. Based on the presumption that the completion of the European Economic Community's (EC) customs union in 1968 would have adverse repercussions for the Pacific economies, in 1967 Prime Minister Takeo Miki proposed the establishment of a Pacific Free Trade Area (PAFTA).[44] In 1968 the JERC organized a conference to consider, and reject, the PAFTA proposal.

But Miki's proposal encouraged the Australian and Japanese private sectors to form the Pacific Basin Economic Council (PEBC), a nongovernmental organization open initially to businessmen from the five Pacific Rim countries and subsequently open also to the participation by businessmen from other Asian states. Currently, more than 400 enterprises have joined and attend annual meetings.

Similarly, Miki's initiative made possible the establishment of the Pacific Trade and Development Conference (PAFTAD), which met for the first time in Tokyo in 1968.[45] This organization eventually gave rise to the Organization for Pacific Trade and Development (OPTAD), which beginning in the late 1970s has brought together Japan, the United States, Canada, Australia, New Zealand, and the ASEAN states.[46] Unlike the many unsuccessful attempts at institution building in the 1960s, all of these initiatives

---

[42] Susumu Yamakage, "Will Japan Seek Regionalism?" in *The Technical Challenges and Opportunities of a United Europe*, ed. Michael S. Steinberg (London: Pinter Publishers, 1990), pp. 152–53.

[43] Susumu Yamakage, personal communication, April 1, 1995; Donald Crone, "Does Hegemony Matter? The Reorganization of the Pacific Political Economy," *World Politics* 45 (July 1993): 513.

[44] Crone, "Does Hegemony Matter?" p. 513.

[45] Ibid., pp. 513–14.

[46] Gerald Segal, *Rethinking the Pacific* (Oxford: Clarendon Press, 1990), pp. 361–63.

were economic and nongovernmental organizations that emphasized personal networking and the exchange of information rather than political negotiations and binding decisions.

By broadening the focus of integration to encompass Asia-Pacific in the late 1970s, Prime Minister Masayoshi Ohira sought to strengthen the sense of an emerging Pacific community with new organizations. The Japanese government proposed a loosely structured organization that would bring together in equal numbers representatives from business, government, and academia. The Pacific Economic Cooperation Conference (PECC) was founded in 1980, through the joint initiative of Prime Minister Ohira and Prime Minister Malcolm Fraser of Australia. Today it has a total membership of twenty states, including the PRC, Russia—which also represents the other members of the Commonwealth of Independent States (CIS)—Mexico, Chile, and Peru. All major Latin American states send observers, and some participate in special task forces. The EU monitors the organization closely as well.[47]

PECC operates through a network of study groups and has been particularly important in pressing the case for what Vinod Aggarwal calls a meta-regime of open regionalism: regional liberalization that remains consistent with the norms and rules of GATT and the WTO but also embodies a regionally based form of multilateralism.[48] In the words of Donald Crone, "the PECC substructure provides an avenue for interest-group politics that connects eventually with governments. While increasing Pacific economic interdependence did not cause institutionalization, it does support it and contribute transnational underpinning to an intergovernmental regime."[49] The PECC's heterogeneity dilutes greatly any direct influence that Japan might wish to exercise on or over it.[50] Japanese policy appears in any case to aim in the opposite direction. In the area of foreign aid, for example, since the late 1970s Japan has shifted decisively toward multilateralism. This is evident even in the ADB. Although Japan has occupied the bank's presidency since its inception in 1965, its voting share has decreased from 20.2 percent in 1972 to 12.3 percent in 1991, despite an increase in capital that Japan has paid into the bank.[51]

[47] Crone, "Does Hegemony Matter?" pp. 514–15.
[48] Vinod K. Aggarwal, "Building International Institutions in Asia-Pacific," *Asian Survey* 32 (November 1993): 1033–35.
[49] Crone, "Does Hegemony Matter?" p. 523.
[50] Frank B. Gibney, "The Promise of the Pacific," *Wilson Quarterly* 16 (Winter 1992): 69–70; Frank B. Gibney, "Creating a Pacific Community," *Foreign Affairs* 72 (November/December 1993): 22; Yamakage, "Will Japan Seek Regionalism?" p. 153.
[51] Kozo Kato, "Uneven Interdependence: International Placements, Domestic Institutions,

Building on the accomplishments of the PECC, and using it as a political base, Australian prime minister Robert Hawke started a year-long diplomatic initiative in 1988. It came to fruition in November 1989 when an even wider regional grouping was created, APEC,[52] which brings together governmental and nongovernmental representatives from Japan, the United States, Canada, the Republic of Korea, Australia, New Zealand, and the six member states of ASEAN. The PRC, Taiwan, and Hong Kong joined in 1992, Papua New Guinea and Mexico in 1993, and Chile in 1994.[53] With a budget of only $2 million and a small secretariat located in Singapore, APEC relies mostly on technical working groups.[54]

APEC is a purely consultative forum. Ironically, writes Aggarwal, "although APEC is a regional accord, at present in its embryonic state it is more oriented toward openness than the GATT itself."[55] In terms of institutionalization APEC is comparable not to the EU but to the second pillar of the Treaty of European Union (TEU), which facilitates negotiations and the coordination of the foreign policies of European states.[56] For some time to come, however, APEC is likely to remain a forum for trade and investment liberalization, not economic integration. Donald Hellmann argues that "APEC is a transitional institution, a hodgepodge of semiformal committees and working groups that are sustained by a shared desire for continued economic growth."[57] Open-ended and outward-looking, APEC is fostering an exchange of information, research, and con-

---

and Development Cooperation Policy in Japan and Germany" (Government Department, Cornell University, 1995), chap. 2, p. 25.

[52] Susumu Yamakage, "An Asia-Pacific Community as a Regional Order: Possibilities and Limitations of APEC," *Asia Pacific Review* 2.1 (1995): 117–26; Richard A. Higgott, Andrew Fenton Cooper, and Jenelle Bonnor, "Asia-Pacific Economic Cooperation: An Evolving Case-Study in Leadership and Co-operation Building," *International Journal* 45 (Autumn 1990): 823–66, and "Cooperation-Building in the Asia-Pacific Region: APEC and the New Institutionalism," Pacific Economic Paper No.199, Australia-Japan Research Centre, Australian National University, Canberra, September 1991; Crone, "Does Hegemony Matter?" pp. 520–24.

[53] Cowhey, "Pacific Trade Relations," p. 19.

[54] Gibney, "Creating a Pacific Community," p. 21; Haggard, "Thinking about Regionalism," pp. 61–63; Cowhey, "Pacific Trade Relations," pp. 15–16,18–20. These groups deal with topics such as trade liberalization, investment regulations, telecommunications, marine resources conservation, marine pollution, fisheries, the environment, and technology transfer.

[55] Aggarwal, "Building International Institutions," p. 1035.

[56] If in the future APEC were to evolve into a negotiating and policymaking body, as one of the initial reports of the Eminent Persons Group (EPG) to the APEC ministers has suggested, the PECC, currently holding observer status at APEC meetings, would likely serve as a private testing ground for government initiatives. Aggarwal, "Building International Institutions"; Crone, "Does Hegemony Matter?" pp. 522–23.

[57] Donald C. Hellmann, "APEC and the Political Economy of the Asia-Pacific: New Myths, Old Realities," *Analysis* 6 (April 1995): 37.

sultation. At least in these respects it is likely to become the Asian counterpart to the Organization for Economic Cooperation and Development (OECD).[58]

It is noteworthy that proposals for a smaller and more exclusively Asian organization have failed where APEC has succeeded. In 1990 Malaysian prime minister Mahathir Mohamad proposed the formation of an Asian forum that could serve as an alternative to APEC. The proposed East Asian Economic Grouping (EAEG) was to consist only of the eleven Asian members of APEC, excluding the United States, Canada, Australia, and New Zealand. Mahathir Mohamad built on the ideas of others. Some Indonesian proposals aiming in this direction date back to the mid-1980s. They were revived by Phisit Pakkasem of Thailand, who in 1988 called for the creation of a Western Pacific Economic Cooperation (WESPEC). The original APEC proposal had actually excluded the United States.[59] Mahathir Mohamad's proposal for the EAEG had three goals: to establish (1) a political balance against the United States and Japan in APEC; (2) an economic balance against China and Japan in Asia; and (3) a counter to emerging economic blocs in the West. Furthermore, the EAEG was consistent with Mahathir's strong identification with the Third World and his leadership in the Group of 15 for South-South Consultation and Cooperation.[60] Strong U.S. opposition,[61] Japan's hesitation, and lukewarm support from most Asian states led to a downgrading of Mahathir Mohamad's idea to the creation of an East Asian Economic Caucus (EAEC).

There exists a shared suspicion among Asian governments that international bureaucratic structures might become independent of their state sponsors.[62] Because the pace of Asian regional integration has perceptibly quickened since the late 1980s, it is worthwhile to compare this Asian

[58] Cowhey, "Pacific Trade Relations," p. 15; Andrew Pollack, "Shellshocked by Yen, Companies in Japan Still Find Ways to Profit," *New York Times*, April 18, 1995, A1, D6; Dan Biers and Craig Forman, "Asia-Pacific Forum Finds Focus: Trade," *Wall Street Journal*, November 14, 1994, A6; Sven Arndt, " 'Open Regionalism' in the Pacific," *Claremont Policy Briefs* 94–03 (Claremont Graduate School, Claremont, Calif., October 1994).
[59] Natasha Hamilton-Hart, "The EAEG Proposal" (Government Department, Cornell University, 1993), p. 6; Haggard, "Thinking about Regionalism," pp. 33–34; Grieco, "Variation in Regional Economic Institutions," p. 9; Linda Low, "East Asian Economic Grouping," *Pacific Review* 4.4 (1991): 375–82.
[60] Crone, "Does Hegemony Matter?" p. 521; Low, "The East Asian Economic Grouping."
[61] The United States opposes Asia-Pacific regional organizations from which it is excluded. Instead, President Clinton called for the creation of a multilateral Pacific Community at the July 1993 Tokyo Summit. Earlier, the United States advocated a bilateral global partnership between the United States and Japan. Derek Shearer, "Transpacific Vision," *Foreign Policy* 92 (Fall 1993): 182.
[62] Crone, "Does Hegemony Matter?" p. 522.

experience with the early years of the West European integration process. West European governments set up the European Coal and Steel Community (ECSC) to internationalize the core of the military-industrial complex that had permitted Germany to fight two destructive wars in less than a generation. Supranationalism, not national autonomy, was the name of the game. After the early fervor of the European integration movement had spent its force with the defeat of the European Defense Community (EDC) in the French Assembly, the fallback option of low rather than high politics, of economic rather than military integration, spawned an institution, the European Economic Community (EEC), which created a supranational authority in three policy sectors (agriculture, transport, and trade), and which committed itself to the elimination of all tariffs within twelve years, a goal that it achieved ahead of schedule. Put differently, European integration expressed supranational rather than intergovernmental aspirations and even in defeat achieved a greater degree of regional integration more quickly than the various initiatives seeking to further Asian integration.

This is hardly surprising. The destructive effect of World War II made Europeans receptive to supranational integration. National liberation struggles, the heady experience of a new found sovereignty, and the overwhelming domestic pressures that poor, nonindustrialized societies and economies put on weak state institutions made international integration an implausible political option in Asia. Whatever the reason, the difference, in the early years of integration, between a Europe that was backing off from integration and an Asia growing closer is a striking demonstration of the institutional weakness of Asian regionalism. It is thus symptomatic that, in the words of Andrew Pollack, APEC's name "does not end with 'organization,' 'association' or a similar noun . . . this attests to the reluctance of its founders to make it an institution. It operates by consensus, without any mechanism for voting, and many members would prefer to see it stay that way."[63] Indeed, the Western concept of community is often associated with organized and institutional structures, but there is no equivalent Chinese translation for this concept of community. Most APEC members, writes a study group of the Carnegie Endowment, thus opt for words that emphasize "loose family-type linkages and avoid the notion of a formal institution."[64]

This conclusion agrees with the findings of others. Joe Grieco

[63] Andrew Pollack, "Asian Nations Wary on Free Trade," *New York Times*, November 11, 1994, A8.
[64] Carnegie Endowment Study Group, *Defining a Pacific Community*, p. 13.

distinguishes three different aspects of regional economic institutionalization: type, scope, and level.[65] Along all three dimensions, and in sharp contrast to European regionalism, Asian regionalism "presents an almost perfect case of the absence of successful regional institutionalization in economic affairs. That is, while some modest efforts have been made to create a stronger institutional manifestation of regional ties—in particular AFTA, EAEG/EAEC, and APEC—these efforts have either failed completely or seem to face uncertain prospects at best."[66] Similarly, Peter Cowhey concludes that "the major regional institutions of the Pacific Rim are so far not in a position to deliver either warring trade blocs or deep regional integration."[67] Stephan Haggard argues that regional organizations in Asia "have played a role as a locus for the formation of transnational networks, but they have not graduated to the status of policy-making institutions, let alone a forum for consideration of the deep integration agenda."[68] Richard Higgott writes that to the extent that the Single European Act (SEA) and the Maastricht treaty require a "pooling of sovereignty, they are qualitatively different from Asia-Pacific economic co-operation."[69] And summarizing the findings of their contributors Jeffrey Frankel and Miles Kahler talk of Asia's "soft" regionalism, closely integrated and centered on the Japanese economy, which differs from the "hard" regionalism of Europe, which is based on politically established discriminatory arrangements.[70] In sum, despite a flurry of activity in recent years, Albert Fishlow and Stephan Haggard are close to the mark when they state that "the puzzle with reference to the Pacific is not to explain the progress of regional initiatives, but their relative weakness."[71]

[65] Building on the integration literature of the 1960s, in "Variation in Regional Economic Institutions" Grieco offers a scale for each of the three aspects of integration: *type* varies from bilateral treaties to supranational integration; *scope* varies from few, unimportant issues to many, important ones; *level* varies from a minimal to a maximal transfer of national power to monitor and verify compliance with cooperative commitments, to coordinate national policies, and to formulate proposals for new policy initiatives.
[66] Ibid., pp. 14–15.
[67] Cowhey, "Pacific Trade Relations," p. 15.
[68] Haggard, "Thinking about Regionalism," p. 61 and pp. 8–12, 60–66.
[69] Higgott, "Economic Co-operation in the Asia Pacific," p. 374.
[70] Jeffrey A. Frankel and Miles Kahler, Introduction, to *Regionalism and Rivalry: Japan and the United States in Pacific Asia*, ed. Frankel and Kahler (Chicago: University of Chicago Press, 1993), p. 4.
[71] Albert Fishlow and Stephan Haggard, *The United States and the Regionalization of the World Economy* (Paris: OECD, 1992), p. 30. See also Robert Gilpin, "Economic Change and the Challenge of Uncertainty," in *East Asia in Transition: Toward a New Regional Order*, ed. Robert S. Ross (Armonk, N.Y.: M. E. Sharpe, 1995), p. 17, and Harry Harding, "International Order and Organization in the Asia-Pacific Region," ibid., pp. 327–28, 335–37; Miles Kahler, *International Institutions and the Political Economy of Integration* (Washington D.C.: Brookings Institution, 1995), pp. 107–9, 111–16; Yuichiro Nagatomi, "New Evolutions in Global

Two Determinants of Asian Regionalism

How can we account for the relative weakness of the formal political institutions of Asian regionalism? A comparison with Europe suggests that the answer can be found by examining two factors: power and norms in the international system, and the character of domestic state structures. First, U.S. foreign policy after 1945 established the principle of multilateralism in Europe and bilateralism in Asia. This has made it much more difficult for Asian states to develop broad, interlocking, institutionalized political arrangements of the kind that have characterized the European experience. Second, the distinctive character of Asian state institutions has militated against the type of integration typical of Europe: sanctioned by public international law and embodied in formal international institutions characterized by sharp boundaries between members and nonmembers.

Measured in relative terms, U.S. power in Asia after 1945 was much greater than in Europe.[72] It was not in the interest of the United States to create institutions that would have constrained independent decision making in Washington. Nor was it in the interest of states in Asia to enter institutions that would not enhance their automony but probably would reduce their access to the benefits of de facto client status with Washington. However, when a gradual shift in relative capabilities brought to an end the extreme hegemony the United States had enjoyed in Asia, a weak institutionalization of an unstable and uncertain order became an attractive option for both the declining hegemon and its allies in Asia.[73] Today it is China and Japan who oppose rapid moves toward a formal institutionalization of regional integration. China fears being trapped in institutions not of its own making; Japan no longer needs formal institutions, as it did in the 1960s, to help it overcome its diplomatic isolation.

Asian regionalism thus centered on a convergence of interests in the provision of some collective goods. By and large bilateral political practices had excluded collectively shared norms of Asian regionalism. For example, political initiatives to create regional trade organizations in Asia typically were bargaining chips, motivated more by an assessment of developments

---

Community of Post-Modernization and Industrialization by Industrialized Countries," Foundation for Advanced Information and Research (FAIR), Working Paper Series No.8, Tokyo, September 18, 1989, pp. 11–12.

[72] In 1950 the combined GNP of Britain, France, Italy, and Germany was equal to 39 percent of the U.S. GNP. In 1965 the combined GNP of Japan, South Korea, Philippines, Singapore, Thailand, Malaysia, and Indonesia still was only 15.9 percent of the U.S. GNP. By 1989 this had grown to 79.8 percent, largely because of the sharp growth in the Japanese GNP. See Crone, "Does Hegemony Matter?" p. 503, note 7, and p. 510.

[73] Crone, "Does Hegemony Matter?" pp. 502–5, 517.

in other regions or in global trade negotiations than in the intrinsic interest of creating Asian trade institutions.[74] Still, bargaining interests were constrained by existing GATT norms, and these, Aggarwal contends, had a significant effect on the evolution of Asian trade organizations.[75]

Significantly, norms matter not only for the prescription of proper conduct, as in the case of trade, but for the construction of a collective identity. "Common notions of the community good" facilitate regional institutionalization; conflicts over values do not.[76] An analysis of Asian regionalism thus needs to pay some attention to the cultural basis of power. Specifically regional integration is more easily institutionalized if political actors subscribe to the notion of forming a distinct community, as was true in Europe, than if they do not, as in Asia. As James Kurth has argued, in the past the values embedded in the Atlantic and the Pacific basins were antithetical. The states of the Atlantic Basin endorsed international liberalism and welfare. The states of the Pacific Basin endorsed national mercantilism and development.[77] Only the values of the Atlantic Basin states lead to political programs and government policies favoring institutionalized forms of regional integration.

After World War II Atlantic cooperation was buttressed by collective notions that tapped into the roots of shared Western culture. Indeed the very concept of a Western community (Christian, democratic, capitalist) became politically prominent in the 1950s. It gave expression to a powerful, collectively shared purpose in Europe's regional institutions that is absent in contemporary Asia.[78] Even as ardent a proponent of a collective Asian identity as Kishore Mahbubani admits that Western critics are correct when they deplore the absence of a sense of community in the Pacific. "There is still a long way to go before it is realized. Nothing like it has been experienced before."[79]

After 1945, as Bruce Cumings argues in Chapter 4 in this book, U.S.

---

[74] Soogil Young, "Globalism and Regionalism: Complements or Competitors?" in *Pacific Dynamism and the International Economic System*, ed. C. Fred Bergsten and Marcus Noland (Washington, D.C.: Institute for International Economics, 1993); Aggarwal, "Building International Institutions," p. 1035; Crone, "Does Hegemony Matter?" pp. 519–20; Haggard, "Thinking about Regionalism," pp. 32–35. Kenneth A. Oye has argued that in the 1980s some of the most significant examples of economic liberalization resulted from discriminatory bilateral or regional strategies. See Oye, *Economic Discrimination and Political Exchange: World Political Economy in the 1930s and 1980s* (Princeton: Princeton University Press, 1992), p. 169.

[75] Aggarwal, "Building International Institutions," pp. 1036, 1040; Crone, "Does Hegemony Matter?" pp. 522–25.

[76] Crone, "Does Hegemony Matter?" pp. 506, 524–25.

[77] James Kurth, "The Pacific Basin versus the Atlantic Alliance: Two Paradigms of International Relations," *The Annals of the American Academy of Political and Social Science* 505 (September 1989): 34–45.

[78] Carnegie Endowment Study Group, *Defining a Pacific Community*, pp. 13, 22–23.

[79] Mahbubani, "The Pacific Way," p. 107.

diplomacy left a legacy in contemporary Asian security relations that has reinforced this difference. Firmly committed to the principle of multilateralism in Europe, the United States weaned that region away from its traditional preference for organizing security and economic relations between states along bilateral lines.[80] Not so in Asia. After 1945 the United States enshrined the principle of bilateralism in its dealings with Japan and other Asian states.[81] The North Atlantic Treaty Organization (NATO) and the Southeast Asia Treaty Organization (SEATO) were both offspring of the cold war strategy of the United States. NATO succeeded in transforming the security relations of its members. Founded in 1954, SEATO remained a paper organization. When it closed its doors in 1977 hardly anybody noticed. Today the absence of historically rooted, multilateral arrangements makes adaptation to global change difficult in Asia. The U.S.-Japan Security Treaty looks anachronistic to many of its critics, but in the absence of alternative institutional arrangements, if the treaty lapsed, Asian states would confront vexing security issues.[82] In the words of John Ruggie, "Whereas today the potential to move beyond balance-of-power politics in its traditional form exists in Europe, a reasonably stable balance is the best that one can hope to achieve in the Asia-pacific region."[83] These institu-

[80] Steve Weber, "Shaping the Postwar Balance of Power: Multilateralism in NATO," in *Multilateralism Matters: The Theory and Praxis of an Institutional Form*, ed. John Gerard Ruggie (New York: Columbia University Press, 1993), pp. 233–92. On the relationship between multilateralism and bilateralism in Europe, see Peter W. Ludlow, "Managing Change: The United States and Europe East and West," in *The Global Economy: America's Role in the Decade Ahead*, ed. William Brock and Robert D. Hormats (New York: W. W. Norton, 1990), pp. 65–68.

[81] Michael Schaller, *The American Occupation of Japan: The Origins of the Cold War in Asia* (New York: Oxford University Press, 1985); J. W. Dower, *Empire and Aftermath: Yoshida Shigeru and the Japanese Experience, 1878–1954* (Cambridge: Harvard University Press, 1988); John Lewis Gaddis, *Strategies of Containment: A Critical Appraisal of Postwar American National Security Policy* (New York: Oxford University Press, 1982), pp. 25–126; Walter LaFeber, *America, Russia, and the Cold War, 1945–84*, 5th ed. (New York: Knopf, 1985), pp. 29–124; Robert M. Blum, *Drawing the Line: The Origin of the American Containment Policy in East Asia* (New York: W. W. Norton, 1982); David Allan Mayers, *Cracking the Monolith: U.S. Policy Against the Sino-Soviet Alliance, 1949–1955* (Baton Rouge: Lousiana State University Press, 1986); David Mayers, *George Kennan and the Dilemmas of U.S. Foreign Policy* (New York: Oxford University Press, 1988). Joseph M. Grieco, "Realism and Regionalism: American Power and German and Japanese Institutional Strategies during and after the Cold War" (paper presented at the 1996 meeting of the American Political Science Association, San Francisco, Calif., August 29–September 1, 1996).

[82] Gerald L. Curtis, ed., *The United States, Japan, and Asia* (New York: W. W. Norton, 1994); June Teufel Dreyer, ed., *Asian-Pacific Regional Security* (Washington, D.C.: Washington Institute Press, 1990); Ramesh Thakur and Carlyle A. Thayer, eds., *Reshaping Regional Relations: Asia-Pacific and the Former Soviet Union* (Boulder, Colo.: Westview Press, 1993); William E. Odom, with contributions by Andy Yan and Perry Wood, *Trial after Triumph: East Asia after the Cold War* (Indianapolis: Hudson Institute, 1992); Sheldon W. Simon, ed., *East Asian Security in the Post-Cold War Era* (Armonk, N.Y.: M. E. Sharpe, 1993).

[83] John G. Ruggie, "Multilateralism: The Anatomy of an Institution," in Ruggie, *Multilateralism Matters*, p. 4. A more optimistic analysis is found in Tong Whan Park, "Multilateralism in Northeast Asian Security: Theoretical and Practical Challenges" (paper presented at the

tional differences between multilateral and bilateral arrangements are reinforced by powerful historical experiences. In Western Europe the cold war was experienced as a long peace, in Asia as a series of destructive wars.

Asian security is shaped by an open regionalism that is influenced by several centers of power. The end of the cold war and the disintegration of the Soviet Union had a different significance in Asia than it did along the central front in Europe. The breakup of the Soviet Union and the redeployment of the Russian navy from a forward to a bastion strategy has diminished global tensions. But it may eventually create new threats for countries such as Japan and Norway, which lie near these bastions, located on the Kola peninsula and in Vladivostock. Furthermore, an accelerating regional arms race in Asia, fueled by unrelated issues, such as the conflict on the Korean peninsula and jurisdictional conflicts in the South China Sea, have been financed by some of the fastest-growing economies in the world.[84] These security issues create multiple political fissures in Asia that make a continued military presence of the U.S. Navy highly likely.[85]

Asia thus is a region that, as Susumu Yamakage argues in Chapter 8, remains open to security links with nonregional powers. For example, as part of the cold war in 1971 the Rim of the Pacific Exercise (RIMPAC) was set up. It provided for integrated naval war exercises involving Australia, Canada, New Zealand, and the United States. No Asian state has joined RIMPAC since.[86] And from the outset ASEAN's institutional growth was impaired by the fact that its members had signed bilateral defense treaties with the United States, Britain, and Australia. ASEAN's initial impetus in 1967 was political and military security, not economic prosperity.

Asian regionalism has some distinctive advantages and disadvantages in the management of security affairs.[87] The European assumption that peace

---

American Political Science Association Meeting, New York, September 1–4, 1994). James T. H. Tang gives a more pessimistic analysis in his article "Multilateralism in Northeast Asia International Security: An Illusion of a Realistic Hope" (paper presented at the NPCSD Workshop on Changing National Military Security Perceptions, organized by the Institute of International Relations, University of British Columbia, and the Research Institute for Peace and Security, Tokyo, Yokohama, August 28–29, 1992).

[84] Michael T. Klare, "The Next Great Arms Race," *Foreign Affairs* 72 (Summer 1993): 136–52. Denny Roy, "Hegemon on the Horizon? China's Threat to East Asian Security," *International Security* 19 (Summer 1994): 149–68.

[85] Richard K. Betts, "Wealth, Power, and Instability: East Asia and the United States after the Cold War," *International Security* 18 (Winter 1993/94): 34–77; Aaron L. Friedberg, "Ripe for Rivalry: Prospects for Peace in a Multipolar Asia," *International Security* 18 (Winter 1993/94): 5–33; Barry Buzan and Gerald Segal, "Rethinking East Asian Security," *Survival* 36 (Summer 1994): 3–21.

[86] From 1980 on, however, Japan held joint exercises with the U.S. Navy on a bilateral basis during, but apart from, RIMPAC naval exercises.

[87] Mahbubani, "The Pacific Way," pp. 105–6.

and prosperity can be secured through institutionalization without much regard to the societies located at the European periphery looks in the 1990s like a huge gamble. In sharp contrast, Asian regionalism resists exclusivist institution-building impulses; it favors instead inclusive networks. It is thus fitting that in the 1990s, despite the absence of formal regional institutions and security arrangements, there exist thirty ongoing, nonofficial security "dialogues" in Asia.[88] Asia-Pacific is moving to integrate the periphery, currently Burma and Vietnam, and eventually perhaps even North Korea. Kishore Mahbubani put the issue this way: "Europe may be accentuating the contrast between the continent and its neighborhood, thus developing potentially destabilizing geopolitical fault lines. By contrast, the geopolitical fault lines in the Asia-Pacific region are gradually being stabilized."[89] In light of the growing crises in the Balkans and in North Africa, recent developments in and around North Korea, Kampuchea, Vietnam, and Burma lend some support to this view.

Yet a conception of security that encompasses more than the traditional balance of power and interstate war makes us aware of Asia's great fragility. With a growing number of Asian polities experiencing economic revolutions and social transformations of hitherto unimaginable speed, the potential for vast economic dislocations and social explosions increases.[90] Robert Ash and Y. Y. Kueh write that "there is a danger that increasing economic integration within Greater China could threaten China's national economic identity, or at least compel re-definition."[91] Asia is currently experiencing large-scale migration, profound environmental degradation, deep societal insecurities, and growing inequalities, not to mention the power struggle within regimes themselves experiencing fundamental change; these are not conditions conducive to international security in Asia.

The comparative weakness in the institutionalization of Asian regionalism can also be traced to the character of Asian state institutions. Some

---

[88] Pauline Kerr, "The Security Dialogue in the Asia-Pacific," *Pacific Review* 7.4 (1994): 407. See also Harry Harding, "Prospects for Cooperative Security Arrangements," in Bundy, Burns, and Weichel, *Future of the Pacific Rim*, pp. 138–55; Joseph S. Nye, "The Case for Deep Engagement," *Foreign Affairs* 74 (July/August, 1995): 90–102; Chalmers Johnson and E. B. Keehn, "The Pentagon's Ossified Strategy," *Foreign Affairs* 74 (July/August, 1995): 103–14.

[89] Mahbubani, "The Pacific Way," p. 106.

[90] Britain took fifty-eight years (from 1870) to double its economic output per person, the United States forty-seven years (from 1839), and Japan thirty-three years (from the 1880s). This compares with seventeen years for Indonesia, eleven for Korea, and ten for China. See Mahbubani, "The Pacific Way," p. 103.

[91] Robert Ash and Y. Y. Kueh, "Economic Integration within Greater China: Trade and Investment Flows between China, Hong Kong and Taiwan," *China Quarterly* 136 (December 1993): 711.

state structures are better suited to deal with public law and formal institutions as the preferred vehicle for regional integration. I call these highly rationalized forms of bureaucratic and legal rule "Weberian states." Despite some important variations in the institutional profile across Europe, with one significant exception, they all belong to the same Weberian species.

Only Greece is singularly ill-equipped institutionally for full participation in the European integration process. Greece was admitted to the EC primarily for ideological reasons. Widely considered by Europeans as the cradle of European culture and civilization,[92] Greece simply could not be excluded once the colonels were deposed in 1974.

Yet the interaction between social and state structures that shaped the political evolution of modern Greece in the nineteenth and twentieth centuries showed strong residues of centuries of Ottoman rule. "Greek constitutionalism at the time of the founding of modern Greece," writes Vassiliki Georgiadou, "had little to do with the liberal-bourgeois constitutional order in Western Europe. . . . Despite the formal constitutional anchors of state and government, the political regime had enormous difficulties to institutionalize principles of Roman law and uncontested property rights."[93] Traditional regional and local powerbrokers—bureaucrats, clerics, and the military—created a state that on the surface may have endorsed West European principles but in its core retained strong elements of Ottoman autocracy and corruption. The bloated Greek civil service and public economy, the lack of a regional system of government, the absence of reliable statistics, the institutional limitations that the state faces in the collection of taxes are some of the political characteristics of the modern Greek state that make it ill-suited for participation in European integration.

On all of these dimensions, furthermore, Greece differs from the other Southern European states.[94] Under the impetus of the European integration process Spain and Portugal have effected far-reaching transformations in their economic and social structures. Greece has not. Greece is changing, but the change is excruciatingly slow and painful for both Greece and its European partners. It is hard to imagine an EU composed of states

---

[92] Michael Herzfeld, *Ours Once More: Folklore, Ideology, and the Making of Modern Greece* (Austin: University of Texas Press, 1982); Suzanne Rudolph, "Religion, the State and Transnational Civil Society," in *Transnational Religion, the State, and Global Civil Society*, ed. Rudolph (forthcoming), pp. 21–22.

[93] Vassiliki Georgiadou, *Griechenlands nicht-kapitalistische Entwicklungsaspekte im 19. Jahrhundert* (Frankfurt: Peter Lang, 1991), pp. 4–5, author's translation.

[94] James Kurth and James Petras, eds., *Mediterranean Paradoxes: The Politics and Social Structure of Southern Europe* (Oxford: Berg, 1993).

resembling modern Greece. Political elites throughout Western Europe are reluctant to admit Turkey to full membership in the EU, not only because of dismay over the human rights record of the Turkish government or fear both of potentially large-scale labor migration and of Islamic fundamentalism, but also because of their experiences in dealing with Greece, a distant cousin of the Ottoman Empire.

Regional integration in Asia is similarly shaped by the character of Asian states. Southeast Asian states, for example, are heirs to British, Dutch, French, Spanish, and U.S. colonialism. Social forces penetrate these postcolonial states deeply and thus create multiple political connections in intricate network structures. These states have inherited the colonial tradition of "the rule by law" rather than the West European tradition of "the rule of law." Southeast Asian states are constituted legally, but the relation between state and society is governed by social norms rather than legal ones.[95]

But the historical roots of Asian states reach deeper than Western colonialism.[96] "Asian history can be deciphered as a succession of greater or lesser empires," writes Wang Gungwu, "bordered and interspersed by polities, fragments of polities, with or without kings, princes, and tribal chiefs of one kind or another."[97] Unlike Europe, contemporary Asian states are shaped by the legacy of universal empires, regional kingdoms, and subcontinental empires, with a history that often predates that of modern Europe by millennia. These empires and kingdoms, Suzanne Rudolph argues,[98] rose and fell by cyclical conceptions of dynastic time not by linear, teleological conceptions of progress in history characteristic of the European intellectual tradition. The notions of unified sovereignty and the monopoly of force, central to the conception of continental European states, does not capture Asian political realities. In Southeast Asia, for example, according to O. W. Wolters, overlapping patchworks of "circles of kings," or *mandalas*, represented "a particular and often unstable political situation in a vaguely definable geographical area without fixed boundaries . . . where smaller centres tended to look in all directions for security."[99]

[95] I am indebted to Takashi Shiraishi for clarification of this point.

[96] This argument is also developed in Peter J. Katzenstein, "Conclusion: National Security in a Changing World," in *The Culture of National Security: Norms and Identity in World Politics*, ed. Katzenstein (New York: Columbia University Press, 1996), pp. 498–537.

[97] Wang Gungwu, "Empires and Anti-empires: Asia in World Politics," in *The Fall of Great Powers: Peace, Stability, and Legitimacy*, ed. Geir Lundestad (Oxford: Oxford University Press, 1994), p. 237.

[98] Suzanne H. Rudolph, "Presidential Address: State Formation in Asia—Prolegomenon to a Comparative Study," *Journal of Asian Studies* 46 (November 1987): 731–46.

[99] O. W. Wolters, *History, Culture, and Region in Southeast Asian Perspectives* (Singapore: Institute of Southeast Asian Studies, 1982), p. 17.

The Chinese and Vietnamese, on the other hand, presupposed that "any state should be associated with rules of dynastic succession and be described by fixed boundaries."[100] But even there, the political center, or king of kings, was no "oriental despot," but rather presided over a self-regulating civil society. To be sure, the center ruled by force at times and did try to extract resources from civil society, but these activities did not define the character of Asian empires and kingdoms.

According to Rudolph the relation of the political center to civil society was custodial and ritualized. And civil society—divided into regions, classes, guilds, religious communities, and subkingdoms—was segmentary. Asia was a patchwork of galactic polities, not absolutist monarchies. In these polities a system of repulsion and attraction kept all units circling in one orbit. At the center of the political universe was not a "sun king" but an all-encompassing sense of order, ritual sovereignty, not effective sovereignty. Clifford Geertz's description of Negara, the theater state in Bali,[101] points to the ceremonial and aesthetic aspects of sovereignty and the importance of encompassing processes of cultural assimilation rather than exclusive formal institutions. These aspects of statehood helped create a common form of life and express an encompassing cosmology. Military penetration and conquest played an important role, but so did social replication through processes of diffusion and emulation. The result was common social and cultural domains tenuously related to the formal control of a political center. Akira Iriye concludes that in China and Japan, for example, "military force was of much less significance than culture as a symbol of authority and greatness."[102]

What is true of Asia in general is true also of Japan in particular. This may be one reason why contemporary Japanese state theory has insisted on coining a series of neologisms designed to transcend the dichotomies of "strong" and "weak" and "public" and "private" when theorizing about politics.[103] Rule by a powerful bureaucracy, legitimated by the long-term domination of Japanese politics by the LDP, is an important part of a polity that links state and society in complex ways. It is difficult to describe these relationships between state and society with categories distilled from the European experience. Japanese scholars and specialists tend to emphasize the network character of the Japanese state and the requirements of reciprocity in the building of a political consensus that combines

---

[100] Ibid., p. 13.
[101] Clifford Geertz, *Negara: The Theatre State in Nineteenth-Century Bali* (Princeton: Princeton University Press, 1980).
[102] Akira Iriye, *China and Japan in the Global Setting* (Cambridge: Harvard University Press, 1992), p. 9.
[103] Peter J. Katzenstein, *Cultural Norms and National Security: Police and Military in Postwar Japan* (Ithaca: Cornell University Press, 1996), chaps. 2 and 3.

considerations of political efficacy with a mixture of economic efficiency and inefficiency. Although it is autonomous in some ways, the Japanese state is both embedded in civil society and penetrated by it. It has the potential, that is, for both strength and weakness.[104] Political and economic network structures that vitiate the distinction between public and private spheres inside Japan are replicated in and externalized to Asia. Unsurprisingly, a nation of networks creates regional integration through networks. "In large part," Walter Hatch and Kozo Yamamura write, "Japanese business and political elites have 'schmoozed' their way to power. They have, in other words, mastered the fine art of networking in Asia."[105]

This line of reasoning is suggestive, not definitive. It points to the need for research into the externalization of institutional models of states that would complement sociological models of the internalization of global models of modernity and proper conduct. It could be refined theoretically and tested empirically in specific Asian settings characterized by different institutions. Such research would have to lead us from deeply ingrained historical patterns to the present through the historical experiences of colonialism, decolonization, nationalism, and sovereign statehood. For the time being, and on the authority of Wolters's and Rudolph's writings, and the recent literature on Japanese and East Asian political economy, this argument offers a plausible explanation for the distinctiveness of Asian regionalism. Pooling exclusive state sovereignties in international institutions, in the interest of regional integration, assumes the monopoly of force as the key defining element of state power and politics. This assumption derives from the European historical experience and the specific character of European state structures. Different state structures may have made Asian states less susceptible to processes of regional integration in formal institutions.[106]

Formal and Informal Regional Integration in Asia

International power and norms and domestic state structures thus may account for both the relative lack of formal political institutions and the

---

[104] I know of no good comparative studies that rank political systems by the efficacy with which they create and sustain a common cultural domain. But Rohlen's interpretation goes further than any other I have read in specifying the various mechanisms by which that common cultural domain can be made amenable to empirical study. See Thomas P. Rohlen, "Order in Japanese Society: Attachment, Authority, and Routine," *Journal of Japanese Studies* 15.1 (1989): 5–40.

[105] Hatch and Yamamura, *Asia in Japan's Embrace*, p. 131.

[106] By extension this argument could also be applied to how Anglo-Saxon states cope with processes of regional integration. These states fall between the endpoints of the continuum defined by Asian and continental European states.

informal network structures that define Asian regional integration. ASEAN exemplifies the first of these two factors, Japan's corporate structures and the network of overseas Chinese the second.

Ironically, as Susumu Yamakage shows in Chapter 8, the one institution that excludes Japan, ASEAN, is the one regional forum that comes close to giving formal political institutions some measure of importance in Asia's regional integration. Since its founding in 1967 ASEAN has seen a notable growth in the volume of interactions among its members.[107] In the early 1990s official ASEAN meetings numbered in excess of 250 a year.[108] As Yuen Foong Khong puts it, "strong networks of ASEAN business executives exist, bilateral and trilateral military exercises are common, every new ASEAN chief executive visits the other ASEAN countries soon after taking office, and intra-ASEAN think tank and academic exchanges have been fully institutionalized."[109]

Compared to Northeast Asia in particular as well as other international institutions in Asia more generally, ASEAN shows astonishing institutional capacity and dynamism. Its comparative strength is arguably due to three factors.[110] First, historical memories of a common colonial past have made all ASEAN member states very respectful of one another's sovereignty. They also fuel resentment of U.S. diplomatic pressure on issues such as human or workers rights and capital or corporal punishment. ASEAN member states tend to emphasize socioeconomic rights and the primacy of community not political rights and the primacy of the individual.[111] While this does not distinguish Southeast Asian politics clearly from the politics of Northeast Asia and China, recent historical memories do. In Northeast Asia Chinese and Korean memories of Japanese imperialism

[107] Davis B. Bobrow, Steve Chan, and Simon Reich, "Southeast Asian Prospects: American Hopes and Fears," *Pacific Review* 9.1 (1996): 1–30. Yuen Foong Khong, "ASEAN and the Idea of a Security Community" (paper presented at the 90th American Political Science Association annual meeting, New York City, September 1–4, 1994), appendix I; Susumu Yamakage, "The Integrative Role of ASEAN in the ASEAN Region: From Symbol to System," in *Twenty Years of ASEAN: Its Survival and Development*, ed. Okabe Tatsumi (Tokyo: Japan Institute of International Affairs, 1988), pp. 143–66; Donald E. Weatherbee, *ASEAN and Pacific Regionalism* (Bangkok, Thailand: Chulalongkorn University, Institute of Security and International Studies, 1989); Sueo Sudo, "Japan-ASEAN Relations: New Dimensions in Japanese Foreign Policy," *Asian Survey* 28 (May 1988): 509–25, and "From Fukuda to Takeshita: A Decade of Japan-ASEAN Relations," *Contemporary Southeast Asia* 10 (September 1988): 119–43; Charles Morrison, "Japan and the ASEAN Countries: The Evolution of Japan's Regional Role," in *The Political Economy of Japan*, vol. 2, *The Changing International Context*, ed. Takashi Inoguchi and Daniel I. Okimoto (Stanford, Calif.: Stanford University Press, 1988), pp. 414–15.
[108] Khong, "ASEAN and the Idea of a Security Community," p. 3.
[109] Yuen Foong Khong, "Pluralistic Security Communities: The Case of ASEAN" (Government Department, Harvard University, 1994), p. 3.
[110] Khong, "ASEAN and the Idea of a Security Community" and "Pluralistic Security Communities."
[111] Khong, "ASEAN and the Idea of a Security Community," p. 3.

remain strong and feed on the conflicts inside Japan over whether or not to acknowledge Japan's war guilt.[112] Second, ASEAN members have learned a common lesson from the Vietnam war. National resilience matters and is created through economic growth and domestic legitimacy. The Northeast Asian states learned different lessons from the Vietnam War. China and Korea participated in the war, on opposite sides. And Japan was torn between the government's support of the U.S. war effort and strong domestic opposition. Finally, all ASEAN members subscribe to the ideology of capitalist growth. In Northeast Asia, until very recently, China has strongly opposed the route to capitalist growth that Japan, South Korea, and Taiwan chose after 1945.

But ASEAN is also a remarkably modest organization with scattered signs of institutional deepening and growth evident only in recent years. No concrete measures to advance economic integration were taken in the first decade of its existence. Prior to the signing of the Treaty of Amity and Cooperation at the ASEAN summit in Bali in 1976, member states committed themselves only to selective, not general, preferential tariff reductions. And the preferences granted and the trade flows in question were both small, thus leaving trade among ASEAN members largely unaffected. Intra-ASEAN trade amounts to less than 20 percent of ASEAN's total external trade.[113] Attempts to reduce non-tariff barriers have been ineffective. And ASEAN has made virtually no headway in the implementation of procedural mechanisms for settling disputes among ASEAN members.

To give ASEAN more economic dynamism, member states committed themselves in 1987 to the creation of the ASEAN Free Trade Area (AFTA) by 1995. In 1993 they committed themselves once again to accelerate what had been very slow progress in order to reach that goal by the year 2008. As has been true of numerous proposals for industrial cooperation, the establishment of a free trade zone will take a long time, especially for Indonesia, the Philippines, and Thailand.[114] ASEAN states have traditionally expressed a preference for managed bilateral over free multilateral trade, while in fact practicing general protection. Only in the 1990s has the move to freer multilateral trade gathered strength.

Nevertheless, private-sector and politically less visible mechanisms do

[112] Nicholas D. Kristof, "Many in Japan Oppose Apology to Asians for War," *New York Times,* March 6, 1995, A9.
[113] James C. Clad, "The Half-Empty Basin," *Wilson Quarterly* 16 (Winter 1992): 79.
[114] Cowhey, "Pacific Trade Relations," pp. 16–17, 20–24; Crone, "Does Hegemony Matter?" p. 519; Linda Y. C. Lim, "Southeast Asia: Success through International Openness," University of Wisconsin, Madison, Working Paper Series on the New International Context of Development No.8, August 1993, pp. 13–14; Mario E. Carranza, "Geo-Economic Regionalism in a Post-Sovereign World: The Future of ASEAN and the European Union" (paper presented at the thirty-sixth annual meeting of the International Studies Association, Chicago, February 21–25, 1995).

support Asian regional integration.[115] In the absence of a sustained move by ASEAN or other international institutions, private business as well as provincial and local governments are pushing ahead with the construction of a regional economy. Relatedly, in the Brand-to-Brand Complementation Scheme (BBC) ASEAN granted automobile companies in 1989 up to 50 percent tariff reductions and credit toward local content for ASEAN trade in auto parts. This policy encourages both regionalization and localization. According to Richard Doner, Japanese assemblers have begun to see in the BBC "a useful channel through which to begin rationalizing their scattered but growing operations in the region."[116] This informal regionalization may lead to further integrative developments.[117] Sectoral rationalization reconfigures local interests that are hurt or helped by trade liberalization and which otherwise may stall or stop formal trade negotiations. Governments interested in larger export revenues may latch onto the economic potential of the BBC as a way of strengthening their liberalization policies. Furthermore, the diffusion of higher quality in regionally traded parts may reinforce notions of best practice that Japanese corporations have tried to institutionalize through their supplier networks, producers' associations, and private-public consultative mechanisms throughout Southeast Asia.[118]

ASEAN is a decentralized intergovernmental and nongovernmental congress that operates incessantly, without accreting centralized powers. Yet it has had some noticeable effects on security issues vital to the interests of its members. For example, after 1979 ASEAN stood by Thailand as a frontline state and closed ranks in pressuring Vietnam to end its occupation of Kampuchea. In 1992 both Vietnam and Laos signed ASEAN's Treaty on Amity and Cooperation, thus signaling their commitment to abide by the norm of a peaceful settlement of disputes. Furthermore, in the form of the ASEAN Regional Forum (ARF) Asia-Pacific recently acquired its first

---

[115] Linda Y. C. Lim, "The Role of the Private Sector in ASEAN Regional Economic Cooperation," in *South-South Co-operation in a Global Perspective*, ed. Lynn K. Mytelka (Paris: OECD, 1994), pp. 125–68.

[116] Richard F. Doner, "Remarks" (paper presented at the workshop on Multinationals and East Asia Integration, Cambridge, Mass., November 18–19, 1994), p. 3; "Limits of State Strength: Toward an Institutionalist View of Economic Development," *World Politics* 44 (April 1992): 427–29; "Japanese Investment and the Creation of a Pacific Asian Region," in Frankel and Kahler, *Regionalism and Rivalry*, pp. 159–214; and *Driving a Bargain: Automobile Industrialization and Japanese Firms in Southeast Asia* (Berkeley and Los Angeles: University of California Press, 1991).

[117] Doner, "Remarks," pp. 6–7; U.S. International Trade Commission, *East Asia*, pp. 101–10.

[118] Also, subregional "growth triangles," such as Johor (Malaysia)-Singapore-Riau (Indonesia), bring together different national and provincial governments in search of foreign investors. They may complement political moves that seek to increase region-wide liberalization. Yuan, *Growth Triangle;* Lim, "Southeast Asia," pp. 11–13.

multilateral forum institutionalizing a regional security dialogue.[119] In sum, ASEAN's history illustrates that, in the words of Kiichi Fujiwara, in Asia's regional integration "state sovereignty and regional cooperation expanded in unison."[120]

The network organization that characterizes the Japanese state gave rise to the distinctive patterns of Japanese penetration of Asian economies.[121] Saya and Takashi Shiraishi have illustrated how, in the early decades of the twentieth century, Japanese colonial communities in Southeast Asia, composed initially of marginal populations of prostitutes and pimps and, subsequently, of shopowners, white-collar workers, clerks, planters, and plantation workers eventually became extensions of a Japanese state that sought to "re-Nipponize" these communities through the activities of local bosses and consulates, the establishment of local Japanese associations, and, eventually, the introduction of Japan's uniform educational system.[122]

After 1945 Japanese influence continued to spread in the form of network extensions of Japanese practices but without a monopoly of state control. After the Pacific War virtually all Japanese living in Southeast Asia returned to Japan, leaving Japanese corporations without direct points of contact. The Japanese who had left Southeast Asia at the end of the war wearing army uniforms returned, however, dressed in business suits, in the late 1950s. This initiated a new era of Asian regional integration, as Japanese economic influence began to spread gradually once more in Asia.[123] Political and personal connections were reknit that in some cases had existed for decades before the war, thus giving Japanese business an edge

---

[119] The ARF was a result of ASEAN's Post-Ministerial Conference (PMC), in which ASEAN foreign ministers, since 1978, have met with their counterparts from their dialogue partners to discuss economic and security issues. This arrangement was formalized in 1993 as the ARF and comprised the ASEAN members, its dialogue partners (the United States, Japan, Canada, the European Union, South Korea, Australia, and New Zealand), as well as Russia, China, Vietnam, Laos, and Papua New Guinea. See Khong, "ASEAN and the Idea of a Security Community," pp. 15–17.

[120] Kiichi Fujiwara, "State Formation and Regional Order: Southeast Asia in the International Environment" (paper presented at the symposium "Peace Building in Asia-Pacific and Australia-Japan Relations," University of Tokyo, Komaba Campus, December 3–4, 1994), p. 1; Kiichi Fujiwara, "Governmental-Parties: Political Parties and the State in North- and Southeast Asia" (paper presented at the International Political Science Association [IPSA] Roundtable, Kyoto, March 26–27, 1994).

[121] Daniel I. Okimoto, *Between MITI and the Market: Japanese Industrial Policy for High Technology* (Stanford, Calif.: Stanford University Press, 1989).

[122] Saya Shiraishi and Takashi Shiraishi, "The Japanese in Colonial Southeast Asia: An Overview," in *The Japanese in Colonial Southeast Asia*, ed. Shiraishi and Shiraishi (Ithaca: Cornell University, Southeast Asia Program, 1993), pp. 5–20.

[123] Masashi Nishihara, *The Japanese and Sukarno's Indonesia: Tokyo-Jarkarta Relations, 1951–1966* (Honolulu: University Press of Hawaii, 1976), offers a vivid case study of this process. For the 1970s and 1980s, see Machado, "Malaysian Cultural Relations," pp. 645–56.

over international competitors who also sought to establish themselves in emerging markets often governed by authoritarian regimes. Profitable business opportunities were pursued to benefit both political leaders in Southeast Asia and Japanese business. Thus Giovanni Arrighi concludes that "it was precisely the 'informal' and 'flexible' nature of the transborder expansion of Japanese capital in the surrounding low-income region that boosted its world competitiveness."[124] And in the words of Edward Lincoln, Japan has moved swiftly toward an "informal and soft form of economic regionalisation with other Asian countries."[125]

Generational turnover and a massive increase in Japanese direct foreign investment in the 1980s changed this picture once again. Put succinctly, Japanese developmentalism has gone regional. By sharply increasing investment in and aid to its Asian neighbors Japan has increased its trade with them, as well; the level of technology transfer has also risen. But since the domestic structures of Japan are much more conducive to the creation of dynamic technological efficiencies than are the domestic structures of the other Asian states, Asia's technological dependence on Japan is also increasing and economic hierarchies are being created not dismantled in the process of high economic growth and industrialization. This is the central point of Hatch and Yamamura's analysis.[126]

The organizational advantages of the keiretsu structure of Japan's large corporations became more apparent over time. As Richard Doner shows in Chapter 6, these corporations rebuilt supplier chains abroad, in textiles and electronics first and in automobiles later. Such chains link myriads of subcontractors and producers of components in complex, multitiered arrangements that had heretofore operated in sheltered domestic markets.[127] Medium-sized Japanese corporations also expanded their operations in Northeast and Southeast Asia and have thus helped to create an integrated regional economy centered for the most part on Japan.[128] Such business

[124] Giovanni Arrighi, "The Rise of East Asia: World-Systemic and Regional Aspects" (paper presented at the conference "L'economia monidale in transformazione," Fondazione Istituto Gramsci, University of Rome, October 6–8, 1994), p. 23; Pollack, "Shellshocked by Yen."
[125] Lincoln, "Japan's Rapidly Emerging Strategy," p. 13.
[126] Hatch and Yamamura, *Asia in Japan's Embrace*. We should add, however, that the Japanese developmentalism now being regionalized lacks the insistence on enhancing national political autonomy, a trademark of Japan's economic policy since the Meiji Restoration.
[127] Dennis J. Encarnation, *Rivals Beyond Trade: America versus Japan in Global Competition* (Ithaca: Cornell University Press, 1992), pp. 147–82; Office of Technology Assessment, U.S. Congress, *Multinationals and the National Interest: Playing by Different Rules*, OTA-ITE-569 (Washington, D.C.: U.S. Government Printing Office, September 1993), pp. 86–94.
[128] Seki, *Beyond the Full-Set Industrial Structure;* David Arase, "Japan in East Asia," in *Japan in the Posthegemonic World*, ed. Tsuneo Akaha and Frank Langdon (Boulder, Colo.: Lynne Rienner, 1993), pp. 113–36; Peter J. Katzenstein and Martin Rouse, "Japan as a Regional Power in Asia," in Frankel and Kahler, *Regionalism and Rivalry*, pp. 217–48; Richard F. Doner, "Jap-

practices have led to a triangular structure of trade.[129] Backed by the largest stock of foreign investment in the region, the largest aid disbursements in Asia, and a high volume of trade, the Japanese government has begun to export its prized system of administrative guidance to influence business operations abroad. In the fall of 1990 MITI started setting up organizations in various Asian countries to make it easier for local businessmen, including Japanese investors, and officials to meet periodically with MITI officials. These organizations are conceived as arenas for offering "local guidance."[130] Good administrative practices come hand in hand with bad ones. Japanese aid programs export the practice of bid rigging (*dango*) common in Japan's domestic public works. The request-based aid process that typifies Japan, writes David Arase, "is well adapted to penetrating developing countries precisely because it allows for graft and corruption while giving the Japanese government deniability."[131] In brief, Japanese business and government have extended the distinct institutional forms of Japanese state-society relations across national borders.

This network form of regional integration brought about by a network state typifies Asia more generally. The web of entrepreneurial relationships through which Greater China has been reintegrating since the late 1980s offers a second example. Takeshi Hamashita offers in Chapter 3 a histor-

---

anese Foreign Investment and the Creation of a Pacific Asian Region," in Frankel and Kahler, *Regionalism and Rivalry*, pp. 191–97; Kiyoshi Kojima, "Japanese and American Direct Investment in Asia: A Comparative Analysis," *Hitotsubashi Journal of Economics* 26 (June 1985): 1–35; Christian Deubner, *Potentiale und Formen eines verstärkten Regionalismus in Ost- und Südostasien und die Rolle Japans* (Ebenhausen, Germany: Stiftung Wissenschaft und Politik, 1985); Arrighi, "Rise of East Asia," pp. 17–26; Satoshi Ikeda, "Japanese Accumulation Structure and the Postwar World-System," *Social Justice* 21 (Summer 1994): 37–42; Shojiro Tokunaga, "Japan's FDI-Promoting Systems and Intra-Asia Networks: New Investment and Trade Systems Created by the Borderless Economy," in *Japan's Foreign Investment and Asian Economic Interdependence: Production, Trade, and Financial Systems*, ed. Shojiro Tokunaga (Tokyo: University of Tokyo Press, 1992), pp. 5–47; Edward J. Lincoln, *Japan's Economic Role in Northeast Asia* (Lanham, Md: University Press of America, Asia Society, 1987); Kunio Yoshihara, *Japanese Investment in Southeast Asia* (Honolulu: University Press of Hawaii, 1978); Mitchell Bernard and John Ravenhill, "Beyond Product Cycles and Flying Geese: Regionalization, Hierarchy, and the Industrialization of East Asia," *World Politics* 47 (January 1995): 171–209; Crone, "Does Hegemony Matter?" p. 511.

[129] Exports and investments by Japan and the East Asian NIEs have made Southeast Asian economies both importers of foreign capital as well as machinery, equipment, parts, and supplies and exporters of final products destined for Western markets. See Lim, "Southeast Asia," pp. 6, 18–20, and Doner, "Japanese Foreign Investment."

[130] Edward J. Lincoln, *Japan's New Global Role* (Washington, D.C.: Brookings Institution, 1993), pp. 125, 127–28, 145–46, 178, 192; Cowhey, "Pacific Trade Relations," pp. 9–12. See also Ippei Yamazawa, "A Vision for the Asia Pacific Economy in the Year 2000 and the Tasks Ahead," in Bundy, Burns, and Weichel, *Future of the Pacific Rim*, pp. 206–20.

[131] David Arase, *Buying Power: The Political Economy of Japan's Foreign Aid* (Boulder, Colo.: Lynne Rienner, 1995), p. 161.

ical analysis that Mark Selden updates in Chapter 9 for the 1980s and 1990s. Even though political connections are part of the economic bargains being struck, what John Kao calls a new Chinese "Commonwealth" is not defined by formal state institutions.[132] That commonwealth has no written charter, but it exists nonetheless and has important political and economic effects. Ethnic ties and family clans establish powerful regional business networks "informal though pervasive, with local variations but essentially stateless, stitched together by capital flows, joint ventures, marriages, political expediency and a common culture and business ethic."[133] An ethnic Chinese network that transcends national boundaries accounts for up to 80 percent of the corporate sector in countries such as Malaysia, Thailand, and Indonesia and for about 40 percent in the Philippines.[134] And about four-fifths of the foreign investments in the PRC are thought to come from regional business networks that link Taiwan, Hong Kong, and parts of Southeast Asia with the PRC.[135]

This process of regional integration is informal and by Japanese, let alone European, standards "underinstitutionalized." It lacks political or economic summits. "It has no head, no organization, no politics, no boundaries," says Peter Kwong-ching Woo, chairman of Hong Kong–based

---

[132] John Kao, "The Worldwide Web of Chinese Business," *Harvard Business Review* 71 (March–April 1993): 24; Marcus W. Brauchli and Dan Biers, "Green Lanterns: Asia's Family Empires Change Their Tactics for a Shrinking World," *Wall Street Journal*, April 19, 1995, A1, A8; Lampton et al., *The Emergence of "Greater China,"* pp. 3–4; Joel Kotkin, *Tribes: How Race, Religion, and Identity Determine Success in the New Global Economy* (New York: Random House, 1993), pp. 165–200; Arrighi, "Rise of East Asia," pp. 31–38; J. A. C. Mackie, "Overseas Chinese Entrepreneurship," *Asian-Pacific Economic Literature* 6 (May 1992): 41–64; Milton J. Esman, "The Chinese Diaspora in Southeast Asia," in *Modern Diasporas in International Politics*, ed. Gabriel Sheffer (New York: St. Martins Press, 1986), pp. 130–63; Susan Shirk, *How China Opened Its Door: The Political Success of the PRC's Foreign Trade and Investment Reforms* (Washington, D.C.: Brookings Institution, 1994); Thomas P. Lyons and Victor Nee, eds., *The Economic Transformation of South China: Reform and Development in the Post-Mao Era*, Cornell East Asia Program no.70 (Ithaca, N.Y.: Mario Einaudi Center for International Studies, 1994); David S. G. Goodman and Gerald Segal, eds., *China Deconstructs: Politics, Trade, and Regionalism* (New York: Routledge, 1994); *China Quarterly*, no. 136 (December 1993).

[133] Henny Sender, "Inside the Overseas Chinese Network," *Institutional Investor*, August 1991, 29.

[134] Nine of the ten largest business groups in Thailand are owned by ethnic Chinese, who account for about 10 percent of the population. In Indonesia, the Chinese population accounts for 4 percent of the population and owns the ten largest business groups. In truth nobody knows the exact size of these business empires. They are extremely complex in their structure and shielded from the scrutiny of any outsider. See Brick, "Emergence of Greater China," pp. 3–4; Murray Weidenbaum, "Greater China: A New Economic Colossus?" *Washington Quarterly* 16 (1993): 71, 76; U.S. International Trade Commission, *East Asia*, pp. 50–51.

[135] Paul Blustein, "Forging 'Greater China': Emigres Help Build an Economic Power," *Washington Post*, December 1, 1992, A30.

Wharf (Holdings) Ltd.[136] These networks are composed mostly of family firms; multinational corporations are largely absent. As Joel Kotkin puts it, "The pattern and fundamental character of the Chinese global extension differs dramatically from those of the Japanese. In contrast to the exceedingly close ties between the Japanese *salarimen* abroad and their home islands, the Chinese global network possesses no fixed national point of origin, no central 'brain.' "[137] After painstaking field research in Thailand, Mitchell Sedgwick concludes similarly that "Japanese multinationals in Thailand have reproduced the atomization of labor and strong centralization of decision-making authority—the 'Fordism'—that they managed to avoid in post-war Japan. . . . Beyond internal plant dynamics, however, the strict centralization is also reflected in the position of subsidiaries vis-à-vis headquarters. Subsidiaries in Thailand are part of a tightly controlled and rigorously hierarchical organizational structure extending down from Japan."[138]

Differences in Japanese and overseas Chinese corporate networks integrating Northeast and Southeast Asia can be traced also in specific industries.[139] In the case of electronics, for example, Michael Borrus argues that Japanese networks rely largely on Japanese sources with similar technical capabilities. In contrast, overseas Chinese networks draw on increasingly high value-added technical specialization throughout Asia. Japanese networks tend to be closed, Japan-centered, and long-term. Chinese networks

---

[136] *Business Week*, November 29, 1993, quoted in Hatch and Yamamura, *Asia in Japan's Embrace.*

[137] Kotkin, *Tribes*, p. 167.

[138] Mitchell W. Sedgwick, "Does the Japanese Management Miracle Travel in Asia? Managerial Technology Transfer at Japanese Multinationals in Thailand" (paper presented at the Workshop on Multinationals and East Asian Integration, MIT Japan Program, Cambridge, Mass. (November 18–19, 1994), p. 8. See also M. K. Chng and R. Hirono, eds. *ASEAN-Japan Industrial Co-Operation: An Overview* (Singapore: Institute of Southeast Asian Studies, 1984). C. Y. Ng, R. Hirono, and Narongchai Akrasanee, eds., *Industrial Restructuring and Adjustment for ASEAN-Japan Investment and Trade Expansion: An Overview* (Singapore: Institute of Southeast Asian Studies, 1987).

[139] David P. Angel, *Restructuring for Innovation: The Remaking of the U.S. Semiconductor Industry* (New York: Guilford Press, 1994); Dieter Ernst, "Network Transactions, Market Structure, and Technology Diffusion—Implications for South-South Co-operation," in *South-South Co-operation in Global Perspective*, ed. Lynn K. Mytelka (Paris: OECD, 1994), pp. 109–12; Dieter Ernst, *What Are the Limits of the Korean Model? The Korean Electronics Industry under Pressure* (Berkeley: University of California, Berkeley Roundtable on the International Economy [BRIE], 1994); Takeshi Aoki, "Japanese FDI and the Forming of Networks in the Asia-Pacific Region: Experience in Malaysia and Its Implications," in *Japan's Foreign Investment and Asian Economic Interdependence*, ed. Shojiro Tokunaga (Tokyo: University of Tokyo Press, 1992), pp. 73–110; Edna Bonacich et al., *Global Production: The Apparel Industry in the Pacific Rim* (Philadelphia: Temple University Press, 1994); Bernard and Ravenhill, "Beyond Product Cycles," pp. 185–88; Eileen M. Doherty, ed., *Japanese Investment in Asia: International Production Strategies in a Rapidly Changing World* (Conference Proceedings, Berkeley Roundtable on the International Economy [BRIE] and the Asia Foundation, San Francisco, September 26–27, 1994).

tend to be open, flexible and disposable.[140] The existence of this alternative network of overseas Chinese has made it possible in the last fifteen years for the U.S. electronics industry to escape from a position of almost total dependence on Japanese firms for component technologies and manufacturing capabilities. This development has reinforced economic links across the Pacific and may have diffused political tensions in U.S.-Japan trade relations. Partly overlapping subregional trade and investment networks thus take the place of a more formal institutionalization of Asian regionalism.[141]

In either its Japanese or overseas Chinese variant, Asia's regionalism thus eschews formal institutions. Asian regionalism takes different forms, marked by weaknesses in international institutions. It is defined primarily in market terms. It operates not only under the auspices of Japanese keiretsu structures together with the Japanese government but also through the efforts of overseas Chinese, who seek to combine their business acumen and financial resources in tightly held, medium-sized, family-owned firms, with the vast natural resources, cheap labor, and pent-up consumer demand of the PRC. Japanese keiretsu organizations and Chinese-owned family firms shape Asian regionalism through the economic integration that they bring about without explicit links to formal international institutions.

International power and norms as well as domestic state structures mitigate against the creation of a closed form of Asian regionalism under

[140] Borrus, "MNC Production Networks and East Asian Integration," p. 3. See also Eileen M. Doherty, "Japanese Production Networks in Asia: International Production Networks in a Rapidly Changing World" (paper prepared with Dieter Ernst, Michael Borrus, Stephen S. Cohen, and John Zysman for the Berkeley Roundtable on the International Economy [BRIE], University of California, Berkeley, 1994), pp. 2–3. Dieter Ernst, *Carriers of Regionalization: The East Asian Production Networks of Japanese Electronics Firms*, Working Paper No. 73 (Berkeley: University of California, Berkeley Roundtable on the International Economy [BRIE], November 1994). Borrus notes that, with the exception of the electronics industry, this ideal-typical characterization is based largely on intuition and awaits further empirical and theoretical work.

[141] Borrus, "MNC Production Networks and East Asian Integration," pp. 5–6. Changes in the electronics industry may well be under way as Eileen Doherty suggests ("Japanese Production Networks in Asia," p. 2). The industry is witnessing a sharp increase in the linkups between Japanese and Asian-based companies. "Such partnerships suggest an emerging Asian regionalism in the industry, a set of increasingly close relationships that provide Asian chip makers with Japanese alternatives to U.S. technology." David P. Hamilton and G. Pierre Goad, "Japan's Chip Makers Pick Partners in Asia: Trading Know-How for Factory Space, They Beat the Yen," *Wall Street Journal*, November 7, 1994, A11. New strategies of Japanese corporations may be a response to their dramatic loss of market share in memory chips to Korean producers. David P. Hamilton and Steve Glain, "Koreans Move to Grab Memory-Chip Market from the Japanese," *Wall Street Journal*, March 14, 1995, A1, A11.

either Japanese or Chinese leadership. Conditions favor instead an open Asian regionalism. Its economic form will be network-like. Its political shape will be multicephalic. And its political definition will remain contested.

Relying on a comparative perspective, I have argued that Asian regionalism is likely to be open. Talk of a second coming of the Co-Prosperity Sphere and the emergence of a yen bloc express the correct intuition that, with the collapse of bipolarity, regionalization is of increasing importance in world politics. But this should not lead us to draw misleading historical analogies with the 1930s. The world today is a vastly different place.

Fearing that it might undercut its global stakes, Japan continues to show some ambivalence toward the regionalization processes that it accelerates through aid, trade, and investment in Asia. For many of Japan's business and political leaders, internationalization and regionalization are not mutually exclusive processes. Asia and Asia-Pacific remain amorphous categories open to different political definitions, approaches, and solutions. A loose and encompassing Pacific community might form around Japan, China, South Korea, Taiwan, ASEAN member states, Russia, the United States, Australia, Canada, and perhaps some Latin American countries. Such a community would probably be restricted to dealing with only a small number of economic issues. Alternatively, and less likely, a deepening of the U.S.-Japanese relationship could create tighter links between the two countries covering a growing range of economic and political issues. Or Japan might find itself drawn into ethnically based capitalist rivalries that could divide Asia while forging closer links to the global economy. Finally, Japan might continue in building ever closer production alliances with the NIEs in Northeast Asia, the ASEAN states in Southeast Asia, and with producers located in the Chinese trading network, thus reinforcing further the Asian links that it has forged while seeking to transform Asia into a Japanese production platform. Each of these scenarios expresses a compelling political logic. But the future is unlikely to replicate any one of them. More likely are political approaches that will seek to combine selected elements from each.

One might also look to the past for intellectual templates that could inform our views on Asian regionalism. Hatch and Yamamura see in Japan's embrace of Asia the emergence of structural dependencies reminiscent of those Nazi Germany brought about in Central Europe in the 1930s.[142] Murray Weidenbaum has looked instead to a more distant Cen-

---

[142] Hatch and Yamamura, *Asia in Japan's Embrace.*

tral European past, to the Hanseatic League as a historical analogue for the political organization of Greater China.[143] The comparison is apt and might be extended to other manifestations of Asian regionalism. The League was not unified by governmental institutions, but government and business leaders from different cities, principalities, and states in Northern Germany and around the Baltic area cooperated on matters of mutual economic concern. Unlike the Hanseatic League Asian regionalism is likely to infuse the nongovernmental organizations with considerable political powers. For state and society in Asia are too intimately tied together to be fully disentangled in the world of "private" diplomacy. Since the future will not replicate the past, such historical analogies are useful for broadening our vision rather than for making predictions.

Future scenarios and historical analogies help stretch our imagination. Here they set the stage for the four parts of this book. Part I situates Japan in Asia by reviewing some important economic and cultural aspects of Asian regionalism. In Chapter 1 T. J. Pempel traces the growing economic and social interdependence of Asian states. Victor Koschmann explores in Chapter 2 the ambivalent cultural legacy of Asian discourse in Japanese politics.

Part II examines Japan's changing relations with Asia and the United States. The Sinocentric world of a comparatively permeable or "suzerain" sovereignty and the British and American worlds of a comparatively impermeable or "pure" sovereignty embody different mixtures of cultural and political elements.[144] In Chapters 3, 4, and 5 Takeshi Hamashita, Bruce Cumings, and Takashi Shiraishi examine the political logics of these two worlds for Japan's position in Asia in the nineteenth and twentieth centuries. Whether relations between the Sinocentric and Anglo-American worlds will lead to historically recurrent frictions or a historically unique fusion is an issue of central importance for Japan, Asia, and the world at large.[145]

Part III analyzes aspects of Asian regional political economy and culture. Richard Doner analyzes in Chapter 6 the institutional extension of Japan in Asia. Intra-industry trade and direct foreign investment offer Japan numerous opportunities, in bilateral settings, of leading from behind in a system of soft rule. Doner also points to the disadvantages that derive from

---

[143] Weidenbaum, "Greater China," pp. 78–79.

[144] Suzerainty provides a past institutional order that partially contradicts contemporary sovereignty. "Pure" sovereignty in the Westphalian system, by way of contrast, contains no alternative institutional order for the society of states. It points only to numerous instances where de jure and de facto sovereignty diverge.

[145] Robert A. Manning and Paula Stern, "The Myth of the Pacific Community," *Foreign Affairs* 73 (November/December 1994): 79–93; Mahbubani, "The Pacific Way."

the tendency of Japanese corporate networks to be exclusive and rigid. This creates distinctive weaknesses in a region of multiple networks and shifting markets.

Processes of Asian regional integration that combine economic and cultural elements merit special attention. Japanese exports of mass culture to Taiwan, Hong Kong, and, more slowly, South Korea offer good illustrations. The export of Japanese TV programs, movies, *pachinko* parlors, karaoke bars, and comic strips are new elements in the evolution of Asian mass culture.[146] In Chapter 7 Saya Shiraishi examines how Japan has innovated in the creation of "image alliances" that have acquired a cultural dynamic of their own. She uncovers carefully the various mechanisms that give Japan in Asia some of the "soft power" that it supposedly lacks for playing on the global stage.[147]

Part IV explores Asian regionalism from the vantage point of the security relations between Japan and the United States as well as the economic relations between China and Japan. Susumu Yamakage argues in Chapter 8 that the relationship between the United States and Japan remains of vital importance for Japan's national security and Asian regional security more generally; however, that central link of Japan and Asia to the larger international system permits a variety of regional arrangements designed to enhance the security of Asian states.

Just as Franco-German relations have become a bedrock of the European integration process, the relations between China and Japan are at the center of any future growth of Asian regionalism.[148] This is the focus of Mark Selden's analysis of the emergence of Greater China and its implications for Japan and Asia in Chapter 9. In particular Selden explores the effects that the economic growth and political power of maritime China will have for the PRC and Asia.

Finally, in the Conclusion, Takashi Shiraishi and I place Japan's role in Asia in a broader comparative perspective. We view Asian regionalism as intimately linked to global processes, see Japan's role in twentieth-century Asia at the margins of both the Sinocentric and the Anglo-American empires, seek to illustrate both the similarities of and differences between Japan and Germany after 1945, and contrast Japan's and Germany's lead-

---

[146] Dan Biers, "Japan's Asian Neighbors, in a Shift, Are Tuning In to Its Cultural Exports," *Wall Street Journal*, October 25, 1994, A12; Funabashi, "The Asianization of Asia," p. 79; Carnegie Endowment Study Group, *Defining a Pacific Community*, p. 23.

[147] Joseph S. Nye, *Bound to Lead: The Changing Nature of American Power* (New York: Basic Books, 1990).

[148] Iriye, *China and Japan*; Chalmers Johnson, *Japan: Who Governs?* (New York: W. W. Norton, 1995), pp. 235–63; Yeng Deng, "Regime Dynamics in Asia-Pacific" (Ph.D. diss., University of Arizona, 1995).

ership with a light hand in open regions since 1945 with the goal of closed regions and brutal aggression in the 1930s and 1940s. Finally, we argue that because the United States remains relevant to regional developments in both Asia and Europe, the mixture of unilateral and multilateral initiatives that it pursues will have an important influence on the strength of political forces that are pushing toward openness, not closure, and the degree of political influence that is exercised by multiple centers of influence rather than one regional hegemon.

I

THE REGIONAL SETTING

1

Transpacific Torii: Japan and the Emerging Asian Regionalism

T. J. PEMPEL

The dynamics of Asian growth have been enthusiastically chronicled. Even more upbeat are projections for the future. The International Monetary Fund expects that of the $7.5 trillion increase (in 1990 dollars) in the gross world product between 1990 and the year 2000, East Asia will contribute half. The World Bank estimates that between 1993 and 2000, Asia as a whole will account for half the growth in world trade.[1]

In the face of past economic growth and projections of more to come, there has been considerable discussion worldwide of Asia. Despite recent slowdowns, the economies of first Japan, then the Four NIEs or Tigers, and subsequently the Emerging Dragons and South China have all advanced at a phenomenal pace. Congruently, considerable speculation has arisen about the possibility that these nation-states are developing ever closer ties and that a much more economically and politically integrated Asian region will result. For many in the West, such an integrated and economically dynamic Asia appears more frightening than welcome.

This image has become more pervasive since Europe enhanced its own economic integration through the European Union, as NAFTA has gained momentum as a North American trade bloc, and because both have been (correctly) perceived as strongly anti-Asian in motivation. Discussion about Asian regionalism has included speculation about neo-Confucian models of development, the creation of a yen bloc, an Asian Free Trade Regime, and at one extreme, what Steven Schlossstein has called "a kinder, gentler,

[1] "A Survey of Asia," *Economist*, October 30, 1993, pp. 3.

East Asian Co-Prosperity Sphere.''[2] According to such notions—based more on the appeals of tripolar symmetry than on in-depth analysis—the world's three most powerful economies, the United States, Germany, and Japan, would each be the central pillar of three regionally based and somewhat antagonistic trade and investment blocs, a scenario vaguely reminiscent of George Orwell's nightmarish dystopia, *1984*.

Notions of Asian integration and Asian regionalism in the 1990s present a striking contrast to Asia since the late 1800s. True, as Takeshi Hamashita makes clear in Chapter 3, a host of trading regimes have existed throughout Asia, linking many great port cities to one another, but during the nineteenth century, in Asia as in the world at large, the central forces affecting the region were the Western powers, modernization, industrialization, colonialism, and military might. Consequently, in the late nineteenth and early twentieth centuries, Asia was largely a fragmented collection of disparate Western colonies: the British controlled Singapore, Burma, Malaya, and Hong Kong (as well as Australia and New Zealand); the Dutch had Indonesia; the French had Indochina; the Portuguese, Goa and Macao; the Philippines belonged first to Spain and then to the United States; Taiwan and Korea were under Japanese control; China, racked by civil war, was occupied, crossed, and recrossed by military forces from virtually all of these powers. Japan and Thailand were the only two Asian countries free, or mostly so, of Western colonial rule. As a consequence, prior to World War II, the only significant collective challenge to Western leadership in Asia, and the only real bid for Asian integration, came under Japan's unsuccessful military bid during the 1930s to form the Greater East Asia Co-Prosperity Sphere.

Such fragmentation continued and was perhaps even exacerbated following World War II. Largely as an outgrowth of the emergent cold war, Northeast and Southeast Asia (not to mention South Asia) were characterized primarily by fragmentation and high levels of mutual hostility. The Korean peninsula, liberated from colonial Japanese rule, was almost immediately cleaved at its midpoint by the United States and the Soviet Union and subsequently plunged into a civil war with the two indigenous sides being used largely as surrogates for the two superpowers. The countries of Indochina underwent a series of wars, first with France, then with the United States, and throughout and subsequently, among themselves. Indonesia experienced a horrifying bloodbath in the mid-1960s, one which was also tied to cold war politics and which left it at odds with many of its immediate neighbors. Guerrilla insurrections swept Thailand,

---

[2] Steven Schlossstein, *Asia's New Little Dragons: The Dynamic Emergence of Indonesia, Thailand, and Malaysia* (Chicago: Contemporary Books, 1991), pp. 281–87.

Malaysia, Burma, and the Philippines. The victory of the Chinese Communists in 1949 followed decades of internal war, and within only a decade, China was witnessing further tumult with the so-called Great Leap Forward (1958–60), which led to the deaths of perhaps 30–50 million Chinese. This was then followed by an unleashing of the Red Guards in the mid-1960s, which led to even greater internal chaos; finally, the democracy movement of the late 1980s ended in the massacre at Tiananmen Square. Some 15 to 20 percent of the Cambodian population was liquidated by the Khmer Rouge during the mid-1970s. And these were just the "big problems" that Asia was forced to confront and which kept it internally divided.[3]

Further operating against any serious regional cohesion in Asia were the alliances forged out of the cold war. The United States sought to create a "grand crescent" of anticommunist regimes housing U.S. military bases from the Aleutian Islands through Japan, South Korea, and Taiwan, and extending further south through the Philippines and South Vietnam.[4] As the leader of this alliance structure, the United States worked assiduously to maintain bilateral relations with its various alliance partners and to resist more than perfunctory efforts at closer intra-Asian ties, which it saw as a potential challenge to U.S. predominance in the region.

Against the United States stood the Soviet Union, the People's Republic of China, North Korea, and North Vietnam. While the two competing military alliances permitted partial integration among its members, there were virtually no links across the ideological chasm that separated the two hostile blocs.

Meanwhile, the smaller states in the region protected themselves by forging ties with their former colonial rulers, building neutral blocs, pitting the superpowers against each other. In sum, Asian regionalism and integration were at best a dream in the face of such overwhelming military and strategic forces pressing toward fragmentation.

If the cold war and international military politics kept Asia divided for the first three decades after World War II, economics and consumerism have been the main engines driving Asia toward integration over the subsequent fifteen years. The global security and military considerations that earlier spawned fragmentation have waned in importance relative to a host of regional economic forces.

And although there is no denying the importance of domestic politics and economics within most of the Asian economic success stories, Japan

---

[3] "Survey of Asia," p. 4.
[4] Bruce Cumings, "Japan's Position in the World System," in *Postwar Japan as History*, ed. Andrew Gordon (Berkeley and Los Angeles: University of California Press, 1993), pp. 34–63.

has been a major factor in the development of the emerging Asian regionalism. As both a developmental model and a practical catalyst, Japan has stood at the center of much of Asia's postwar moves toward both rapid economic advancement and greater integration.[5] Furthermore, it promises to be a central player in any future regional developments.

This poses something of a dilemma for Japan. Japan's relationship with Asia has of course been complicated, but Japan's simultaneous relationship with the West has added further to this complexity. This duality has been an essential feature of Japanese foreign policy for the last century and more. At times, as Victor Koschmann points out in Chapter 2, Japan has reached out to embrace its Asian neighbors and to speak and act forcefully as the self-appointed spokesman for the region. Frequently, this has meant an overt rejection of the West, especially during the period of xenophobic anti-Western regionalism that Japan sought to advance during the 1930s and 1940s. At other times, Japan has linked its future unambiguously to the West, ranging from the country's initial welcome of Francis Xavier and Christianity, to the Tokugawa fascination with "Dutch learning" gained through the trading port of Nagasaki, and on to the enchantment of many Meiji leaders with Western technology, to the more contemporary embrace of American baseball, Madonna, and Coca-Cola or the welcoming of Europeanism in the form of Beethoven, soccer, and Mercedes Benz.

The debate continues. Today the argument within Japan centers on whether the country's future should be "Asian" or "Western." Many, stressing Japan's political parliamentarism, its economic and technological sophistication, and its international interests, argue for giving primacy to Japan's links to the West. These, they hold, were critical to Japan's economic success following World War II and will continue to provide the logical direction that Japan should take in the future. The rest of Asia, they contend, will not be able to play a major role in Japan's future for at least two or three decades. Others, however, as is manifested in the popularity of the book by Malaysian Prime Minister Mahathir Mohamad and Japanese nationalist Shintaro Ishihara, *The Asia That Can Say No*, point to anti-Japan sentiments in the West and argue that Japan cannot escape its cultural roots and its geographical neighbors. Japan's future, they contend, lies primarily in contributing to the creation of an economically dynamic, and ever growing, counterweight to the increasingly anti-Asian West.

[5] My thoughts on this process can be found in T. J. Pempel, "Japan's Changing Political Economy," *NBR Analysis* 4.5 (1993): 19–31; "The Developmental Regime in a Changing World Economy," in *The Developmental State*, ed. Meredith Woo-Cumings (forthcoming); and "The Enticement of Corporatism: Appeals of the 'Japanese Model' in Developing Asia," in *Capitalism and Corporatism in Korea: Comparative Perspectives*, ed. Dennis McNamara (forthcoming).

My view lies between these extremes. I suggest that the most fitting image of Japan's proper role is the torii, the large wooden gate that stands at key points outside a Shinto shrine and which consists of two large columns joined by an equally strong lintel. For many Japanese, their country is the ideal lintel—the top beam or crossbar uniting the otherwise isolated columns, which represent Asia and the West. Japan is ideally positioned economically and culturally to be the "bridge between East and West." It stands between and brings together two otherwise insulated and incomprehensible worlds. Developing and maintaining such a role, however, is by no means automatic, natural, or without immense problems, including strong reluctance by many in both the West and Asia to accept Japan in such a position; however, I believe that if Japan withdraws into either camp, the results are likely to be even more problematic, both for Japan and for the rest of Asia.

Stages in the Emerging Asian Regionalism

Two distinct stages can be identified in the growing economic integration of Asia. Both stages are closely linked to changes in Japan's domestic political economy, and the consequent changes in Japan's foreign economic policy. The first stage was driven primarily by trade and aid, the second by foreign direct investment (FDI). In addition, the first of these stages had Japan clearly at the center of a series of bilateral linkages—much as had been true of the U.S. security policies vis-à-vis Asia during the first thirty years after World War II. The second stage, meanwhile, has been far more multilateral in character.

In this second stage, which has by no means seen a massive diminution in Japanese presence in Asia, additional investors, primarily from Taiwan, Hong Kong, and South Korea, have moved into subsidiary, but nonetheless important, roles as lieutenants in the march toward Asian integration. Trade patterns have become more multilateral. The result is a much more complicated criss-crossing and interpenetration of economic forces than the earlier pattern, in which Japan was the center and the other countries of Asia were at the periphery, connected to one another primarily through Tokyo.

Most Japanese policymakers and business leaders long ago accepted a regionally based model of economic development for Asia. But as Koschmann points out in his treatment of Japanese pan-Asianism in Chapter 2, all such early models were predicated around an integration that situated Japan at the center of any Asian success. The most prominent manifestation during the 1930s was the Greater East Asian Co-Prosperity Sphere. Far less overtly imperialistic was the "flying geese model," initially advanced by Japanese professor Kaname Akamatsu in the 1930s and subsequently made more famous in the writings of Kiyoshi Kojima during the 1970s in a formulation Kojima called the catching-up product cycle.[6]

In this model, Japan was to be the "lead goose," the Asian originator of new industrial sectors. Heading a "flying V" of Asian economic geese, Japan was to pull the region forward with its own successes in industrialization and manufacturing. The other Asian countries were to follow Japan's lead, and a succession of Asian "geese" was to replicate Japan's developmental experiences and those of the other "geese" ahead of them in formation, moving steadily forward in their levels of manufacturing sophistication.

This model was closely linked to particular industrial sectors. Hence, as rising labor costs and other factors of production drove Japanese manufacturers out of certain industries in which they could no longer operate profitably, these industries were to be developed by slightly less sophisticated successors in other Asian countries, whose own economic advancements would follow in due course. Over time, the Asian nations would move collectively and in a geese-like formation toward ever more sophisticated levels of development and industrialization, the end result being greater manufacturing sophistication, international competitiveness, and economic well-being. Japan, of course, was to remain the leader in regional development, controlling all leading technologies and industries, but by following Japan's lead along a common trajectory, other countries would quickly benefit.[7]

The message of the"flying geese" model to the rest of Asia was quite simple: follow Japan's example, stay in line and don't try to get too close;

[6] See, for example, Kaname Akamatsu, "Shinkoku kogyokoku no sangyo hatten" [Industrial development in newly industrializing countries], in *Ueda Teijiro Hakushi Kinen Rombunsho* [Collected essays in honor of Ueda Teijiro], vol. 4 (Tokyo: Kagakushugi Kosyosho, 1943); see also Kaname Akamatsu, "A Historical Pattern of Economic Growth in Developing Countries," *The Developing Economies* 1 (March–August 1962): 3–25. Kiyoshi Kojima, "Reorganization of North-South Trade: Japan's Foreign Economic Policy in the 1970s," *Hitotsubashi Journal of Economics* 13.2 (1973): 1–28, and *Japanese Direct Foreign Investment: A Model of Multinational Business Operations* (Tokyo: Tuttle, 1978).

[7] It was Bruce Cumings, in "The Origins and Development of the Northeast Asian Political Economy: Industrial Sector, Product Cycles and Political Consequences," *International Organization* 38 (Winter 1984), who linked the flying geese model to the product cycle. For a critique and substantial elaboration of Cumings's argument, see Mitchell Bernard and John Ravenhill, "Beyond Flying Geese and Product Cycles: Regionalization, Hierarchy, and the Industrialization of East Asia," *World Politics* 47 (January 1995): 171–209.

eventually, you too will fly into the kind of successful economy we are in the process of leaving behind. The implicit arrogance of a permanent place at the front of the avian Asian advance was never mentioned by its Japanese advocates. Its underlying logic, however, seemed to undergird Japanese policies toward Asia for at least the first thirty or thirty-five years after World War II.

Indeed, the image has not lost its power even in the 1990s. Thus, in 1990, the Japanese Ministry of Finance's Committee on Asia Pacific Economic Research declared: "It is necessary that what Japan used to do should be done by the Asian NIEs, what the Asian NIEs used to do should be done by ASEAN countries."[8]

At the same time, all such thinking about Japan and Asia was complicated by Japan's relationship with the West. The dualistic pulls for Japan's focus was particularly strong during the early postwar years. This in turn grew primarily out of the conditions of Japanese domestic politics and the foreign policy constraints that flowed from them. As Figure 1-1 indicates, Japan had been quite heavily linked to Asia through trade during the prewar years with nearly 52 percent of Japanese exports going to Asia and 36 percent of Japan's imports coming from Asia. Western trade played a far less substantial role as the war approached. This balance was rather quickly reversed for Japan following the loss of the country's colonies and its domestic economic prowess in World War II. As a consequence, during the 1940s and 1950s, Asia receded in economic and strategic significance, and the West, particularly the United States, gained much greater predominance.

It was during this period that Japan opted, under Prime Minister Shigeru Yoshida, for a politics of very limited military spending and a focus on domestic economic revitalization, all under the nuclear and security umbrella of the United States, combined with virtually undiluted access to the rich U.S. market for Japanese goods. With Asia economically prostrate and divided by the cold war, its appeal to Japan diminished correspondingly.

Yoshida's emphasis on the United States was by no means a consensual choice within Japan. The country was divided into at least three major groupings. On the ideological right stood many unreconstructed nationalists, anxious to erase the stigma of military defeat and to rewrite Japan's constitution to restore the preeminence of the emperor, to rewrite Article IX to allow Japan to maintain larger military forces with no constitutional

---

[8] Foundation for Advanced Information and Research (FAIR), *Interim Report of Asia-Pacific Economic Research* (Tokyo: Foundation for Advanced Information and Research, 1990), p. 64, as quoted in Bernard and Ravenhill, "Beyond Flying Geese and Product Cycles," p. 182.

Figure 1-1. Japanese exports and imports, 1934–1936 and 1994

Japanese Exports

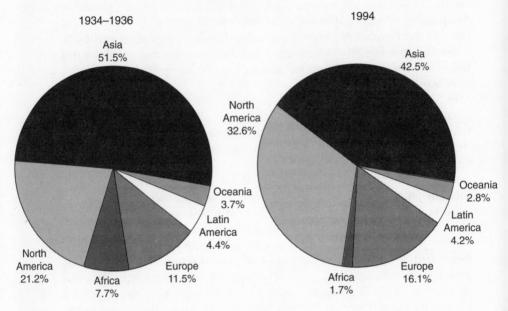

1934–1936

Asia
51.5%

North
America
32.6%

Oceania
3.7%

Latin
America
4.4%

North
America
21.2%

Africa
7.7%

Europe
11.5%

1994

Asia
42.5%

Oceania
2.8%

Latin
America
4.2%

Africa
1.7%

Europe
16.1%

Japanese Imports

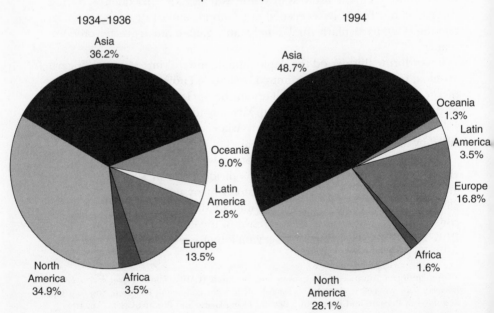

1934–1936

Asia
36.2%

Oceania
9.0%

Latin
America
2.8%

Europe
13.5%

North
America
34.9%

Africa
3.5%

1994

Asia
48.7%

Oceania
1.3%

Latin
America
3.5%

Europe
16.8%

Africa
1.6%

North
America
28.1%

Source: Based on data in *Nihon Kokusei Zue* (Japan national almanac) (Tokyo: Kokuseisha, 1995), p. 368.

ambiguities, and to roll back many of the "democratic excesses," forced, in their eyes, on a defeated and powerless Japan. Implicit in most of their arguments was a strongly pro-Asian focus.

On the left, meanwhile, was a strong socialist (and to a lesser extent, communist) movement, opposed to Japan's close foreign policy ties to the United States and to its capitalist economic system and vocal in its denunciation of all political groups to its ideological right, whom it uniformly castigated as advocating a return to prewar authoritarianism. Favoring either "unarmed neutrality" or closer ties to the Soviet Union and China, the left was uniformly hostile to Japan's alliance structure with the United States and to the presence of U.S. troops on Japanese soil.

Still a third pole was represented largely by Prime Minister Yoshida and his followers. This group saw close ties to the United States as either ideal in their own right or as the price Japan must pay to retain its capitalist economy and its conservatively democratic politics and to prevent a socialist takeover, whether domestically driven or foreign imposed. Focusing primarily on revitalizing Japan's domestic economy, this group favored a minimal foreign policy beyond that of following the U.S. lead on most major questions. Attempting to revise the constitution seemed to this group an unnecessary or foolish way to empower the left, given the deeply entrenched pacifism of the Japanese public. Access to U.S. markets held out an economic appeal that balanced strategic considerations.

Yoshida's policies eventually won out within Japan's conservative camp, and constitutional revision was put off soon after the formation of the Liberal Democratic Party in 1955. The battle between Japan's "progressives" and "conservatives" continued into the late 1950s and early 1960s. A series of business-government actions defeated the most militant elements in Japan's labor movement, while the stormy passage in 1960 of the revised U.S.–Japan Security Treaty, from the vantage point of history, solidified the links between U.S. and Japanese defense systems and laid the groundwork for the eventual acceptance by the broader Japanese public of its inevitability, if not necessarily its desirability.[9] The victory of Yoshida's policies meant not only a low military posture in Japan's foreign policy, but also an emphasis on economic linkages to the United States and the West, not Asia.

Thus, starting in 1960, Japan began its march toward economic success with little serious opposition from domestic political forces. In 1960, Prime Minister Hayato Ikeda, a Yoshida disciple, announced that he would pursue a "low politics" with limited attention to divisive issues such as military

[9] Hideo Otake, *Futatsu no sengo—Doitsu to Nihon* [Two postwars—Germany and Japan] (Tokyo: NHK Books, 1992), chap. 7.

expansion, ties to the United States, or constitutional revision. Instead, he opted for policies aimed at doubling the national income in ten years. And by 1964, Japan had committed itself to a major expansion in trade liberalization and had reestablished convertibility of the yen. In addition, it had joined the Organization for Economic Cooperation and Development, become an Article 8 member of the International Monetary Fund, hosted the Olympics, and introduced the world famous "bullet train," to highlight only a few of the country's clearly "economic" successes. Japanese foreign policy, and indeed, much of its domestic politics, had become the politics and policy of rapid economic growth. And for the most part, it was the West and most especially the United States (not Asia) that served as the primary pillar supporting Japan's overall policy orientation.

Asia was by no means ignored; yet within the context of Japan's broad focus on rapid economic growth, trade and aid became the principal mechanisms for Japan's developing involvement with its Asian neighbors. This took the form, first, of Japanese wartime reparations. Between 1955 and 1965, Japan had negotiated agreements with a total of ten East and Southeast Asian countries, transferring about $1.5 billion in reparations and economic and technical assistance. The bulk of this money was tied to the purchase of Japanese goods and services, thereby opening these markets to Japanese companies and creating ever more important bilateral economic links between these countries and Japan. Included in the arrangements was the 1965 normalization of Japan's relationship with South Korea, thereby solving—in the form of a half-billion dollars in grants and loans—one of the country's few remaining foreign policy issues.

This was quite congruent with Japan's broader economic strategy for the first thirty years after World War II which relied primarily on importing raw materials, largely from Asia and the Middle East, and then utilizing these materials for the production of manufactured goods by a host of ever more sophisticated plants within Japan. These products were then sold both within the Japanese domestic market and also exported, primarily to the United States and only secondarily to the rest of Asia. Early postwar Japanese political economy had a clearly U.S. bias to its direction.

Still, Pacific Asia[10] accounted for one-quarter of Japan's exports and twenty-four percent of Japan's imports in the late 1950s, well below prewar levels.[11] These percentages remained relatively constant over the succeeding years, despite dramatic improvements in the internal composition of Japan's economy. For the bulk of this period, Japan concentrated heavily

[10] Australia, Burma, China, Hong Kong, Indonesia, South Korea, Malaysia, New Zealand, Philippines, Singapore, Taiwan, and Thailand.
[11] Thomas Kerschner, *Japanese Foreign Trade* (Lexington, Mass: D. C. Heath, 1975), p. 22.

on the purchase of raw materials and unfinished products from the region, offsetting such purchases with exports of light manufactured goods and consumer products.

During this time, there was relatively little real intra-Asian trade to speak of. Most of the Asian states traded heavily with Japan (as well as with the United States) but not terribly much with one another. At the time Asian "regionalism" meant largely that a number of countries in the Asian region had similar bilateral economic links to Japan and the United States; there was little complex economic activity across the region as a whole. Certainly, trade between the "capitalist" and "communist" economies of Asia was quite limited as a result of U.S. and Soviet policies affecting the region.

In government aid, Japan also had a very visible presence in Asia, although its contributions were far less significant than those of the United States. Approximately 70 percent of Japan's aid was sent to Asian countries, with the remaining thirty percent divided relatively equally among Africa, the Middle East, and Latin America. This "aid" was almost invariably linked to the development and expansion of markets for Japanese companies. The Japanese government gradually became the principal donor of aid throughout Asia as the United States reduced its presence in the region following its military defeat in Vietnam and the articulation of the Guam Doctrine by Richard Nixon in 1969.

In short, for most of the first three decades following World War II, Japan was linked primarily to the United States and only secondarily to Asia. Relations between Japan and the rest of Asia were highly asymmetrical. Asia was principally a source of raw materials for Japan as well as an outlet for Japan's manufactured goods. Most state-to-state relationships were bilateral—a series of individual countries in two-way links to Japan. There was relatively little cross-national economic integration. It is also worth noting that intra-Asian relations were not particularly advanced by much intra-regional tourism, technology transfer, research and development, or cultural exchange.

In addition, with the exception of ASEAN, formed in 1967, and the creation of the Asia Development Bank (ADB) in the same year, there was relatively little institutionalization of the emerging regional economic linkages. All of this began to change in the mid-1970s and then expanded rapidly in the middle of the 1980s following the dramatic rise in total Japanese investment and in the growing complexity of trade and investment patterns.

Japanese politics began to change significantly with the breakdown of the Bretton Woods monetary system in 1971, followed by the quadrupling of world oil prices in 1973. Japanese firms scrambled to deal with the increased value of the yen and the rampant inflation that beset Japan during the mid-1970s.[12] Moreover, as Japan began to develop increasingly massive trade surpluses with the United States and, to a lesser extent, Western Europe, and as many U.S. industries began to feel the effects of competition from Japanese imports across a range of goods from textiles to steel, autos, and electronics, economic relations between the United States and Japan began to deteriorate.[13]

In reaction to pressures from the West as well as from Japan's most competitive industries, the Japanese government stepped up the country's economic liberalization. Simultaneously, as pollution problems beset many regions of the country, Japanese consumers began to question the merits of unchecked economic growth. Moreover, as Japanese businesses became more and more successful, and as they began to face increasing protectionist barriers in foreign markets, many of them chose to invest abroad.

The cumulative result of these multiple trends was a twofold shift in Japanese foreign economic policy. First, foreign direct investment (FDI) by Japanese firms gradually became more important than simple trade.[14] And second, Asia became more important to Japan's overall economic strategies. This period thus marked a second stage in Asian regionalism, one driven quite distinctly by Japan's FDI and ushering in a much greater economic integration throughout Pacific Asia. This investment began in the mid-1970s and included efforts by Japan to move its dirtiest industries to Taiwan and South Korea. But it accelerated vigorously following the Plaza Accord of 1985 and the consequent 40 percent appreciation in the value of the Japanese yen by 1987. (See Figure 1-2 and Table 1-1.) The result was an even more massive acceleration of Japanese FDI and a deeper integration of Japanese manufacturing across Asian borders.

Japanese FDI was relatively small prior to the 1970s and concentrated on the extraction of raw materials; following the jump in the value of the

[12] One of the major responses to inflation was a series of agreements between Japanese business and labor that resulted in a trade-off between employment guarantees and job retraining for workers in exchange for low or no wage increases as a means to allow Japanese manufacturing firms to remain internationally competitive. See Toshimitsu Shinkawa, "Senkyu hyaku nanaju gonen shunto to keizai kiki kanri" [The 1975 spring offensive and the management of economic crisis], in *Nihon Seiji no Shoten*[Problems in Japanese politics], ed. Otake Hideo (Tokyo: Sanichi Shobo, 1984), pp. 189–232; Ikuo Kume, "Changing Relations among the Government, Labor, and Business in Japan after the Oil Crisis," *International Organization* 42 (Autumn 1988): 659–87.

[13] Atsushi Kusano, *NichiBei—Massatsu no Kozo* [United States–Japan: The structure of friction] (Tokyo: PHP Kenkyujo, 1984).

[14] See T. J. Pempel, "From Exporter to Investor: Japanese Foreign Economic Policy," in *Japan's Foreign Policy: After the Cold War, Coping With Change*, ed. Gerald L. Curtis (Armonk, N.Y.: M. E. Sharpe, 1993).

Figure 1-2. Direct investment in Asia by Japan, 1980–1993

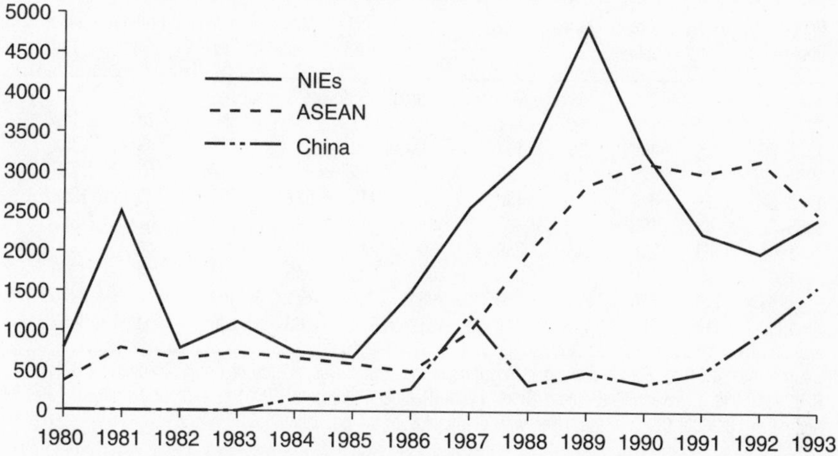

Sources: Ministry of Finance, *Financial Statistics of Japan* (Tokyo: MOF, various years); Keizai Koho Center, *Japan 1995: An International Comparison* (Tokyo: Keizai Koho Center, 1994), p. 61.

yen, it became economically suicidal for Japanese firms not to invest abroad, including the country's manufacturing and service industries, not just those devoted to extracting raw materials. The incentives for Japanese companies to continue manufacturing at home diminished as the costs of investing abroad dropped dramatically in yen terms. In effect, the rest of the world's land prices, labor rates, and corporate valuations had been slashed in half. Why not buy?

From 1951 until 1971, total Japanese foreign direct investment totaled just slightly over $4 billion, with nearly 60 percent of that coming in the last three years of the period. Nearly three-quarters of Japan's limited overseas investments were in nonmanufactured items. As the impact of the breakdown of Bretton Woods began to be felt, Japanese capital moved abroad with an ever-accelerating speed. Thus, the total investment for the years 1973–76 was virtually double that for the preceding twenty years.[15] This expansion continued with $4.7 billion invested in 1980. By 1985 this figure had nearly tripled to $12.2 billion.

Yet it was after 1985 that investment truly began to skyrocket. Spearheaded by Japanese banks and securities corporations, Japanese FDI in 1986 was nearly double that of 1985. By 1988 the figure had doubled once again and it peaked in 1989 at $67.5 billion, some five times greater

[15] Keizai Koho Center, *Japan 1987: An International Comparison* (Tokyo: Japan Institute for Social and Economic Affairs, 1987), p. 56.

Table 1-1 Japanese Manufacturing FDI in Asia, by Major Host Country (1973–1990)

Period (inclusive)	Hong Kong	Sing- apore	Korea	Taiwan	China	Thai- land	Malay- sia	Indon- esia	Philip- pines	Asia Total
				Millions of current US dollars						
1973–76	64	146	292	111	0	71	154	550	78	1496
1977–80	85	467	295	134	1	120	251	843	143	2353
1981–82	30	323	59	96	8	99	77	476	55	1230
1983–84	19	342	69	130	22	118	227	268	20	1258
1985–86	66	198	178	385	46	112	97	93	57	1265
1987	108	268	247	339	30	210	148	295	na	2370
1988	85	179	254	303	203	625	346	298	na	2370
1989	116	678	257	360	206	784	471	167	na	3220
1990	114	270	147	513	161	714	592	536	na	3053

Source: Adapted from *Pacific Economic Relations in the 1990s: Cooperation or Conflict?* edited by R. Higgott, R. Leaver, and J. Ravenhill. (Boulder Colo.: Lynne Rienner Publishers, 1993) p. 125. Copyright © 1993 by Australian Fulbright Commission. Used with permission of the publisher.

than it had been just five years earlier.[16] While the bulk of this investment went to North America, principally the United States, roughly one-quarter was targeted for the rest of Asia, making a profound impact on economies throughout the region. (See Figures 1-3 and 1-4.) Further, between 50 and 60 percent of Japan's Asian investment was in manufacturing. Numerous Japanese firms, particularly those in the consumer electronics and automobile industries began moving toward an expanded, intra-industry division of labor throughout the Asian region, one which, it was presupposed, would to be favorable to Japan.

Japan also took on an increasingly important role in all international financing during this period. In the late 1970s, Japanese investors accounted for 6 percent of direct investment outflows from the major industrial nations, 2 percent of equities outflows, 15 percent of bond outflows and 12 percent of short-term bank outflows. By the late 1980s, these figures had swollen to 20 percent of international FDI, 25 percent of equities, 55 percent of bonds, and 50 percent of short-term bank loans.[17] In 1991, 19 percent of all Japanese banks' overseas lending went to Asia; three years later that had risen to 26 percent (Figure 1-5).

Japan's investment expansion in Asia was extraordinary[18] and continued

[16] Keizai Koho Center, *Japan 1994: An International Comparison* (Tokyo, Japan Institute for Social and Economic Affairs, 1994), p. 54.

[17] Jeffrey A. Frieden, "Domestic Politics and Regional Cooperation: The United States, Japan, and Pacific Money and Finance," in *Regionalism and Rivalry: Japan and the United States in Pacific Asia*, ed. Jeffrey A. Frankel and Miles Kahler (Chicago: University of Chicago Press, 1993), p. 434.

[18] Thus, in 1989, Japanese firms were investing four times as much money in Taiwan as they

Figure 1-3. Japanese new foreign direct investment

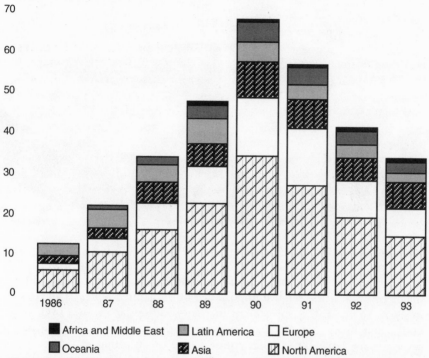

Africa and Middle East ▪ Latin America □ Europe
Oceania ▨ Asia ▨ North America

Source: Adapted from "Japanese Manufacturing: Asian Promise," *The Economist,* June 12, 1994, p. 77.

into the 1990s. As of mid-1993, Asia accounted for 19 percent of Japan's outstanding FDI, up from 12 percent in 1990.[19] Moreover, when the focus is on single-year investment, rather than total investment, Japan's recent Asian focus is even more noteworthy. For the single year 1993, Asian FDI by Japan accounted for a much higher 33 percent of total Japanese FDI.[20]

---

had in 1985, five times as much in Malaysia, five times as much in South Korea, six times as much in Singapore, fifteen times as much in Hong Kong, and twenty-five times as much in Thailand. Kenneth Courtis, "Japan in the 1990s," *Business and the Contemporary World* (Winter 1992), as cited in James Fallows, *Looking at the Sun: The Rise of the New East Asian Economics and Political System* (New York: Pantheon, 1994).

[19] "Japanese Manufacturing: Asian Promise," *Economist,* June 12, 1993, pp. 74–77.
[20] Isao Kubota, "Economic Integration Is Increasing in Asia," *Japan Times,* June 20, 1994. (In contrast, the U.S. and European shares of outstanding Japanese FDI have fallen from 46 percent to 40.5 percent and from 25 percent to 21 percent over the period 1990–1993.)

Figure 1-4. Japan's foreign direct investment by region, 1994

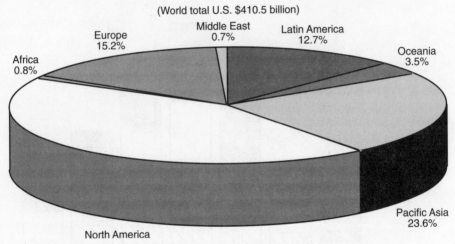

(World total U.S. $410.5 billion)

Europe 15.2%

Middle East 0.7%

Latin America 12.7%

Africa 0.8%

Oceania 3.5%

Pacific Asia 23.6%

North America

Source: Ministry of Finance, *Financial Statistics of Japan* (Tokyo: MOF, 1995), p. 106.

The rapidly growing Japanese investment in Asia corresponded with a major reversal in the relative importance of the United States as an Asian investor. In 1980, U.S. investment in Asia—outside Japan—was over one and a half times that of Japanese firms in the same area. For the past several years, Japanese FDI has continued to outstrip that of U.S. corporations in Asia by about three to one. With the U.S. focus apparently shifting away from the Pacific, Japan has become a preeminent source of capital if only by default.[21]

Furthermore, about one-half of U.S. investment in Asia continues to be for natural resource extraction, especially oil and natural gas, and is particularly concentrated in Indonesia and Malaysia; when these figures are taken out of consideration, Japan's increasing dominance in Asian manufacturing becomes even more conspicuous. All of these data support claims that Japan is becoming "more Asian" and also that any increasingly integrated Asia has become highly dependent on Japan at its center.

Interestingly, even though U.S. investment has not been growing terribly rapidly, that of Taiwan, South Korea, and Hong Kong have been. All three have become significant sources of capital investment throughout the region, thus complicated any image of an emerging "yen bloc."[22] Korean

[21] Richard P. Cronin, "Japan's Expanding Role and Influence in the Asia-Pacific Region: Implications for U.S. Interests and Policy" (Washington, D.C.: Congressional Research Service, Library of Congress, 1990), p. CRS-2; cited in Fallows, *Looking at the Sun*, p. 485.
[22] "Survey of Asia," p. 14.

Figure 1-5. Japanese banks' overseas lending

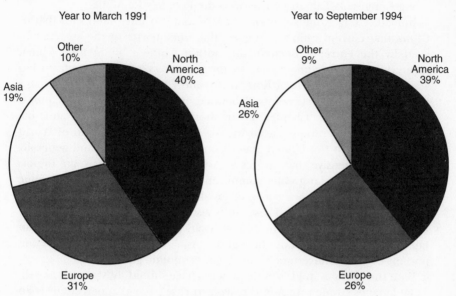

Source: Adapted from "Riding for Another Fall," *The Economist*, December 17, 1994, p. 76.

and Taiwanese FDI were substantially affected, although not immediately, by the currency revaluations that followed the Plaza Accord: the Taiwanese NT dollar rose by 28 percent from 1985 to 1987 and the Korean won rose by 17 percent from 1986 to 1988. Japan's share of the total stake in Asian FDI dropped steadily from 1990 to 1993 to a mere 14 percent of the total investment capital pouring into the region; other Asian investment monies were over 58 percent.[23]

In addition to the presence of South Korea and Taiwan as individual investing countries, Asia has seen the emergence of a network of FDI that suggests, in economic terms, the reemergence of "greater China." This

[23] Investment data from *International Economic Data Bank, Australian National University.* Taiwanese and Korean investments in ASEAN have been spectacular. In the three years from 1987 to 1990, Taiwanese investment in manufacturing within ASEAN rose more than tenfold (with electronics as the single most important area of investment). The *cumulative* Korean investment in ASEAN as of 1985 amounted to only $42 million; in 1989 alone, *new* investment from Korea amounted to $132 million. By the end of the decade Taiwan had replaced the United States as the second major investor in ASEAN and had overtaken Japan as the largest investor in Malaysia. The combined share of the four Asian NICs in ASEAN (except Thailand) is now greater than that of Japan. Bernard and Ravenhill, "Beyond Flying Geese and Product Cycles," p. 182.

investment trend involves capital from Chinese investors in Singapore, Hong Kong, and Taiwan moving into the People's Republic.

Indeed, Hong Kong's economy has become so integrated with that of China that current estimates suggest that one-quarter of the currency issued by the entrepôt is circulating within Chinese boundaries. China, meanwhile, has become home to three-quarters of the manufacturing workers employed by Hong Kong firms, and China is by far Hong Kong's biggest trading partner, points elaborated by Richard Doner in Chapter 6 and Mark Selden in Chapter 9.[24] In short, while Japan has certainly become far more centrally placed in Asia than it was at the end of World War II, its ties to the United States remain quite extensive and generally more comprehensive than its ties to Asia. Furthermore, there are important indications of far greater complications and overlaps in the economic patterns of Asia than are conveyed by the earlier pattern of bilateralism and Japanese dominance. These shifts also make it clear that a decreased U.S. investment presence, in and of itself, does not automatically mean Japanese capital hegemony throughout Asia. There are many other important economic investors in the Asian economic game today.[25]

With the changes in FDI, trade patterns have shifted substantially as well. Total Japanese trade with Asia (Figure 1-6) rose from 31.3 percent in 1980 to 38.1 percent in 1994.[26] Exports rose, although with fits and starts, during the decade of the 1980s. Significantly, in 1991, for the first time in decades, Japanese exports to Asia were greater than Japanese exports to the United States.[27]

The more noteworthy change came in Japanese imports from Asia. And here the trend was in fact down, rather dramatically, from 57.2 percent in 1980 to 41.9 percent in 1990 but then retracing back up somewhat in 1995 to 45.7 percent.[28] Japan has hardly been an automatic market for Asian exports. Thus, as Figure 1-7 makes clear, total ASEAN trade has become less dependent on Japan; Japan's share of ASEAN market fell from

[24] "Survey of Asia," p. 11
[25] A final point that should be made concerning direct investment is that the returns on Japanese investment in Asia have been incredible. One survey showed that 80 percent of multinationals' investments in Asia had become profitable within two years compared with only 20 percent of the investments in the United States. Ibid., p. 14.
[26] These figures are dollar-based and are as reported in Tsusho Sangyosho, *Tsusho Hakusho, 1994* [white paper on trade] (Tokyo: Tsusho Sangyosho, 1994), 2:6–7.
[27] Ibid., 1:176.
[28] These figures based on data in *Nihon Kokusei Zue 1996/97* [Japan national almanac], (Tokyo: Kokuseisha, 1996), p. 357, and Nihon Kokuseisha, *Suji de miru Nihon no Hyakunen* [100 years of Japanese statistics] (Tokyo: Nihon Kokuseisha, 1993), pp. 323–24, and *Nihon Tokei Geppo* [Japan statistical monthly], December 1994, pp. 78–82.

Figure 1-6. Major trading partners

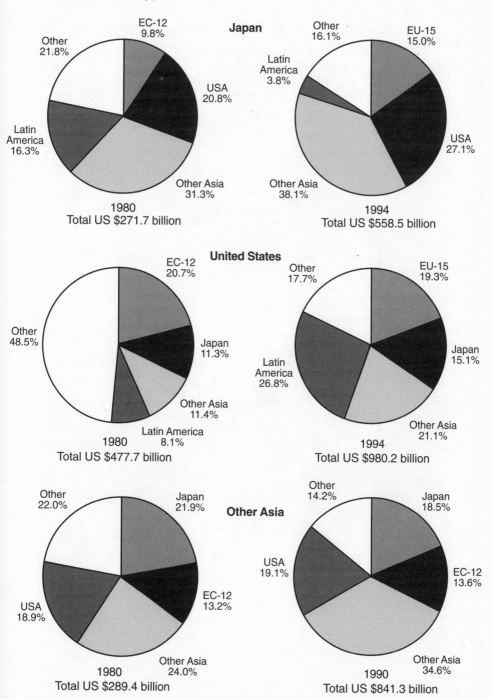

Japan

Other
21.8%

EC-12
9.8%

USA
20.8%

Latin
America
16.3%

Other Asia
31.3%

1980
Total US $271.7 billion

Other
16.1%

EU-15
15.0%

Latin
America
3.8%

USA
27.1%

Other Asia
38.1%

1994
Total US $558.5 billion

United States

EC-12
20.7%

Other
48.5%

Japan
11.3%

Other Asia
11.4%

Latin America
8.1%

1980
Total US $477.7 billion

Other
17.7%

EU-15
19.3%

Latin
America
26.8%

Japan
15.1%

Other Asia
21.1%

1994
Total US $980.2 billion

Other Asia

Other
22.0%

Japan
21.9%

USA
18.9%

EC-12
13.2%

Other Asia
24.0%

1980
Total US $289.4 billion

Other
14.2%

Japan
18.5%

USA
19.1%

EC-12
13.6%

Other Asia
34.6%

1990
Total US $841.3 billion

Sources: IMF, *Direction of Trade Statistics Yearbooks, 1987, 1991,* and *1995* (Washington, D.C., IMF, annual).

Figure 1-7.   Composition of ASEAN trade

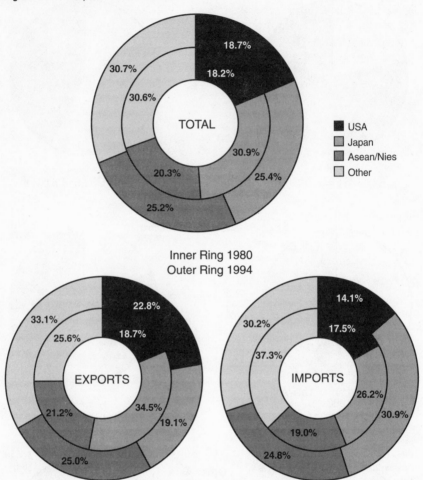

Source: Compiled from IMF, *Direction of Trade Statistics Yearbook* (Washington, D.C.: IMF, 1995).

30.9 percent in 1980 to 25.4 percent in 1994. ASEAN trade with the NIEs in contrast rose from 20.3 percent to 25.2 percent over the same period.

The major conclusion to be drawn from this mass of data is that trade patterns in Asia have become less Japan-centric than they were in the early 1950s. Past patterns of trade saw Japan in a series of bilateral relations with most of Asia. In effect, Japan was the largest or second largest trade partner of virtually every other Asian country and there was relatively little other intra-Asian trade. Asia trade patterns have become vastly more intricate since that time.[29]

In short, while Japan remains quite obviously a major trading and capital-rich power throughout the Asian region, much of its trade is now linked to the investment in manufacturing plants of Japanese-owned factories, especially in ASEAN and China. Simultaneously, however, there are signs of ever increasing trade and investment ties among various of the other Asian economies with one another, many of these independent of any Japanese role as a trade or capital hub.

Japanese aid has also shown important changes. While Japanese aid was relatively niggardly in size, primarily bilateral, and heavily tied to Japanese purchases during the first four decades after World War II, that picture changed substantially in the last decade. Japan's share of official development aid grew rapidly from the mid-1980s onward and in various years Japan has been the largest or the second largest contributor worldwide. Today, an increasing portion of Japanese aid is given via international financial institutions such as World Bank and Asia Development Bank. Formally, by 1989, only 17 percent of Japan's bilateral aid was fully or partially tied, in contrast to the OECD group average of 39 percent and the U.S. average of 58 percent.[30] At the same time, Japanese companies

[29] For example, Hong Kong currently sends 25 percent of its exports to China and 24 percent to the United States, whereas Japan gets only 6 percent. China, meanwhile, sends 43 percent of its exports to Hong Kong, 15 percent to Japan, and 8 percent to the United States. Both Malaysia and the United States serve as larger export markets for Singapore than does Japan, and Thailand is closing quickly on Japan's third-place spot. Taiwan sends 32 percent of its exports to the United States, but it too has been caught up in the Hong Kong–China link and its next largest export market is Hong Kong with 13 percent of total exports. Japan lags at 12 percent. Malaysia sends 23 percent of its exports to Singapore, 17 percent to the United States, 15 percent to Japan, and 5 percent to South Korea. For Thailand, the United States remains the largest market and Japan is second, but Singapore has gained an important position. *Nihon Kokusei Zue, 1993*, pp. 405–6.

[30] James W. Morley, "Japan and the Asia-Pacific: Defining a New Role," *Asian Update* (New York: Asia Society, May 1993), p. 5. At the same time in a discussion I had with a Bangladeshi financial official in March 1994, he indicated that though formally untied, most Japanese aid to Bangladesh is at least implicitly expected to be used for purchases from Japanese companies, often at inflated prices guaranteed to give them a substantial profit.

continued to do well as a result of governmental aid projects; in the year to March 1992, for example, Japanese firms won 31 percent of the contracts financed by Japanese assistance. And this figure probably understates the linkage, since it does not include joint-venture partners of Japanese firms or infrastructural projects that subsequently benefit Japanese companies.[31]

Furthermore, as the economies of Korea, Taiwan, and Singapore have improved, their demand for, and Japan's willingness to grant, aid has disappeared; such Asian countries are no longer dependent on Japanese aid for their well-being or for capital. Not all the countries of Asia, however, have been weaned from Japanese aid, and Asian countries remain the primary destination of about 70 percent of Japanese aid (six of Japan's largest ten recipients are Asian—Indonesia, India, China, the Philippines, Thailand, and Sri Lanka). Japanese foreign assistance still is seen primarily as "economic cooperation," in which many Japanese loans are bilateral and are designated for massive infrastructural projects in which Japanese engineering, construction, and trading companies are the principal contractors.

Nonetheless, it is important to note that in 1994 six of Japan's ten largest recipients—Egypt, Syria, Pakistan, Bangladesh, India, and Sri Lanka—lie outside Japan's more traditional "Asian" sphere. In past years, all ten, or at least nine of the ten were East or Southeast Asian. In short, there has been an increased internationalization to Japanese foreign aid and the direct ties to creating dependencies by Asian countries on Japan have been somewhat diminished.

The notion of an "Asian region" as little more than the Greater East Asia Co-Prosperity Sphere advanced by abacus rather than samurai sword is further complicated when one considers that Australia and New Zealand, despite their European cultural heritage, now increasingly define their economic future as intimately tied to the Asian region to their north. Once Britain joined the European Community in 1973, it was incumbent on both countries, but New Zealand particularly, to find new markets. They found many of them in Asia. Thus Japan is now the recipient of 25 percent of Australia's and 16 percent of New Zealand's exports, while these two countries receive 18 percent and 16 percent of their total imports from Japan. Japan is the largest recipient of Australian exports and the second largest recipient of New Zealand exports; it is the second largest source of Australia's imports and the third largest source of New Zealand's.[32] Within both countries, Asian investment and Asian tourism have

[31] "Japan Ties Up the Asian Market," *Economist*, April 24, 1992, pp. 33–34.
[32] *Nihon Kokusei Zue, 1993*, p. 405–6.

become quite important; this is reflected in the dramatic increase in studies of Asian languages and Asian cultures (particularly Japanese) in the secondary schools of both countries. As economically significant, industrialized democracies, Australia and New Zealand are also poised to play an increasingly Asian role.

Finally, it is important to note that there has been an increase in the institutionalization of Asian regionalism. Much of this has involved informal, nonofficial institutions such as the Pacific Economic Cooperation Council (PECC), the Pacific Basin Economic Council (PBEC), and the Pacific Trade and Development Conference (PAFTAD). Following up on ASEAN, perhaps the most important governmental development organizationally was APEC (the Asia-Pacific Economic Community). The earliest evidence of interest in such a group developed in Australia during the mid-1960s. It was not formally created until 1989 however, again at Australian initiative. But the recognition given to APEC within Asia, and more important, President Clinton's hosting of the APEC summit in Seattle in late 1993, and subsequent meetings in Bogor and Osaka, have all served to suggest the beginnings of a regional institutionalization that had been lacking before.

Thus signs of a vastly more complicated set of investment, trade, and institutional relationships than are congruent with simple notions of Japanese dominance are emerging rapidly. As Mark Selden makes clear in Chapter 9, China is now moving to become part of the Asian economic colossus, drawing increasingly on money from Chinese investors in Hong Kong, Singapore, and even Taiwan—with parts of South China embracing variations of capitalism as the means to do so. Russian Asia is also potentially a part of the Asian region—and South Korean economic assistance has served to bring that emerging power increasingly into the Asian sphere. And finally, as noted, to the extent that Australia and New Zealand are seen as parts of an emerging Asian region, there are consequently multiple counterweights to any unchecked Japanese influence.

Japan: Economic Gulliver in a Region of Lilliputs

Economics is by no means the only currency in which international or regional power is exchanged. Bruce Cumings makes it very clear in Chapter 4 that although Japan's influence is clearly rising throughout Asia, it would be a mistake to ignore the continuation of U.S. hegemony, based on that country's nuclear and other strategic capabilities, its dominant role in various international organizations, and its technological and industrial capabilities, as well as its preeminent influence over much of the world's "discursive regime," known as culture. Russia remains a nuclear power; India, which already has a strong military, is developing a blue-water navy and a space program that could lead to forward projection capabilities. North Korea could easily destabilize any Asian balance by acquiring (and brandishing) nuclear weapons. In Chapter 9 Selden makes the strong argument that Chinese political and military might will give it a preeminent role in Northeast and East Asia in the decades to come, and one recent poll in Japan even showed that 55 percent of Japanese citizens predicted that China would be the most powerful country in the region by 2005.[33] In short, there are many contenders for power and influence in Asia, particularly when power and influence are considered in their traditional guises.

At the same time, in recent years, economic might has begun to play a disproportionately larger role in international affairs, and nowhere is this more evident than in Asia, as even Yamakage makes very evident in Chapter 8. And it is in economics that Japanese preeminence in the region seems most dramatic. Thus, even as trade and investment patterns become someone less Japan-centric, and as other powers identify themselves as "Asian," Japan's economic preeminence in the region remains overwhelming.

Japan in 1995 was the leading source of imports for Taiwan, Korea, Indonesia, Thailand, Malaysia, the Philippines, and Singapore. It was the leading or second leading export market for Australia, Indonesia, South Korea, and China.[34] Clearly Japan continues to play a preeminent role in the trade policies of all of these countries, despite the increased variegation of trade throughout the region.

On foreign aid, Japan's role also remains critical to many Asian countries. Japan is still the primary aid donor for all six ASEAN nations as well as China and Burma. Looking at individual countries, Japan's share as a proportion of total aid received runs from 78 percent in Burma and 70 percent in Thailand to 68 percent in the Philippines, 66 percent in Indonesia, and 56 percent in China. With the exception of the Philippines, U.S. aid to the Asian region is relatively insignificant (and is clearly on the downturn). Through the late 1980s, Japanese aid represented 15 to 20 percent of the entire budget expenditures of almost every country in the region.[35] And given the decline in U.S. aid, Japan is now supplying roughly

---

[33] As reported in *Tsingtao Daily*, April 24, 1995. Survey originally conducted by *Nihon Keizai Shimbun* and *Wall Street Journal*.

[34] Based on calculations from *Nihon Kokusei Zue, 1996/97*, pp. 387–388; Tsusho Sangyosho, *Tsusho Hakusho, 1996*, vol 2.

[35] Robert M. Orr, "The Rising Sum—What Makes Japan Give?" *The International Economy*, September–October 1989, p. 83.

two-thirds of the aid received by ASEAN and about one-half that received by China.[36] Such economic leverage over the entire national economies of so many of these countries clearly puts Japan in an exceptionally powerful position within the region. At a minimum, it suggests a major mechanism by which to exercise the same type of cross-national cronyism articulated by Takashi Shiraishi in Chapter 5.

What is most striking is that economically Japan stands in a uniquely superior position to the rest of the countries of Asia. Japan remains the finely engineered Lexus in a region dominated by functional, cheap, but still somewhat clunky Kias and Proton Sagas. With only 10 percent of the region's population and an even smaller proportion of its total land mass, Japan accounts for about two-thirds of the region's total Gross National Product (GNP). Japan has an economy that is more than ten times greater than that of the second largest economy in Asia, China. Australia's total economy is only one-fifteenth that of Japan's. As to the NIEs, Japan's economy is about twenty times as large as Taiwan's and fifteen times as large as Korea's, not to mention being about thirty times larger than Indonesia's and nearly one hundred times larger than Singapore's. The Japanese GNP is about six times greater than the combined GNPs of Taiwan, South Korea, Singapore, and Hong Kong.

As a member of various international economic policymaking bodies, most particularly the G-5 and G-7, the Japanese state is organizationally positioned to play an important role in the making of internationally influential economic policies on matters of trade, exchange rates, capital movements, and the like; those of the rest of Asia are not. Clearly, such surface comparisons demand that Japan be recognized as one of the major "capitalist democracies," having a powerful presence in "the West," as well as its increasingly well-recognized presence in Asia. No other Asian country comes close to having such trans-regional economic muscle.

Thus, while many South Korean companies are quite large by so-called Third World standards, only eight were listed among the Fortune 500 largest companies in the world in 1995, whereas Taiwan has two and no other East or Southeast Asian country makes the list. In contrast, there are 149 Japanese companies on the list, a number which is not far behind the United States, which leads with 151.[37]

Citizens of Hong Kong and Singapore, despite the quite small total economies of these two entrepots, still enjoy reasonably satisfactory lifestyles, with the per capita incomes of each being above those for Spain

---

[36] Shafiqul Islan, "Foreign Aid and Burden Sharing: Is Japan Free Riding to a Co-Prosperity Sphere in Pacific Asia?" in Frankel and Kahler, *Regionalism and Rivalry*, pp. 338–39.
[37] "Fortune's Global 500," *Fortune*, August 7, 1995, pp. F37–40.

and Ireland, for example. In Asian terms, citizens of these two countries live quite comfortably. Yet their lives are by no means on a par with the citizens of Japan, who still enjoy per capita incomes at least twice theirs. Meanwhile, the per capita GNP and the standards of living of the citizens of South Korea and Taiwan are even further behind, at levels perhaps 10 percent those of Hong Kong and Singapore. Though many pundits tout China's longterm economic potential, and there is no denying that such a populous nation could soon have a massive GNP, it is important to remember that annual per capita GNP in rapidly growing China is in the neighborhood of $325 versus $27,000 per person in Japan.

Japanese tourist companies organize trips to Korea or Thailand for cheap sex or to Hong Kong and Singapore for duty-free electronics goods, but the citizens of these countries look to Japan for education, investment, technology, and jobs and the manufacturers there look to Japan's extensive market. Consequently, although much of Asia seems to be emulating Japan, it is important to realize just how great an economic distance still exists between Japan and the rest of its imitative neighbors. As just one simple measure, the Asian Development Bank, in operation since 1967, invariably has a Japanese president.

Japan clearly merits inclusion with the advanced democracies of Europe and North America on most counts, and failure to see Japan as at least as "Western" as it is "Asian" is a serious comparative mistake. Politically, culturally, and economically, Japan ceased to be exclusively Asian in anything other than geographic terms decades ago.[38] Nevertheless, even if it is not "of" Asia, Japan is certainly "in" Asia. Much of the trade, aid, and investment strategy Japan has followed since the early 1970s has involved Asia; the bulk of its Overseas Development Assistance goes to the countries of Asia; for most of the 1980s, Japan was the largest or second largest trading partner of all of the Asian NICs and near NICs. Its economic im-

---

[38] This message was brought home to me in a brutally frank way when I was interviewing the executive vice-president of a major Japanese manufacturing company. At the time I was the director of Cornell University's China-Japan Program, an organization whose name was the simple evolutionary consequence of a "China Program" having expanded to include "Japan specialists." In traditional fashion, I presented my name card, feeling culturally comfortable with the fact that unlike many of my Western colleagues, my card had English on one side and Japanese on the other. My interviewee was quite stunned. "Why," he asked, "does a major university like Cornell waste money on a program that puts Japan and China on an equal footing? China is an economic backwater, a retrograde dictatorship, and a country mired in the nineteenth century. Japan is an advanced industrial democracy that has nothing in common with such a place. If you wish to have any credibility in Japan, you should get rid of such a program and start treating Japan as an advanced country." On my return, I successfully proposed a name change to "East Asia Program," which didn't quite meet my guest's needs, but I also dropped the entire item from the name cards I used in Japan.

pact on the countries of the region is undeniable. Meanwhile, the countries of the region, sometimes reluctantly, must, if only because there are no viable alternatives, look primarily to Japan for the capital, technology, managerial skills, markets, and political leadership that they hope will allow them some chance to imitate Japan's success.

Former MITI vice-minister Naohiro Amaya once stated that "Asia is only a geographical word. Asian nations share nothing in common."[39] At one level he is unquestionably correct; yet, what these Lilliputian nations do share is the presence of a Japanese Gulliver in their midst, something none of them can safely ignore, despite modest trends toward a more complicated interdependence throughout the region and the growing presence of possible counterweights to Japanese influence.

Furthermore, it is a gargantuan presence that is likely to reap great future benefits from the past patterns of its investment and interaction with its Asian neighbors. Despite the bursting of Japan's "bubble economy" in 1990, the Japanese economy remains quite strong structurally. Japan is still a net creditor of some $350 billion; it has a continually strong currency; in 1996 its foreign reserves were over $200 billion, compared to $85 billion for Germany and $73 billion for the United States; its manufacturing plants are among the best in the world.

Kenneth Courtis, a leading investment analyst, for example, expects that the major world increase in auto demand over next decade will be in Asia. He anticipates that as many as sixteen new plants are likely—each producing 200,000 cars per year. One, maybe two, will be American; the same, he holds, will be true for European manufacturers. At least ten will be Japanese, if not twelve to fourteen. This will enable Japanese auto manufacturers to move from their current 38 percent world market share to 45 percent by decade's end.[40]

The implications of such a possibility become clear from a recent experience with Japan's Mitsubishi Corporation. Apparently, Mitsubishi, which is involved in supporting the Malaysian auto industry, was asked to submit an automobile industry "master plan" to the Vietnamese government in late 1992. The Mitsubishi report, which listed companies that could produce components for Vietnam's future automobile manufacturers, allegedly mentioned only Japanese firms, many of which are tied to the Mitsubishi corporate family.[41] In short, the Vietnamese government was given a strong push toward "Japanizing" any auto industry it sought

[39] As quoted in Sam Jameson, "Peace Brings Prosperity to Asia," *Japan Times,* July 16, 1992.
[40] James Fallows, *Looking at the Sun: The Rise of the New East Asian Economic and Political System* (New York: Pantheon, 1994), p. 246; "Survey of Asia," p. 15.
[41] Murray Hiebert and Susumu Awanohara, "Gearing Up for a Fight," *Far Eastern Economic Review,* August 19, 1993, p. 46.

to develop, primarily as a result of the very presence of Mitsubishi in Southeast Asia. In effect, the current preeminence of Japanese firms in Asia will almost certainly enhance the continued preeminence of Japanese firms throughout the region.

Infrastructural growth in Asia is exploding with $1.5 trillion to be invested between 1996 and 2006. Asia is currently installing the equivalent of Japan's entire present telephone switching capacity (or two-fifths of that in the United States). By 1997 Asian telecom purchases should equal those of entire OECD minus Germany. A similar situation is developing in electricity-generating equipment, for which Asia will be accounting for more than a third of world demand. Ten Asian airports are already under construction, with ten more likely to follow before the decade is out. Aircraft makers expect Asia to buy 1000 passenger aircraft spending $40–50 billion between 1993 and 1998.[42] Furthermore, Japan is likely to be involved in financing energy and infrastructure projects in ASEAN, Hong Kong, and Taiwan; energy projects alone in these three are likely to require some $40–50 billion between 1992 and 1997.[43]

In short, Asia's markets are likely to grow rapidly, perhaps exponentially, in the next ten to twenty years, and the principal economic beneficiaries are most probably going to be those companies and countries currently preeminent in Asia. To date, these firms have largely been Japanese.

Though Japan's presence is undeniable, it is not clear how welcome that presence is or and is likely to remain. As Leon Hollerman puts it: "Japan's ... strategy is not a policy of world domination; no nation has been coerced into accepting its leadership. The nations that accept Japan's guidance, trade, finance, and direct investment do so willingly out of self-interest. In serving their own aspirations, they serve those of Japan."[44] To an extent, of course, this is true. But in fact Hollerman overlooks the narrow range of choices available to those who "choose" to accept Japanese economic leadership.

In much of Asia today there may be widespread admiration for the economic accomplishments of Japan but there is far less admiration for or desire to join Japanese society. This provides a stark contrast, for example, to those who live in Central America and Mexico, where disdain for "gringo" or "yanqui" dominance is offset by the strong desire of many to head for the border at the first sign of economic problems in their own countries. It is also a contrast to the situation in much of Europe, where

---

[42] "Survey of Asia," p. 16.
[43] Anthony Rowley, "In Their Own Backyard," *Far Eastern Economic Review*, March 19, 1992, p. 41.
[44] Leon Hollerman, "The Headquarters Nation," *National Interest* 25 (Fall 1991): 16.

those who live in the poorer countries of, for example, southeastern Europe, anxiously await the opportunity to emigrate to the economically more well-to-do countries of the north and west.

Certainly, Japanese economics drives much of Asia, but Japanese culture does not. There are, of course, counterexamples: the Japanese youth magazines *Bruttus* and *Popeye* are popular among many Asian youth, and as Saya Shiraishi notes in Chapter 7, Japanese comic characters are known Asia-wide. *Karaoke* has become one of Japan's more successful, if obnoxious, exports throughout the region. Tourism is up, with many Asians traveling, both legally and illegally, to Japan. The number of foreign students in Japan increased about sevenfold between 1981 and 1995.[45]

Yet the Japanese language is nowhere near becoming the *lingua franca* of the region; English and Chinese are far more widely used. (And the implications of the language problem can be seen in the problems Vietnam and Burma had joining ASEAN. Despite good will on all sides, delegates from both countries find it exceptionally difficult to function in the daily ASEAN meetings, which are held almost exclusively in English.) Asian parents are still far more likely to send their high-school and college-aged children for educations to the United States than to Japan (and Japanese schools are far less likely to welcome them than their U.S. counterparts are). The worldwide explosion of telecommunications and computer softwear has been essentially an English language phenomenon. E-mail and the Internet remain principally English-language communications tools, and these are dramatically less widespread in Japan than in North America or Europe, which is somewhat surprising given Japan's preeminence in electronics. Satellite television is a relative rarity in Japan itself; Japanese broadcasts and movies are not widely received through Asia. Indeed, the first trans-Asian satellite project, Star Cable, was begun in Hong Kong; and CNN provides by far the area's most widespread international programming. In short, Japan's position as a Gulliver in an Asian Lilliput is based far more on its economic prowess than on its cultural standing throughout the region.

Not surprisingly, reactions to Japan differ greatly throughout Asia. Memories of wartime Japanese atrocities remain relatively strong in China, Korea, Singapore, and the Philippines, for example. Such memories are far less vivid or relevant in Thailand, Burma, Indonesia, or even Malaysia, and are hardly a factor in India and the rest of South Asia. As the wartime generation dies out throughout Asia, reactions to Japan as a regional leader based on distant wartime memories are sure to fade. Yet just as

---

[45] *Japan Times*, February 9, 1991, p. 3. Jetro, *Nippon 1996* (Tokyo, Jetro, 1996), p. 155. It should be noted that about 90 percent of the foreign students in Japan in 1990 were self-sponsored.

many in the West have long doubted the wisdom of either opening their markets to Japanese products or of "learning from Japan," there is widespread skepticism in much of Asia about the wisdom of emulating any alleged "Japanese model," following Japan's leadership, or allowing Japan to be Asia's main bridge to the West.

The ambiguous relationship between Japan and the other countries of Asia is captured in an anecdote, perhaps apocryphal, about the impact of Japanese investment. Allegedly, the new prime minister of one ASEAN country was embarrassed and astonished to find that across from the official residence was a huge blinking sign for Japan's electronics giant, Sony. In a fit of nationalism, he called the president of Sony and requested that the neon sign be shut down. The Japanese chief executive was quick to comply and the sign was dimmed. Three weeks later the prime minister called back requesting that the sign be turned back on. It seems that the crime rate around the official residence had risen sharply in the interim, since the blinking neon was the only source of electric light in the neighborhood.

This in a nutshell is the dilemma of Japan in Asia: the disparity in capital, technology, and power is so great that the other nations of the region can nor live without it. But the likelihood remains that Japan's powerful presence will generate resentment.

Asian Regionalism: Pan-Asian or Pan-Pacific?

Recent Asian economic success has been almost uniformly dependent on exports. Indeed, export-oriented development has become so linked in the public mind with the hypergrowth of Pacific Asia that the connection has become "a new development orthodoxy."[46] Consequently, Asian successes, combined with geographical proximity and a host of common traits related to political and economic organization and to social structures have led contemporary theorists to group the nations of East Asia under umbrella terms such as "the developmental state."[47]

Despite having tried a variety of alternative approaches, all the successful

[46] Stephan Haggard, "The Newly Industrializing Countries in the International System," *World Politics* 38 (January 1986): 344.

[47] The term "capitalist development state" was to my knowledge first used by Chalmers Johnson in *MITI and the Japanese Miracle* (Stanford: Stanford University Press, 1982). Johnson broadened the application to include Korea and Taiwan; Chalmers Johnson, "Political Institutions and Economic Performance: The Government-Business Relationship in Japan, South Korea and Taiwan," in *The Political Economy of the New Asian Industrialism*, ed. Frederick Deyo (Ithaca: Cornell University Press, 1987), pp. 136–64. My evaluation of the concept, along with a reformulation can be found in my article "The Developmental Regime in a Changing World Economy," in Woo-Cumings, *Developmental State*.

Table 1-2. U.S. and Japanese Shares in East Asian Exports of Manufactured Goods (percent)

Exporter	1980		1984		1990	
	U.S.	Japan	U.S.	Japan	U.S.	Japan
Hong Kong	34.13	2.76	45.98	3.29	30.71	4.93
South Korea	28.90	13.28	38.56	10.12	32.45	15.43
Singapore	20.96	8.12	32.52	3.58	28.35	5.54
Taiwan	38.37	7.31	53.66	6.30	39.49	8.89
China	9.04	11.02	18.68	10.79	22.92	8.79
Malaysia	31.66	5.70	41.28	5.91	28.31	5.35
Thailand	17.46	7.14	29.39	6.77	27.81	13.29

Source: Adapted from *Pacific Economic Relations in the 1990s: Cooperation or Conflict?* ed. R. Higgott, R. Leaver, and J. Ravenhill (Boulder, Colo.: Lynne Rienner Publishers, 1993), p. 128. Copyright © 1993 by Australian Fulbright Commission. Used with permission of the publisher.

Asian economies have relied heavily on exports outside the region to advance their longterm development. There has been a substantial increase in intra-Asian trade over the past decade, but intra-Asian exports are still vastly below the levels of intra-Western hemisphere or intra-European trade.[48]

Furthermore, with the exception of Japan and Indonesia with populations of 120 million and 190 million, and China with one billion or more, the other Asian countries have very limited domestic markets. As a consequence, all have been forced to conceptualize "markets" in nondomestic terms and to produce with an eye toward international standards, world competition, and selected niches. But for most of these countries, "international" has hardly meant "worldwide."

Virtually all of the Asian economic success stories have relied heavily on exports to North America. (See Figure 1-6 and Table 1-2.) Thus, despite the growing economic linkages among the various Asian countries through both trade and investment, Asia as a whole would face economic catastrophe if it were to become a "closed" rather than an "open" region.

In this same context, Japan has demonstrated neither the desire nor the ability to become the major absorber of manufactured exports from the rest of Asia. Figure 1-7 makes it clear that while ASEAN imports from Japan increased from 1980 to 1994, ASEAN exports to Japan fell from 34.5 percent to 19.1 percent during that same period. The picture is even more stark for manufactured exports from all of Asia. In 1993, Japan absorbed less than 10 percent of Asia's manufactured exports, a sharp contrast to

---

[48] Intra-Asian exports comprise about 30 percent of total regional trade, as opposed to 50 percent and 70 percent for the western hemisphere and Europe. Mark Borthwick, *Pacific Century: The Emergence of Modern Pacific Asia* (Boulder, Colo.: Westview Press, 1992), p. 530.

the 37.3 percent destined for other Asian countries, the 26.4 percent that went to the United States, or even the 15.5 percent that went to the EEC-12.[49]

The high growth rates of the Asian NICs and the ASEAN countries have depended increasingly on the import of Japanese capital goods. The end result has been the gradual erosion in the mid-1990s of ASEAN's once favorable trade balance with Japan; the Asian NICs have long since run comparably driven deficits. In fiscal 1993, Japan's trade surplus with Asia jumped 25 percent over the previous years to $56 billion, for the first time exceeding its surplus with the United States. Thus most Asian countries with the exception of China, Thailand, and Malaysia now have substantial trade deficits with Japan.[50]

The character of Japanese FDI has also resulted in a somewhat asymmetrical trade picture with the rest of Asia. The four NICs—Hong Kong, Singapore, South Korea, and Taiwan—have grown increasingly dependent on Japan for industrial goods to produce their higher-value products and to upgrade their factories. To the extent that many of these upgraded factories remain in non-Japanese hands, however, the exports of these countries have found it difficult to penetrate the Japanese market.

A good deal has been written about the extent to which the Japanese market has opened up to take in more Asian exports, particularly those of Japanese-owned firms. Indeed, it is far easier for an import to enter Japan when it bears the label "Sony," "Sharp," or "Sumitomo," than when the label says "Black and Decker" or "Cincinnati Milacron." In 1980, Asian subsidiaries of Japanese firms exported 9.8 percent of their output back to Japan; by 1987 this share had risen to 16.7 percent.[51] But typically, Japanese-owned firms in the rest of Asia are not producing goods that are no longer made in Japan due to shifts in the product life-cycle; rather, as both Richard Doner and Takashi Shiraishi make clear in Chapters 6 and 5, the huge inflow of industrial products from Japan to most of the ASEAN countries and China has frequently been linked to purchases by Japanese-owned firms in these areas.[52] Such firms are becoming part of a much

---

[49] Walter Hatch and Kozo Yamamura, *Asia in Japan's Embrace: Building a Regional Production Alliance* (Cambridge: Cambridge University Press, 1996), p. 181.

[50] For the first half of 1994 Japan ran its largest Asian surpluses with Hong Kong ($21 billion), Singapore ($13 billion), and Taiwan ($13 billion); the total surplus with Asia was $31.4 billion, still exceeding that with the United States, which was $27 billion. Nikkei Weekly, *Japan Economic Almanac, 1995* (Tokyo: Nihon Keizai Shimbun, 1995), p. 30.

[51] Marcus Noland, *Pacific Basin Developing Countries: Prospects for the Future* (Washington, D.C.: Institute for International Economics, 1990), p. 152.

[52] There has been a big jump in Japanese exports to ASEAN, for example, from 26.7 percent of Japanese exports in 1989 to 32.5 percent in 1993. Tsusho Sangyosho, *Tsusho hakusho, 1994*, p. 267.

broader regionalization of Japanese production.[53]

As a result, much of Asian trade retains a very strongly vertical character, with Japan at the top. The two Asian countries that enjoy trade surpluses with Japan are the Philippines and Indonesia, both of which are poor countries exporting raw materials; Malaysia and Thailand have positive surpluses heavily fueled by exports from Japanese-owned plants back to the homeland; the more advanced economies, such as Taiwan and South Korea, struggle under massive trade deficits. Korean had a trade deficit of $9.5 billion in 1991, of which $8.8 billion was with Japan; Taiwan's deficit with Japan was almost as large. At the same time, Japan enjoyed a massive trade surplus with all of Southeast Asia—largely in exports of capital goods. Currently, that surplus runs around $40 billion annually.[54] Far more compelling is the extent to which Asian exports continue to depend heavily on the North American, and to a lesser extent the European, market. Thus, as Table 1-2 shows clearly, most of the Asian exporters send at least twice as much, and in some cases as much as six times as much, of their exports to the United States as to Japan.

To this day Japan itself follows this pattern. Japan sends 32 percent of its exports to the United States and only 6 percent to its next largest export partner—Hong Kong.[55] Thus Japan is a "world economic superstar" mostly in terms of its GNP, capital holdings, and per capita income. It is far less a world economic power in terms of diversified market capabilities. Historically, Japan has hardly welcomed foreign direct investment; this reluctance, although it has weakened somewhat by the mid-1990s, remains extremely strong. Consequently, while FDI in Germany totals approximately $1500 per capita; that in the United Kingdom, $3500 per capita; and that in the United States, $1700 per capita; FDI in Japan is only $135 per capita.

Japan's relatively closed home economy and dependence on exports to the United States is hardly unique among the Asian economic success stories. In 1990 South Korea relied on the United States to take 30 percent of its exports; its second largest partner, Japan, took only 19 percent. Tai-

---

[53] Louise do Rosado, "Engines of Growth: 'Made in Asia'—on a Japanese Machine," *Far Eastern Economic Review* May 21, 1992, p. 38. See also Hatch and Yamamura, *Asia in Japan's Embrace*, pp. 175–191.

[54] The Bank of Japan argues that this is linked to the flow of capital and technical and personnel assistance from Japan to southeast Asia and not just exports. Anthony Rowley, "No Balancing Act in View," *Far Eastern Economic Review*, June 18, 1992, pp. 50–52.

[55] Hong Kong recently replaced South Korea as Japan's second largest market, and Korea in turn had alternated with Germany for several years. None of the three countries has ever accounted for more than 6 percent or so of total Japanese exports, regardless of their respective positions.

wan sold 32 percent of its exports to the United States; its second largest partner, Hong Kong, took only 13 percent; Japan, its third largest partner, only 12 percent. Twenty-one percent of Singapore's exports wound up in the United States; Japan took only 9 percent. The United States was also a larger export market than Japan for Thailand or Malaysia. What such figures make clear is that current Asian regionalism is not self-sufficient economically at present and is not likely to become so in the near future. Its economic success depends heavily on access to outside markets, most particularly those of the United States.[56] The U.S. market has been vital for the export successes of most Asian countries, with Japan only gradually becoming a second export market for many.

Taiwan, Japan, and South Korea depend heavily on the United States not only for foreign direct investments and other capital linkages but also for security. This dependence makes it clear that although they demonstrate a great deal of domestic independence, these states have nowhere near the level of autonomy idealized in most literature on state theory. The regimes in all three countries are highly dependent on the United States while Korea and Taiwan are similarly dependent on Japan.

There is undoubtedly an emerging "asianism" among many Japanese leaders. As James Morley describes it: "On the right, [there are the] old pan-Asianists who seek a return to Japanese supremacy; on the left, [the] old socialists who hold deep sympathy for Asia; and in the center, a group of young intellectuals and business leaders whose respect for the United States has declined as their confidence in themselves has grown."[57]

At the same time it is also clear that most Japanese government officials want Japan to be more than just an Asian regional power. Japan does live in two economic worlds and to deny one while focusing exclusively on the other is to miss a reality far more complex than that captured by the model of three closed blocs. Thus, while just over 27 percent of Japanese foreign direct investment goes to Asia and Oceania, fully 43 percent goes to North America and an additional 15 percent to Europe. (Also see Figure 1-4.) Asian trade in the mid 1990s represented about 29 percent of Japan's total trade; trade with the United States and Europe totaled 44 percent.[58] Japan's government and business elites are clearly sensitive to the importance of maintaining close links to the United States and Europe for mar-

---

[56] *Nihon Kokusei Zue, 1990*, p. 404.
[57] Morley, *Japan and the Asia-Pacific* p. 6.
[58] Anthony Rowley, "Slowly Off the Trade Blocs," *Far Eastern Economic Review*, June 18, 1992, p. 44.

kets, technology, capital, and culture. Consequently, as MITI officials put it, "We have a regional policy for Asia but not a policy on regionalism."[59]

Furthermore, Japan's investments increasingly involve the creation of alliances among major multinational corporations on all three continents. General Motors and Toyota, Ford and Mazda, and Mitsubishi and Daimler Benz are but a few of the more noteworthy. But what these ties portend is twofold: first, an even smaller likelihood that the major corporations in any of the three potential "blocs" will be oriented toward exclusivity of either trade or investment within those blocs; and second, the likelihood that future economic activities throughout the world will be increasingly driven by such cross-bloc alliances, further reducing regional economic isolation.

In this regard, a rather significant battle was won when APEC was founded. APEC quite explicitly defines "Asia-Pacific" to include the United States, Canada, New Zealand and Australia. Malaysian prime minister Mahathir Mohamad, responding to the implicit anti-Asianism of a united Europe and a NAFTA that excludes Asia, opposed APEC and called instead for the creation of an East Asian Economic Caucus that would explicitly not include the United States, Canada, Australia, and New Zealand and would include all three Chinas ("a caucus without Caucasians" as one wag noted). Mahathir believed that such a racially based, and economically closed, Asian economic bloc would serve as a counterweight to the rather closed European Economic Union and NAFTA. (The final compromise, to make the EAEC a caucus within APEC, has proved satisfactory so far.) In reality, no such regional bloc is possible for Asia. The developmental states of Asia are simply too dependent on outside markets.

What this leaves is a vastly more complicated portrait of Asian regionalism than that implied by the Orwellian vision. It is clear that Japan stands at the economic center of much that is happening in Asia, but at the same time, there are growing tiers of intra-Asian dependencies that bypass Japan completely. Any emerging Asian regional ties will surely include an important role for Japan as the region's most powerful economy. At the same time, future Asian regional developments are not likely to depend heavily on Japanese trade, technology, capital, or culture.

At the same time, throughout most of Asia, and with increasing institutionalization to back it up, there is a recognition that Asian regionalism must be open to, and linked with, the West. Intra-regional autarky is impossible. This reality is clearly understood within Japan, and so, Japan will

---

[59] Ibid., p. 46.

continue to live in two worlds. As the rest of Asia advances economically, these nations too will continue to be highly dependent on the United States and its markets, and to a lesser extent perhaps on Europe. Any emerging Asian regionalism will most probably be Pan-Pacific and open, rather than Pan-Asian and closed.

2

Asianism's Ambivalent Legacy

J. VICTOR KOSCHMANN

Without the West there is no East. The very idea of Asia is ultimately empty and variously exploitable. The ideology of Asianism rejects that emptiness by attributing positive, essential meaning to Asia, however it might be conceived geographically. In the context of modern Japan, Asianism proclaims that the Japanese and some combination of other peoples and nation-states in the region share an identity and a destiny, natural or constructed. Although not intrinsically aggressive or imperialistic, this ideology is implicated in modern Japanese expansionism and continues even in the present to offer a tempting rationale for Japan's regional "leadership."

Greater Asia and the West

The "Orient" emerged initially as the Other of Europe. The Occidental identity constructed by modern Europeans required a contrasting pole and therefore necessarily involved the subordination of a second term.[1] As a result, in post-Enlightenment European discourse, the Orient, or Asia, was inevitably marked as secondary, and thus "particular," in relation to the European "universal." Indeed, that discourse often denied that Orientals had any history at all as a result of their putative lack of "subjective aware-

[1] For one discussion of this point, see Ernesto Laclau, *New Reflections on the Revolution of Our Time* (London: Verso, 1990), pp. 32–33.

ness" (G. W. F. Hegel) or their immersion in a so-called Asiatic mode of production (Karl Marx).

Nineteenth-century Japanese intellectuals adopted the distinctions between East and West from European writers, whose authority derived from imperialist power, and proceeded initially to narrate their own history in terms of European categories and assumptions. By doing so, they were accepting a basically unilinear narrative of world history whose informing values were civilization and enlightenment and which relegated Japan to a backward, subordinate position relative to the United States and the major countries of Western Europe. Of course, this unilinear paradigm was extremely useful to Japanese leaders in the Meiji period, who were seeking both legitimacy and a way to strengthen their society and thus to preserve its independence against the threat of imperialism. Historical reconstructions of European growth led to the identification of specific priorities for resource allocation that would facilitate Japan's modernization process.[2]

During this early period, for about thirty years up to the end of the Sino-Japanese War, Dai-Ajiashugi (Greater-Asianism) arose as a counter to modernization within the Eurocentric paradigm. According to Teruo Ito,

> Greater-Asianism was able to serve as a kind of antithesis to the Meiji government's series of aggressive policies [toward the Ryukyus, Korea and Taiwan]. However, that was possible only by virtue of the fact that Japan along with other Asian countries was being subjected to aggression by the Great Powers. Once that condition disappeared, Greater Asianism lost its ideological viability. That occurred decisively following the Sino-Japanese War, when Japan began its aggression toward China and the rush toward annexation of Korea.[3]

Ito finds evidence of the resistance mounted by Greater-Asianism against Meiji Japan's aggressive foreign policy in works by a range of figures, including Takamori Saigo, Emori Ueki, Toten Miyazaki, and Ikki Kita. Yet Greater-Asianist thought was by no means innocent of complicity in that policy. For example, based on a study of the various permutations of Asianism in this period, historian Young-jae Park contends that "[no] one ar-

---

[2] See Yukichi Fukuzawa, *An Outline of a Theory of Civilization* (Tokyo: Sophia University, 1973); Soho Tokutomi, *The Future Japan*, ed. and trans. Vinh Sinh (Edmonton: University of Alberta Press, 1989); and *Meiroku Zasshi: Journal of Japanese Enlightenment*, ed. and trans. William Braisted (Tokyo: University of Tokyo Press, 1976).

[3] Teruo Ito, "Kaisetsu: Ajia to kindai Nihon" [Introduction: Asia and Modern Japan], in *Ajia to kindai Nihon: Han-shinryaku no shiso to undo* [Asia and Modern Japan: Thought and Movements in opposition to invasion], ed. Teruo Ito (Tokyo: Shakai Hyoronsha, 1992), p. 286.

gues for relations of equality between the peoples of Asia and Japan; they invariably place Japan at the apex of a vertical relationship."[4]

In the meantime, because a national identity seems to require a national history, Japanese historians and philosophers eventually embarked on the task of retrieving Japan's history from the Eurocentric paradigm. To accomplish this they had to confront their location in "Asia" and their reputedly "Asian" nature in the eyes of the West. Meiji educator Yukichi Fukuzawa's approach to this difficult issue in the mid-1880s had been to separate Japan from Asia and everything pejorative associated with it—in effect, to leave Asia and join the West for all purposes except the strictly geographical.[5] The approach of prominent Japanese historians of Asia beginning around the turn of the twentieth century, on the other hand, was to reappropriate the Orient as a value-laden category and to define Japan's world-historical emergence in relation to it. For them Asia, or the East (*toyo*), as a cultural, geographical and historical concept was a potential antidote to the loss of history and identity that had accompanied the integration of Japan into the Eurocentric world. Through their new discipline of Toyoshi (history of the East), they strove to overcome the Orient's putative inferiority to Europe by demonstrating its fundamental equivalence. The East was to be an equal counterpart to the West. Yet this did not mean that all nations and peoples were necessarily equal *within* Asia. Indeed, these historians accepted as a matter of course that in Asia only Japan, as the sole nation of the region to become constitutional as well as industrial, could actually be considered equivalent to the European nations and the United States. Thus, for Japan, the elevation of the East to world-historical parity always implied Japanese leadership within the East.

It is important to note that for the Toyoshi scholars the East never included what was later to be called Southeast Asia and for all practical purposes was limited to China and Inner Asia.[6] Moreover, whereas Europeans had figured the Orient as the origin of "world" history and, thus, of the Occident itself, the Toyoshi historians situated *toyo* as Japan's origin. Rather than Europe's Orient, China was now Japan's *toyo*.[7] In a manner

---

[4] Park Young-jae, "Kindai Nihon no Ajia ninshiki: Datsu-Ajiashugi to Ajiashugi" [Modern Japan's perception of Asia: Asianism and arguments for transcending Asia], in *Nichiro senso zengo no Nihon no Kankoku shinryaku* [Japan's invasion of Korea in the era of the Russo-Japanese War], ed. Rekishigakkai (Seoul: Itchokaku-kan, n.d.), p. 64.

[5] See Yukichi Fukuzawa, "On De-Asianization," in *Meiji Japan through Contemporary Sources*, ed. Center for East Asian Cultural Studies (Tokyo: Center for East Asian Cultural Studies, 1973), 3:129–33.

[6] Stefan Tanaka, *Japan's Orient: Rendering Pasts into History* (Berkeley and Los Angeles: University of California Press, 1993), p. 107.

[7] Ibid., pp. 81, 87.

broadly parallel to the way French and British Orientalists related their own civilization to that of Egypt and the rest of the Near East,[8] these Japanese Orientalists found in China the origin of a civilization—in this case Confucian—that had been abandoned in modern China but was later to come to full maturity in Japan. Rather than resulting, as it had in China, in a conservative structure that inhibited change, Confucianism in Japan became a "progressive ideal" that facilitated social development even as it reinforced cohesion. Thus, out of Confucian "filial piety" the Japanese were duty-bound to help China to rediscover this revitalized Confucian heritage and reverse its modern decline.[9]

Belief in China's decadence was pervasive among a wide range of Japanese intellectuals, and to some extent among Chinese as well. *Asahi shimbun* editor Tenshu Nishimura, who "throughout his life . . . believed that, because the Japanese and Chinese were of a 'common culture and common race,' the two peoples should maintain good neighborly relations,"[10] concluded during a visit to China at the behest of the General Staff Office of the Japanese Army that the Chinese "were not good at keeping up their own tradition" and that the dilapidated state of Chinese buildings provided clues to the "deterioration of Chinese civilization." Moreover, he was apparently able to persuade the Chinese official Chih-tung Chang that, in Chang's words, China and its neighbors were "gradually becom[ing] conservative and feeble." Nishimura argued that Chinese should take advantage of Japan's prior success in adapting Western knowledge to Asian conditions by sending Chinese students to study in Japan rather than in Europe: "If you follow the Japanese model, you can get twice the result with half the effort and expense."[11]

Japanese scholars concluded on the basis of their research that "China was not a state but merely a civilization."[12] As early as 1911 the conservative philosopher Tetsujiro Inoue had observed that although the Chinese respected filial piety in the context of family life they had no "national family system" such as that embodied in the Japanese emperor system; therefore, the Chinese moral system did not include loyalty to the emperor, which was the "most fundamental value of the Japanese nation-state."[13] In 1914

[8] Edward Said, *Orientalism* (New York: Pantheon, 1978), pp. 71, 92, 121, and passim.
[9] Tanaka, *Japan's Orient*, pp. 115–16.
[10] Tao De-min, "Nishimura Tenshu's Journey to the Yangtze Basin in 1897–98," *Sino-Japanese Studies* 4 (October 1991):29.
[11] Ibid., pp. 33–37.
[12] Kimitada Miwa, "Japanese Policies and Concepts for a Regional Order in Asia, 1938–1940," in *The Ambivalence of Nationalism: Modern Japan between East and West*, ed. James W. White, Michio Umegaki, and Thomas R. H. Havens (Lanham, Md.: University Press of America, 1990), p. 135.
[13] Tanaka, *Japan's Orient*, pp. 132–33.

the Toyoshi scholar Konan Naito argued that there were no significant organizations in China above the "village community or . . . extended family," and that therefore the Chinese had no "spirit of independence and patriotism relative to foreign countries."[14] In the early 1920s the historian of China Jin'ichi Yano published two essays on the theme that "China is not a nation," and Yano's views were apparently incorporated into the infamous "Tanaka Memorial" of 1927. According to Kimitada Miwa, "Yano's thesis that China was not a nation was instrumental in making the 'non-governmental' idealism of the 1920s surface in the 1930s as national policy. In this sense it became the theoretical premise of a regionalist concept designed to rescue Japan from its growing isolation in international opinion."[15] By the beginning of the 1930s, therefore, both scholarship and Asianist romanticism had become closely linked to Japanese expansion on the continent.

Asianism as Official Policy

Because of recent suggestions that Japan's relationship with Asia is again moving in the direction of something like the Greater East Asian Co-Prosperity Sphere, it is worthwhile to go into particular detail regarding notions of Asianism in the period when they merged with national policy, that is, in the late 1930s and during the Pacific War. An understanding of Asianism under the New Order in East Asia (1938) and the Greater East Asian Co-Prosperity Sphere (1940) is necessary for the assessment of the relevance of present-day Japanese Asianism. Even in the era of the New Order and the Co-Prosperity Sphere there existed complicitous forms of Asianism that were liberal in orientation, and influential streams of liberal Japanese Asianism in the 1980s and 1990s do not differ radically or fundamentally from their prewar counterparts. In the present, as in the 1930s and during the war, conceptions of a uniquely Asian mode of thought and behavior whose most advanced form prevails in Japan are capable of providing a rationale for Japanese economic exploitation and perhaps even a degree of political domination.

The "Asianism" of the 1930s was hardly homogeneous. A distinction adopted by philosopher and critic Osamu Kuno in his study of Japanese ultranationalism may help clarify the discursive range of the term. Kuno points out that the role of the emperor in the Meiji state system was understood differently at different levels of society:

---

[14] Miwa, "Japanese Policies," p. 136.
[15] Ibid., p. 137.

The emperor appeared to have absolute authority and autonomy only to the masses. The public education in elementary and middle schools, and particularly in the military, thoroughly indoctrinated the people in that point of view. Due to the powerful influence of such institutions, belief in the emperor's authority was second nature to the average Japanese. Those in advisory organs or otherwise close to the emperor, however, understood his authority as being just symbolic and nominal. Accordingly, there emerged a system in which almost all real power was distributed among elite members of advisory organs and exercised by them on the emperor's behalf.

The emperor's authority and power, then, were interpreted in two ways. The successful working of the Meiji state depended on a subtle balance between an ideology for public consumption, the *kenkyo*, or exoteric ideology, and an elitist belief in a more restricted definition of imperial power, the *mikkyo*, or esoteric ideology. The exoteric, public, ideology operated to maintain the emperor as absolute monarch with unlimited authority and power. The esoteric canon, on the other hand, placed the authority and power of the emperor in a framework of limitations formed by the constitution and other considerations. The distinction between the two served to mobilize the energy of the people in service to a monarch in whom they could believe without qualification, while the government was run on the basis of a doctrine of constitutional monarchy.

This system might have continued to work smoothly had it not been for the military, especially the so-called Imperial Way Faction:

> Among the groups at the top of the power structure, only the military continued to cling to the exoteric belief system concerning the emperor. By using the Ministry of Education, which was entrusted with responsibility for elementary education, the military waged a campaign against the esoteric "understanding," a drive that became known as the Movement to Clarify the National Polity. . . . The military campaign, the growth of political awareness on the part of the "masses" educated in the exoteric belief, and their mobilization against the "eggheads" who espoused the organ theory, were all necessary preconditions to the rise of ultranationalism.[16]

The campaign Kuno refers to resulted in the so-called Minobe Affair of 1935, in which the most authoritative interpreter of the theory of the emperor as an organ of the state, retired University of Tokyo law professor

---

[16] Osamu Kuno, "The Meiji State, Minponshugi, and Ultranationalism," in *Authority and the Individual in Japan: Citizen Protest in Historical Perspective*, ed. J. Victor Koschmann (Tokyo: University of Tokyo Press, 1978), pp. 64–65.

Tatsukichi Minobe, was forced to resign from the House of Peers and all other public positions.[17] As Kuno explains this crisis:

> When faced with an attack by these allied forces, the organ theory of the emperor—the interpretation of the Meiji state as a constitutional monarchy which had been officially but tacitly sanctioned since the latter years of Meiji—crumbled irrespective of the will of the emperor himself. This fate was perhaps inevitable for an elite understanding that had been kept secret from the people at large. The esoteric belief remained persuasive only in the upper echelons of the society and never captured the minds of the people.[18]

These two ideologies, whose coexistence was the very substance of the Meiji system and whose incompatibility brought that system down in the mid-1930s, extended beyond the question of the emperor to affect other dimensions of imperial Japanese ideology, including conceptions of Japan's relationship to Asia. By the mid-1930s there were exoteric and esoteric forms of Asianism. These might initially be illustrated in the two organizations cited by historian Kimitada Miwa as centrally involved in the formulation of Prime Minister Fumimaro Konoe's 1938 proclamation of the New Order in East Asia.

The Greater Asia Association (Dai-Ajia Kyokai), or GAA, can be taken to represent the exoteric conception of Asianism. Formed in 1933 as the successor to the Pan-Asia Association (Han-Ajia Kyokai), the GAA took its name from Sun Yat-sen's famous speech in Kobe in 1924, which he organized around the notion of "Greater Asianism."[19] Members of the GAA premised their hopes for Asian unity on "East Asian ethical values" and were "more traditional" than other members of the elite, to the extent of espousing "anti-modern theories of the state based upon the historical intellectual heritage of an indigenous village community."[20] A representative member of the group, who was to become personally involved in drafting Konoe's proclamation of the New Order in East Asia, was Masaru Nakayama. Nakayama had attended the To-A Dobun Shoin (East Asia Common Culture Academy) in Shanghai, which "ensconced the teachings

---

[17] For details, see Frank O. Miller, *Minobe Tatsukichi: Interpreter of Constitutionalism in Japan* (Berkeley and Los Angeles: University of California Press, 1965), chap. 7.

[18] Kuno, "Meiji State," p. 65.

[19] For details on Sun's speech, see J. Y. Wong, "Sun Yatsen and Pan-Asianism," *International Studies* 2 (June 1987): 17–32. Also, Yoko Miyakawa Mathews, "Formulating a New Asia: Sun Yat-sen and Japanese Intellectuals in the 1930s" (Department of History, Cornell University, May 1994).

[20] Miwa, "Japan's Policies," pp. 138–40.

of Confucius as the basis of moral education." He called for "return to a classical East Asia, a new-found antithesis to the modern industrial society of the West."[21]

Thus, broadly speaking, the exoteric form of Asianism emphasized the harmonious, more or less natural continuity from family, to village, to Volk/nation, to Greater Asian community based on racial and cultural affinities between Chinese and Japanese, of the sort captured in the slogan *dobun-doshu* (same culture, same race). Exoteric Asianism is also usually linked with the vision of Japan shared by the "Japanists" (Nihonshugisha), such as Tetsujiro Inoue, that is, the restoration and perfection of Japan as an ethical, "family-state" under the divine imperial patriarch.

Also organized informally in 1933 was the Showa Research Association (Showa Kenkyukai), or SRA, whose members typically espoused esoteric ideology. Unlike the GAA, which tended to be aligned with the military's Imperial Way faction (*Kodoha*), the SRA supported the Control faction (*Toseiha*). According to Miwa's view, a representative member of the SRA was the political scientist Masamichi Royama, who in the late 1930s was exploring German conceptions of geopolitics.[22] But the SRA's contribution to Asianism was philosophical and cultural as well as social-scientific.

In 1938, philosopher Kiyoshi Miki was asked to head the SRA's newly formed Cultural Problems Research Group (Bunka Mondai Kenkyukai), and it was in conjunction with this SRA subgroup that he produced his highly influential philosophical reflections on the future East Asian Community.[23] Miki had been deeply involved in Marxist thought, and his brushes with left-wing politics had led to his arrest and incarceration for several months in 1930, ostensibly for contributing money to the Communist Party. By 1938 he considered Marxism alone to be inadequate as a philosophy of history and praxis and was working on a study of imagination and technology. His developing philosophy of *techne* greatly influenced his conception of Asianism, a conception that aptly illustrates the esoteric counterpart to philosophical naturalism and mystical restorationism. Indeed, the SRA's contribution to Asianism should be understood as a reform-oriented alternative to the exoteric views of the status of the emperor and of Japan's "manifest destiny" in Asia that were gaining ground within the Japanese establishment.

[21] Ibid., pp. 141–42.
[22] Ibid., pp. 138.
[23] On Kiyoshi Miki and the SRA, see William Miles Fletcher III, "Intellectuals and Fascism in Early Shōwa Japan," *Journal of Asian Studies* (November 1979): 39–63, and *The Search for a New Order: Intellectuals and Fascism in Prewar Japan* (Chapel Hill: University of North Carolina Press, 1982).

The Philosophy of East Asian Community

The initial result of Miki's affiliation with the SRA's cultural subgroup was the essay "Shin-Nihon no shiso genri" (Philosophical principles for the new Japan), published anonymously by the SRA in January 1939. A continuation was published in September of the same year. The initial essay is linked explicitly to the outbreak of hostilities between Japan and China in 1937 and the subsequent Japanese invasion—the so-called China Incident—and attempts to show the potential world-historical significance of this "incident." Miki argued that the conquest of China could lead to the "unification of Asia" and, ultimately, of the world, on principles more inclusive than the one-sided Eurocentrism that had previously comprised the limit of world history.

Miki argued against simplistic forms of naturalism that treated the Japanese nation as an ahistorical given. He insisted that the unification of East Asia could never be achieved through reliance on tradition alone:

> The culture of the East Asian Community must be connected to the East Asian cultural tradition. However, we must remain keenly aware that this tradition of so-called Oriental culture is haunted by feudalism. In order to rid itself of that feudal element the communal (Gemeinschaft-like) dimension of Oriental culture must be laced with modern (Gesellschaft-like) culture. [In that sense], the culture of the East Asian Community must be a newly created culture rather than merely a revival of the feudalistic. If it is to be called a revival of Oriental culture, this revival must be tantamount to the creation of a new East Asian culture, just as in the West the revival of Greek and Roman culture that was called the Renaissance was certainly not a simple revival of ancient culture but rather the creation of an entirely new, modern one.[24]

This new East Asian culture would require a thorough modernization of China conducted with the involvement of or by Japan.[25] Accordingly, because of their traditionalist orientation, Sun Yat-sen's "three principles of the people"—people's nationalism (*minzokushugi*), people's rights (*min-*

---

[24] Kiyoshi Miki, "Shin-Nihon no shiso genri," [Philosophical principles of a new Japan], *Miki Kiyoshi zenshu* [Complete works of Kiyoshi Miki]. (Tokyo: Iwanami Shoten, 1968), 17:515. I have profited from Kiyoshi Miki, "Principles of Thought for a New Japan," trans. Lewis E. Harrington (Department of Asian Studies, Cornell University, June 1993), but the translations in the text are my own.

[25] Miki, "Shin-Nihon no shiso genri," p. 510.

kenshugi), and people's livelihood (*minseishugi*)—were entirely inadequate as a blueprint for China's transformation.[26]

Miki criticizes what had come to be called Japanism (*Nihonshugi*)—hermetic, hypostatized conceptions of Japanese history and culture typical of the exoteric discourse—for the "self-righteousness" and "narrow-minded xenophobia" that were evident in the tendency to define Japanese culture as an ahistorical abstraction that had to be resurrected or restored. Miki insists rather on historicizing Japanese culture in relation to the zeitgeist of each period, viewing it not as a fixed entity but as a constructive, creative process: "The Japanese spirit must be formed anew as today's zeitgeist and work toward the creation of new culture with global significance."[27] Moreover, rather than exclusive and closed, Japanese culture, premised on the *kokutai* of imperial sovereignty, tended to be open and inclusive:

> The culture of ancient Japan was developed by assimilating elements from the Chinese and Indian, and then Western culture. Moreover, as it took in these elements it did not forcibly unify them into a fixed form but was tolerant to the point of allowing different elements to coexist side by side. Belief in Shinto and belief in Buddhism were carried on in parallel among Japanese without contradiction, and Japanese and Western art could be viewed on the walls of the same room without a sense of incongruity. Indeed, the depth and breadth of the Japanese mind are aptly revealed in this practical unification of objectively incompatible entities.

Drawing a parallel between his inclusive, pluralistic notion of Japanese culture and the new Asian community, he says: "Precisely such a spirit is essential to the new community, as it must animate the cultural particularity of each East Asian people and must not force any into a single pattern."[28]

In order to retain the freedom and individuality of the elements while at the same time actualizing a transnational community, nationalism—including Japanese nationalism—had to be limited.

> Because the East Asian Community aims at communal relations among peoples, its philosophy must transcend the standpoint of simple nationalism [Volkism = *minzokushugi*]. At the same time, within the community, the special nature of each people must be recognized. Therefore . . . , the philosophy of Volkism retains significance in that it asserts the particularity of

---

[26] Ibid., pp. 526–28.
[27] Ibid., p. 529.
[28] Ibid., pp. 530–31.

each people. Moreover . . . , there must be some truth in nationalism because every world-historical movement is initiated by a single people. Similarly, the East Asian Community has taken shape as a result of the initiative of the Japanese people. Yet Japan itself must enter into and submit to the principles of this community which has been formed under its own leadership. Accordingly, it is natural that Japan must accept limits on its own nationalism.[29]

By the same token, "Inasmuch as within the community the special characteristics of each people are to be allowed full expression, by the same logic it is important to respect the individuality of each person within each of those peoples. . . . The inability of a whole to recognize the individuality of each of its parts must be taken as a sign of weakness."[30] Miki adds in the continuation of his essay, "if the individual is not free, the harmony of the whole cannot be true harmony. . . . True harmony can obtain only among independent entities."[31]

It is important to note that, despite its manifest lack of realism, given the full-scale battles and Japanese atrocities under way on the continent, Miki's philosophical perspective on the China war was by no means arbitrary or merely opportunistic. His philosophical orientation paralleled in many of its aspects the contemporaneous work of Martin Heidegger, with which he was quite familiar; it also was broadly in tune with that of Miki's teacher and Japan's most respected philosopher, Kitaro Nishida.

As William Haver has lucidly pointed out, Nishida clearly registered his objection to exoteric theories of continuity among the various levels of "biological" race, genealogical "house" (*ie*) or family, ethnic nation or Volk (*minzoku*), and state. He is especially critical of the contention that family, *minzoku*, and state formed a single continuous corporate entity.[32] For Nishida, the *minzoku* was by no means natural, but could only result from self-conscious creation in history. A *minzoku* existed only when its members believed and acted as if it existed. (For Nishida, the nation had indeed to be an "imagined community"!)[33] The *minzoku* was a historical

[29] Ibid., pp. 516–17.
[30] Ibid., p. 519.
[31] Kiyoshi Miki, "Shin-Nihon no shiso genri: Zokuhen—kyodoshugi no tetsugakuteki kiban," [Philosophical principles of a new Japan, continued: The philosophical foundations of cooperativism], in *Miki Kiyoshi zenshu*, 17:561.
[32] *Nishida Kitaro zenshu* [Complete works of Kitaro Nishida] (Tokyo: Iwanami Shoten, 1979), 12:416–19; cited in William Haver, "The Body of This Death: A Polemic on the Ground of Historical Consciousness in the Time of AIDS" (Department of History, SUNY, Binghamton), pp. 39–66.
[33] Nishida did not use the term, which is Benedict Anderson's; see Anderson, *Imagined Communities: Reflections on the Origin and Spread of Nationalism* (London: Verso, 1983).

entity par excellence. Yet a *minzoku* became a state only when it entered into relations with other *minzoku* in a shared world and rationalized itself and its relations with the others.[34]

Given his conception of the Volkisch state, Nishida could figure the "new world order" only in terms of a kind of pluralism. Each *minzoku* had both to express itself in a unique national mission and at the same time to transcend itself in the creation of a world order. Contrary to the Wilsonian conception of nationality, whose origins Nishida associates with the eighteenth century, there could only be global unity if the new world order allowed national *minzoku* to transcend themselves within a regional context. Globalism had to be the ultimate objective of the Greater East Asian Co-Prosperity Sphere, as well. That is, the East Asian nations that had been subjected to European colonial rule must now transcend their own narrow interests to construct a regional order and on that basis contribute to the formation of a "single historical world."[35]

It is also worth noting that intellectuals unconnected to Nishida or Miki also proposed that members of the emerging East Asian imperium should retain freedom of choice. Masayoshi Miyazaki, an economist who did not belong to the SRA but acted as adviser to the Control faction leader, Kanji Ishiwara, wrote in 1938 concerning his conception of an East Asian League:

> Inasmuch as the objective of the League would be the liberation of the people of East Asia, it must guarantee completely the right of political independence of those who have been liberated. In addition to working for the freedom of Asian peoples who have not yet been liberated, Japan and the other member countries must assure freedom of choice, leaving it entirely up to the newly liberated nation to decide whether to join the League or remain completely independent. The right to secede from the League must also be guaranteed. The East Asian League shall be a firm pledge entered into voluntarily by the nations of East Asia and based on relations of mutual economic and political reliance among Japan and other members. It will not be a coercive order.[36]

Miki's East Asian Community thesis as well as Miyazaki's East Asian League proposal were criticized by ideologues of the Imperial Way faction and by Pan-Asianists, most of whom espoused some version of the exoteric view.

---

[34] Haver, "Body of this Death," p. 44.

[35] Cited in ibid., p. 52.

[36] Bunso Hashikawa, "Japanese Perspectives on Asia: From Dissociation to Coprosperity," in *The Chinese and the Japanese: Essays in Political and Cultural Interactions*, ed. Akira Iriye (Princeton: Princeton University Press, 1980), p. 352.

Indeed, according to Bunso Hashikawa, Miyazaki's conception of the League was attacked because it supposedly "ignored Japan's position as the leader of Greater East Asia,"[37] but others have pointed out that Miyazaki's ultimate objective was a Japan-China alliance under the Japanese emperor.[38]

Despite their relative sophistication and the criticism they attracted from proponents of the exoteric view, esoteric conceptions of East Asian unity probably contributed as much as the exoteric to Japanese aggression and exploitation of peoples in the Co-Prosperity Sphere. The war responsibility of esotericist intellectuals has been argued exhaustively elsewhere.[39] Yet the issue of their complicity is perhaps more complicated than has been recognized. For example, in his illuminating explication of racist ideology in Japan during the Pacific War, John Dower refers in passing to the views of such esoteric theorists as Keiji Nishitani and others of the Kyoto School of philosophers. He credits them with being more sophisticated than shrilly exoteric publicists like Chikao Fujisawa, but in the end lumps both together on the basis that "for all their abstract theorizing . . . the Kyoto School also made it clear that the current conflict represented Japan's ascension as the leading 'world-historical race.' "[40] Yet the term "race" Dower refers to is not *jinshu* ("biological" race; *Rasse* in German) but *minzoku*, which Dower himself considers to be the equivalent of *Volk*, defined as "natural and spiritual communities which shared a common destiny" but not necessarily a common ancestry.[41] Kyoto School philosophers, virtually all of whom were protégés of Kitaro Nishida, generally used *minzoku* in the sense Nishida insisted upon, that is, as a historically contingent rather than naturally existing body, "imaginary" rather than objectively "biological." Therefore, it seems to be a mistake to conflate the esoteric with the exoteric form of Asianism on the basis of the loosely racial connotations of the term *minzoku*.

---

[37] Bunso, Hashikawa, " 'Dai to-A kyoeiken' no rinen to jittai," [Ideals and realities of the Greater East Asia Co-Prosperity Sphere], *Nihon no rekishi* [History of Japan] (Tokyo: Iwanami Shoten, 1977), 21:293; quoted in Mathews, "Formulating a New Asia," p. 13.

[38] Mathews, "Formulating a New Asia," p. 14.

[39] M. Fletcher, "Intellectuals and Fascism" and *Search for a New Order;* James B. Crowley, "A New Asian Order: Some Notes on Prewar Japanese Nationalism," in *Japan in Crisis: Essays on Taisho Democracy,* ed. Bernard S. Silberman and H. D. Harootunian (Princeton: Princeton University Press, 1974), pp. 270–98; and Crowley, "Intellectuals as Visionaries of the New Asian Order," in *Dilemmas of Growth in Prewar Japan,* ed. James W. Morley (Princeton: Princeton University Press, 1971), pp. 319–73.

[40] John Dower, *War without Mercy: Race and Power in the Pacific War* (New York: Pantheon, 1986), p. 227.

[41] For the translation of "world-historical race" as *sekaishiteki minzoku,* see ibid., p. 351, note 47; for explication of the meaning of *minzoku* in contrast to *jinshu,* see ibid., pp. 267–68.

Indeed, in its Japanese wartime usage the term *minzoku* was rendered increasingly polysemous in the course of Japan's modern expansion, as initially the peoples of Hokkaido and the Ryukyus, and then of Korea and Taiwan, were integrated securely into the modern Japanese state and accordingly, for some purposes at least, into the Japanese *minzoku* as well. Thus,

> The identity of "the Japanese" as conveyed in the term "Japanese *minzoku*" came to refer to the totality of all who were ruled by and belonged to the Japanese state. They formed a community integrated according to some principle other than racial/ethnic particularism. That is, "Japanese *minzoku*" came to mean something like "citizen of the Greater Japanese empire" (aside from whether such a term was possible in a legal sense). . . . At the same time, it is also true that "Japanese *minzoku*" was thought of as something quite different from the Korean *minzoku* or the various *minzoku* of Taiwan.

In other words, in opposition to "the West," the people of Japan's entire Greater East Asian community could be thought of as a single *minzoku*, whose racial, ethnic, and class differences were all dissolved in the benevolent gaze of the emperor (*isshi dojin*), but this universalism did not prevent various forms of discrimination within that community between "Japanese" defined more narrowly and the others.[42]

It also seems misleading to treat all wartime documents mentioning "liberation" and autonomy as merely deceptive and obfuscating. Often, no doubt, such terms were used cynically, but in the esoteric discourse their provenance included the major European thinkers of the nineteenth and twentieth centuries, many of whom are canonical figures in the genealogy of liberalism. Not only Hegel but Kant and Locke, among others, insisted that true freedom entailed subjection to law and other forms of authority;[43] thus freedom could be construed to mean obedience to the state and, at

---

[42] Naoki Sakai, " 'Toyo' no jiritsu to daito-A kyoeiken," [Autonomy of Asia and the Greater East Asia Co-Prosperity Sphere], *Jokyo* 48 (December 1994): 9–10.

[43] To adequately support this argument would require more extensive demonstration than is possible here, but perhaps a few quotations will be suggestive. Hegel wrote, for example, that "it is the moral Whole, the *State*, which is that form of reality in which the individual has and enjoys his freedom; but on the condition of his recognizing, believing in, and willing that which is common to the Whole." Georg Wilhelm Friedrich Hegel, *The Philosophy of History*, trans. J. Sibree (New York: Dover Publications, 1956), p. 38. Kant wrote, "What else then can freedom of will be but autonomy. . . . Thus a free will and a will under moral laws are one and the same." Immanuel Kant, *Groundwork of the Metaphysic of Morals*, trans. H. J. Paton (New York: Harper Torchbooks, 1954), p. 114. Locke wrote, "However it may be mistaken, the end of law is not to abolish or restrain but to preserve and enlarge freedom; for in all the

the transnational level, the voluntary subjection of Asian nations to Japanese leadership. It can be further argued that Nishida, Miki, and others were faithful to and, indeed, sometimes more sophisticated than, this tradition of political philosophy, and that their rationale for the Co-Prosperity Sphere was an extension of that tradition, not merely an ad hoc, apology for imperialism.[44] Of course, such an argument implies that the liberal-pluralistic conceptions of Asian unity now prevalent in Japan are implicated in the creation of a new structure of Japanese exploitation in Asia.

Other members of the SRA whose endeavors were more social-scientific than philosophical were also focusing their research on the question of East Asian unity. In a manner broadly parallel to Miki's argument, the political scientist Masamichi Royama argued in 1938 that the "China Incident" signified the world-historical possibility of a new global order premised on regionalism rather than on atomistic relations among autonomous nation-states. The League of Nations had imposed on the world an order that presupposed the modern theory of state sovereignty and the principle of national self-determination as expressed in the principle of "one nation, one state."

> It was the League organization in Geneva that universalized the West and sought to incorporate the countries of the East into this universal system. It credited regionalism only in the specific case of the U.S. Monroe Doctrine whereas, with respect to the East, . . . it recognized no regional unities. Behind the League's orientation was not just a belief in the West's universality but also the actual force exerted by England and France, which had already reached the stage of commercial and financial imperialism and therefore were interested in having an East . . . that was nationally divided.[45]

The China Incident and Japan's incipient bid to form a new Asian order foretold the possibility of a new world order that would give full credence and initiative to an Asian regional unit. In other words, the Japanese nationalism that was expressed in Japan's "development" on the continent would in fact provide the motive force for the transcendence of nation-

---

states of created beings capable of laws, where there is no law, there is no freedom." John Locke, *The Second Treatise of Government*, ed. Thomas P. Peardon (New York: The Liberal Arts Press, 1952), p. 32.

[44] The prewar Japanese philosopher/critic who most eloquently and thoroughly demonstrated the continuity between liberalism and fascism in the prewar Japanese context was Jun Tosaka. See Tosaka, *Nippon ideologii-ron* [On Japanese Ideology] (1936; Tokyo: Iwanami Bunko, 1977).

[45] Masamichi Royama, "To-A kyodotai no riron" [A theory of the Greater East Asia Co-Prosperity Sphere], *Kaizo* (November 1938): 8.

alism by catalyzing the construction of an Asian community. Unfortunately, the Chinese had misjudged Japan's intentions, considering the Japanese moves as merely another case of capitalistic imperialism. Yet Japan's advance supposedly differed fundamentally from imperialism: Japan aimed not at unilateral dominion but rather at a community, perhaps organized federally. Such a community would respect the heterogeneity that was intrinsic to the region and recognize the various "national" (*minzokuteki*) sentiments it encompassed; it could not rely on given geographical factors, which did not necessarily favor Asian unity, but would strive gradually to construct a new administrative order with functional links to those natural, geographical conditions. Economically, moreover, the community should not aim at autarchy or a bloc economy, but rather strive to contribute to a new global economy that would bring peace and "the coexistence and common prosperity of all peoples."

Overall, Royama recognized clearly that even a new order encompassing only Northeast Asia would require a great deal of effort, and thus he emphasized the need for what he calls a political approach—one that is instrumental and constructivist, ready to provide the "great deal of technical and administrative innovation and creativity" that would be required.[46] In other words, because Asia does not exist as a region already integrated through economic interaction, Royama proposes that it must first be invented and consolidated politically (and, by extension, ideologically) as a bounded community before it can be integrated economically.

Miwa speculates that this article, and the persuasiveness of Royama's views more generally, led Konoe to issue the proclamation regarding the New Order in East Asia. Yet it seems that the proclamation was actually drafted by the Pan-Asianist Masaru Nakayama, who was in Peking at the time. Miwa's explanation for why Konoe, whose own views were more in line with Royama's, went to Nakayama for the draft is provocative in light of the opposition between exoteric and esoteric views of the emperor and of Asianism. That is, Konoe believed that Nakayama's "tradition-rooted and emotion-bound expressions of neighborly relations and racial affinity" would be more persuasive to the Japanese public and also to the Chinese than Royama's esoteric reasoning based on economic analysis and geopolitics.[47] In sum, just as since the Meiji period the bureaucratic and intellectual elite had been content to disseminate emperor worship and notions of the family-state to elementary students while reserving the scientific worldview for those who went on to higher schools and university, Konoe now "disguised" Royama's social-scientific conclusions regarding

---

[46] Ibid., pp. 21–23.
[47] Miwa, "Japanese Policies," p. 148.

the new Asian order under Nakayama's Pan-Asianist appeal to "kingly way" (*wang-tao*) philosophy.[48]

Greater East Asia Co-Prosperity Sphere

Miwa argues that what I have called the esoteric thought of members of the SRA also influenced the thinking behind Foreign Minister Yosuke Matsuoka's August 1940 allusion to a Greater East Asia Co-Prosperity Sphere, a community that was to "include such southern regions as the Dutch East Indies and French Indochina."[49] Yet as many have pointed out, much of the original rationale for the New Order did not apply to the Co-Prosperity Sphere's "southern regions," whose relationship to Japan was historically quite different from those between Japan and its closer neighbors, China and Manchuria. Indeed, Royama's economistic notions of geopolitics led him to the same conclusion. In a March 1941 essay he argued that Southeast Asia was geopolitically and economically a very different region from Northeast Asia, and that Japan's economic relations with the southerly region had historically been relatively shallow. Moreover, he noted that the proposed Co-Prosperity Sphere overlapped the economic spheres of influence of the United States and Great Britain. Royama again contended that prior to becoming a viable economic region, Greater East Asia would first have to be consolidated as a political entity.[50]

The questions raised by the inclusion of Southeast Asia in the Co-Prosperity Sphere were not just economic or geopolitical. Asianists in the Meiji period had been concerned only in passing with areas south of China,[51] although Tenshin Okakura was a notable exception,[52] and despite Matsuoka's optimism, Northeast Asia continued to be given conceptual priority in the era of the Co-Prosperity Sphere as well.[53] W. G. Beasley

---

[48] Ibid., p. 149.

[49] Quoted in ibid., p. 151. The entire text of Matsuoka's proclamation, conveniently alongside Konoe's declaration of the New Order, is reprinted in English in *Japan's Greater East Asia Co-prosperity Sphere in World War II: Selected Readings and Documents*, ed. by Joyce C. Lebra (Kuala Lumpur: Oxford University Press, 1975), pp. 68–72.

[50] Masamichi Royama, "Daito-A kyoeiken no chiseigakuteki kosatsu," [A Geographical Consideration of the Greater East Asia Co-prosperity Sphere], *Kaizo* (March 1941): 102–4; Miwa, "Japanese Policies," pp. 151–52.

[51] Toru Yano, "Kindai Nihon no nanpo kanyo" [Modern Japan's involvement in the South Pacific], in *Tonan Ajia to Nihon* [Southeast Asia and Japan], ed. Toru Yano, Koza Tonan Ajia 10 (Tokyo: Kobundo, 1991), pp. 7–8.

[52] Kakuzo Okakura, *The Ideals of the East* (New York: E. P. Dutton, 1905).

[53] W. G. Beasley, "Japan and Pan-Asianism: Problems of Definition," *International Studies* 2 (June 1987): 12.

argues that pan-Asianism's focus on the northeast was "ideological" in the sense that Asianist ideals relied so heavily on a Confucian idiom that they could not readily be applied to non-Confucianist cultures. Moreover, in the absence of Confucianism's ethical influence, such cultures "did not possess the qualities that would make them partners with Japan on anything like terms of equality. They needed 'guidance.' "[54]

Perceptions of the two areas seem to have differed among the general public as well. Ken'ichiro Hirano illustrates the different Japanese perceptions of Northeast and Southeast Asia by comparing two popular prewar cartoon characters, "Norakuro" (Stray Dog Blacky) and "Boken Dankichi" (Adventurer Dankichi). The former is sent as a member of the dog army to the continent where, although bullied by his superiors, he fights and wins many battles against the enemy pigs. The latter drifts accidently southward to a savage island somewhere in Nan'yo (the South Seas). There, the black natives make him king, and he provides them with a railroad and a postal service. According to Hirano,

> *Norakuro* and *Boken Dankichi* were replicas of those Japanese who went northward and southward. The northward movement was primarily militaristic and state-supported. On the other hand, most of the Japanese who went to Southeast Asia before the war received less backing from the state: *Dankichi* was almost alone. *Dankichi* . . . reflected the Japanese attitude that Japanese could be well-accepted leaders of a native people and could lead the natives into modern life by virtue of Japan's earlier modernization. He also exemplified the simple-minded notion of . . . superiority over other Asian nations.[55]

Yet clearly esoteric concepts and guidelines that had been developed earlier in conjunction with the formation of the New Order continued to be developed by members of the SRA and other intellectuals after 1940 and were often applied in the effort to legitimate the Greater East Asian Co-Prosperity Sphere. In a 1943 publication, Michio Murayama echoed Miki in his contention that the Japanese national character had always been open to infusions of different groups from outside, and was devoid of racial prejudice. Japanese society was a veritable "melting pot."[56] In

[54] Ibid., p. 13. Also see Beasley, *Japanese Imperialism, 1894–1945* (Oxford: Oxford University Press, 1987), chap. 14.

[55] Ken'ichiro Hirano, "The Japanese in Asia," Institute of International Relations for Advanced Studies on Peace and Development in Asia, Series A-7, Sophia University, Tokyo, (n.d.), p. 8. Also see Hidetoshi Kato, "The Trend toward Affirmation of War: 'Norakuro,' " *The Japan Interpreter* 7 (Spring 1971): 179–86.

[56] Michio Murayama, *Daito-A kensetsuron* [On the construction of Greater East Asia] (Tokyo: n.p., 1943); quoted in Sakai, " 'Toyo' no jiritsu," pp. 9–10.

other words, Murayama agreed with Nishida that a *minzoku* is historically constructed rather than naturally given. Therefore, it could be expected to change over time. Of course, such a conception of the Japanese nation was by no means new in the 1930s. Indeed, the liberal leader of the Meiji Enlightenment, Yukichi Fukuzawa, had identified the national essence (*kokutai*) with the historically contingent concept of "nationality."[57] In that sense, one must see the ideas of the SRA and the Nishida school as following in a fundamentally liberal tradition. Such a view clearly conflicted directly with the exoteric view of the Japanese *minzoku* as eternally a single (racially defined) entity since its founding "2,600 years ago."

Like Royama, the Kyoto University philosopher Masa'aki Kosaka insisted upon distinguishing between Japan's leading role in Asia on the one hand and imperialism on the other. Sakai quotes Kosaka:

This ideal of a Co-Prosperity Sphere should not take the form of the old imperialism. Imperialism does not *give life to* other countries through *mediation*, but merely *uses* them as *means*. This was the British method. Even when they gave a colony its independence, it was for the purpose of using it. It remained a means of extending and expanding Great Britain. However, we must distinguish *mediation* from *means*. *Means* implies using the other as a *thing*, while *mediation* entails recognizing the other as an independent *subject*. An autonomous, self-conscious entity should not be treated as a means but as mediation. One should not rule it, but rather be its representative. We can locate ourselves at the center of the many peoples that surround us only as their "representation."[58]

Imperialism is unilateral and instrumental; mediation is interactive and representational. Yet, as Sakai points out, the Co-Prosperity Sphere was, indeed, announced and imposed unilaterally, so how did ideologues and executors of the Co-Prosperity Sphere attempt to convince themselves and others that it nevertheless differed from imperialism? Sakai concludes that—like Snow White's wicked stepmother demanding praise from the magic mirror—they manifested a kind of "narcissism" that compelled them incessantly to cite cases in which, supposedly, members of nations in the Co-Prosperity Sphere expressed support for and invested hopes in the Japanese. By repeating such cases, often misleadingly, they sought to present the Co-Prosperity Sphere as the result of the collective will of all its member peoples rather than just of the Japanese, and to present themselves not as the ruler of those peoples but as their "representative."[59]

---

[57] Fukuzawa, *Outline*, pp. 23–28.
[58] Sakai, " 'Toyo' no jiritsu," p. 13.
[59] Ibid., p. 14.

What emerges, therefore, is a kind of duplicity within the wartime, "antir-acist" discourse—what I have called the esoteric discourse—by which a benign, enlightened vision of the Co-Prosperity Sphere is preserved at one level even as doubts are resolved through narcissistic elicitation of Asian support at another. Of course, in cases where subordinates in the Co-Prosperity Sphere even implicitly refused that support, their narcissistic "leaders" turned paranoic and punished them severely.[60]

Esoteric concepts filtered down to the local administrative level as well, often apparently in combination with exoteric notions. The document "Daito-A kyoeiken-ron" (On the Greater East Asia Co-Prosperity Sphere), compiled in 1942 by the intelligence section of the Ministry of the Navy, suggests how the Co-Prosperity Sphere was envisioned as a whole. It divides the components of the Sphere into five categories: (1) Japan, the "leading country"; (2) independent countries (Republic of China [Nanking], Man-chukuo, and Thailand), (3) independent protectorates (*dokuritsu hogo-koku*) (Burma, Philippines, Java), (4) directly administered areas (*chokkatsuryo*) that were "key points in the defense of Greater East Asia," and (5) colonies under the sovereignty of powers outside the Sphere (French Indochina, Portuguese Timor, and so on).

In the context of the Co-Prosperity Sphere, "independence" was always qualified. Even those countries in the second category were subject to the "mediating leadership" (*shido baikai*) or "internal guidance" (*naizai shido*) of Japan. Regarding the third category of "independent protectorates," the document makes clear that, while for propaganda purposes these could be called "independent," it was to be clearly understood that they remained subject to the higher sovereignty of the leading country, Japan. Moreover, in a manner reminiscent of relations between feudal domains and the Edo regime during the Tokugawa period (1603–1868), compo-nent elements of the Sphere were prohibited from interacting directly with each other: they were to be connected to one another only via the "me-diating leadership" of Japan.[61]

Terms such as "mediating leadership" and other language used in de-scribing the unity of the Co-Prosperity Sphere suggest the influence of both esoteric and exoteric outlooks. The document declares that, instead of liberty as it was supposedly conceived of in Europe, that is, as a "cen-trifugal splitting among the various *minzoku*," the Co-Prosperity Sphere would employ the more typically Asian sense of that term as "centripetal

[60] Ibid., pp. 13, 18.
[61] Ken'ichi Goto, "Kindai Nihon-Tonan Ajia kankei shiron josetsu," [On the history of Japan-Southeast Asian relations], in *Nashonarizumu to kokumin kokka* [Nationalism and the modern nation state] ed. Tsuchiya Kenji, *Koza gendai Ajia* 1 (Tokyo: Tokyo Daigaku Shuppankai, 1994), pp. 38–40.

unity." It also specifies that, "we do not recognize mechanistic forms of vicious equality [*akubyodo*] or atomistic freedom," but would rather adhere to "organic unity as a totality, in which each element is given its proper place according to its abilities, values, and standard of life."[62] Here it is worth recalling that Kiyoshi Miki had explicitly rejected not only familial metaphors but "organic unity" as implying an unacceptably direct sub-ordination of the parts to the whole.[63] The rhetoric of "proper place," of course, evokes the principles of familism typical of exoteric conceptions of Japanese society as well as of the relationship between Japanese and the natives.[64]

Finally, the document very candidly illustrates the manner in which ide-als of all kinds were ultimately jettisoned in favor of stark "realism." It notes that until the war was won, the peoples of occupied areas would have to endure material privation along with the Japanese, and therefore for several years it would most likely be more a matter of "co-poverty" than "co-prosperity." To compensate them for their material suffering, the report recommends that they should be given the "spiritual" satisfac-tion of being "reborn as people of the New East Asia."[65]

Postwar Asianism and the Present Situation

In the post–World War II era, while under occupation by U.S. forces rep-resenting the Allies, Japan underwent a massive reform program designed to "Westernize" Japanese society. Ideologically Japanese went through an-other Enlightenment comparable to that of the early Meiji period. Indeed, by the time the U.S.–Japan Security Treaty was signed along with the peace treaty, it seemed that Japan would again "de-Asianize," with few regrets for the time being because Asia symbolized disillusionment and war guilt.

Nevertheless, the new alignment of Japan with "the West" in the emerg-ing cold war inevitably stimulated an Asianist reaction that recalls the Greater-Asianist resistance against Eurocentrism in the Meiji period. Led intellectually by the specialist in Chinese literature, Yoshimi Takeuchi, and increasingly persuasive on the Left, this postwar Asianism focused almost exclusively on China and, more specifically, the Communist revolutionary movement there. It is important to note, however, that Takeuchi's own conception of Asia was radically nonessentialist. As Sakai notes, for Tak-

[62] Ibid., pp. 40–41.
[63] Miki, "Shin-Nihon no shiso genri: Zokuhen," pp. 560–61.
[64] See the discussion in Dower, *War without Mercy*, chap. 10.
[65] Goto, 'Kindai Nihon-Tonan Ajia kankei," p. 41.

euchi, "the Orient does not connote any internal commonality among the [entities] subsumed under it. . . . The principle of its unity lies outside itself."[66] Therefore, to an extent exceeding even that of such prewar esoteric Asianists as Kiyoshi Miki and Masamichi Royama, Takeuchi's orientation to Asia strained the bounds of "Asianism" defined as the perception of a shared Asian identity and destiny.

Beginning in January 1950, when the Cominform criticized the Japanese Communist Party for collaborating with U.S. imperialism, the party turned in some ways toward the thought of Mao Zedong and the Chinese revolutionary model. This move initiated a broad and frequently shifting association between Sinocentric Asianism and the Japanese Left, whether communist or left-wing socialist, that lasted for over a decade. Politically and diplomatically, the major target was the U.S.-imposed barrier that isolated Japan from China and other socialist states on the continent. Ideologically, this left-wing Asianism revived familiar, prewar conceptions of Asian identity, including the tired canard of "same culture, same race."

Left-wing Asianism centering on China lasted until the early 1970s, when a series of events, including Sino-Soviet wrangling, the violence and disorder caused by China's Cultural Revolution, Lin Biao's attempt to assassinate Mao Zedong, rapprochement between China and the United States, and then, in 1973, the normalization of relations between Japan and China, led to disillusionment with Maoism and set the stage for a rather pale, postwar version of the prewar cooptation of Asianism as "national policy."

In the meantime, as Takashi Shiraishi points out in Chapter 5, elements of Japan's business and bureaucratic establishment had already returned in fact if not entirely in concept to Southeast Asia in the early postwar period. Against the background of reparations talks, Prime Minister Shigeru Yoshida made an official visit to Southeast Asia in 1954, and in 1957 Nobusuke Kishi responded to the urging of Japanese business leaders and diplomats by going south twice more, visiting twelve countries. As trade increased, "friendship" societies were formed one after another, and Japanese travel to Asia expanded. The first yen-credit agreement between postwar Japan and an Asian country was signed with India in 1958, and by the mid-1960s, such agreements had been concluded with several other Asian nations.[67]

[66] Naoki Sakai, "Modernity and Its Critique: The Problem of Universalism and Particularism," in *Postmodernism and Japan*, ed. Masao Miyoshi and H. D. Harootunian (Durham, N.C.: Duke University Press, 1989), p. 117.

[67] Lawrence Olson, *Japan in Postwar Asia* (New York: Praeger Publishers, 1970), pp. 13–43.

In the late 1980s, in the wake of the yen's appreciation following the 1985 Plaza Accords and massive Japanese investment and economic aid in Southeast Asia, there was a new wave of deliberation about Asia among members of the government-business establishment.[68] Several government ministries launched major studies of Japan-Asian relations. One, undertaken by the Ministry of Finance at the behest of Prime Minister Masayoshi Ohira, was organized by Yuichiro Nagatomi, who already in 1980 had gathered 130 leading intellectuals and 89 top bureaucrats to carry out a study of Japan's agenda for the twenty-first century.[69] In the latter half of the 1980s, he formed the Committee for Asia-Pacific Economic Research, which, like the Ohira brain trust, included leading, mainstream intellectuals from universities, government, and business.

Although their scale was grander and their membership more uniformly mainstream, the agenda and function of these groups made them in some ways comparable to the Showa Research Association. Whether the recommendations made by these commissions and other such groups in the 1980s can be compared to those of the SRA half a century earlier is a matter of judgment, but at least superficially some of their proposals recall the esoteric thought of the 1930s. As Kenneth Pyle sums up their conclusions,

Such bureaucratic thinking envisions a kind of "benign division of labor" coordinated and presided over by Japan. The favorite metaphor for this pattern of development is the "flying geese" formation, a phrase coined by Akamatsu Kaname, a prewar Japanese economist, but more recently popularized by former foreign minister Okita Saburo. This pattern of regional development prescribes a lead economy with others ranked behind in the order of their economic strength and technical sophistication. This analogy suggests a vertical division of labor, not wholly unlike what was envisioned in Japan's prewar pan-Asian ideology. The report of MOF's Committee on Asia-Pacific Economic Research, for example, foresees a three-tier division of labor in Asia composed of: (1) Japan; (2) the newly industrializing economies (NIEs), that is, South Korea, Hong Kong, Taiwan, and Singapore; and (3) the ASEAN countries and China. While denying that this would be a fixed structure, the report seems to minimize the possibility of changing the order of countries when it describes future development in the region.[70]

---

[68] For discussion of recent Japanese views of Asia, see *Japan Echo* 20 (Special Issue 1993).
[69] Kenneth B. Pyle, *The Japanese Question: Power and Purpose in a New Era* (Washington, D.C.: AEI Press, 1992), p. 70.
[70] Ibid., pp. 134–35.

The regional hierarchy proposed here is not the same as that designed for the Co-Prosperity Sphere, but, as Pyle remarks, it is not "wholly unlike" it either. Japan is permanently the leader, and other countries in the region are ranked according not only to "economic strength" but "technical sophistication." Clearly, much elite discourse in Japan is still premised on an enduring, if by no means pervasive, assumption of Japan's superiority over other Asian nations (whether by virtue of "national character," environment, or history) and therefore its capacity to represent and/or lead Asia.

It is not only an implicit belief in Japan's superiority that seems to connect contemporary Asianism with its prewar predecessor but also certain world-historical pretensions, according to which Japan is destined in the twenty-first century to transcend the modern era and move to the forefront of not only Asia but the world. Such a view was put variously in a number of reports of the Ohira and Ministry of Finance study groups of the early-1980s,[71] and was expounded more recently by the influential economist Yasusuke Murakami, among others. In 1988, Murakami observed that "the Cartesian underpinnings of modern Western thought," which have been most clearly manifest among Americans, were being eclipsed by an "Asian challenge" based in an anti-Cartesian, hermeneutic mode of understanding, whose effectiveness in the contemporary world is best exemplified in the successes of modern Japan.[72] Then, in an argument for "polymorphic liberalism" as an alternative to classical economics, Murakami gave more extended treatment to the contrast between Cartesian "transcendental reflection" and the "hermeneutic reflection" that is supposedly favored by Japanese.[73] What is most striking about Murakami's conceptual scheme is the global confrontation it posits between an "hermeneutic" approach whose world-historical vehicle is modern Japan (heading the "Asian challenge") and the "transcendental" approach asserted most forcefully by the United States. It would appear that the new, bipolar world system is to be premised on epistemology and culture rather than ideology in the manner of the cold war.

A parallel impression is conveyed by observations culled almost at ran-

[71] Yuichiro Nagatomi, *Kindai o koete* [Transcending the modern] (Tokyo: Okura Zaimu Kyokai, 1983); *Sofuto mikksu fuoroappu kenkyukai hokokusho* [Report of the Soft-Mix Follow-up Study Group] (Tokyo: Okurasho, 1985–89). For a critique, see H. D. Harootunian, "Visible Discourses/Invisible Ideologies," in Miyoshi and Harootunian, *Postmodernism and Japan*, pp. 63–92.
[72] Yasusuke Murakami, "The Debt Comes Due for Higher Education," *Japan Echo* 15 (Autumn 1988): 78–80.
[73] Yasusuke Murakami, *An Anticlassical Political-Economic Analysis: A Vision for the Next Century* (Stanford: Stanford University Press, 1996), pp. 390-27.

dom from a selection of recent working papers produced by a study group, the Kokka Senryaku Kenkyukai (Research Group on State Strategy), whose official membership of fourteen includes not only the omnipresent Nagatomi but business and financial executives, journalists, government bureaucrats, and academics. A July 1994 statement of purpose issued by the Group focuses on the relationship between the United States and Japan in Asia, observing that "among conscientious Japanese, virtually no one thinks that Japan should exercise hegemony in place of the United States." On the contrary, "Japan intends to provide advice and cooperation to the countries of Asia as an equal and a friend, with no thought for becoming their Number One leader."

The report adds, however, that the United States finds it difficult to deal with others on an equal basis. Because of the peculiar circumstances that obtained during their growth as a nation, the Americans tend to strive incessantly for the top position and to consider anything less as failure. They reacted defensively to Malaysian Prime Minister Mahathir Mohamad's proposal for an East Asian Economic Community because they saw it as a threat to U.S. hegemony. They accuse the Japanese of trying to replace them as the hegemonic power and chastise them for not adhering to universally accepted norms of economic behavior. Yet, according to the statement, in the real world it is the American approach that is unusual: "It appears that Americans are irritated by cultural differences between the U.S. and Asia. The Americans' thought patterns and customs, which were nurtured in the course of American history—survival of the fittest based on thorough-going individualism, free competition, and a sense of personal responsibility—are themselves 'peculiar,' to the point of being unmatched anywhere else on earth." The United States tends to impose its own way of thinking on the assumption that it is universally valid but, in fact, it is "the Japanese system, emphasizing 'conciliation' and 'compromise' [*kyocho*], that has universality." Of course, the report goes on, neither approach is perfect, but above all it is necessary to persuade the United States to be more relativistic and to try to understand Asia, while also working to dispel anti-American feelings among Asians.[74]

The strategy-group paper and Murakami's works are typically Asianist in the sense that they hypostatize an Asian culture and situate Japan as its representative. Apparently, global theorists like Murakami no longer see the need even to distinguish between Northeast and Southeast Asia: an "Asian" way of thinking exemplified in Japan confronts a Cartesian/Western way of thinking typified by the United States. Such a confrontation

[74] "Keizai kozo kaikaku kenkyukai/Kokka senryaku kenkyukai no shushi" [Research Group on Economic Structural Reform/Research Group on State Strategy], July 12, 1994.

underlies the various problems faced by Japan in Asia, and overcoming it will solve those problems. Moreover, they argue that the "Asian" mode of understanding is the wave of the future, and although Asians should to some degree accommodate the American approach, the global confrontation can ultimately be transcended only when the United States adopts the more "universal" Asian approach.

Once set forth in this manner, the new bipolar structure suggested, with minor variations, by Murakami and the study group begins to resemble that proposed by the United States in the infamous "Japan 2000" report, produced with CIA funding at the Rochester Institute of Technology and leaked to the press in June 1991.[75] The latter report situates the United States at the center of the "Western world paradigm," which is diametrically opposed to the "Japanese paradigm." Whereas the Japanese State Strategy group posits that the United States cannot imagine being other than "Number One," "Japan 2000" says of the Japanese that "unequivocal dominance is their goal."[76] It is interesting how the United States and Japan each objectify the other as its own opposite, while paranoically projecting its own hostility. Yet neither side can demonstrate the homogeneity of its own bloc ("Asia" or the "Western world") except by asserting the fundamental difference of that bloc from the other.

It is certainly true that Japanese versions of the new bipolar structure are usually phrased much more moderately than "Japan 2000." They always make a point of declaring that openness and pluralism must be the sine qua non of any new regional political economy under Japanese leadership and emphasize the need to respect difference. As a Japanese report in 1992 put it, "When faced with others who are different from us, we need to feel an active interest in what makes them different and learn to coexist with them."[77] Yet, as we have seen, a sincere commitment to liberal pluralism does not in itself distinguish this new ideology for relating to Asia from that put forward in the late-1930s and early-1940s by esoteric theorists of the SRA. In themselves, these statements by no means guarantee that the new Asianism will be all that new. The question remains, therefore, whether, in the context of Japan's preponderant economic interest and involvement in Southeast Asia since the late 1980s, the liberal

---

[75] See "C.I.A. Report on Japan Economy Creates Furor at Institute," *New York Times,* June 5, 1991. Also see Bruce Cumings, "C.I.A.'s *Japan 2000* Caper," *Nation,* September 30, 1991, pp. 366–68.

[76] Andrew J. Dougherty, "Japan 2000" (Rochester Institute of Technology, February 11, 1991), p. 153.

[77] The Round Table on Japan and the Asia-Pacific Region in the 21st Century, "Japan and the Asia-Pacific Region in the 21st Century: Promotion of Openness and Respect for Plurality," December 25, 1992, unpublished, unofficial translation, 27.

Asianism of Murakami and others is providing intellectual respectability to the construction of Japanese hegemony in the region.

First, it is important to remember that there remains even in elite circles an "exoteric" discourse on Japan's relations with Asia that is much more blunt than Murakami and the study-group reports about Japan's emerging Asian opportunities. In 1991, the right-wing Japanese politician, Shintaro Ishihara, remarked cheerfully that Japan was naturally "the nucleus of Asia," and that although the earlier Co-Prosperity Sphere, based on military subordination, had failed miserably, "now is the right time" to establish a new Sphere premised on Japan's technological and cultural preponderance in the region.[78] More liberal Asianists, of course, are outwardly concerned to defeat such notions and whatever plans or projects they might reinforce. At the same time, such rhetoric plays upon assumptions regarding Japanese superiority and natural leadership role that are common fare among liberals.

Second, as other chapters amply demonstrate, the historical situation in Asia is very different from that of the late-1930s. Most obviously, postwar Japan continues to adhere in principle to the "peace Constitution" (although many in and out of the government are calling for a larger Japanese security role in Asia).[79] More important, the United States remains the dominant military power as well as a major economic force in the area, and liberal Japanese Asianists in the 1980s and 1990s clearly recognize and even welcome the U.S. military presence. As Bruce Cumings argues in Chapter 4, the United States appears to be in a position to limit how high the Japanese "goose" can fly. Less clear, however, are how the relationship between Japan and the United States will develop in Asia and what role the logic of contemporary Asianist discourse is to play in that relationship.

Murakami and some members of the State Strategy group apparently presume that similarity in worldview is the fundamental condition for successful relations; yet in the real world, such similarity can be constructed only through the externalization of difference: cultural and other differences among Asians can be shown to be minor and thus nondivisive only if they are relativized in relation to the major cultural difference that supposedly divides "Asia" from the "West." Therefore, for Japanese, Japan's difference from the United States becomes the fundamental condition of its identity with Asia. The apparent result is a zero-sum game in which

[78] Shintaro Ishihara, "Tahara Soichiro no batoru intabiu: Ima koso jitsugen dekiru 'daito-A kyoeiken' " [Battle interview with Soichiro Tahara: The Greater East Asia Co-prosperity Sphere that can now be established], *Sansara* 13 (July 1991): 52–54.
[79] For example, see Hisahiko Okazaki, "Southeast Asia in Japan's National Strategy," *Japan Echo* 20 (Special Issue, 1993): 54–55.

proximity to the "Asian" mode of behavior implies distance from the U.S. mode, and vice versa. Surely, Japan's position in the triangular relations among itself, the United States, and the other Asian nations must be extremely ambivalent so long as close relations with the Asians depends on dissimilarity from the United States.

When seen through the lens of the Asianists' oppositional logic, therefore, the rationale that posits U.S. hegemony as the main systemic constraint on Japan's intentions in Asia offers few grounds for complacency. U.S. interests and involvement in Asia might indeed presently constrain Japan's options in various ways (Cumings), and Japanese business and government decision makers might prefer it that way (Shiraishi, Yamakage). But the liberal Japanese Asianist (and American ethnocentrist) interpretation of the relationship between the United States/"West" and Japan/"Asia" as a global confrontation of worldviews ("paradigms") will make it ever more difficult to contain the effects of economic tension between the United States and Japan. If that tension were to make cooperation between Japan and the United States in Asia ultimately impossible, the liberal Asianist logic of cultural bipolarity might again be enlisted to provide a rationale for unilateral Japanese domination. Under hostile circumstances, would not U.S. "constraint" of Japan play into the hands of Japanese advocates of a new Co-Prosperity Sphere? In Japan as elsewhere, liberal, ostensibly internationalist discourse remains quite capable of accommodating, and even promoting, imperialism.

II

FROM PAST TO FUTURE

3

The Intra-regional System in East Asia in Modern Times

TAKESHI HAMASHITA

East Asia entered modern times not because of the coming of European powers but because of the dynamism inherent in the traditional, Sinocentric tributary system. The Ch'ing dynasty's attempt to impose its own mercantilist control over tribute met resistance from overseas Chinese traders to its trade policy and led to the expansion of overseas Chinese private trade. This in turn forced the Ch'ing state to shift its policy from trade monopoly enforcement to tax collection. European powers entered this changing tributary system in the nineteenth century and exploited it to expand their own influence. Japan seized the opportunity to detach itself from the Sinocentric tributary system, opted for westernization as a way of modernization, and then attempted to "reenter" East Asia, only to get caught between the resilient Sinocentric system and the emerging Westphalian international system.

My purpose here is to understand East Asia as a historically constituted region with its own hegemonic structure. To do this we must examine how the states and areas that found themselves in this East Asian system tried to cope with the transformation of the long-established, Sinocentric, tributary system in the nineteenth and twentieth centuries. The traditional historiographic categories of Western "impact" and Asian "responses" cannot adequately address the structural transformations in the East Asian hegemonic system. East Asian history in modern times must be examined in its own terms, with special attention to how its internal dynamism led to its transformation and how it accommodated the "impact" of the coming of European powers and the rise of a new international system.

Traditionally, the tributary system, central to the maintenance of the Sinocentric system of suzerainty, has been understood narrowly, as the recognition and investiture of a king in each tributary state. The system, however, understood more broadly, was the external expression of hierarchical domestic relations of control, extending downward and outward from the imperial center. In other words, the tributary system was an organic network of relations, between the center and the periphery, which includes the provinces and dependencies of the empire, rulers of native tribes and districts, tributary states, and even trading partners. This tributary system in a broader sense constituted the arena in which the states and other entities of Southeast, Northeast, Central, and Northwest Asia operated in their relations with China.

Reassessing East Asian Historiography in Modern Times

Recent advances in the study of modern East Asian history invite us to reassess orthodox historiography and to reinterpret East Asian history in new perspectives. The most important development in historical studies of East Asia for our purpose is the shift in emphasis from the study of the central governing systems to the study of peripheral areas. Local relations with neighboring countries have begun to attract scholarly interest. The larger regions are also drawing more attention. Research into the trading networks between the Ryukyus, Tsushima and Ezo, and foreign countries, for instance, have largely undermined the assumption of Japan's unity and autonomy as a state, nation, territory, and culture and underlined the importance of multiple trading networks in the East Asia region. These studies require us to analyze the tributary system and China's external relations in a new light and to examine its ceremonial and diplomatic dimension, economic relations, and the use of military might (or military relations) in terms of relative shift in the balance of power between the center and peripheries, between north and south, and between the Sinocentric geopolitics of suzerainty and international power politics. Three areas of interest are especially pertinent to our discussion.

First, studies of Japan's seclusion policy in the Edo period (1603–1867) in the East Asian historical context have underlined the importance of Satsuma-Ryukyu and Tsushima-Korean trade relations and demonstrated the relative openness of Japan's "closure." This discovery has resulted from the recent attempt to understand Japanese history in a larger regional context. Earlier studies on Japanese history invariably treated Japan's domestic history and its external relations separately. The recent attempt to study Japanese internal and external relations in an integrated perspective thus marks a significant historiographical departure. Japan was "closed" in the Edo period because of the "closed nature" of Japanese historical studies. Light cast on the core of Japanese history from the outside, from Asia outside Japan, suggests that it is now time to do away with the institutional and intellectual divides that have long segregated Japanese, Oriental (Eastern), and Western histories.

Second, studies on imperial systems in the North China at the eastern edge of the Eurasian continent have shown that a loose system of rule was constructed over East and Southeast Asia with tributary and "imperial title-awarding" relations as its central institution. The historical transformation of this larger region needs to be examined in light of the regional unity that was constituted and sustained by the tributary system.

Third, recent studies on relations between Europe and Asia have demonstrated that European powers participated in the historically constituted, Sinocentric regional order without reorganizing, let alone destroying, it. As Europeans made their way to East Asia via Islamic, Indian, and Southeast Asian spheres, they absorbed elements from each sphere and deployed them to their own advantage.

Crucial in this emerging new perspective is the "discovery" of maritime Asia. Historically, there existed several maritime regions that stretched from Northeast Asia to East Asia and then from Southeast Asia to Oceania. Within this vast area countries, regions, and trading centers and subcenters interacted with one another. This vast area is not one large expanse of water like the Indian and Pacific Oceans, but is constituted by a series of seas connected by straits. (See Figure 3-1.)

This series of seas extends from Northeast Asia to the southeast of Australia and includes the seas of Okhotsk and Japan, the Yellow Sea, the East China Sea, the South China Sea, the Java Sea, the Banda Sea, the Arafura Sea just north of Australia, the Coral Sea, and the Tasman Sea between southeast Australia and New Zealand. Maritime Asia is far larger, at least as complex, and much more diverse than the Mediterranean.

The landmasses surrounding the seas are thus separated from one another and have their own histories. The states, regions, and cities located along the periphery of each sea zone are close enough to influence one another but too far apart to be assimilated into a larger entity. Autonomy in this sense formed a major condition for the establishment of the looser form of political integration known as the tributary system.

This geographical context requires us to study Asian regional history as the history of Asian seas. In this history, each sea zone saw the rise and

Figure 3-1. Maritime zones of Asia

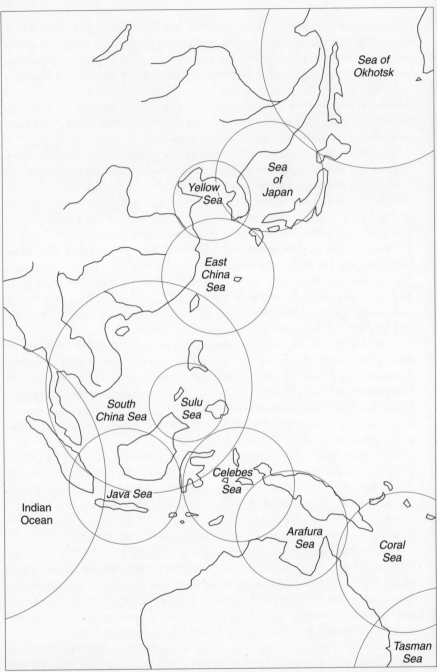

Source: Takeshi Hamashita, *China-Centered World Order in Modern Times* (Tokyo: University of Tokyo Press, 1990). Used by permission of the publisher.

fall of political and economic powers. Attempts were also made to build closer intraregional ties. The evolution of the South China Economic Zone, nowadays a lively topic of discussion, is inseparable from the historically constituted area of South China Sea. The same is true of the regions centered on the Sea of Japan and the Yellow Sea.

"Western impact" did not destroy this maritime Asia or the Sinocentric tributary system embedded in it. When was it then that China abandoned its tributary system of suzerainty and adopted the principle of national sovereignty? How did its former tributary states respond? And what remains of the traditional tributary system in the modern and contemporary East Asian international order?

Given that the tributary principle reigned in East Asia and Southeast Asia for over a thousand years, it is difficult to conclude that that local incident known as the Opium War ended it. One might argue that the master-vassal relationship centered on China ended when China began signing treaties with Western nations, such as the trilateral agreement signed by Japan, China, and the United States concerning the opening of Korean ports in the latter half of the nineteenth century and the Sino-French and Sino-British treaties, which determined the status of Vietnam, Siam, Burma, and Tibet. But from the Chinese perspective, the tributary system was still very much alive, and in the case of Korea, China sent military assistance and political advisers to post-treaty Korea after the mutual confirmation of their master-vassal relationship.

The tributary system changed from within, as three developments in modern East Asia suggest. First, "tributary" states and "equal" trading partners had asserted themselves as "middle kingdoms" in their own right, to create a zone of autonomy and to resist China's hegemony, long before the Opium War. Second, the tributary trade, run on the governmental level, had become less and less profitable in the nineteenth century, because the Ch'ing government pursued a policy of currency inflation. This policy invited growing discontent among tributary states, led to a flourishing private trade, and reduced tributary exchange to nominal levels. And finally, former tributary states adopted Westphalian international principles and methods and turned them against China. China, in the end, gave up the Sinocentric tributary system in the early twentieth century with the rise of Han nationalist movement to overthrow the Manchus and the rallying of overseas Chinese merchants under Chinese nationalism, which was soon to become the founding principle of the Republic of China, that is, the "Middle" Republic. Since then, China's "middleness" has become strongly tinged with ethnic Han nationalism.

The Tributary System and Its Transformation

The core principle of Sinocentrism was the unitary benevolence and dignity of the imperial institution and its ultimate extension to "all under Heaven." In the center, power was concentrated in the person of the Emperor, under whom a Grand Secretariat (or Council of State in the Ch'ing period) acted as a "cabinet" to supervise the Six Boards. Locally, the "government" was represented by eight Governors-General and sixteen Provincial Governors.

This domestic political structure may be characterized as follows. First, central and local institutions coexisted and their powers overlapped. Governors-General and Provincial Governors were on the same level with such central institutions as the Six Boards, with no superior-subordinate relations between them. The Treasurers too had the independent right to report directly to the Emperor, though they were ostensibly under the control of the Governors-General and the Provincial Governors. The Board of Revenue was located at the institutional center, but its management was largely left in the hands of the Provincial Governors.

Second, there was a sharp distinction between the officialdom and the population. At the prefectural and district levels, officials were not allowed to hold office in their home areas, lest they become too closely connected with the local population. This system was maintained to keep local officials from becoming hostages of social organizations such as clans and "hometown" associations and to protect the basic financial integrity of the state.[1]

The Board of Ceremonies was in charge of China's external relations; a special bureau, the Mongolian Superintendency, was responsible for the control and "management" of Mongolian tribes, Tibetan affairs, and the Lamaist hierarchy. In the late Ch'ing period, a new department, the Yamen of Foreign Affairs, was established to manage all official relations with Western countries.

On China's southeastern periphery, the Ch'ing government appointed local rulers as "Administrators of the Natives" and "Native Officials."[2] This approach to peripheral control started in the T'ang period, was inherited by the Yuan, and was fully institutionalized under the Ming. In the Ch'ing period, Administrators of the Natives and Native Officials were responsible for both military and civil affairs.

---

[1] To investigate center and local issues here means to analyze center-local relations from the viewpoint of the strengths of local society. See Chu T'ung-chu, *Local Government in China under the Ch'ing* (Cambridge: Harvard University Press, 1962).

[2] She I-che, *Chung-kuo T'u-ssu Chih-tu* [Official ranks to minorities' leaders in Chinese history] (Peking: Association for Periphery Studies, 1947).

Though nominally "voluntary," native tribute was just another form of tax payment, and the tributary system shared some features with domestic control. Besides, the general pattern of overlapping powers between central and local institutions prevailed in the peripheral "native" regions as well. Local powers thus had some room for maneuver and initiative despite the apparent concentration of power in the central institutions. It is possible to argue that the policy governing China's external relations was not very different from that governing its domestic relations. Indeed, the continuity in its domestic and external policies is quite striking.

Another way of considering China's geographic environment is to look at how China classified the surrounding maritime areas into Eastern Seas, Western Seas, and Southern Seas (see Map 3-1). Still, China's priority lay in Sinocentered relations, not in its geographical classifications.[3]

Its hegemonic structure consisted of a center, the domestic local areas considered most important from the center's perspective, "minorities" under Administrators of the Natives and Native Officials, areas in tributary relations with China, subdued groups, and finally trade partners in the Sinocentric tributary system. Under the tributary system a local ruler either visited or sent an emissary to visit the Emperor, who recognized the tributary group and hence legitimized its ruler. The "loyal" countries, areas, and tribes were then expected to pay regular tribute to the center.

Tributary countries are described in the Ming institutional code as falling under the following six areas or groups: (1) the first category of southeastern barbarians, that is, Korea, Japan, the Liu-ch'ius (Ryukyus), Annam, Cambodia, Siam, Champa, Java, and others, eighteen countries in all; (2) the second category of southeastern barbarians, that is, Sulu, Malacca, Sri Lanka, and others, forty-four countries in all; (3) the northern barbarians, that is, kings and rulers of Da-tan, eight altogether; (4) the northeastern barbarians, that is, the Nu-zhi; (5) the first category of western barbarians, fifty-eight groups from the west of Lan-chou in Shen-hsi Province, including thirty-eight from the western regions; and (6) the second category of western barbarians, fourteen groups altogether from the Tur-fan region.[4] In the Ch'ing period, China added more tributary countries and restructed its categories. The Ch'ing institutional code includes Laos, Vietnam, and Burma, as well as Portugal and the Netherlands. It also stipulated the routes tributary missions should take: the Korean mission was to pass through the Shan-hai customs barrier of Feng-t'ien Province; the Liu-ch'iu

---

[3] Huang Sheng-tseng, *Hsi-Yang Ch'ao-keng Tien-Iu* [Records of tribute from west sea] (Peking: The China Publisher, 1982).
[4] *Ming Hui-tien* [Grand Record of Ming dynasty], Cabinet ed., vols. 105–108 (Ch'ao-keng [tributary countries], 1502).

(Ryukyu) mission, through Fou-chou; the Annamese, through the Chen-
nan barrier of Chiang-hsi Province; the Cambodian and Burmese, through
Yun-nan; the Sulu mission, through Hsia-men; the Dutch through Kuang-
tung; and the Portuguese and British missions, through Macao.[5] As we will
see, it is important to remember when seeking to understand China's relations with European powers in modern times that these routes and points
of entry, whether by sea or by land, were simultaneously trade routes and
trade ports.

Given the complex historical and institutional significance of the tributary
system, it is useful to examine how tributary relations functioned in reality.
The tributary system as normally understood consisted of a network of
bilateral relationships between China and each tribute-paying country,
with tribute and imperial "gift" as the mediums of exchange and the
Chinese capital as the center. Matters were never that straightforward.
There also existed several other lesser or satellite tributary networks not
directly connected with China, which made the system of reciprocal relationship significantly more complex. The tributary system in reality encompassed both inclusive and competitive relations extending web-like over a
large area. One good example is the Ryukyus or Liu-ch'iu, whose kings
sent tribute missions both to Beijing and Satsuma in the Ch'ing period,
which placed China and Japan in a competitive relationship. Korea also
sent missions to Japan, although it was a tributary of China. Laos was a
tributary of Vietnam, itself a tributary of China. All these countries maintained satellite tributary relations with one another as well.[6]

The other fundamental feature of the tributary system to be kept in
mind is its basis in commercial transactions. The tributary system paralleled or was in symbiosis with a network of commercial trade relations.
Trade between Siam, Japan, and southern China, for instance, was maintained for many years on the profitable basis provided by tributary missions, even when much of the nontributary, commercial, trade was hardly
remunerative. When the rice trade from Siam to Kuang-tung and Hsia-
men became unprofitable in the eighteenth century, traders shifted their

---

[5] *Ch'in-ting Ta-Ch'ing hiu-tien shih-li* [Historical record of regulations of great Ch'ing dynasty],
Cabinet ed., vol. 503 (Ch'ao-keng, 1812); John E. Wills, Jr., *Embassies and Illusions, Dutch and
Portuguese Envoys to K'ang-hsi, 1666–1687* (Cambridge: Harvard University Press., 1984).

[6] Kaneyoshi Uehara, *Sakoku to Han boeki* [The closing-up policy and (Liu-ch'iu-Satsuma) pro-
vincial trade] (Naha: Yaeyam Shobou, 1981); Fusataka Nakamura, *Nissen Kankeishi no Kenkyu*
[Research into the History of Japan-Korean Relations] (Tokyo: Yoshikawa Kobunkan, 1969);
Ryoji Takeda, "Gencho Shoki no Shin to no Kankei [Vietnam and Ch'ing relation in the
early Nguyen dynasty], 1802–1870," in *Vietnam-Chugoku Kankeishi* [Historical relations between
Vietnam and China], ed. Tatsuro Yamamoto (Tokyo: Yamakawa Shuppan, 1975).

commercial focus from Liu-ch'iu and Nagasaki and thus maintained and even strengthened the general multilateral trade relationship.[7] Commercial penetration of Chinese traders and the emigration of "overseas Chinese" into Southeast Asia is, needless to say, historically intertwined with the expansion of this trading network. Commercial expansion and the development of the tributary trading network proceeded together. Trade relations in East and Southeast Asia expanded as tributary relations expanded.[8]

This tributary trade system also functioned as a form of trade between European and East Asian countries. In the records of trade from the Netherlands and Portugal to China in the K'ang Hsi period, several European-made cotton textiles are listed together with woolens. European-made cotton textiles are also mentioned in lists of tribute articles from Southeast Asian countries to China. Thus the tributary system in fact constituted a multilateral trading network capable of absorbing commodities from outside itself.

These aspects of the tributary trading system became more pronounced in the transition from Ming to Ch'ing in the sixteenth and seventeenth centuries. First, the ideal of Sinocentric unity was expanded and consolidated, strongly affecting Korea, Japan, and Vietnam. Second, tributary trade was expanded with the participation of European countries. And third, private trade expanded along with the tributary trade, and trade-related institutions such as trade settlement and tax collection underwent further sophistication.

China has considered itself the "center" for many centuries, surrounded by "barbarians" who are to be enlightened through the virtuous rule of the Emperor. The influence of the civilized center gradually spread outward and downward onto the surrounding areas in concentric circles (see Figure 3-2). The relationship between center and periphery was a unilateral and unified order in China's perspective. Seen in functional terms, however, this hegemonic structure consisted of (1) indirect rule by designating rulers of minority tribes as regional officials (*tusi, tuguan*); (2) rule over foreign peoples under the jurisdiction of Lifanyuan, a good example being the rule over the Mongols; (3) looser rule based on tributary

---

[7] Sarasin Viraphol, *Tribute and Profit: Sino-Siamese Trade, 1652–1853* (Cambridge: Harvard University Press, 1977), chap. 4; Harukatsu Hayashi and Nobuatsu Hayashi, eds., *Ka-i hentai* [Cyclical changes between Sinocentrism and barbarism] (Tokyo: Heibonsha, 1958–59).

[8] Hisanori Wada, "Tonan Ajia ni okeru Shoki kakyo shakai" [The early history of Overseas Chinese Society in Southwest Asia] (Tokyo: Tokyo Gakuho, 1959), and "Jugo-seiki no Jawa ni okeru Chugoku-jin no Tsu-sho Katsudo"[Chinese commercial activities in Java in the fifteenth century], in *Ronshu Kindai Chugoku Kenkyu* [Collected articles on modern Chinese studies] editorial committee ed. (Tokyo: Yamakawa Shuppan, 1981).

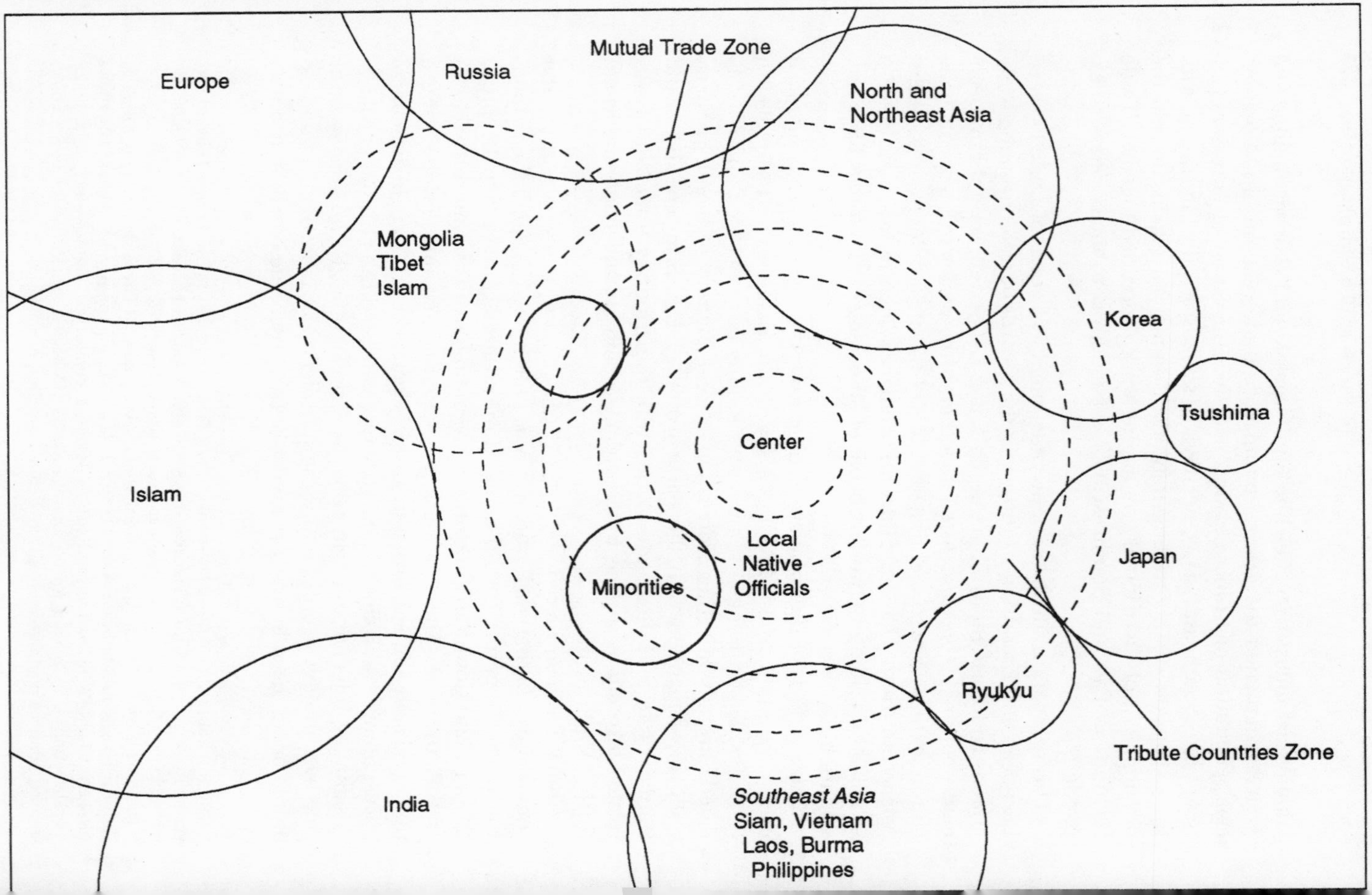

Figure 3-2. Sino-centric world and interregional relations in Asia

relations; (4) "equal" trade partners (with implication of independent relations) on the remotest periphery; and (5) the *huawai*, the area "outside of enlightenment (civilization), which the Emperor's virtue did not reach.

This concentric structure, based on the degree of strength in relational terms, shows that the tributary relationship in its original meaning was only part of the overall structure of suzerainty. This suggests that traditionally scholarship in this area has interpreted the "tributary" relations broadly in geographical terms to include relations beyond the original Chinese category and linked it directly to the principle of the "Middle Kingdom," and in doing so, extended the "tributary" relationship to mean the fundamental and centripetal governing principle.

The relationship between the tributary system and the centripetal governing principle of China may be accidental. The "tributary" relationship was dominant in East Asia, and perhaps for this reason, the Sinocentric order came to be identified in the literature with the tributary system. But this identification of the tributary system with the idea of the Middle Kingdom may be an oversimplification. As we have seen, the governing structure based on the order of the Middle Kingdom was characterized by several governing principles, including indirect rule, tribute rule, and "equal" trading partnership. The unifying principle that governed the entire Sinocentric order was the idea of the Middle Kingdom. It was an abstract principle for governing larger relations between China as the center and the other states and entities on its periphery, encompassing several different governing principles. It was not so much centripetal as comprehensive and intermediary.

Tributary states also shared the ideal of "Middle Kingdom" and were fully aware of their participation in the system. This is demonstrated historically by Vietnam, Korea, and Japan, which allowed China to intervene in their courts; these states asserted their legitimacy as peripheral states and acted as smaller-scale "Middle Kingdoms" in their immediate regions. Vietnam, for instance, required tribute from Laos. Korea insisted on the continuation of orthodox Sinocentrism under the Ch'ing dynasty, which it saw initially as a "barbarian" dynasty. China criticized Vietnam for using Nam Viet [south Yue] which existed in ancient China and forced to use Viet Nam [Yue south]. These cases show how tributary countries, acting from their own understanding of Sinocentrism, began to assert their own "national" identities vis-à-vis China.[9] The ideal of Sinocentrism was

[9] Park Chi-won, *Yeol ha ilqi* [Journal of the journey to Hot River City] (Seoul, 1780), trans. Yoshio Imamura (Tokyo: Heibonsha, 1975), p. 5; Ryoji Takeda, "Gencho Shoki"; *Batavia jo nishi* [Diaries of Batavia], vols. 1–3, trans. Naojiro Murakami (Tokyo: Heibonsha, 1983);

therefore not solely China's preoccupation, but one shared throughout the Sinocentric world. "Nationalism" in this sense was born in Asia from within the system and through the common ideal of tributary relations. Satellite tributary zones that surrounded the Chinese-dominated core had historically constituted identities of their own, on the basis of which they went on to their own modernization.

How did the tributary system work? What was the driving force of the networks in the system? Tributary trade consisted for the most part in the following: (1) two-way exchange of formal tribute submitted by tributary missions and "gifts" bestowed by the imperial center; (2) licensed trade in the Peking Assembly Hall by the limited group of merchants allowed to accompany tribute missions; and (3) frontier trade between merchants along China's land frontiers and in specified Chinese ports.

The form and frequency of tributary missions varied according to the degree of intimacy between the country sending the mission and China. Tribute from "native tribes and Districts" was required once a year, once every other year, or once every three years. These missions were allowed to open markets in the Peking Assembly Hall under the jurisdiction of the Board of Ceremonies, and their major tribute articles were horses and gold and silver vessels. In the early Ming period, Emperor Yung-le carried out the policy of "pacification" in the Northeast (Manchurian) area. Later, Manchu groups in the area who accepted Ch'ing control were organized into a "Pacification Guard" and established tributary relations with the Ch'ing dynasty. This tribute was as compulsory as the tax payment of other subjects. Tribute articles consisted mainly of horses and fur products. Korea maintained the closest relationship of all the tributaries with China. Tributary missions from Korea to the Ming Court were initiated in the second year of Hong-wu (1369). After a brief pause in tribute missions in the period of chaos at the end of the Ming dynasty, the Korean Yi dynasty started paying tribute again in 1636 and reopened the market at Yi-chou on the Sino-Korean border. The first tribute articles to the Ch'ing consisted of one hundred taels of gold, one thousand taels of silver, paper, furs and skins, cotton textiles, medicine (ginseng), rice and other items, twenty-eight categories of articles altogether. Gold and silver became tribute items when the circulation of silver in China became more frequent and when silver became a medium of exchange along with silk and brocade.[10]

Chang Tsun-wu, *Ch'ing-han tsung-fang mao-i, 1637–1894* [Sino-Korean Tributary Trade, 1637–1894] (Taipei: Academia Sinica, 1978); Yoshiharu Tsuboi, *L'Empire Vietnamien: face a la France et a la Chine* [Confrontation of the Vietnam empire with France and China], 1847–1885 (Paris: L'Harmattan, 1986).

[10] *Ch'in-ting Ta-ch'ing hui-tien shih-li*, vol. 503 (Ch'ao-keng).

In the tribute transactions described here, the relationship between trib- ute goods and "gifts" was largely one of selling and purchasing and the tribute exchange can be seen as a commercial transaction. Even the Chi- nese court thus acted as a party to business transactions. Its mode of pay- ment was often Chinese currency, whether paper money or silver. In economic terms, tribute was thus managed as an exchange between seller and buyer with the "prices" of commodities fixed. According to Shigeo Sakuma, "Price standards were determined, albeit loosely, by market prices in Peking."[11] Given the nature of this transaction, it can be argued that the entire tributary trade formation was determined by the price struc- ture of China and that the tributary trade zone formed an integrated "sil- ver zone" in which silver was used as the medium of trade settlement. The key to the functioning of the tributary trade as a system was the difference between the prices inside China and those outside China.

The tributary countries and Chinese merchants often had cause for complaint under this system because the stipulated "prices" of tribute commodities often fell below market prices. And when China paid in pa- per currency, the profits accruing from tribute articles were pushed down by currency debasement, which limited the ability of the tributary missions and embassies to purchase Chinese goods. Despite these problems, the private, informal, trade that accompanied tribute missions expanded, in- creasing silver circulation and leading to the absorption of silver both from Europe and the Americas. On the whole, this tributary trade system took on the attributes of a silver circulating zone with multilateral channels of trade settlement in which silver was used as the chief medium of exchange.[12]

Tributary states thus grew increasingly discontented economically, be- cause China has "rigged" tributary trade for its own fiscal convenience. The Ch'ing government demanded more tributary goods in larger vol- umes, but the goods it gave in exchange were not always those desired by the tributary states. The Ch'ing court often gave paper currency as its "gift," which depressed the value of tribute goods. The Ch'ing govern- ment also imposed tighter trade controls. Chinese merchants engaged in the tributary trade in and around China thus grew increasing critical of the situation. In the meantime, private trade along sea coasts, which had long accompanied the tributary trade, expanded with the emergence of Asia-wide commercial networks, and threatened to surpass the tributary

[11] Shigeo Sakuma, "Mindai no gaikoku boeki—kohaku boeki no suji" [Foreign trade of Ming dynasty], in *Wada hakushi kanreki kinen toyo-shi ronshu* [1Collected articles of Oriental history commemorating the sixtieth birthday of Dr. Wada], (Tokyo, 1951).
[12] Takeshi Hamashita, "Kindai ajia boekiken ni okeru ginryutsu—Ajia keizaishi-zo ni kansuru ichi-koso" [Silver circulation in modern Asian trade zone], in *Shakai keizai shigaku* [Socioec- onomic history] 51.1 (1985): 4.

trade in importance. This development was yet another factor contributing to the change in the Sinocentric tributary relationship.

"Western impact" needs to be understood in this changing historical context. It was in fact exploited by Siam, Burma, Tibet, Vietnam (Indochina), Japan, Korea, and other countries in China's vicinity to resist China and adopt "modernization" policies to become more autonomous within the framework of the traditional tributary relations in East Asia. European powers encouraged this path of "Asian modernization," but never replaced the traditional principle of order with their own and did not intend to do so except for extending the sovereignty principle of the Westphalian international system in their own relationships with Asian states.

Having reached East and Southeast Asia, European powers sought to conclude advantageous treaties with local states, but they encountered two major problems. One was how to decide whether the party they were negotiating with actually represented the legitimate power in its locality. The other was how to make sure that agreements concluded were honored. As long as the Sinocentric relationship in East Asia continued, bilateral treaties with local states that ignored their relations with China, especially when negotiating with states near or bordering China, were simply ineffective. European powers were forced to take into account the regional "tributary sphere," the East Asian regional order of suzerainty. They tried to establish treaty relations with East and Southeast Asian states while tacitly recognizing the presence of their master-vassal relationship with China. The tributary system and the international treaty relationship existed side by side simultaneously.

As we have seen earlier, the Western countries were not seen as outside the tributary system in the general Sinocentric scheme of things. They were caught in the logic of tributary relations, and geographically speaking, they were seen as located at some indeterminate distance beyond China's frontiers. In Kuang-tung, for instance, Britain was not even identified by Chinese officials as the same country that had sent diplomatic representation to Tibet. When European powers dealt with Asia, therefore, they had little choice but to deal with the tributary relations that formed the basis of all relations in the region.

This is beautifully illustrated by Owen N. Denny's remarks concerning the opening of Korean ports in the second half of the nineteenth century. Denny, former U.S. consul at Tianjin whom the Korean king had invited to Korea as his diplomatic adviser in July 1885, thought of Korea as a tributary state of China. According to Denny, in the past the tribute relationships were sustained by a faith unshakable as long as China's treatment of its tributaries remained gentle, cordial, and fair and did not seek to interfere either with another country's system of tributary relationships or with its sovereignty and independence.[13]

This remark clearly shows that Denny did not consider the tributary system and treaty relations as incompatible, but that he was not sure whether or not Korean state sovereignty existed at all. The Western countries, fearing the expansion of Japanese influence, tacitly approved the continuation of Korea as a tributary (vassal) state of Ch'ing China. To enforce Korea's vassal status, the minister of northern sea trade, Li Hong-zhang, appointed Paul G. von Mollendorff as head of the Korean customs office and Yuan Shi-kai as political adviser to the king of Korea to supervise the signing of the treaty opening Korean ports.

When the Spanish and the Portuguese arrived in Asia, they had to participate in the already-established intra-Asian trade network. This restricted the direct exchange between East and West, since Westerners were obliged to pay in silver or by barter for what they wanted. The Dutch and the British found that they too had to come to terms with, adapt to, and learn to exploit the existing Asian tributary trade system. Consequently, the nature of Western "expansion" in and its "impact" on Asia was conditioned by the existence and the character of this Asian trade zone.

China and the Asian tributary trade system responded to Western powers and the treaties they imposed from within the system. It is difficult, therefore, to define the emergence of modern Asia neatly as the shift from the tributary system to the treaty system.[14] British penetration into Asia began in the seventeenth century through her East India Comapany. British ships carried Asian products, such as rice, to China, products that had previously been imported to China through tributary trade relations, which they sold to purchase Chinese products such as tea and silk.

In the nineteenth century, European powers began producing raw materials such as rubber in Asia to meet their own industrial needs and to sell their industrial products to Asia. For this purpose they had to link the

---

[13] Takehiko Okudaira, *Chosen Kaikoku Kosho Simatsu* [A history of negotiations over the opening of Korea] (Tokyo: Toko Shoten, 1935), pp. 172–73.

[14] H. B. Morse, *The Chronicles of the East India Company Trading to China, 1635–1843*, 5 vols. (Oxford: Oxford University Press, 1926–29); John K. Fairbank, "The Early Treaty System," in *The Chinese World Order* (Cambridge: Harvard University Press, 1968); Kim Key-Kiuk, *The Last Phase of the East Asian World Order: Korea, Japan, and the Chinese Empire, 1860–1882* (Berkeley and Los Angeles: University of California Press, 1980). J. K. Fairbank and S. Y. Teng, "On the Ch'ing Tributary System," in *Harvard Journal of Asiatic Studies*, no. 6 (1941); J. K. Fairbank, ed., *Trade and Diplomacy on the China Coast: The Opening of the Treaty Ports, 1842–1854* (Cambridge: Harvard University Press, 1953); J. K. Fairbank, ed., *The Chinese World Order, Traditional China's Foreign Relations* (Cambridge: Harvard University Press, 1968); Morris Rossabi, ed., *China among Equals: The Middle Kingdom and Its Neighbors, 10th–14th Centuries* (Berkeley and Los Angeles: University of California Press, 1983).

intra-Asian trade with the international market by establishing ports where balanced trade between two quite distinct markets could be conducted. These ports, Hong Kong and Singapore, which inherited the historical trading centers of Canton and Malacca, respectively, eventually absorbed a huge amount of capital from overseas Chinese.[15] This led to the closer integration of the Southeast Asian and southern Chinese economies and to their extension into the Indian Ocean trade zone. Nevertheless, the marketing structure in the European colonies in Asia continued to display the characteristics of the traditional intra-Asian trade associated with the tributary system. Elements of domestic, intermediate, and international markets all were present in Singapore and Hong Kong.[16]

Sino-Japanese Relations in Modern Times

With this brief description of the relationship between the Asian tributary trade system and the West, we may now turn to the question of Sino-Japanese relations in modern times. How did they start? Previous studies on the subject have concentrated on the differences in how the Japanese and the Chinese modernized under "Western impact."[17] Such a focus— on Japan's adoption of the national strengthening policy and on its imperialist expansion into China during the Sino-Japanese War in 1894— traces the history of modern Japan only from the perspective of "Westernization" and understands the history of moden Japan as the emergence of a "small West" in Asia. But to be more fully comprehended Japanese modernization needs to be examined in terms of its generation from within the Sinocentric tributary system. From this perspective Japanese modernization was an attempt to move the center of the tributary trade structure to Japan. In other words, the main issues in Japanese modernization were how to cope with the Chinese dominance over commercial relations in Asia, the dominance that had functioned as the base for Sinocentric economic integration through the tributary trade relationship, and how to reorganize relations among Japan, China, Korea, and Liu-ch'iu (Ryukyu) in a way that put Japan at the center.

First, let us consider these questions from the economic perspective. In

---

[15] Cheng K'uan-ying, *Nan-yu Jih-chi* [Diary of the journey to the South Sea], 1967, p. 33.

[16] Chiang Hai Ding, *A History of Straits Settlements Foreign Trade, 1870–1915* (Singapore: National Museum, 1978).

[17] K. N. Chaudhuri, *Trade and Civilisation in the Indian Ocean* (Cambridge: Cambridge University Press, 1985); Wong Lin Ken, "The Trade of Singapore, 1819–69," *Journal of the Malayan Branch of the Royal Asiatic Society* 33.4 (December 1960): 11–12.

the literature Japanese modernization is described as a matter of industrialization and the recovery of autonomy in tariff matters, that is, in terms of the formation of a national economy and the achievement of full national sovereignty. Analyses of these questions usually start with explaining how Japan achieved "national wealth and power." Yet if we ask why Japan chose to industrialize in the first place, however, studies are not very convincing. Although the details of Japanese industrialization have been much discussed, there is hardly any inquiry into why Japan opted for industrialization as it did. Because the course of Japan's modernization has been studied as a process of overcoming its subordination to Western powers or achieving its independence from the West, the importance to Japan of the historical relationship between Japan and China has been largely ignored. To understand the direction and nature of Japanese modernization, however, it is crucial to recognize that Japan opted for industrialization after the opening of its ports because of its location in a web of commercial relations with China.

Japan opted for industrialization as it did, because its attempts to expand its commercial relations with China had been defeated. Japanese merchants could not compete with the entrenched overseas Chinese merchants who ruled the Dejima trade in Nagasaki in the Edo period. Chinese merchants held a monopoly on the export business for seafood and native commodities that Japanese traders simply could not break.

When the Japanese consul in Hong Kong, Suzuki, emphasized the importance of the Hong Kong market in 1890 in a report he sent to the Japanese Ministry of Foreign Affairs, he commented on the low morale of Japanese traders in Hong Kong and pointed out the following: (1) Chinese merchants were united and had a long-term strategy that went beyond short-term profit; (2) Japanese merchants were undercapitalized and when they suffered even a single loss, had to withdraw; and (3) there were indications that Japanese producers sold their products Chinese people were fond of to Chinese merchants much cheaper than to Japanese merchants.[18]

According to the consul's report, Chinese merchants not only controlled the local market but even extended their influence to Japanese producers, and he was very pessimistic about Japanese merchants entering the Hong Kong market. It was under such circumstances—the commercial power of Chinese merchants and their influence in Japan—that the need for cultivating the Chinese market increased. And it was from Chinese merchants

---

[18] Frances V. Moulder, *Japan, China and the Modern World Economy* (Cambridge: Cambridge University Press, 1977), chap. 1.

in Japan that Japanese obtained the information needed to start a modern cotton textile industry capable of competing with Western cotton textiles for a share of the Chinese market.

In the nineteenth year of Meiji (1887), Chinese merchants in Yokohama started buying cotton cloth produced in Saitama prefecture. The parties concerned pressed the authorities to promote exports to the Chinese market and asked the Japanese consul in Hong Kong about future possibilities. Prominent Chinese merchants in Hong Kong advised the Japanese to produce cloth in bolts as wide as that sold by the West, both plain and striped, at a competitive price. Based on this advice, production and export to China got under way.[19] This example is representative of the general course of Japanese industrialization, which started with the production of substitutes for Western textiles in Asia. Competition among Japan, China, and India in the production of cotton textiles also started at about this time.

Increased foreign trade with Western countries through foreign firms also provided an impetus to Japan's industrialization. The expansion of new exports like silk and coal, along with such traditional items as seafood, accelerated its industrial development.[20] Although this was due to the commercial activities of Western firms, the main aim of such firms was not to export industrial products of their own countries, but to import Asian products. The opening of the Japanese market thus did not change its trade relations with East Asia significantly.

Political relations between Japan and China in the early Meiji period can now be reinterpreted in this light. Previous studies of the Sino-Japanese treaty of May 13, 1871, have generally concluded that the treaty represented the equality of the two nations as demonstrated by the approval of mutual consular jurisdictions. It is pointed out that the treaty embodied the idea of equality of nations common to modern international intercourse and that it marked the opening of the modern era in international relations in East Asia.[21] It is doubtful, however, whether the equality Japan supposedly obtained was recognized as such by Ch'ing China. China's dealings with other states were informed by its long-established idea of a hierarchy of dignity with the Emperor at the top. "Equality" with the Emperor was unthinkable, indeed impossible, in Chinese scheme of

[19] Otojiro Okuda, *Meiji shonen ni okeru honkon nihon jin* [Japanese in Hong Kong in the early years of Meiji] (Taipei: Taiwan Government, 1937), pp. 275–81.
[20] Ibid., pp. 244–247.
[21] Kanji Ishii, *Kindai nihon to igirisu shihon; Jadin-maseson shokai wo chushin ni* [Modern Japan and British capital: A history of the Jardine-Matheson Company in Japan] (Tokyo: University of Tokyo Press, 1984), chap. 2.

things. The Kiakhta Treaty of 1727 with Russia can serve as an example of this problematic.

Article 6 of the Kiakhta Treaty, which concerned the exchange of official letters, included a clause that implied "equality" between the signatories. The article provided that such letters should be exchanged between the Russian Senate and the Ch'ing Colonial Office.[22] Compared with the one-sided nature of the tributary system in which China was clearly dominant, the exchange of letters under the Kiakhta arrangement appears evenhanded. Yet China did not really see Russia as an equal; after all, the mandate of the Colonial Office was to control the affairs of the Mongols. The treaty also provided for the opening of mutual trade on the frontier in place of trade in the Assembly Hall in Peking. Although this stipulation also seems to imply equality between the two countries, the trade in question was originally conducted as part of the tributary trade. We can also find a good deal of evidence to show that knowledgeable Chinese believed the Emperor was merely doing a favor to Russia.

Given this historical precedence about "equality," how should we interpret the significance of the Sino-Japanese Treaty of 1871? The Chinese party concerned with the treaty negotiations was the Yamen of Foreign Affairs. The duties of the Yamen were similar to those of a ministry of foreign affairs. Established under strong pressure from Western powers to replace the Ministry of Ceremony, the Yamen included among its members some of the ministers of the Council of State and was thus far more powerful than the Colonial Office or the Mongolian Superintendency. But it did not have the power to bind Governors-General and Provincial Governors responsible for policy implementation. It is hard to imagine that when the Yamen signed treaties with foreign countries, China recognized them as equal.[23] It was Japan who exploited this expression of "equality" as if it were a concession from China to reorganize international relations in East Asia to its own advantage.

In view of these factors, which were implicit in the tributary system and not part of the "Western impact," we can argue that Japan's moderniza-

---

[22] Michio Fujimura, "Meiji shoki ni okeru nisshin kosho no ichi danmen: ryukyu bunto joyaku wo megutte" [Sino-Japanese negotiation on the Ryukyus] (I), *Nagoya daigaku bungakubu kenkyu ronshu, shigaku* [Journal of the Faculty of Arts of Nagoya University] 16 (1968). M. Fujimura, "Meiji ishin gaiko no kyu kokusai kankei eno taio: Nisshin shukojoki no seiritsu wo megutte" [The foreign policy of the Meiji government toward traditional international relations of Asia], ibid., 14 (1966).

[23] Kin'ichi Yoshida, *Kindai roshin kankei shi* [Sino-Russian relations in modern times] (Tokyo: Kondo Shuppan, 1974), chap. 3; Eric Widmer, *The Russian Ecclesiastical Mission to Peking during the 18th Century* (Cambridge: Harvard University Press, 1976).

tion was initiated in a fairly unstable international environment. After Japan emerged from the isolation of the Edo period, it launched the project of abolishing the tributary system (of which it had previously been a part) and reentering into East Asian relations on a new basis. Japan confronted the tributary system when it tried to reconstruct its relationship with Korea and the Ryukyus. Historically speaking, its attempt to do away with a system that is still largely intact throughout East Asia ultimately proved fatal.

Migration and Chinese Nationalism

Large-scale Chinese emigration started in the 1860s, after treaties signed in 1858 and 1860 legalized overseas travel by Chinese workers. The treaties were a product of the desire on the part of Britain, France, and the Netherlands to obtain Chinese labor in their colonies to offset the international labor shortage that followed the abolition of the African slave trade. In 1866, Britain and France signed the Chinese Labor Immigration Agreement with China and started what became known as the coolie trade or the pig trade, the supply of Chinese indentured labor.

The Ch'ing attitude to these treaties was less of respect for the results of diplomatic negotiations than a reluctant concession to satisfy the demands of foreign powers. The Ch'ing government had long prohibited Chinese emigration for moral reasons. From then on, however, there was a remarkable increase in the number of emigrants working on rubber and sugar plantations and in tin mines in Southeast Asia. Between the mid-1880s and the mid-1910s, Chinese emigration to British Malaya totaled 4.1 million to Singapore (an average of 120,000 a year) and 1.57 million to Penang (an average of 44,000).[24]

It is well known that Sun Yat-sen was supported by overseas Chinese, and Sun himself actively sought to mobilize overseas Chinese support to advance his cause. In his lectures on nationalism, Sun referred to many different aspects of the Chinese tributary system and tried to reinterpret its historical significance within the national-international framework. He argued: "As to justice, even in the days of her greatest power, China never completely destroyed another state. For instance, former Korea was nom-

[24] Ta Chen, *Chinese Migrations, with Special Reference to Labor Conditions* (Washington, D.C.: U.S. Department of Labor, 1923), pp. 4–21. Yen Ching-hwang, *Coolies and Mandarins: China's Protection of Overseas Chinese during the Late Ch'ing Period, 1851–1911* (Singapore: Singapore University Press, 1985).

inally a tributary of China, but in reality she was independent. She lost her independence only in the last ten or twenty years.''[25]

After pointing out the historical significance of the Sino-Japanese War for the tributary system in East Asia, Sun Yat-sen summarized the role of the system as follows:

> Let us again [go back a little further] and speak of territories lost earlier: Korea, Formosa, and Pescadores. These territories were ceded to Japan after the Sino-Japanese War [1894–95]. It was this Sino-Japanese War which induced the great powers to start to talk about dividing up China. . . . In the first year of the Republic [1921], Nepal was still bringing tribute into Szechwan. Since then no more tribute has been paid, because the roads through Tibet have been obstructed.''[26]

Thus, when China was strongest, her political strength inspired awe in all her neighbors. The nations in the south and west of Asia considered it an honor to be a feudatory state [of China] and to pay tribute. At that time European imperialism had not yet penetrated into Asia, and the only country in Asia that deserved to be considered imperialistic was China. That is why the weaker and smaller countries feared China; they feared lest they be crushed by her political force. Even at the present time, none of the weaker and smaller Asiatic races feels absolutely secure in regard to China.[27]

Sun Yat-sen thus replaced the Chinese tributary relations with territorial issues in relation to foreign powers and equated suzerainty with imperialism, but retained some basic features of the Sinocentric tributary system, which was based on authority relations, not treaty relations. Although the major thrust of his argument was anti-Manchu, anti-imperialist Chinese nationalism, it is clear that his basic idea about China's new external relations with its surrounding area is to some extent coterminous with the historical Sinocentric tributary zone. He explained this point thus:

> When we held our recent Nationalist Conference in Canton, Mongolia sent representatives to ascertain whether the Southern Government was continuing the imperialistic traditions toward the foreign countries. As soon as these representatives arrived and saw that the policy adopted by our Conference was to assist the weaker and smaller races and was utterly devoid of imperialistic tendencies, they heartily approved [our plan] and proposed to

unite [with us] in order to form a Great Eastern Nation. Not only did Mongolia approve our policy, but all other weaker and smaller races did likewise.[28]

This shows that the widest sphere of Sun's nationalism or the unified area in terms of space was imagined as being closely related to the sphere of the historical tributary system.

Generally speaking, Chinese emigration, despite its diversity, had the following common traits: (1) the maintenance of family and communal ties with home country, with considerable traffic between homeland and the host country; (2) the maintenance of traditional social units, customs, and lifestyles in the host country; and (3) well-developed social organizations for facilitating emigration. With these traits, Chinese communities developed their entrenched economic position in Southeast Asia. To promote the anti-imperialist movement in China and obtain financial support, Sun actively raised issues important to overseas Chinese. In his National Reconstruction plan, he wrote:

Encouragement must be given to the education of overseas Chinese and our overseas cultural work, so that they may succeed to the fine cultural heritage of their fatherland. Special facilities will be afforded to those young Chinese abroad who return to China to study or work.[29]

Tribute and emigration thus became the two basic factors that conditioned the Asian character of Sun Yat-sen's idea of nationalism in its extended form.

How then, does modern Chinese nationalism differ from this extended nationalism and from xenophobic antiforeignism? The answer to this question, as posed at the beginning of the twentieth century, might be found in the social structure of China, above all, in the relationship between the state, the "race," and society. Sun Yat-sen himself also tried to establish nationalism on the basis of these foundations. But in China the state has always proved too fragile to support this sort of nationalism; and the other two elements, "race" and society, are not adequate to the task. Without a durable state, the core value of race quickly broke down, as Sun had warned that it would, into family ties, local social ties, and provincialism.

Tribute, trade, and migration, on the other hand, reinforced national consciousness among overseas Chinese under colonial domination. The overseas Chinese found their unity in the shared experience of living as

[28] Ibid., p. 95.
[29] Ibid., p. 262.

an ethnic minority. Thus, Chinese nationalism was created in the periphery among the overseas Chinese, where attachment to China and national consciousness was strong, not in the center. Overseas Chinese have also maintained the historical idea of a wider Sinocentric regionalism derived from the traditional idea of a "Middle Kingdom" and loosely related to long-term tribute relations in East and Southeast Asia.

The Chinese diaspora as a whole is strengthened and unified by an interlocking system of family ties, local and regional ties, national ties, and the historical notion of a "Middle Kingdom." Currently, the Chinese diaspora looks to South China as its economic and regional center, and South China itself is renewing its historical connections to Southeast Asia.

The Sinocentric world is thousands of years old, not hundreds. Over its history it has turned toward and away from maritime Asia. These broad swings have always had a deep impact both on Chinese affairs and on the affairs of Asia as a whole. After an interval of two hundred years, China has begun looking south again. The economic and political weight of South China and maritime Asia is likely to increase further with the return of Hong Kong to China in 1997. Such a reorientation of China may set in train developments that will reorganize Chinese relations with Singapore and the other Southeast Asia states as well as with Korea and Japan. An Asian maritime order, for better or for worse, is likely to intersect in new and unpredictable ways with the maritime order centered around the United States. In a larger historical perspective the United States is a very recent upstart in Asia. How it comes to terms with the ascendance of maritime China will have a profound effect on the evolution of Japan's position in Asia.

4

Japan and Northeast Asia into the Twenty-first Century

BRUCE CUMINGS

In this chapter I explore Japan and Northeast Asia first through the optic of conventional liberal analysis and then through the optic of twentieth-century history, looking forward to the twenty-first, while pondering questions of continuity and discontinuity. Japan and some other parts of the Northeast Asian region, I maintain, nested through almost all of the twentieth century in an international structure that offered the United Kingdom and the United States a diffuse, outer-limit leverage over their behavior; further, this structure will last at least into the first couple of decades of the twenty-first century.

For purposes of argument I divide this international structure into four aspects: the system of states, a regime of technology, a regime of resources, and a discursive regime that includes most of what is commonly called "culture," "civilization," "state vs. market," "state vs. civil society," and the like.[1] I also seek to include in all four aspects the arrow of world time, the effects of which are important but difficult to understand, together with more obvious considerations of global space.[2] These four aspects are

I thank Peter Katzenstein, Takashi Shiraishi, Giovanni Arrighi, Brett de Bary, Tom Christensen, Rick Doner, Victor Nee, T. J. Pempel, and Mark Selden for their comments on my paper (even when I disagreed with them).

[1] The argument I make here draws on my forthcoming *Industrial Behemoth: The Northeast Asian Political Economy in the Twentieth Century*, to be published by Cornell University Press. By "system of states" I mean the international system defined by the nation-states that make it up, in the conventional analysis. The norms and practices of this system go under the name diplomacy, but I see it as just one of several international systems. Least of all do I argue for a "state-centered" analysis, as one critic of this essay asserted.

[2] My most recent attempt to lay out some of these ideas is in "Archaeology, Descent, Emer-

part of a connected chain that changes over time, as Louis Althusser correctly argued, and in which the empirical existence and verification of structure and the transference of meaning from structure to action through metaphor (otherwise known as language and culture), each carry an equal weight.

Hegemony is the name of the American game, but hegemony is a complex human practice that cannot be defined precisely. Our world has a hierarchical structure where those on top get the most of what there is to get, but the hierarchy is by no means one of domination, subordination, direct dependence, closed opportunity for others, or a matter of winning all the time. (Obviously Japan has been "winning" in trade for many years, but it is not hegemonic. It is very hard is to *distinguish* hegemony from crude Hobbesian notions of power and to mark the critical turning point at which winning actually changes to losing.) The "policy" of the hegemon often consists of establishing outer limits on the behavior of those within the hegemonic realm; the outer limits must be wide enough to allow talent to rise or the system will not last (it will polarize and explode) and strong enough to prevent orientation away from the realm. But we can hardly call this practice humdrum day-to-day "policy," since the last structural change in the system of U.S.–Northeast Asian relations came with the Allied victory in World War II and its consequences in the period 1945–50, and since this structure still defines the situation today.

Hegemonic power is ultimately conditioned by technological and industrial power, which helps us understand its beginnings; that advantage is locked in by military power, which helps us understand the long middle years of a hegemonic cycle; and the requirements of military supremacy and a probable later tendency toward financial speculation and resulting capitalist torpor helps us grasp its decline.[3] But just as no episode of industrialization has been identical to a previous one, as Alexander Gerschenkron (who understood the arrow of time) endeavored to teach us, so no two hegemonies are exactly alike: what happened to Great Britain may or may not help us to understand the U.S. hegemonic cycle. Daniel Moynihan once said that we don't know how we achieve consensus but we

---

gence: Japan in British-American Hegemony, 1900–1950," in *Japan in the World*, ed. H. D. Harootunian and Masao Miyoshi (Durham, N.C.: Duke University Press, 1993).

[3] If I had the space I would say much more, but I must also acknowledge a debt to Immanuel Wallerstein and Giovanni Arrighi, whose analyses have shaped my view of hegemony. I say "probable" in the text because it is by no means clear to me that the rampant financial speculation of the 1980s–1990s can be isolated as an element of hegemonic decline, given that we are in the midst of a technological revolution worthy of the steam engine, namely, the information revolution, led by the United States and clearly an element of hegemonic advance.

certainly know when it is gone; similarly there is no magic path to hegemony, but we do know when it is gone. Indeed, we can date it precisely in our time: the baton was passed when Dean Acheson got a message from the British' ambassador in February 1947 saying Britain could no longer defend Greece and Turkey, and then walked off to a club for lunch, remarking to a friend that there were only two powers now (the United States and the Soviet Union). If today it were a Japanese Prime Minister bailing out the Mexican peso or choosing the new head of the World Bank or holding a summit in Moscow instead of Bill Clinton, we would know that U.S. hegemony had ended. Of course it hasn't: Japan is still a piker in the system of states and the regime of resources, a comer in the regime of technology, and a cipher in the global regime of culture.

The strong system and the ideal hegemony, as Antonio Gramsci and any aristocrat worth his salt understood, is that realm in which people do the right thing out of habit, that is, by inhaling the ethos, exhaling social action, and thinking that their action is voluntary and comes from within. The weak hegemony wields the knout and opens the jails and the gallows, a signal that power is unsure and defensive. (This is in fact no hegemony at all; imperative domination or subordination is the better name.) Hegemony prevails when people do what you want them to do, without having to be told or better yet, asked. I argue that Japan, South Korea, and Taiwan have done what the United States wanted them to do for most of the postwar period, that the People's Republic of China moved dramatically away from its prior path and toward an U.S.-shaped path after 1978, and that the preeminent industrial power in Northeast Asia, Japan, has followed either the Anglo-American core or the European continental alternative (for example, the German model) in most of its industrial development since 1868.

If I try to understand how realms of autonomy open up within this international system, particularly for the parallel organization of capitalist profit-making—and on that point I make absolutely no distinction between "market-driven" capitalism and "state-driven" capitalism, for both have existed in both Japan and the United States, for example, if at different times—I find that much of the existing analysis in this vein either chases its own tail or reinvents the wheel from decade to decade. As the U.S. capacity unilaterally to manage the global system declined in the 1970s, a clear realm of enhanced autonomy did open for Japan, and instantly a new duality afflicted the U.S.-Japan relationship: Japan should do well, yes . . . but not so well that it hurt U.S. interests. This is not, of course, a duality that the United States can dominate or control, since people are people, their comparative advantages come and go, and things change; it merely tells us that the U.S.-Japan relationship has entered a new and less predictable phase. U.S. thinking about Japan remains firmly within that duality today, a "double vision" symbolized by the inability of elites and pundits to do more than oscillate between lauding free trade and criticizing protectionism, between admiration for Japan's success and alarm at its new prowess.[4] Intellectually, it takes the form of putative watershed divisions between Japanese and American capitalism.

Dark Spots on the Sun? On Our Eyes?

> When after a forceful attempt to gaze on the sun we turn away blinded, we see dark spots before our eyes, as a cure.[5]

The mainstream "liberal" view is not one held by an American known as a "liberal" like Senator Ted Kennedy (although he may hold it). By "liberal" I mean the worldview of Anglo-Saxon positivism (Mill, Bentham, and all that), the idea that politics is vote driven, and the assumption that economic activity is or ought to be market driven. The leading American interpreter of Japan in the 1990s, James Fallows (it will not please Japan scholars to hear this, but it is true), is also the leading exemplar of the liberal view of Japan, which, without too much oversimplification, can be summarized as follows: modern Japan is a successful market-driven democracy and a responsible member of international society, unless it is not. The simultaneous illogic and truth of this sentence calls up the mirrored gaze of the American liberal, a sort of partially occluded bifocal optic, in which the clear, acute lens on the top locates something familiar in the "near abroad" (which is to say the whole world), whereupon the mirror lens on the bottom declares it to be liberal and therefore Good. Or, the clear lens locates something unfamiliar and the mirrored lens declares it illiberal and therefore Bad. With the demise of the Soviet bloc the liberal lens cleared dramatically, finding democracy and the market almost everywhere: except in 1990s Japan.

Fallows is smart enough not to lather his recent book, *Looking at the Sun*, with a lot of rhetoric about the economic and civilizational threat from a Japan that organizes itself so differently from the United States that it has raised up a new, heterodox and dangerous form of capitalism, thus to turn "Japan" into the Other that the United States lost with the collapse of the

---

[4] A contemporary example would be Adam Smith's review of two new books on the Japanese political economy in *New York Times Book Review*, March 19, 1995.

[5] Friedrich Nietzsche, *The Birth of Tragedy*, trans. Walter Kaufmann (New York: Vintage Books, 1967), p. 67.

Soviet Union. But that is basically what he thinks. He begins one chapter with a story that I would guess is apocryphal, about finding an English translation of Friedrich List's *Natural System of Political Economy* in a bookshop near Hitotsubashi University. He said it had taken him five years to find an English version of List's thought (several are sitting on the same library floor where I am writing), and upon doing so he exclaims his version of Eureka: *"Friedrich List!!!"*[6] He goes on to argue that List, not Adam Smith, was Japan's economic guru.

Now compare Japan scholar E. H. Norman, writing in 1941, who began a passage about Prussian influence on post-Restoration Japan by saying, "It is a commonplace that Ito modelled the Japanese constitution [and much else] very closely upon the Prussian."[7] Or compare Karl Marx, who in 1857 noted that the only original American economist was Henry Carey, a follower of List who saw the United States as a late-developing industrial power, needing strong protection for its market and its nascent industries, and who thought Harvard economists were hopelessly Smithian.[8] Since Carey's *Principles of Social Science* was widely read in Japan in the 1880s,[9] perhaps Fallows ought also to exclaim, "Henry Carey!!!" In a mere few sentences we have uncovered not a truth about civilizational "difference," but a circular argument that ignores capitalist similarity and the influences of temporal stages and international competition on industrial policy: thus Fallows reinvents Norman's wheel.

Fallows has many useful things to say in this book, but he has conceived the problem of U.S.–East Asian competition badly. Taking "culture" as a key category, he mistakes Japan's differential Western learning (from the continent and from the Anglo-American realm) for essential cultural difference and contemporary industrial rivalry for a basically nonexistent *kulturkampf*. Conceiving of places called "Japan" and "Korea" as separate and distinct from the U.S. hegemonic realm, he constantly gets the context of action and decision wrong. Fallows has dark spots before his eyes that ultimately show little more than his lack of historical sensibility—thus illustrating that it is always better to grind one's lens than one's axe.

To return to the focal metaphor and now to eyeball the system of states,

[6] James Fallows, *Looking at the Sun: The Rise of the New East Asian Economic and Political System* (New York: Pantheon Books, 1994), p. 179.

[7] E. H. Norman, *Origins of the Modern Japanese State*, ed. John Dower (New York: Pantheon Books, 1975), p. 451.

[8] Karl Marx, "Bastiat and Carey," in *Grundrisse: Foundations of the Critique of Political Economy*, trans. Martin Nicolaus (New York: Vintage Books, 1973), pp. 883–93.

[9] Robert Schwantes, "America and Japan," in *American–East Asian Relations: A Survey*, ed. Ernest R. May and James C. Thomson, Jr. (Cambridge: Harvard University Press, 1972), p. 122.

again we find a bifocal or bifurcated stare, and again we find not difference but similarity in the American and Japanese experiences. To begin with, in both nations we can derive a dialectic of to-the-world or away-from-the-world. Louis Hartz located this as the primary pattern in the American relationship to the world, launching out to transform the world in the American image, followed by a predictable failure and a retreat into some form of isolation;[10] his is the best explanation we have of the curious welling up of 1990s-style isolationism amid global hyper capitalism. Hartz and Tocqueville understood that this was not a back-and-forth orientation to the geographic external world, but an oscillation about the European world: center of civilization, Americans ran toward it (Anglophilia, Atlanticism, and "Europe-first") or away from it (Anglophobia, the New Order for the Ages,[11] the frontier, and "Asia first").[12] For the leaders of U.S. foreign policy roughly since the War of 1812, the Atlanticist gaze did not avert, spots did not grow on the eyes; instead the gaze was soothing (if shaded by the Royal Navy), like watching a setting sun sink into the horizon on a lazy August evening (it *is* an old world; we *are* the new; patience is our virtue).

Curiously, Japan has a similar optic and a similar pattern of involvement and disengagement with the external world. Perhaps this is because island Japan and "island" America gather comfortably in the shelter of great oceans, with eyes and ears fixed on imagined threats and distant thunder, while the domestic order remains unperturbed and imperturbable (save for a civil war from time to time). Or perhaps it is because both the United States *and* Japan announce to the twentieth century a New Order for the Ages. Like the United States, Japan also had a choice between worlds: the dialectic was "to the West" or "to Asia"; liberal reformer Yukichi Fukuzawa coined Japan's version of "Europe first" (*datsu-a* or "away from Asia") and thereby warmed the cockles of liberal hearts ever since. And, of course, Japan has never lacked for "Asia firsters": nationalist Shintaro Ishihara, coauthor of the 1989 potboiler *The Japan That Can Say No*, got together recently with Malaysian Prime Minister Mahathir Mohamad to

---

[10] Louis Hartz, *The Liberal Tradition in America* (New York: 1955), chap. 9.

[11] *Novus ordo seclorum* is on the U.S. national seal and the dollar bill, although in the latter case it resides under a cyclops eye hovering above a pyramid, a Masonic or Illuminati symbol that has drawn the beady stares of American conspiracy theorists from the origin of the nation right down to the local-yokel "militias" that came to the media's attention in the aftermath of the 1995 Oklahoma City bombing.

[12] Richard Drinnon's *Facing West: The Metaphysics of Empire-Building and Indian-Hating* (Minneapolis: University of Minnesota Press, 1980) is a marvelous recreation of the motive forces driving Americans away from Europe.

write *The Asia That Can Say No,* amid much hyperbole about Japan's dangerously deepening economic position in East and Southeast Asia.[13] Even more curious, both Japan and the United States have preferred a West-first to an Asia-first orientation except for two disastrous expeditions (plunges into China at the Marco Polo Bridge in 1937 and the Yalu River in 1950),[14] with each choice morally valenced by the liberal mainstream as "internationalism vs. nationalism."[15]

For both the United States and Japan this choice was between a new world (modernity as industrialism defined it) and an old world (civilization as Europe or China defined it). Japan's choice was much more acute, however, because it posed a completely unknown Western modernity against the long-standing authenticity of the Sinic world order. Japan's "East" was China, just as America's "West" was England. Both Japan and America are derivative civilizations and they know it (both embody certain elements of a barbarian periphery),[16] but the American remove from Europe was into a perceived wilderness whereas the Japanese choice for Asia was a walk back into the woods, toward a deeply known and revered civilization. European and American modernity was the sun upon which Japan could not gaze for long without seeing spots; China was the agreeable and familiar setting sun that one could contemplate with relative equanimity, even when it was the very Red sun of Mao Zedong (after all, the sun reddens as it sets). Only the Sun-King of Korea discomfited Japan, owing to the mad fear that Kim Il Sung's North Korea was a risen sun whose country did "Japan" better than the Japanese do.

Japan's nineteenth-century choice (and Korea's, too) was *not* between a Western international system and no system, but between a Western system predicated on the sovereign equality of nations but seeking to subordinate Japan, Korea, and China and an East Asian international system centuries old predicated on the sovereign hierarchies of the Middle Kingdom but affording nearly complete autonomy to Japan and Korea. It is amazing to

---

[13] For example, the cover article, "Japan's New Identity," in *Business Week*, April 10, 1995, pp. 108–20.

[14] If the second reference seems obscure, I refer the reader to my *Origins of the Korean War vol. 2, The Roaring of the Cataract, 1947–1950* (Princeton: Princeton University Press, 1990), chap. 21 and 22. A plunge long blamed on Asia-firster MacArthur, the Yalu debacle destroyed the Truman administration and shaped U.S. security policy down to the end of the cold war. At the time Korea was widely viewed as the first war the United States ever lost.

[15] Akira Iriye uses precisely these terms in his *Power and Culture: The Japanese-American War, 1941–45* (Cambridge: Harvard University Press, 1981).

[16] Clemenceau once remarked that "America is the only nation in history which miraculously has gone directly from barbarism to degeneration without the usual interval of civilization." Korean Confucians looked upon Japan's rapid westernization in the 1870s as yet more evidence that it had never fully participated in or understood Sinic civilization.

see how even the experts on late nineteenth-century East Asia take the Western theory as the norm and cannot get it through their heads that there *was* an international system (and therefore a norm) in East Asia, one that had lasted for centuries. China, Japan, and Korea knew one another, cross-fertilized one another, and traded with one another, whereas in the mid-nineteenth century it was the Western system that was utterly new, deeply threatening, and entirely untried and unproved in East Asia.[17]

After transcending the unequal treaties and the threat of direct subordination, Good Japan looked to find itself mirrored and admired in the hegemonic lens, a wish requited by the British imperial looking glass of the early part of this century,[18] and by the American looking glass in the 1920s ("Taisho democracy"), and again from 1945 to 1970 (modernization theory). Since trade conflict began in the early 1970s, double vision has afflicted both Japan and the United States, but this is still merely double vision, a long and remediable stage before blindness. Oddly enough, Bad Japan also wants to see its reflection in the hegemonic lens—a dead giveaway that even the baddest of Japanese cannot avoid the measure of the hegemonic eye (something both John Dower and Akira Iriye have argued, in very different ways).[19]

Today Americans also get sunspots. Fallows's *Looking at the Sun* is a continuous back-and-forth glance between the Japanese sun and the American spots on his eyes. The scholarly counterpart to Fallows in the field of political economy is perhaps Chalmers Johnson, but Johnson never needed to be told about List-in-Japan. For the system of states it is clearly Robert Scalapino, whose large *ouevre* on U.S.-Japan relation operates on a discursive plane far removed from the fundamentals of this relationship. Speaking usually in the passive voice, which permits the "agent" to act without regard to the "principal" and vice-versa, Scalapino finds things happening over time in this relationship that may occasion a smile here and a frown there, here a shimmer and there a sunspot, but from 1945 to the present the U.S.-Japan relationship mostly yields a twinkle in his eye.

In a *locus classicus* for this liberal optic circa 1977, "Perspectives on Modern Japanese Foreign Policy,"[20] Scalapino finds a Japan firmly committed

[17] See, for example, Peter Duus, *The Abacus and the Sword: The Japanese Penetration of Korea, 1895–1910* (Berkeley and Los Angeles: University of California Press, 1995). Compare Professor Hamashita's work on the tributary system in Chapter 3.

[18] See various quotations and citations from British *Japonoiserie* at the turn of the century in Cumings, "Archaeology, Descent, Emergence."

[19] Dower argues in *War without Mercy* (New York: Pantheon Books, 1986) that wartime Japanese stereotypes of Americans sought to elevate Japanese to the American level; Iriye wrote that even in the most pronounced years of Japan's self-conscious estrangement, namely, the early 1940s, its leaders complained about being captured by Anglo-American ideas.

[20] Robert Scalapino, "Perspectives on Modern Japanese Foreign Policy," in *The Foreign Policy*

to internationalism and to the internationalist ideology of those years, trilateralism;[21] some might fret about a return to "xenophobia and exclusiveness," he wrote, and others about a declension to "continental involvement" (connoted in 1977 as "Pan-Asianism"), but any venture in such directions would be "hopelessly unrealistic," he thought.[22] His essays rarely tell the reader why things happen in this relationship: they just happen, with no particular origin and no particular structure.

Every once in a while Professor Scalapino delivers himself of a value judgment, however—for example in the second sentence of this same essay: "In the early nineteenth century, the Japanese islands were in a remote, nearly inaccessible part of the world, totally removed from a larger economic or political context." It is my belief that the Japanese islands were located then exactly where they are now, but that is not the Eurocentric picture—that is not the optic that sees Perry's black steamships "opening" Japan in 1853, and so on. This all-seeing liberal eye also floats above the realities of postwar U.S.–Japan relations, on a discursive plane that reflects only what it wishes the reader to see (with some things front-and-center and others in the shade). Scalapino's essays on this theme are representative of an entire policy-related literature that could reverse all the valences of approval/disapproval the minute Washington or Tokyo acted to change the fundamentals hammered out after World War II. Perhaps the best proof of this point is that no Japanese, no matter how pro-American or committed to internationalism, can write with the same blithe disregard for origin and structure.

Thus in the same collection we find mainstream political scientist Seisaburo Sato saying that nineteenth-century Japan was indeed remote—*to the Western powers*—and therefore too remote and too unpromising "to subjugate effectively." (Perry may have "opened" Japan, but all he wanted was coaling stations.) This, of course, is a world-system dictum that the imperial powers gazed upon Japan long enough to energize its reformers, but not strongly enough to seriously contemplate incorporating it, and therefore Japan got the precious systemic "breathing space" that E. H. Norman was the first to highlight,[23] and which distinguishes Japan from China and Korea in the modern period.[24]

---

of Modern Japan, ed. Scalapino (Berkeley and Los Angeles: University of California Press, 1977), pp. 391–412.

[21] Ibid., p. 400.

[22] Ibid, pp. 399, 407.

[23] Norman, *Origins of the Modern Japanese State,* pp. 118, 144.

[24] Compare Scalapino: Japan's "uniform spread of common culture . . . may even have been the decisive factor that enabled Japan to avoid the kinds of subordination to the West that affected much of Asia." "Perspectives," p. 395.

From Sato we learn also of a regime of technology and resources, in which for most of the twentieth century Japan has been dependent on advanced Western technology, for all of the postwar period has depended on the United States for its defense and its military technology, and for all of the century has depended on crucial imported raw materials, especially oil. And here we get a punch line: according to Sato it was oil that made the difference in Japan's singularly autonomous foreign policy decision, namely, the "move South" in July 1941 which culminated in Pearl Harbor. In 1977 Sato thought that Japan remained a fundamentally weak country among the hallowed circle of advanced industrial states, and could not *but* cooperate in any regime the other powers developed, whether it be trilateralism, NAFTA-APEC, the newly formed World Trade Organization, or something else. Scalapino's docile and compliant Japanese foreign policy becomes Sato's "irresponsible immobilism"—"ad hoc, reacting, and equivocating."[25] (It is well to remind the 1990s reader who watched Japan's catatonia at the time of the Gulf War or Prime Minister Morihiro Hosokawa's handwringing or Prime Minister Tsutomu Hata's empty rhetoric about Japan becoming a "normal power" or Prime Minister Tomiichi Murayama's "socialist" recapitulation of all three, that Sato wrote these lines almost two decades ago.)

Professor Sato also had a mathematically precise conception of Japan's place in the twentieth-century hierarchy of states: number 8 after it defeated Russia in 1905, number 3 under the Washington system of the 1920s, and number 2 (maybe) in 1977. Furthermore, he wrote, Japan almost always sought an alliance with a stronger industrial country: Britain from 1902 to 1923, the U.S.-defined Washington System from 1922 to 1931, Germany from 1940 to 1945, and the United States throughout the postwar period.[26] These same emphases can be found in the work of Akira Iriye, the dean of diplomatic historians working on East Asian-American relations.[27]

Elsewhere I have argued that if we excavate "Japan as Number Two" in the international realm, where states are arrayed in a hierarchy of power, sometimes known as the balance of power, and states are both autonomous

[25] Sato, "The Foundations of Modern Japanese Foreign Policy," in Scalapino, *Foreign Policy of Modern Japan*, pp. 372, 374, 379–83, 388–89.

[26] Ibid., p. 379.

[27] Especially in *Across the Pacific: An Inner History of American-East Asian Relations* (New York: Harcourt, Brace & World, 1967), his most brilliant and original book; but see also *Pacific Estrangement: Japanese and American Expansion, 1897–1911* (Cambridge: Harvard University Press, 1972), *After Imperialism* (Cambridge: Harvard University Press, 1965), and the deeply revisionist *Power and Culture*. All these books operate on the terrain of intercultural imagery and conflict.

and penetrated (their structures being the outcome of both domestic and international forces), we get the deep structure of a world system in which Japan has been an important but always subordinate part.[28] An archaeology of Japan in the twentieth-century system, for example, unearths the following timelines:

A. 1900 to 1922: Japan in British–U.S. hegemony
B. 1922 to 1941: Japan in U.S.-British hegemony
C. 1941 to 1945: Japan as regional hegemon in East Asia
D. 1945 to 1970: Japan in U.S. hegemony
E. 1970 to the 1990s: Japan in U.S.-European hegemony

There are always problems with a division of human history by years and decades; I am just as capable as the reader of pointing out inconsistencies or errant facts in this one, and there are many in the decade of the 1930s. Like every other division into decades, this one is driven by a conception more than by daily empirical fact; I justify it in *Industrial Behemoth* (forthcoming). For my purposes here the schema has the virtue of highlighting an important aspect of the international structure that most other conceptions miss: three of the periods (A, B, and E) are trilateral partnerships, and none is one of colonial or imperial domination. A bilateral regime is predictable in a temporary phase of comprehensive advantage where the hegemon towers over the rest (from 1945 to 1970 for the United States), and a trilateral regime is predictable in the rising and declining phases of transitional hegemonies (from 1902 to 1941 for Britain; from 1970 to some time in the next century for the United States).

The U.S. trajectory is instructive for grasping the historical system known as hegemony and the turning point in the early 1920s that Iriye called the Washington system. By 1900 if not earlier the United States was the dominant industrial power in the world. Shortly after World War I it came to be the dominant diplomatic partner in the trilateral hegemonic partnership that had existed in East Asia since the 1890s. In the early 1920s U.S. banks also became dominant in the world economy;[29] Iriye rightly judged the United States at that time, in spite of its presumed isolationism, to have been "the key to postwar international relations . . . its capital, technology, and commodities sustained the world economic system throughout the 1920s . . . as the financial, business, and political center of the

---

[28] Cumings, "Archaeology, Descent, Emergence."
[29] See Carl P. Parrini, *Heir to Empire: The United States Economic Diplomacy, 1916–1923* (Pittsburgh: University of Pittsburgh Press, 1969).

world.''[30] The Anglo-Japanese alliance had became tattered, and the United States now became more important than Britain to Japanese diplomacy. The Washington naval system of 1922 was explicitly trilateral, in that the United States and Britain kept their naval superiority, while Japan, the United States, and Britain all cooperated to keep China a subordinate actor in the East Asian system. It is only in 1941, however, that we can see a conscious U.S. drive to hegemony under Roosevelt, and only in 1947 did it finally replace Britain as the hegemonic power (with no terrible result for Britain, just an U.S.-cushioned decline to the point where now Britain's only comparative advantage seems to be in the editorship of American magazines).

Japan was content to "prosper in the collective informal empire" of the British and the Americans throughout the first third of the century and to feed off a British-American technological regime without making any significant technological innovations of its own until the late 1920s—and then only in textiles, an industry already in incipient decline in Britain and the United States. Before the late 1920s Pratt Machines from England had supported the developing Japanese textile industry, General Electric was dominant in the delivery of electricity, and as early as the 1890s Standard Oil had placed both Japan and China well within the world oil regime (refined as kerosene then), which was increasingly dominated by U.S. firms by midcentury. The great transnational oil firms are indelible examples of Anglo-Saxon hegemony and perhaps the best symbol of the joint British-American technical condominium was the British-American Tobacco Company, a subsidiary of the Duke tobacco interests in North Carolina, which got Japan and China hooked on a cigarette habit so deep that "nonsmoking sections" can hardly be found anywhere in either country today.[31] Even the spearhead for Japan's penetration of Manchuria, the South Manchurian Railway Company, got its reputation for advanced and efficient service by importing thousands of the latest American locomotives and railway cars, not to mention tons of American steel railway ties, all known for decades as the best in the world.[32]

---

[30] Iriye, *Power and Culture*, p. 15.
[31] James B. Duke formed BAT in 1902, in league with a chief rival, the British Imperial Tobacco Company; Duke held two-thirds of the stock. By 1915, BAT had almost $17 million in investments in China and was one of its two largest employers. Michael H. Hunt, *The Making of a Special Relationship: The United States and China to 1914* (New York: Columbia University Press, 1983), pp. 282–83.
[32] William Wray, "Japan's Big-Three Service Enterprises in China, 1896–1936," in *The Japanese Informal Empire in China, 1895–1937*, ed. Peter Duus, Ramon H. Myers, and Mark Peattie (Princeton: Princeton University Press, 1989), pp. 35, 57–59; also Myers, "Japanese Imperi-

Neither the British nor the Americans were happy with the nationalist Japan that *began* to emerge in 1931 (which is why I use 1941 and not 1931, the conventional dating for Japan's unilateralism), and they complained about it mightily while doing next to nothing to halt Japanese aggression in Manchuria. Japan industrialized its way out of the Depression; in the midst of the global doldrums and shrunken world trade Japan's total exports more than doubled from 1932 to 1937, and "appeared to flood world markets." Cotton yarn, woven goods, toys, and iron and steel led the advance. Yet Japan did not register a trade surplus until 1935, when its exports were but 3 percent of the world total, compared to ten percent for the United States. Despite that, Japan's trade partners became obsessed with Japan's export activity. The U.S. economist Miriam Farley explained this by saying Japan had merely "picked the wrong century in which to industrialize," not a bad observation. By 1936 every major nation had curtailed the influx of Japanese exports, yet Japanese business groups still "tried to induce Americans to invest in Manchuria" as late as the late 1930s, and were more successful than generally recognized.[33] Meanwhile U.S. textile concerns "lobbied for restraints on exports to the U.S. despite a massive trade surplus with Japan."[34] So it goes.

As I have argued elsewhere,[35] the dynamic mechanism that moves within the regime of technology both temporally and geographically is the product cycle: U.S. rolling stock in Manchuria in the 1910s, U.S. technology in Japanese mines in the 1920s, U.S.-designed refineries in Wonsan, Korea, in the 1930s,[36] U.S. steel and electronic technology in Japan in the 1950s, Japanese light electronic technology in Korea in the 1960s, Japanese steel technology in P'ohang, South Korea, in the 1970s, Japanese technology requested by the *North* Koreans to renovate old Japanese mines in the

---

alism in Manchuria: The South Manchurian Railway Company, 1906–1933," in Duus, Myers, and Peattie, *Japanese Informal Empire*, pp. 105–7.

[33] A student of mine, Haruo Iguchi, is completing a dissertation on the "new zaibatsu" groups in Manchuria; his archival researches have turned up a great deal of U.S. business involvement behind the presumedly "closed door" of Manchukuo. See also William Miles Fletcher III, *The Japanese Business Community and National Trade Policy, 1920–1942* (Chapel Hill: University of North Carolina Press, 1989), p. 2, who argues that Japanese business groups "tried to induce Americans to invest in Manchuria" in the late 1930s.

[34] Fletcher, *Japanese Business Community*, pp. 2, 98–99.

[35] For more elaboration see Cumings, "The Origins and Development of the Northeast Asian Political Economy," *International Organization* 38 (Winter 1984): 1–40.

[36] In the late 1930s Japanese technicians installed an oil refinery at Wonsan based on U.S. "blueprints and consultations"; the Russians took it over in 1945 and then placed it in a Russian-Korean joint stock company. At some point after 1950 it became a North Korean national oil refinery. See MacArthur Archives, RG6, box 78, Allied Translator and Interpreter Service, Issue No. 23, February 15, 1951, quoting original documents captured in Wonsan in October 1950.

1980s, Japanese technology in Manchuria in the 1990s. Because Japan has been the core of this regional product- and technology-proliferation system, some like Kaname Akamatsu came to see it as the lead goose in a flying v—which is the truth but not the whole truth. It is true only if one's optic misses the real lead goose or the ceiling above which the regional v formation does not fly. And here, of course, we can see why the "flying geese" formation much talked about today is not and will not be the Greater East Asia Co-Prosperity Sphere revisited until the world (and not just Korea or Taiwan or Thailand) sources its technology from a hegemonic Japan.

In 1941 the real lead goose exercised the outer limits of its hegemonic power by imposing an embargo on oil to Japan, which came as a tremendous psychological shock and made its leaders assume that the only alternative was war. Yet even in the midst of that terrible war the leaders of Japan's "New Order" complained that Anglo-American ideas "cling to us like fleas," and there never was substance to either the philosophy or the reality of the "Co-Prosperity Sphere."[37] You had to go all the way to Burma to find an Asian people that believed Japan's wartime ideology. (Apparently the rising sun looked better at a great distance). As H. D. Harootunian has pointed out, Imperial Japan's ideologues failed miserably at a *shutaisei* (*chuch'esông* in South Korean, *Juche* in North Korean) program for being both Asian and modern at the same time. As for its coercive autonomy, Japan's failed attempt at unilateral regional hegemony was visible on the sea after Midway (July 1942) and on land after Guadalcanal (December 1942); by mid 1943 a small cadre of "internationalists" in Japan and the U.S. State Department were moving on remarkably parallel lines to reintegrate Japan into the U.S. hegemonic regime.[38] This finally came to pass with the "reverse course" in 1947 and after, as Japan became an American-positioned engine in a productivist coalition designed to restart the postwar world economy.

The Great Crescent and the Kennan Restoration

Japan's place in the postwar world was defined by 1950,[39] and this definition still governs the situation today. It was in that period that the tec-

[37] Iriye, *Power and Culture*, pp. 65, 68. Iriye comments upon the "orthodoxly Western" nature of Japan's development in Northeast Asia after 1941 and finds various Japanese "cultural essence" arguments to be vacuous (p. 95). *Shutaisei* means something like a master principle of putting Japan (or Korea) first in all things, being ever subjective about and absorbed with each people's putative uniqueness and eternal essence, and so on.
[38] Ibid., pp. 15, 25–27, 65, 81, 83, 97, 148–49.
[39] I have written about this period in several places, but the most detailed analysis is in my

tonic plates of the international structure found their resting place after the earthquake of World War II. Dean Acheson, George Kennan, and John Foster Dulles—to take three of the most important U.S. planners—wished to situate Japan structurally in a global system shaped by the United States, so that Japan would do what it should without having to be told—by remote control, as it were.[40] In so doing they placed distinct outer limits on Japan's behavior, and these limits persist today.

Japan was demilitarized and democratized during the early Occupation years, if less thoroughly than the proponents of the policy had hoped for. It is thus proper to view the years 1945–47 as an exception to the general thrust of U.S. policy toward Japan in the postwar period, a policy elaborated during the war years by Japanophiles in the State Department, who looked forward to reforms that would quickly restore Japan's position in the world economy, and which would not penalize Japan's industrial leaders for their support of the war. Indeed, these plans were first drawn up within six months of Pearl Harbor, which illustrates the point that 1941 was seen as a brief, temporary hiatus in the general pattern of hegemony in East Asia.[41] It is also important to remember, however, that the twin goals of democratization and demilitarization were not antithetical to the subsequent strategy,[42] but in fact represent the extraordinary reach of U.S. hegemony in the late 1940s: restructuring both the world economy and the internal political economies of major industrial competitors Japan and Germany (something Britain had tried but failed to do with Germany after World War I).

The United States was the one great power with the central economic, financial, and technical force to restore the health of the world economy. Although hegemony usually connotes "relative dominance" within the group of core states,[43] by 1947 it was apparent that the United States would have to exercise unilateral dominance for some time, given the gross asymmetry between the robustness of the U.S. industrial system and the poverty of nearly all the others. It was this critical problem of industrial revival,

---

Origins of the Korean War, vol. 2, *The Roaring of the Cataract, 1947–1950* (Princeton: Princeton University Press, 1990), chaps. 1–4.

[40] At the time the leader of the small "Japan Lobby," Harry Kern, said of the U.S.-Japan relationship, " 'remote control' is best." Harry Kern, "American Policy toward Japan," 1948, a privately circulated paper, in Pratt Papers, box 2. Kern put "remote control" in quotation marks because it was originally George Sansom's term.

[41] Cumings, *Origins*, vol. 1, chap. 3; Iriye has made similar points in *Power and Culture*.

[42] The exception would be industrial reparations policy, which was a key element in the early development of the cold war in Europe, and which was rejected outright in East Asia by late 1946 because it would benefit Japan's communist or communizing neighbors at the expense of democratizing Japan.

[43] Wallerstein, *Historical Capitalism* (London: Verso, 1983), p. 58.

spanning Western Europe and Japan, which set off the basic shifts in 1947; the so-called reverse course in Japan was thus an outcome of global policy—as William Borden has aptly demonstrated. The new goal was the reconstitution and restoration of flourishing German and Japanese industrial economies, but in ways that would not threaten hegemonic interests.[44] But the revival of Axis industry also spelled out a new regional policy.

The U.S.-Soviet conflict in Central Europe erected barriers to almost any exchange across the great divide known to Americans as the Iron Curtain. This divide fragmented up marketing and exchange patterns that had underpinned important regional economies. The bulwarks dropped across the central front in Europe, and the developing cold war in Asia cut the Western European and Japanese economies off from peripheral and semiperipheral sources of food, raw materials, and labor—in Eastern Europe, grain from Poland and Hungary, meat and potatoes from Poland, oil and coal from Rumania and Silesia; in East Asia, rice and minerals from North Korea, coking coal and soybeans from Manchuria, tungsten from South China. With the European recovery so sluggish, Japan still dormant, and communist parties threatening in Italy and France, China and Korea, this structural problem was newly perceived and demanded action in 1947. The East Asian expression of this policy turned on an elegant metaphor.

Containment was to be effected in East Asia by the metaphor of a "great crescent" stretching from Japan through Southeast Asia and around India, ultimately to the oil fields of the Persian Gulf.[45] Although containment was thought to be preeminently a security strategy against communist expansion, in East Asia it mingled power and plenty inextricably. To complement and to achieve their security goals, U.S. planners envisioned a regional economy driven by revived Japanese industry, with assured continental access to markets and raw materials for its exports. This would kill several birds with one stone: it would link together nations threatened by socialist state-controlled economies, make Japan self-supporting, weave sinews of economic interdependence between Japan

[44] See William S. Borden, *The Pacific Alliance: United States Foreign Economic Policy and Japanese Trade Recovery, 1947–1955* (Madison: University of Wisconsin Press, 1984); Charles Maier, "The Politics of Productivity," in *Between Power and Plenty: Foreign Economic Policies of Armed Industrial States*, ed. Peter Katzenstein (Madison: University of Wisconsin Press, 1979), pp. 23–50; also Joan Spero, *The Politics of International Economic Relations*, 2d. ed (New York: St. Martin's Press, 1981), pp. 37–41.

[45] William Borden and Michael Schaller have done original work on the "great crescent" program (Acheson and the State Department used the term several times in 1949–50). See Borden, *Pacific Alliance*, and Michael Schaller, *The American Occupation of Japan: The Origins of the Cold War in Asia* (New York: Oxford University Press, 1985). I have set out my ideas here at greater length in *Origins*, vol 2, chaps. 2 and 5, and in *Industrial Behemoth.*

and the United States, and help draw down the European colonies by getting a Japanese and U.S. foot in the door of the pound and franc blocs in Asia.

The archaeology of the Great Crescent uncovers a world-system conception of multiple, overlapping tripartite hierarchies: if the United States was the dominant core economy in the world, Japan and Germany would underpin regional core systems and help reintegrate peripheral areas as exclusively held empires disintegrated. The "high-tech" industries of the 1940s, represented in world-competitive U.S. firms such as Westinghouse, General Electric, IBM, General Motors, Ford, Lockheed, and the multinational oil firms, had nothing to fear from Japan and Germany, as long as both countries were kept dependent politically and technologically and in matters pertaing to defense and the access to resources. As the Rooseveltian design of enmeshing the Soviet Union in the world economy failed, Acheson and others devised a second-best strategy of regional concentrations of strength within the noncommunist "grand area," to forestall the greater catastrophe of further expansion by exclusively held, independent, state-controlled socialist economies. (Of course, they were also dead set against a less formidable type of political economy, the nationalist autarkies of the 1930s.)

After the victory of the Chinese revolution, the search for Japan's hinterland was conducted mostly in Southeast Asia, but in 1947–48 Korea, Manchuria, and North China were all targets of potential reintegration with Japan. In a stunning intervention at the beginning of the famous "fifteen weeks" that inaugurated the Truman Doctrine and the Marshall Plan, Secretary of State George Marshall himself scribbled a note to Acheson that said, "Please have plan drafted of policy to organize a definite government of So. Korea and connect up [sic] its economy with that of Japan," a pearl that cannot be brought to the surface and examined without demolishing much of the diplomatic history on Korea in this period.[46] It captures with pith and foresight the future direction of U.S. policy toward Korea from 1947 to the normalization with Japan in 1965.

The irony, of course, is that Japan never really developed markets or intimate core-periphery linkages in East and Southeast Asia until the 1960s. It was the Korean War and its manifold procurements, not the "great crescent," that pushed Japan forward along its march toward industrial prowess (indeed, some have called the Korean procurements "Japan's Marshall Plan"). A war that killed three million Koreans was

<hr>

[46] National Archives, 740.0019 Control (Korea) file, box 3827, Marshall's note to Acheson of January 29, 1947, attached to Vincent to Acheson, January 27, 1947.

described by Prime Minister Yoshida as "a gift of the Gods,"[47] giving the critical boost to Japan's economy. The Tokyo stock market fluctuated for three years according to "peace scares" in Korea. Yet the logic of an Asian hinterland persisted through the Korean War; it is remarkable to see how vexed the Eisenhower administration still was with "the restoration of Japan's lost colonial empire."[48] Ultimately this logic explains the deep reinvolvement of Japanese economic influence in Korea and Taiwan from the 1960s onward, as we will see.

In short, Japan in the postwar period has been a workshop of the world economy, an "economic animal" defined by the United States and shorn of its prewar military and political clout. Japan's sun was to rise high but not too high: high enough to cause trade problems for the allies in declining industries (textiles, light electronics, automobiles, steel), but not so high that it threatened leading-edge industries, let alone conferred comprehensive industrial advantage. The logic for such a policy was hammered out in 1947, coterminous with the emergence of the cold war, and it deepened as Japan benefited from America's wars to lock in an Asian hinterland for Japan and the "free world" in Korea and Vietnam. In this era, which ran from Truman through Johnson, Japan was a dutiful partner to the United States, which was tickled pink at Japan's economic success. U.S. planners may have fretted about Japanese, Korean, and Taiwanese import substitution and the strong roles for the state in their economies, but the United States supported and indulged these same Northeast Asian allies with massive and unprecedented transfers of technology and capital.[49]

Some have spoken of a "long peace" in the postwar era, while neglecting the security underpinnings of that peace, in a system of *dual containment*: containment of the communist enemy and the capitalist ally. Here

---

[47] Dower, *Empire and Aftermath*, p. 316. Japan lost about two million people during the Pacific War.

[48] At the 139th meeting of the NSC, April 8, 1953, "The President expressed the belief that there was no future for Japan unless access were provided for it to the markets and raw materials of Manchuria and North China." Secretary of Treasury Humphrey wanted the United States to be "aggressive" in providing Japan and West Germany with secure positions where they could "thrive, and have scope for their virile populations." In some respects, it seemed to him, "we had licked the two wrong nations in the last war." Whereupon, "Mr. Cutler [Special Assistant to the President] inquired whether the Council wished to go further than this and adopt a policy which would look to the restoration of Japan's lost colonial empire." Ike said no, probably not. Eisenhower Library, Eisenhower Papers (Whitman file), National Security Council Series, box 4.

[49] Jung-en Woo (Meredith Woo-Cumings), *Race to the Swift: State and Finance in Korean Industrialization* (New York: Columbia University Press, 1991), chap. 3.

was what I have called "the Kennan Restoration," and George Kennan played the key role in conceiving the logic of this security structure—first in papers written in 1947, and then in long negotiations with MacArthur in Tokyo in 1948. The real reason for the long peace between the super-powers was that the Soviet Union shared hidden U.S. security goals to a much greater degree than is generally recognized. Stalin's doctrine, which became the life-long doctrine of Foreign Minister Andrei Gromyko, was to contain not just the United States but also any hint of *revanche* in Germany and Japan. While the United States laid seige to the Soviet bloc, Moscow laid seige against West Germany (by stationing 360,000 Soviet soldiers in East Germany) and against Japan (by stationing 10,000 Soviet soldiers on windswept Iturup, plus much else in the Kamchatka Peninsula region).

Thus when the United States found itself in the best of all possible worlds in the 1990s, having won the cold war but still retaining significant leverage vis-à-vis Germany and Japan, it was not by accident, because the cold war had consisted of two systems: the containment project, which provided security against both the enemy and the ally, and the hegemonic project, which provided for U.S. leverage over the necessary resources of our industrial rivals. Both the hegemonic project and the allied-containment system survive today.

The postwar settlement is also the reason why present-day Northeast Asia, when compared to Europe, has so few multilateral institutions and mechanisms, and had even fewer through most of the postwar period. This outcome was the result of a unilateral U.S. military occupation of defeated Japan in 1945, followed within five years by a general division of the region along the fault line of the cold war. General Douglas MacArthur issued General Order Number 1 on 15 August 1945, excluding allied powers from the occupation of Japan, dividing Korea at the thirty-eighth parallel and Vietnam at the seventeenth parallel, and seeking to unify China under Chiang Kai-shek's rule by requiring Japanese soldiers to surrender to Na-tionalist forces. The only part of that East Asian military division that did not hold was China, and as the Communists cleared the mainland in 1948–49 a new division took place: that between Taiwan and the main-land. MacArthur ruled Japan as a benevolent emperor, while policing the fault lines of great power conflict in Korea and China.

The Korean War erupted in June 1950, resulting in a vastly deepened division of Northeast Asia. A heavily fortified demilitarized zone replaced the 38th parallel in Korea and remains to this day as a museum of the defunct global cold war. The two Koreas remade themselves as garrison states, with very high military-to-civilian population ratios. For a generation China was excluded from the postwar global system by blockade and threats of war. Japan also remilitarized, if modestly, as a result of the Korean War. Above all, the Korean War left an archipelago of U.S. military installations throughout the noncommunist part of the region, bases rarely discussed in the literature but which were the coercive structure that locked in the U.S. position in Northeast Asia, offering a diffuse leverage that I once called "a light hold on the Japanese jugular."

The long-term result of this U.S. unilateralism may be summarized as follows: the capitalist countries of the region tended to communicate with one another *through the United States*, a vertical regime solidifed through bilateral defense treaties (with Japan, South Korea, Taiwan, and the Philippines) and conducted by a State Department that towered over the foreign ministries of these four countries. All became semisovereign states, deeply penetrated by U.S. military structures (operational control of the South Korean armed forces, Seventh Fleet patrolling of the Taiwan Straits, defense dependencies for all four countries, military bases on their territory) and incapable of independent foreign policy or defense initiatives. All were in a sense contemporary "hermit kingdoms" vis-à-vis one another, if not in relation to the United States.

The capitalist countries "communicated" with the communist countries primarily through the U.S. military, symbolized by the military talks at Panmunjom, the developing war in Vietnam, minicrises like Quemoy and Matsu in the Taiwan Straits, chronic threats exchanged between the United States and the PRC, periodic fracases with North Korea (the Pueblo in 1968, the EC-121 in 1969, and the "tree-cutting incident" in 1976), and all-round containment of the (relatively weak) Soviet position in Northeast Asia. There were minor démarches through the military curtain beginning in the mid-1950s, such as low levels of trade between Japan and China, or Japan and North Korea. But the dominant tendency until the 1970s was a unilateral U.S. regime heavily biased toward military forms of communication, and correspondingly biased against the multilateral mechanisms that emerged in Europe.

There was no NATO. There was a SEATO, but it never amounted to much, never spawned a NEATO, and died after two decades. There was a rump Marshall Plan (the ECA or Economic Cooperation Administration, which aided South Korea and Taiwan from 1947 onward). Like the Marshall Plan itself, it was superseded by the revival of the advanced industrial economies, in this case the only one in the region, Japan. (That also began not in 1947 but with the Korean War.) Still, until the mid-1960s the political economy of the region was primarily bilateral with the United States, with the smaller countries sustained by U.S. bulk aid grants (five-sixths of ROK imports in the late 1950s, for example).

The Regime of Technology

Throughout the postwar period, as new work by Richard Samuels illustrates,[50] the technological regime was one of the few places that Japan could seek autonomy, given that autonomy in the system of states was off-limits, thereby denying to this resource-bereft island nation autonomy in the regime of resources (and I don't even want to start with discursive autonomy,[51] which Japan has never achieved in the modern era). Japan therefore took the path of least resistance, assiduously acquiring and husbanding technology from the 1950s down to the present—with results even today that I see as decidedly mixed (Japan number 1 here, number 2 there, number 3 in the next place). Of course, this was only the path of least resistance relative to the others; the United States kept its best technologies from Japanese hands, just as Japan has long tried to keep its Asian neighbors technologically dependent, and just as South Korea now tries to work North Korea into technological dependency via the "light water reactor" controversy of 1994–95.

Although I cannot prove my case here, I do not think Japan in the mid-1990s is significantly or irreversibly ahead of the United States in any important technology. Jean-Claude Derian saw this coming in 1990,[52] a time when the Clyde Prestowitzes of the world were railing on about Japan being ahead in every significant technology and about to become the hegemonic power of the globe, if it wasn't already.[53] Furthermore, Derian expressed worries about the United States's technological lead in several areas that by now have been overcome or no longer matter, like semiconducters, supercomputers, gigaflop processers, high-definition television, and the airbus. But he was generally optimistic that the United States would retain or regain the global technological lead because of critical Japanese weaknesses in what he calls the "sheltered culture" of technology.

---

[50] Richard Samuels, *"Rich Nation, Strong Army"* (Ithaca: Cornell University Press, 1994).

[51] Discursive autonomy is another privilege of hegemony; the hegemonic power always has the right to speak (and in the case of England and the United States speaks some version of Anglo-Saxon positivism), whereas the "right to speak" of everyone else in the system ranges from not fully guaranteed to nonexistent. Thus we get Ishihara's 1989 best-seller under the title *The Japan That Can Say No.*

[52] Jean Claude Derian, *America's Struggle for Leadership in Technology*, trans. Severen Schaeffer (Cambridge: MIT Press, 1990).

[53] Clyde Prestowitz, *Trading Places* (New York: Basic Books, 1989). Prestowitz wrote as if Japan were already hegemonic and claimed that the United States "had effectively lost its consumer electronics industry by the mid-1970s" and faced a "crisis" in the semiconductor industry in 1985 (pp. 92–93).

Japan has a weak scientific tradition, few Nobel prizewinners, and significantly low absolute levels of research and development expenditure when compared to the United States. It is in the "exposed" technological culture that Japan has done well, where technical acquisition and product innovation rather than discovery of new technologies is the key. Furthermore, Derian argued, the United States held two trump cards that Japan did not: the first was its prowess in both the sheltered and the exposed culture, a result in part of enormous U.S. military-related spending, and the second was its hegemonic birthright: the privileged position of the dollar as "the cornerstone of the world monetary system." By allowing the dollar to decline, according to Derian, the United States rebuilt its exports and since 1985 has "forced the rest of the world . . . to share the cost of reestablishing the U.S. balance of trade." If many economists would quibble with Derian, he is right to point out that no other nation has seen prices of some of its exports decline by 50 percent in two years in its competitor's markets.[54] Of course, his argument looks even better in 1995, as the dollar plunges to new postwar lows against the yen while central bankers file their fingernails. At this writing the yen was eighty to the dollar, but yen-denominated world trade was a mere 9 percent of world foreign exchange, compared to 55 percent for the presumably decrepit dollar.[55]

In the late 1980s globe-straddling giant IBM seemed threatened by NEC,[56] only to get savaged at home by small, entrepreneurial companies that put computers in everyone's office or home, and supercomputers on the desktop. Boeing remains preeminent in global aircraft and has backorders well past the year 2000, in spite of much 1980s punditry about its inevitable decline in the 1990s. American chips, from Intel Pentiums to gigaflops, are as good as or better than the Japanese, and in software (which is after all the brains of a computer), the United States has a gigantic lead and a flagship monopoly every bit as good as Standard Oil or U.S. Steel in 1900, namely, Microsoft. Even American automobiles and even early 1980s weak-sister Chrysler are back. I could go on with this, and there are important counterpoints to my argument made by T. J. Pempel and others in this book, but even if I may be wrong about technology I am not wrong about the other three regimes—state system, resources; and discourse—where Japan remains a secondary partner.

---

[54] Derian, *America's Struggle*, pp. 5–6, 175, 267.
[55] Figures from David D. Hale, Kemper Financial Services, quoted in *Business Week*, April 10, 1995, p. 120.
[56] Derian, *America's Struggle*, p. 285.

Japan in Northeast Asia, 1960s–1990s

The decade of the 1960s was a watershed in beginning the transformation back to "normality" of the Northeast Asian system. Thenceforth and down to the present, economic exchange would be the driving force restoring the ties among the nations of the region. The Kennedy administration was pivotal in this regard, inaugurating many policies directed toward drawing down the "multi-furcated" military structures and bringing into play new economic relationships. In some ways this was a fulfillment of the "great crescent" conception linking Tokyo, "island Asia," and the Middle East, which was temporarily demolished by the North Korean invasion in 1950; and in others this was an anticipation of changes later implemented by the Nixon administration—especially the Nixon Doctrine and the opening of China. It was also in the Kennedy period that for the first time U.S. leaders began criticizing Japan for its "free ride" in security affairs.[57] (It is daunting to realize that this rhetoric now is entering its fourth decade, with Japan still recalcitrantly limiting defense spending to about one percent of its GNP, and with U.S. politicians still carping about it.)

The leitmotif of Kennedy's strategy, one scripted by national security adviser W. W. Rostow, was to restore Japan's economic influence in the region. This resulted in the normalization of Japan-ROK relations in 1965 (under enormous U.S. pressure) and the industrialization of both Taiwan and South Korea under the banner of export-led development, typically using obsolescent Japanese light-industrial technology.[58] The International Monetary Fund and the World Bank became involved, in a kind of transnational planning that was particularly evident in the case of South Korea's second five-year plan in the mid-1960s and its recovery from the export-led doldrums in the mid-1980s. Nixon opened relations with China in 1971, initially to draw down U.S. involvement in the Vietnam War and to contain communism by communism, but after the normalization of relations and the epochal reforms instituted by Deng Xiaoping (both policies were decided in December 1978), the economic character of China's interaction with East Asia and the world economy became the dominant

[57] Senator Frank Church's speech of April 22, 1963, was probably the opening scene in this long-running drama. See Makoto Momoi, "Basic Trends in Japanese Security Policies," in Scalapino, *Foreign Policy of Modern Japan*, p. 353.

[58] See the analysis of documents from the Kennedy Library in Woo-Cumings, *Race to the Swift*. A neglected older source on this period is Kim Kwan Bong, *The Korea-Japan Treaty Crisis and the Instability of the Korean Political System* (New York: Praeger, 1968). For Scalapino, Japan's new economic influence in the 1960s also "just happened" to have occurred: "Within less than three decades [after World War 2], Japan had reemerged on the Asian mainland. In Northeast Asia, reemergence took the form of a commanding economic presence in South Korea." Scalapino, "Persepectives," p. 397.

tendency. Once again, the World Bank and the IMF stepped in, this time to help reform a communist economy. The 1990s have seen the further inclusion of Vietnam and a relaxation of North Korea's economic isolation through joint ventures and limited foreign investment. Since the mid-1960s, in short, economic forces drove past or ran roughshod over the previously impervious security barriers hardened by the Korean War. Japan has been the major regional leader in providing that economic force, but it is still not close to being the regional political or military hegemon. Indeed, the U.S. cold war military structure still dominates in matters of regional security, even as the cold war's abrupt end fades into history.

Furthermore, when compared to the European Community even today Northeast Asia lacks intense horizontal connections and the expected multilateral institutions. The Asian Pacific Economic Cooperation council (APEC) had a big splash at the Vancouver summit in November 1993 and its members account for 35 percent of world trade, but it remains a merely consultative grouping, a weak assemblage of eighteen countries that do not interact with one another well or often. (Malaysia's preferred option of an exclusive regional economic grouping generates a lot of heat and attention, but it is much less advanced compared to APEC; indeed it appears to be going nowhere, while attracting the occasional attentions of Japanese nationalists.) There is no NAFTA equivalent, but if a NEAFTA comes into being it will most likely be an extension of NAFTA to include selected Northeast Asian or Pacific Rim economies. Thus it is right to conclude that the Asian "web of interdependence" is weak; "Asia appears strikingly under-institutionalized," without the "rich 'alphabet soup' of international agencies."[59] The temporary result of the 1985 Plaza Accord (which greatly boosted the yen's value) was a vastly enhanced Japanese position in Southeast Asia (in 1989 Japanese firms on average opened one new factory for every working day in Thailand). All this suggested that if any tightly linked interdependence emerged it would be Japan-led, predictably raising again the specter of the Greater East Asian Co-Prosperity Sphere.[60] From the standpoint of the mid-1990s this also seems to be a typically overblown and alarmist reaction, and Japanese investment retains a global rather than purely regional direction, recent punditry connected to the yen's resurgent strength notwithstanding.

Today the main organization linking the Northeast region together is still the private business firm, and it is business firms that drive the dynam-

[59] Aaron L. Friedberg, "Ripe for Rivalry: Prospects for Peace in a Multipolar Asia," *International Security* 18 (Winter 1993/94): 19–23.
[60] Lester Thurow, *Head to Head: The Coming Economic Battle among Japan, Europe, and America* (New York: Morrow, 1992), p. 84. This account seems quite dated now.

ics of the region (for example, in June 1994 a huge coalition of U.S. firms ended the Clinton policy of linking most-favored-nation status for China to its domestic human rights situation). There is nothing like the European Customs Union or the European Parliament or the Organization on Security and Cooperation in Europe (OSCE), although there was some activity toward creating a OSCE-like forum in the latter part of 1993.[61] Travel is no longer restricted for businessmen traversing the region, as it is still for ordinary citizens who may wish to go from Taiwan to China, or South Korea to China, let alone from South Korea to North Korea or vice-versa. External observers might think that China, Korea, and Japan are linked by a common written language in Chinese idiographs, but in fact the common language of the region is English. China uses simplified characters whereas Taiwan does not; South Korea seeks to eliminate characters from its written language altogether, and North Korea did so in 1948. Meanwhile, Japanese and Chinese are as different grammatically as two languages can be (by comparison French, Italian, and Spanish seem like dialects of English). Even the presumed common cultural background in Confucianism does not create cultural ties between, say, Korea and Japan or Japan and China; the lingering animosities of colonialism and war, combined with the dominance of American mass culture, tend to override this traditional heritage and to make of the Northeast Asian discursive regime a hodge-podge of national constructions united only by American pop songs and rock videos.[62]

Above all, apart from the regional momentum of economic development it is still the United States that drives the countries of the region together (or helps to keep them apart, as with North and South Korea). The APEC summit held in Vancouver in November 1993 reflected another lurch by Washington toward a "fundamental shift" in U.S. foreign policy from the Atlantic to the Pacific (the first try since MacArthur's era was during the Reagan administration in the mid-1980s), but the dominant tendency is more a diminution of Atlanticism than a real shift toward the Pacific. In March 1994, U.S. Treasury Department officials exuberantly compared the significance of the contemporary growth spurts in East and

[61] See the *New York Times*, May 23 and July 24, 1993; some observers also thought they saw a coalescence of the small states of ASEAN against Chinese military expansion. Takashi Inoguchi offers some additional cogent reasons for the lack of regional integration in Northeast Asia, in "Dialectics of World Order," in *Whose World Order? Uneven Globalization and the End of the Cold War*, ed. George Sorenson and Hans-Henrik Holm (Boulder, Colo: Westview Press, in press), pp. 10–12.

[62] On this point see the excellent discussion by Masao Miyoshi in *Off Center: Power and Culture Relations between Japan and the United States* (Cambridge: Harvard University Press, 1991), pp. 217–31.

Southeast Asia to "the Industrial Revolution and the Renaissance," a rhetorical flourish showing that a little history is a bad thing. (The article admitted that "the finance ministers of these economies have never met all together in one room.")[63] In the same vein, the only tangible result of the November 1993 APEC meetings was that East Asian heads of state met with a U.S. president in one room for the first time. This merely underlines the point that multilateral relations, even today, are still at an incipient stage in Northeast Asia.

Post–Cold War Northeast Asia: "The Linchpin That Holds Japan in Place"

Simply because U.S. hegemony has defined the region since 1945 does not mean it will continue to do so indefinitely. Indeed, many analysts see an impending shift in the balance of power in East Asia, which almost all of them lament—because they are Americans.

There is an ineffable triumphalism affecting almost every American in the 1990s, beginning with superficial judgments about how the cold war was won, why the Soviet Union collapsed, and what it all means for an American liberalism now said to be the solution to everyone's problems. (In a sense the American gaze has temporarily lost its bifocal quality; the all-seeing liberal eye cannot find significant "difference" and therefore neither can the Pentagon, yielding marginally lower defense spending). The American Century, thought to be waning in the 1980s, is once again at high tide. In many ways the cold war ended in East Asia a generation ago (except for Korea), and tendencies already well under way in recent decades have merely deepened in the 1990s. But that does not stop U.S. analysts—most of them from the "realpolitik" school—from smugness over Northeast Asia, either.

We can see it in Richard Betts's condescending statement: "So should we want China to get rich or not?" or his frank recommendation that Americans should continue being "voluntary Hessians" for Japan for "as

---

[63] *New York Times*, March 19, 1994; Treasury Secretary Lloyd Bentsen told a California audience that "Asia is a continent that economically could be larger than Europe and the U.S. combined within the next fifty years." Such exaggerations assume that current growth rates can be extrapolated into the future. Similarly, in 1993 IMF claimed that China's economy was four times larger than usually thought, and therefore ranked third in the world; others have suggested that China might be the biggest economy in the world by year 2010. Left unexplained is how this will happen while 70 percent of the population remains tied to a peasant agrarian economy, or what industrial or urban jobs will accommodate them if they don't. See Steven Greenhouse, "New Tally of World's Economy Catapults China into Third Place," *New York Times*, May 20, 1993. For similar hyperbole, see "When China Wakes," *Economist*, November 28, 1992.

long as possible," since the only alternative is for Tokyo to "start spending blood as well as its treasure to support international order," and when that time comes "it will justifiably become interested in much more control over that order." It is a lot better, in other words, if the United States polices the world and lets Japan remain, in Betts's words, "a unidimensional superpower"; otherwise, he says, mixing metaphors, "a truncated End of History in East Asia could be destabilizing rather than pacifying." Stability is equated with a revived U.S. hegemony. Meanwhile the United States should continue enmeshing Japan in mechanisms of "neoliberal institutionalism."[64] The pièce de résistance, though, is Betts's assertion that "a China, Japan, or Russia that grows strong enough to overturn a regional balance of power would necessarily also be a global power that would reestablish bipolarity on the highest level"[65]—in other words, no matter which of them came to commensurable power with the United States, it would be our enemy.

Aaron Friedberg also argues that the United States must remain the key player in East Asia; in spite of the end of the Soviet threat it must keep its troops deployed in East Asia, because "American power is the linchpin that holds Japan in place."[66] Samuel Huntington characteristically outdoes everyone else in claiming that continued U.S. hegemony is in not merely the national interest but also the world's: "No other country can make comparable contributions to international order and stability." Japan, however, is not to be trusted because it unremittingly pursues "economic warfare" against the rest of the world and is already dangerously close to hegemonic predominance.[67]

Yet Huntington's argument is looking like yesterday's porridge. If in the recent past most U.S. foreign policy analysts focused on Japan as the rising power—even on "the coming war with Japan"[68]—many now think China is more threatening. Here is Betts again: "The state most likely over time to disturb equilibrium in the region—and the world—is China." Betts seems to think that if current projections hold up, China will not only

---

[64] Richard K. Betts, "Wealth, Power, and Instability: East Asia and the United States after the Cold War," *International Security* 18 (Winter 1993–94): pp. 55–59.

[65] Ibid., p. 74.

[66] Friedberg, "Ripe for Rivalry," pp. 31–32.

[67] Samuel Huntington, "Why International Primacy Matters," *International Security* 17 (Spring 1993): 72–73, 82.

[68] George Friedman and Meredith LeBard, *The Coming War with Japan* (New York: St. Martin's Press, 1991). This would be a remarkably astute book if we were still in the geopolitical milieu of the 1930s, but for the 1990s it is remarkably stupid, not to mention needlessly provocative. For other (more intelligent) suggestions that Japan might be replacing the United States as global hegemon, see Ezra Vogel, "Pax Nipponica," *Foreign Affairs* 64 (Spring 1986): 752–67, and Ron Morse, "Japan's Drive to Pre-Eminence," *Foreign Policy* 69 (Winter 1987–88): 3–21.

soon be rich, but will be "the clear hegemonic power in the region."[69] Pentagon planners, ever in search of enemies now that the Soviet Union has disappeared, have even gone so far as to suggest that U.S. war plans be rewritten to target China and other Third World "renegade states."[70] A national public opinion survey conducted in late 1994 disclosed that while the U.S. public still worries mightily about Japanese economic competition, only 21 percent of foreign policy elites think likewise; far more worry about China's rise to global power.[71]

Once again, however, Japanese political scientists simply cannot agree with the American realists. Takashi Inoguchi, like Sato and Iriye above, somehow finds a way to voice what Betts and Huntington would prefer that we forget in the U.S.-Japan relationship. Inoguchi has suggested, for example, that U.S. hegemony will give way to a cooperative "bigemony" with Japan long before it devolves into serious conflict,[72] which would be the predictable result of declining hegemony, just as for decades Britain reached out to the United States for a partnership, thus to restrain the rising power. In the post–cold war era, Inoguchi finds the United States seeking to use its security position to prolong its hegemony and to push its own trade philosophy in Northeast Asia.[73] He and other Japanese and Korean political scientists also have a far more benign view of China's contemporary emergence as a regional power; from the regional perspective it is not such a terrible thing if Chinese military power balances Japanese economic power, since it is a guarantee that what happened in the 1930s will not happen again.

I disagree with the assembled "realists" who have told us how much we will miss the bipolar stability and "long peace" of the cold war, some of whom are cited above. Elsewhere I have argued that if we go "back to basics," we can sketch a world system that is for the first time since 1917 structured as follows:[74]

---

[69] Betts, "Wealth, Power, and Instability," p. 61.
[70] A Brookings Institution researcher sent me a Pentagon document, based on a 1993 consultants' report on developing a new "SIOP" (Standard Integrated Operations Plan) for 1994, in which the section "SIOP Echo" suggested the necessity for a "nuclear expeditionary force" on call twenty-four hours a day, and directed at "China and other third world states."
[71] John Reilly, ed., *American Foreign Policy and Public Opinion, 1995* (Chicago: Chicago Council on Foreign Relations, 1995).
[72] See his "Four Japanese Scenarios for the Future," *International Affairs* 65 (Winter 1988–89): 27.
[73] Takashi Inoguchi, "Developments on the Korean Peninsula and Japan's Korea Policy," *Korean Journal of Defense Analysis* 5 (Summer 1993): 34.
[74] Bruce Cumings, "The Seventy Years' Crisis and the Logic of Trilateralism in the New World Order," *World Policy Journal* 8 (Spring 1991), and "Comment," *World Policy Journal* 11 (Spring 1994).

• It is fully capitalist, there no longer being an effective socialist challenge or an alternative socialist common market.
• It has six advanced capitalist economies (the United States, Japan, Germany, the United Kingdom, France, and Italy) that are reasonably prosperous and cooperative, and that have no compelling *revanchist* grievances (unlike Germany at the end of World War I).[75]
• The main threat to the system, the cold war, is over; the bipolar system has been replaced by the prospect of a truly plural world politics.
• A divided Europe and a divided Germany, both outcomes of the 1945 settlement and representing the greatest threat to peace throughout the cold war, are now reunited (or are reuniting).
• The system has a United Nations that is fully inclusive and that is supported by the United States and Russia, and that in August 1990 successfully implemented a collective security response to Iraq's aggression, and has followed that up with less effective but no less collective responses to disorder in Somalia, civil war in Bosnia, and the threat of nuclear arms proliferation in North Korea.
• The Third World is fully decolonized, a process also set in motion by the end of World War I and greatly hastened by World War II, and has widely if not completely realized the principle of self-determination.

If we now look at the domestic scene, inside the nations that make up the world system, we find much to encourage us. All the advanced industrial states are democracies, Western Europe before World War I, in Eastern Europe after World War I, or in many other places throughout the world in the 1930s. The conflicts between capital and labor are by and large contained within established systems and mechanisms for negotiation and accommodation, especially when contrasted to the class struggles that erupted prior to World War II. The ideological divides are shallow compared to those before World War II; today's Left cannot but accommodate to capital and today's Right cannot but accommodate to social welfare entitlements. In all the advanced industrial countries (but especially in Western Europe),[76] well-organized people's movements of various types condition and constrain state power; and the ongoing technological rev-

---

[75] Readers may wonder why Russia is not listed here. The reasons are given in Vladislav M. Zubok, "Russia: Between Peace and Conflict," in Sorenson and Holm, *Whose World Order?* p. 164, where Zubok argues that Russia has probably already sunk into the semiperiphery of the world economy.

[76] This point is emphasized by Mary Kaldor, who argues that people's movements in Western and Eastern Europe were essential in bringing down the Iron Curtain and ending the cold war. See "After the Cold War," *New Left Review*, no. 180 (March–April 1990): 25–40.

olution in communications has made each domestic economy acutely aware of its interdependence with every other economy, especially in the round-the-clock global stock market.

Seven decades ago, after the terrible bloodletting of "the war to end all wars," Woodrow Wilson and V. I. Lenin offered competing models for a new world system that nonetheless had much in common: both held to an internationalist vision, to opposition to Old World imperialism, and to self-determination for colonial peoples. Today Bill Clinton, John Major, Helmut Kohl, Ryutaro Hashimoto, and even Boris Yeltsin do not compete so much as unite on principles of internationalism, collective security, open systems, and a world under law—the last being the personification of the unfulfilled vision of Wilsonian idealism.

Like the long peace of the nineteenth century, today we also find several great powers of roughly equivalent weight, with a stronger interest in creating wealth than in accumulating power. It is remarkable that in 1993 Britain, France, and Italy all had economies hovering around a $1 trillion GNP; allegedly gargantuan Germany was at $1.7 trillion.[77] Over time Germany may come to dominate its historic terrain in Eastern Europe, but it will have many competitors: American, British, French and Italian investors, not to mention Japanese and South Korean. In other words it is unlikely that one nation will have its way in Europe, given that the other industrial economies, whether alone or in concert, are also formidable.

The domestic social configuration in the advanced industrial countries is also vastly different from that of the prewar period. The very idiosyncrasies through which the "withdrawals" from the world system of the 1930s were defined and by which fascist and communist revolutions were detonated in several explosive domestic configurations[78] no longer exist. These idiosyncrasies had their origin in the different social formations that prevailed in the various countries, and if Western Europe's ultimate trajectory was liberal, that was not clear until 1945.[79] Until that time liberal progressivism had to contend with romantic reaction on the right and social revolution on the left, both of them anti-market; out of this collision came Nazi Germany and militarist Japan. The Second World War finished off this conjuncture, however, leaving universal bourgeois democracy in Western Europe. Liberal hegemony had been realized, and the revolutionary prospect slowly faded away. I cite this analysis also to suggest why the "dis-

---

[77] Figures from Betts, "Wealth, Power, and Instability."

[78] Karl Polanyi, *The Great Transformation* (Boston: Beacon Books, 1944), p. 133.

[79] See Perry Anderson, "Modernity and Revolution," *New Left Review*, no. 144 (March–April 1984): 96–113.

course of eternal mistrust [of Japan and Germany]" is likely to fade: they have had their democratic revolutions, even if it took World War II to get them.

Realists, as we have just seen, have been quick to argue that "West-West" conflicts would quickly replace the East-West conflict,[80] and others worry that Germany and Japan have not fully learned the lessons of their defeat in World War II,[81] or that rivalry among capitalists will only be deepened by the end of the cold war, or that a "reemergent threat" will take over Russia. As of 1996, however, we can say that West-West conflict has not deepened since 1989; rather it has lessened. Germany and Japan have given little evidence that their postwar democratic revolutions are in jeopardy; the neo-Right in Germany is more worrisome than anything that has happened in Japan, however, where the cold war structure of conservative political rule collapsed in 1993, thus deepening Japan's democratic commitments and even bringing the eternally oppositional socialists to power (whereupon they jettisoned their socialism, which makes my point about a Left that cannot but accommodate). In short, a "realistic" comparison of our 1990s world with that of the past seven decades illustrates why cooperation among the advanced capitalist countries is predictable, at least for the near term of the next decade or two. (One critic of an earlier draft suggested that by saying this I moved from a "structural" to a "liberal" analysis; my argument is that changes in the structure of the world system since 1989–91 have produced a world that corresponds to the one liberals going back to Woodrow Wilson have always wanted to see, and that today global capitalism has an interest in peace as strong as or stronger than it did in the nineteenth century. These two factors combined finally make possible something that looks like a liberal world order.[82]

---

[80] Above all John Mearsheimer, in his widely cited "Back to the Future: Instability in Europe After the Cold War," *International Security* 15 (Summer 1990): 5–36.

[81] Preeminently Karel van Wolferen, whose *Enigma of Japanese Power* (New York: Alfred A. Knopf, 1989) not only revives prewar stereotypes about Japan and sees no watershed changes after World War II, but who uses the words "German" and "Nazi" interchangeably. The best scholarship on Germany, however, argues that Germans have learned the lessons of the European civil war and not only wish to live comfortably within a plural and diverse Europe, but to have a political system structured to yield that outcome. Peter Katzenstein terms the Federal Republic a "semisovereign state," penetrated by NATO security mechanisms, "deeply enmeshed" in multilateral economic institutions like the European Community, and unyielding to reactionary attempts to rekindle a strong nationalism. It is "semisovereign" at home as well, through a political system that is remarkably decentralized and thoroughly democratized. Peter J. Katzenstein, *Policy and Politics in West Germany: The Growth of a Semisovereign State* (Philadelphia: Temple University Press, 1987), pp. 9–10, 15–23, 371–85.

[82] Of course, one who has not read and understood Polanyi's *Great Transformation* will be able to grasp neither what I am saying about the late twentieth century, nor what he argued about

Realists have also argued that the world economy would separate into three great regional blocs, and even in 1994 it was still not unusual to hear analysts assert the continuing tripartite breakup of the world economy.[83] But much of this commentary dissipated when Europe's "1992" turned out to be merely 1992; the European Community was never likely to be a regional economy to put the rest of the world in the shade anyway and thus stir regional counteraction elsewhere. Furthermore, this community will be no larger (and probably smaller) than the combined markets of North America and the middle and laboring classes of Latin America, or the Pacific community embracing Northeast Asia, capitalist-connected regions of China, the ASEAN countries, and Australia.[84] Movement toward enhanced integration has continued in Europe, of course, but with the late-1993 GATT agreements, there is little to suggest that the EC will cut itself off from non-European markets. All three great markets are, will be, and will strive to continue to be interdependent with one another. Of course, the United States and Japan do tower over other industrial economies in their respective regions. Japan has a GDP of $3.5 trillion, compared to South Korea's nearly $350 billion (three-fourths the size of Spain's). No economy in the Americas comes close to the nearly $7 trillion of the United States. Nevertheless, the U.S. market is still so essential to Japan that cooperation is much more likely than conflict and the emergence of regional blocs.

This is the essence of my argument about West-West cooperation in the post–cold war era. All we have so far in the way of evidence, of course, is the history of the years since the "revolutions of 1989," but that history bears out the virtue of my position, and that of Peter Katzenstein and other scholars who peer inside the "black box" of the nation—which hardly can be said for the predictions of the hard-nosed realists.

Japan and its neighbors in Northeast Asia (mainly Korea and Taiwan) have nested for most of this century in a Western hegemonic regime and are nowhere near the self-definition and comprehensive autonomy that local

---

the nineteenth. I might add that there are more ways of thinking about the world than the American discourse on "realism" versus "idealism."

[83] Thus Aaron Friedberg begins his recent article with the assertion that "the dominant trend in world politics today is toward regionalization rather than globalization," somehow forgetting to offer evidence supporting his assertion in the rest of the article. See Friedberg, "Ripe for Rivalry," p. 5.

[84] The *Far Eastern Economic Review* has estimated this Pacific community of consumers also at around 330 million, and that does not include the 150 to 200 million consumers capable of consumer-durable purchases in coastal and urban China.

nationalists have long sought. How long this regime will last is not "any-body's guess," but will depend on when the United States truly enters its period of hegemonic decline and when, accordingly, Japan escapes from the postwar settlement. Both are, in other words, questions for the next century.

In the mid-1990s this is not necessarily descriptive of how East Asia sees itself. In Japan, South Korea, and now China, it is not hard to find a mirror image of American triumphalism, with many commentators dismissing the United States as yesterday's problem: a declining power, a decrepit econ-omy, a mass culture that cannot compare to the heritage of East Asian civilization. China in particular chose to confront the United States on several issues in the mid-1990s, beginning with the glimmering possibility that Taiwan might once again gain substantial U.S. and international rec-ognition. The current Chinese regime, however, is every bit as ham-handed, brittle, and badly led an authoritarian system as that of Park Chung Hee in the 1970s; mistaking a newfound economic strength for real weight, it overplays its hand at almost every opportunity. The over-whelming influence on China is not its current political regime or its 1990s growth spurt, but the dramatic undertow and gravity of a world capitalist system finally getting its way in this vast and legendary market. Japan is far closer to hegemonic transition than China, and for many years to come will remain the most important factor in East Asia.

Still, the regime of technology may soon be cresting in Japan, but it hasn't yet, and this is but one transnational regime: otherwise, Japan re-mains weak. If the archipelago of U.S. military bases in Northeast Asia appears in the 1990s to have the classic attribute of the Schumpeterian definition of imperialism as an atavism, that is an illusion caused by our former fixation with containing communism. The Pentagon and its bases may indeed be Schumpeter's perpetual motion machine, but they do have a function and it is not new: containing Japan. American liberals may get sunspots when they gaze upon Japan and the United States may be on the cusp of hegemonic decline, but it is the only hegemonic power also to have been a continental economy and it only fully completed its national market with the industrialization of the Western states in World War II. From that standpoint, 1941 may indeed have been the beginning of the American Century (as Henry Luce had it), and American industry may still be driving Americans "from the rising to the setting sun," in John Fiske's words.[85] The sun that sets in the Seattle of Microsoft and Boeing rises in Japan's east, and a restless America is still there on the horizon just as it was in 1853.

[85] Drinnon, *Facing West*, pp. 241, 315–18.

5

Japan and Southeast Asia

TAKASHI SHIRAISHI

What is Japan's position in Southeast Asia in this post-cold war era? This question seems simple at first glance. Since the mid-1980s, Southeast Asia's largest investor, largest exporter, largest foreign aid donor, largest buyer of raw materials such as oil, natural gas, and timber, and largest source of tourism has been Japan. As T. J. Pempel aptly puts it, Japan is Gulliver in a region of Lilliputs. But what is happening in this region of Lilliputs, what is this Gulliver doing and intending to do there?

Several recent articles in the U.S. popular press have argued that a "kinder, gentler co-prosperity sphere," in Steven Schlossstein's words, is now in the making in East and Southeast Asia, though for obvious reasons hardly anyone claims that Co-Prosperity Part 2 will be a Japan-centered, self-sustaining, autarchic Asian economic bloc.[1] As Kent Calder rightly

---

[1] Steven Schlossstein, *Asia's New Little Dragons: The Dynamic Emergence of Indonesia, Thailand, and Malaysia* (Chicago: Contemporary Books, 1991), p. 22. For journalistic reporting on "Co-Prosperity Sphere Part 2," see, for instance, "Sayonara, America," *Newsweek*, August 5, 1991, pp. 16–17; David E. Sanger, "Power of the Yen Winning Asia: New 'Co-Prosperity' Is Displacing the U.S.," *New York Times*, December 5, 1991, D1 and D22; and *Japan in Asia*, ed. Nigel Holloway (Hong Kong: Far Eastern Economic Review, 1993). U.S. diplomatic historians working on the 1940s and the 1950s also tend to play with this "Co-Prosperity Sphere" theme less cautiously. See William S. Borden, *The Pacific Alliance: U.S. Foreign Economic Policy and Japanese Trade Recovery, 1947–1955* (Madison: University of Wisconsin Press, 1984); Michael Schaller, *The American Occupation of Japan: The Origins of the Cold War in Asia* (New York: Oxford University Press, 1985); and Andrew J. Rotter, *The Path to Vietnam: Origins of the American Commitment to Southeast Asia* (Ithaca: Cornell University Press, 1987). But see Sayuri Shimizu's excellent dissertation, "Creating People of Plenty: The United States and Japan's Economic Alternatives, 1953–1958" (Department of History, Cornell University, 1991), for a useful antidote.

points out, non-Japanese, including Americans, are investing aggressively in the region. Collectively, since the late 1980s investment from the newly industrialized economies (NIEs), South Korea, Taiwan, Hong Kong, and Singapore, has been larger than Japanese investment. The current Asian economic dynamism is crucially dependent on the U.S. market, even though intra-regional trade has been growing more rapidly and is now larger than trade across the Pacific. No East or Southeast Asian country wants to see Japanese dominance in the region. And Japanese are too divided among themselves to dominate the region politically, or even to present a common front economically.[2]

If it is not a self-sustaining, Japan-centered autarchic economic bloc that is in the making in East and Southeast Asia, what is happening? How are we to understand the current Asian regionalism? Is it, as Calder put it, "the kind of pluralistic constellation of economic forces most consistent with stable interdependence"?[3] Or should we see, as James Fallows does, "a practical reality," in which "as a political version of the phototropism that keeps growing plants directed toward the sun—most countries on the East Asian arc are redirecting their plans toward a future in which Japan is the center of technology, money, and ideas about how to succeed"—in short, the rise of the new East Asian economic and political system?[4]

My understanding is closer to Calder's, but I am more interested in the historical evolution of Japan's presence in Southeast Asia than in its present character. The current Japanese position in Southeast Asia has evolved from its postwar return to the region in a developmental state mode. But it cannot be understood in terms of its developmental state mode, let alone its more distant Greater East Asian Co-Prosperity Sphere past. Japan is not the light of Asia, and however much Japanese chauvinists such as Shintaro Ishihara would love to see it become such, that is a role that Japan cannot pull off. To make this point, two ghosts must be put to rest: the wartime Co-Prosperity Sphere and the postwar developmental state.

To perform this double exorcism, we must keep in mind Japan's position in the region's hegemonic structure. Japan has historically operated in a regional hegemonic system not of its own making, maneuvered to exploit it to its own advantage, and attempted to test and extend outer limits imposed on it whenever an opportunity offered itself. Up to the mid-nineteenth century, the regional hegemonic structure in place was Sino-

---

[2] Kent E. Calder, *Japan's Changing Role in Asia: Emerging Co-Prosperity?* (New York: Japan Society, 1991), pp. 11–13. See also James Fallows, *Looking at the Sun: The Rise of the New East Asian Economic and Political System* (New York: Pantheon, 1994), pp. 247–49.

[3] Calder, *Japan's Changing Role in Asia*, p. 11.

[4] Fallows, *Looking at the Sun*, p. 249.

centric, as Takeshi Hamashita argues, and Tokugawa Japan's answer to the Ch'ing-dominated system of suzerainty was to close its ports and become a smaller-scale middle kingdom. Since the late nineteenth century, as Bruce Cumings tells us, the Anglo-American-dominated Westphalian international system has replaced the Sinocentric world, if not in inland China, certainly in maritime Asia. This development was a blessing in disguise for Japan. It looked threatening initially, but it allowed Japan to detach itself from the Sinocentric world and to become an "equal" with China. Japan then exploited the British-led collective, informal imperialist system in China to its fullest in the first quarter of the twentieth century in its empire building. In the cold war era when the Japanese empire was dismantled and China went communist, U.S. hegemony replaced British informal empire in Asia. Japan again exploited this new U.S. hegemonic system to achieve economic prosperity and social peace. The only fatal mistake Japan has made in modern times, which led to the collapse of its empire, was in the 1930s and the first half of the 1940s when the British-dominated, informal collective, imperialism in China was in a systemic crisis and Japan went continental into Manchuria and China south of the Great Wall and then tried to become the regional hegemon and create a new international order in Asia. Japan's strategic visions that informed the wartime Co-Prosperity Sphere and the postwar "economic cooperation" with Southeast Asia need to be examined in this structural context, that is, whether they challenge or conform to the hegemonic structure in which Japan found itself.

Another point that needs to be kept in mind is the significance of Southeast Asia, *nanyo* or *nanpo* in prewar Japanese parlance and *Tonan Ajia* in postwar, for Japan. The region has repeatedly figured as a "solution" for Japan in crisis. It appeared to offer a way out of the mess Japan found itself in in China toward the end of the 1930s. It seemed to offer a solution for Japan's economic recovery when China was closed in the 1950s and 1960s. And the region is again seen in Japan as a way out of the current predicament, the enormous appreciation of the yen since 1985, which has threatened Japan's international competitiveness and hence its politics of economic growth. Whether Southeast Asia was or is a solution to Japan's predicament is a question that needs to be looked at, but it is important to note at the outset that Southeast Asia has historically figured as an arena for Japan to define its position vis-à-vis the hegemonic structure, maneuver to exploit it to its advantage, and test and extend the outer limits imposed on it. It is in this perspective that I examine Japan's postwar Southeast Asia policy here to show that Japan's current policy can best be understood in terms of the extension of its postwar politics of productivity into Southeast Asia in the name of economic cooperation.

The Greater East Asia Co-Prosperity Sphere

Let us start with examining Japan's prewar and wartime past. We do not need to dwell for long on the Greater East Asia Co-Prosperity Sphere except to note that it was originally conceived as the East Asia Co-Prosperity Sphere (*Toa Kyoei Ken*, that is, without "Greater") in the early 1930s to answer two major strategic questions then confronting the Japanese empire.

One question derived from the lesson Japanese army officers drew from the Great European War that the next world war would be total: how to create a self-sufficient, self-sustaining, autarchic economic bloc out of Japan (which in prewar years included Korea, Taiwan, and Southern Sakhalin) and Manchuria and to make Japan "Asia's America"? Colonel Kanji Ishiwara, essentially the "creator" of Japanese-dominated Manchukuo, believed and most forcefully promoted his belief that the final war would be fought between Japan and the Anglo-Saxons.[5]

The other, more pressing question was the "China problem." As Peter Duus persuasively argues, modern Sino-Japanese relations developed within the context of "the unequal treaty system."[6] Japan did very well in this system, and on the eve of the Manchurian incident in 1931 it had displaced Britain as the paramount foreign economic power in China by almost every measure. By that time, however, the system was in crisis, because it had become the target of increasingly powerful Chinese nationalism.

The British showed a willingness to accept the slow demise of the system, but the Japanese had a great more to lose. After the assassination of Chang Tso-lin in 1928 a new political coalition of forces advocating a "strong" China policy took shape. To overcome the fundamental caution of the Tokyo government, the Kwantung Army forced its hands by precipitating the Manchurian incident. Their objective was to prevent the spread of Chinese anti-imperialism north of the Great Wall. Their concern was not to maintain the informal empire but to consolidate Japanese assets and protect Japanese strategic interests in northeastern China as a hedge against a collapse of the collaborative structure in China proper.

The establishment of Manchukuo—neither a formal colony nor a sphere of influence, but a separate state under Chinese leaders who took

---

[5] See Shin'ichi Yamamuro, *Kimera: Manshukoku no Shozo* [Chimera: A portrait of Manchukuo] (Tokyo: Chuo-Koron-sha, 1993), especially chap. 2.

[6] Peter Duus, "Introduction: Japan's Informal Empire in China, 1895–1937: An Overview," in *The Japanese Informal Empire in China, 1895–1937*, ed. Peter Duus, Ramon H. Myers, and Mark R. Peattie (Princeton: Princeton University Press, 1989), pp. xi–xxix. The following argument on the "China problem" is entirely based on his essay.

their orders from Japanese army officers and civilian officials—was the answer to these questions.[7] But there were internal contradictions in this strategic vision. It was extremely expensive in both financial and human capital. It made Japan the target of anti-imperialist Chinese nationalism, which drew Japan into a wider, far more costly war in China proper. And it set in motion a process that ended in the collapse of the collective informal empire, which put Japan in direct conflict with the U.S. Open Door Policy, while making it more dependent on the United States and Britain for raw materials, especially scrap iron and oil, needed for the creation of an autarchic sphere.

As Victor Koschmann points out in Chapter 2, Southeast Asia was outside the original scope of the East Asia Co-Prosperity sphere, not only because the region was then under European and U.S. colonial domination, but also because the region simply did not belong to the historical tradition Japanese Pan-Asianist ideologues had invoked in the 1930s to justify the East Asia Co-Prosperity Sphere. In fact, while "East," *toyo*, was as ideologically and emotionally charged a term as its antonym, "West," *seiyo*, "South," *nanyo* or *nampo*, had hardly any ideological significance in the prewar Japanese political language. Nor were Japanese interests in colonial Southeast Asia of any imperial concern. But the South was known to be rich in natural resources (oil, iron, tin, rubber, sugar, rice, and so on) and populated by docile "natives" exploited by Europeans and overseas Chinese. The only way to avoid giving in to Chinese nationalism, the Anglo-Saxon powers, and the loss of its imperial possessions in China thus seemed to be to move south, to take over the Dutch East Indies, rich in natural resources, above all in oil, and to make the empire self-sufficient and self-sustaining. Hence "Greater" was added to "East Asia Co-Prosperity Sphere" in 1939, when the French were defeated by the Germans, and Japan eventually made the decision to take the South to "save" the now bankrupt strategic vision that had initially informed the establishment of Manchukuo.[8]

---

[7] See Duus's insightful observation that Manchukuo closely resembled the satellite states that Soviet imperialism created in Eastern Europe after the war. Ibid., p. xxviii.

[8] For the Greater East Asia Co-Prosperity Sphere, see Takafusa Nakamura, *Showa-shi I* [History of Showa I] (Tokyo: Toyo Keizai Shinpo-sha, 1993), chap. 3, and *Showa Keizai-shi* [Economic history of Showa] (Tokyo: Iwanami Shoten, 1986), chaps. 3 and 4; Hideo Kobayashi, *Dai Toa Kyoei Ken no Keisei to Hokai* [The formation and collapse of the Greater East Asia Co-Prosperity Sphere] (Tokyo: Ochanomizu Shobo, 1975); and W. G. Beasley, *Japanese Imperialism, 1894-1945* (New York: Oxford University Press, 1987). Given that Japan was confronted with anti-imperialist, anti-Japanese Chinese nationalism in China and Southeast Asia, one might as well wonder whether Japanese occupation authorities sought to foster a variant of ethnic nationalism in Southeast Asia during the war, promoting "native" interests against the Chinese, and cite as evidence mass killings of Chinese in Malaya and Singapore and the mobi-

It was the decision to stake the fate of the Japanese empire on a gamble. Confronted with the U.S. trade embargo, the Japanese government took a hard look at the resource situation in October 1941. Japan then had 8.4 million liters of oil, which according to its estimate was enough to sustain Japan's war machine for two years. If Japan succeeded in taking the entire region of Southeast Asia, it would obtain in its estimate a little less than 1 million liters (0.22 million gallons) of oil for the first year, but 2.6 million liters (0.57 million gallons) of oil for the second and 5.3 million liters (1.25 million gallons) of oil for the third year, enough to sustain Japan's war effort.[9] The timing to go to war against the United States and Britain was dictated by this calculation, and when the Japanese military took the entire region in half a year, there was euphoria. But there was fatal miscalculation in this equation. For one thing, the estimate of resource exploitation in Southeast Asia was too optimistic: Japanese corporations running "enemy assets" as war booty in the region never met production targets in oil, rubber, or other resources. It was also estimated in October 1941 that three million tons of ships would be needed for civilian use to transport strategic resources from China and Southeast Asia to Japan. But Japan lost more than four millions tons of ships in 1944, which effectively broke the back of Japan's transportation capability. Japan lost the war in 1944, but fought on for almost another full year without any hope of victory.[10]

The Greater East Asia Co-Prosperity Sphere (*Dai Toa Kyoei Ken*) was thus a phantom vision conjured up in a moment of desperation when the empire was confronted with the bankruptcy of its original strategic vision, which had pushed it to the creation of Manchukuo. The word "Greater" (*Dai*) betrayed its bankruptcy, for in a very real sense it signified the shift in its imperial focus from China (where Japan had long been in a mess) to the South (where it was not yet in a mess) and not confronting anew the two major questions that initially led to "the fifteen-year war" that started in China's northeast.

---

lization of Malays against predominantly Chinese, anti-Japanese guerrillas in Japanese occupied Malaya. But the development of mounting ethnic antagonisms in Malaya between Malays and Chinese in the war years was not due to a conscious Japanese policy but because the Japanese military authority simply inherited the British-created state structure and relied on predominantly Malay administrative officials and police forces (as well as Japanese troops) to fight anti-Japanese Chinese guerrillas. Besides, in many places, including Malaya, there soon developed relations of cozy collusion between Japanese officers and officials, "native" officials, and collaborating Chinese traders.

[9] Nakamura, *Showa Keizai-shi*, pp. 129–131.
[10] Ibid., pp. 129–47.

Postwar Return

A different strategic vision informed Japan's return to Southeast Asia in the postwar era. The fundamental facts of postwar Asia were the dissolution of the Japanese empire, the establishment of the People's Republic of China, and the creation of an informal U.S. empire in "Free Asia." When Japan regained independence in 1952, it did so as a U.S. protégé and under the leadership of an internationalist (that is, non-Asianist), conservative coalition of the state bureaucracy, big business and finance, and conservative politicians, who soon formed the LDP in 1955 and achieved the alliance of steel and rice to the exclusion of the left and organized labor.

In line with U.S. policy to make Japan "the workshop of Asia," the politics of productivity informed the overall strategic vision of the conservative coalition. As Charles Maier put it, it was a politics to transform political issues into problems of output, to adjourn class conflict for a consensus on growth.[11] In postwar Japan, where this politics began in earnest in the mid-1950s, it was predicated, as T. J. Pempel points out, on the conservative, pro-business conception of the national interest. Central in this conception were the twin goals of economic growth and industrial transformation, with MITI as a key mover. Foreign economic policies were integral to this overall growth. Its commercial policy rested on an export strategy demanding reasonably free access to world markets; Japan's monetary policy hinged on a fixed and undervalued exchange rate for the yen; foreign capital, foreign managerial control, and "overly competitive" imports were kept out; foreign technology was actively and successfully acquired; and domestic capital was kept within national boundaries to avoid any adverse impact on the balance of payments.[12] Southeast Asia became a major target for its trade promotion and natural resource procurement. Japan's economic penetration into the region is evidence of its success. And the current anomaly of its position in the region can also be understood in terms of its success, which has resulted in the increasingly vacuous center of "Economic General Staff" Ministry of International Trade and Industry (MITI) under circumstances in which the Japanese state can no longer function as the gatekeeper of the Japanese economy.

[11] Charles S. Maier, "The Politics of Productivity: Foundations of American International Economic Policy after World War II," in *Between Power and Plenty: Foreign Economic Policies of Advanced Industrial States,* ed. Peter J. Katzenstein (Madison: University of Wisconsin Press, 1978), p. 23.
[12] T. J. Pempel, "Japanese Foreign Economic Policy: The Domestic Bases for International Behavior," in Katzenstein, *Between Power and Plenty,* pp. 139–90.

How then *did* Japan come back to Southeast Asia? Japan no doubt benefited enormously from the U.S. policy to use Japan as a dynamo of wider regional recovery in Free Asia, rebuilding Japan as the workshop in Asia and restoring its economic ties with primary producing areas in the region.[13] But the price was also high, or so it seemed then, because being a U.S. satellite, Japan established diplomatic relations with Taiwan and supported the U.S. containment policy against China, effectively giving up its access to the mainland, one of its two most important prewar markets.[14] Throughout the 1950s and 1960s, China remained closed, and Sino-Japanese trade remained insignificant. For the ruling conservative coalition this development destroyed any real charm of Asianist thinking (for the left it was another story), while Japan established its beachheads in Southeast Asia in the same years. Nothing shows this point more clearly than the emergence of simultaneously "pro-American" and "Asianist" Nobusuke Kishi, who was a leading "reformist" bureaucrat in the early days of the ministry of commerce and industry, one-time chief of Manchurian industrialization in the 1930s, Hideki Tojo's minister of commerce and industry, and a war criminal, and as prime minister in the late 1950s most instrumental in Japan's comeback in Southeast Asia. In postwar Kishi, internationalism ("pro-Americanism") and Asianism, anticommunism and Japanese commercialism, coexisted in happy harmony.[15]

China's closure also meant that the Asia Japan returned to was America's Asia. Without access to China, Japan in the 1950s was utterly dependent on the United States not only for its security but also for its economic survival. Japan could make up its dollar gap with the United States only with its special procurement that is the American purchase of Japanese goods and services in Japan for the U.S. military.[16] Japan sought a way out of this confining role by concluding war reparations agreements and normalizing diplomatic relations with the countries of Southeast Asia in order to regain access to their markets and natural resources. Washington encouraged this move, because this would promote Japanese economic recovery, eventually reduce Japan's dependence on the United States, and

---

[13] Borden, *Pacific Alliance*, p. 10.

[14] Japan's trade with China amounted to 20.0 percent of its total trade in 1926–30 and 18.4 percent in 1931–36, while it amounted only to 1.3 percent in the period from 1951 to 1960. See The Bank of Japan, Statistics Department, *Hundred-Year Statistics of the Japanese Economy* (Tokyo: Bank of Japan, n.d.).

[15] For Kishi, see Yoshihisa Hara, *Kishi Nobusuke: Kensei no Seijika* [Kishi Nobusuke: A politician of hegemonic power] (Tokyo: Iwanami Shoten, Iwanami Shinsho 368, 1995).

[16] For the importance of U.S. special procurement, see Takafusa Nakamura, *Showa-shi II* [History of Showa II] (Tokyo: Toyo Keizai Shinpo-sha, 1993), chaps. 5 and 6.

make Japan "the workshop in Asia" as it envisioned as early as the late 1940s.

Yet Japan's return to Southeast Asia was not easy and its immediate benefit ambiguous, even with U.S. encouragement and patronage. Prime Minister Shigeru Yoshida, who was most instrumental in setting Japan's postwar trading state strategy, was not at all convinced of the importance of Southeast Asia. When he met with Secretary of State John Foster Dulles in Washington in 1954, Dulles suggested that the reparations agreements should be regarded as an investment for future good will and trade relations. In response, Yoshida asked whether the U.S. government might guarantee the reparations settlement so that "in case they proved too great a burden for the Japanese economy the claimants could be paid."[17] Yet even after this exchange, Yoshida remarked, in the wake of his visit to Southeast Asia in late 1954, that Japan should trade with "rich men, not beggars."[18]

It was Kishi (prime minister from 1957 to 1960) who set the basic pattern for Japan's return to Southeast Asia. Kishi knew that in Southeast Asia Japan could pursue an "independent" diplomacy and play "the leader of Asia" without deviating from the U.S. policy of rebuilding Japan as the workshop in Asia. He also understood well the long-term importance of regaining economic access to the region. And he knew there were ways to obtain direct and immediate benefit to Japanese business and himself. The ways he found were "reparations" and aid, which came in the form of export credits, tied loans, plant exports, and long-term, above all oil-related, investment projects.

MITI's 1958 White Paper spelled out the two objectives of economic cooperation: the establishment of stable markets for Japanese goods and the securing of reliable sources of raw materials. In the same year Ministry of Foreign Affairs (MOFA), MITI, and Ministry of Finance (MOF) established subdivisions in charge of overseeing and promoting economic cooperation activities. The Asian Economic Research Institute (Ajia Keizai Kenkyusho, the Institute of Developing Economies) was founded by MITI. In 1958 Kishi also placed 5 billion yen, $13.9 million, in the Export-Import Bank, specifically earmarked for economic cooperation with South and Southeast Asia, which evolved into an Overseas Economic Cooperation Fund (OECF) in 1961. This grew out of his proposal for a Southeast Asia

---

[17] Shimizu, "Creating People of Plenty," p. 306. Dulles sensibly reminded Yoshida that his suggestion would not be "either in the Japanese interest or in ours" and that if "all those countries with claims against Japan thought that we would guarantee Japanese payment, their claims would skyrocket."

[18] Borden, *Pacific Alliance*, p. 214.

Development Fund. Its original idea was that the United States would contribute the capital, U.S. $300 million, the Japanese the personnel and the
skills, and the Southeast Asians the resources. But the U.S. government
was understandably unenthusiastic, for the Eisenhower administration
knew well that "Japanese self-interest will fully take care of that."[19]

As this episode suggests, what was important was not U.S. funding but
U.S. support and encouragement for Japan's economic cooperation with
Southeast Asia, which made it possible for Japan to play "the leader of
Asia" within the outer limits set by the U.S. hegemony in Asia. "Free Asia"
in this sense constituted the region to which Japan was to return, the
region sustained by the U.S.-Japan security treaty and US military commitments in the region with its bases in the Philippines, Thailand, and
South Vietnam. It is no surprise, then, that Kishi could happily be internationalist (pro-American) and Asianist simultaneously, because his "independent" Southeast Asian diplomacy was fully anchored in the U.S.
scheme of triangular relations between the United States, Japan, and
Southeast Asia.

Thus started Japan's economic cooperation with Southeast Asia. Reparations and economic aid provided Japan with access to needed raw materials in the region and export markets for Japanese products. Export
credits, tied commodity loans, plant exports, and long-term investment
credits were of direct and immediate benefit to Japanese business. Equally
important, they benefited a variety of individual politicians and businessmen on both sides of the reparations and aid negotiations. Old Asia hands
who had forged close personal ties with Southeast Asian politicians during
the war returned to the region as trading company executives, brokers,
and fixers. Personal ties and networks started to grow, knitting together
politicians from the Liberal Democratic Party (LDP), Japanese business
leaders, Southeast Asian politicians, and their business associates with wartime officers and officials as intermediaries.

Thanks to Masashi Nishihara's research, we now know the nature of
personal networks that started to evolve in Japan-Indonesia relations in the
late 1950s and early 1960s. The kingpins were Kishi, Shojiro Kawashima
(LDP secretary general under Prime Minister Eisaku Sato, Kishi's brother,
whom Dewi Sukarno called "papa"), and Sukarno, but the network also
included Japan's top business leaders, trade offices in Jakarta (which grew
from sixteen in 1958 to sixty in 1965), wartime officers and officials, brokers, and Indonesian politicians in Sukarno's inner circle. The North Su-

---

[19] Shimizu, "Creating People of Plenty," p. 341. See also J. Alexander Caldwell, "The Evolution of Japanese Economic Cooperation, 1950–1970," in *The Pacific Basin Development: American Interests*, ed. Harold B. Malmgren (Lexington, Mass: Lexington Books, 1972).

matra Oil Development Cooperation Company (NOSODECO), a child of the Japan-Indonesian oil lobby and established in 1960 with OECF loans, for instance, included ex-bureaucrats from MITI and MOF, business representatives from Mitsui and Mitsubishi, and an "Indonesian expert," who as head of its Jakarta office acted as a troubleshooter thanks to his excellent connections with Indonesian politicians such as minister of basic industries Chairul Saleh and minister of trade Adam Malik.[20]

This was the beginning of Japan's postwar economic penetration into Southeast Asia. The key word was "economic cooperation," which meant trade promotion and resources procurement. MITI was in charge of it. (It started its white paper on economic cooperation in 1958, whereas it was not until the early 1970s that MOFA started its own white paper on official development aid.) Institutions were created—the Overseas Economic Cooperation Fund (OECF, created in 1961), the Overseas Technical Cooperation Agency (the future JICA, created in 1962), and the Institute of Developing Economies. The close cooperation between government and the private financial and commercial sectors was the hallmark of economic cooperation. Reparations were combined with soft loans, both private and official. Transnational politico-business alliances were forged among LDP politicians (with Kishi naturally as the central figure), Japanese business leaders, and Southeast Asian politicians (Sukarno in Indonesia, Jose P. Laurel in the Philippines, U Nu in Burma), and their business associates, with Japanese trading firms as intermediaries to integrate and expand those networks.

Postwar Relations between Japan and Southeast Asia

With the relative decline of the United States as the hegemonic power in Asia and the emergence of Japan as an economic powerhouse, Japan's position in Southeast Asia naturally underwent significant changes from the mid-1960s to the mid-1980s. But it is important to note at the outset that these changes can best be understood in evolutionary terms, because the basic pattern as well as the basic thinking that informed Japan's Southeast Asia policy remained more or less in place well into the 1980s.

First of all, although the twin goals of trade promotion and resources procument remained crucial for Japan's economic cooperation with Southeast Asia, the Japanese government was well aware that the Asia to which Japan had returned was America's Asia, and therefore, not surpris-

---

[20] Masashi Nishihara, *The Japanese and Sukarno's Indonesia: Tokyo-Jakarta Relations, 1951–1966* (Honolulu: University Press of Hawaii, 1975), pp. 120–21.

ingly but certainly with U.S. prodding, it made "burden-sharing" for the maintenance of "Free Asia" a major component of its foreign policy in the mid-1960s. Or to put it more precisely, the Japanese government geared itself to promoting trade and procuring resources while placating the U.S. demand for burden-sharing.

This is clearly seen in Japan's aid policy. In the 1950s and early 1960s, Japan provided reparations and economic aid to each Southeast Asian country bilaterally for trade promotion and resources procurement. By the mid-1960s, however, Japan had emerged as an economic "power," thanks to its high economic growth and its steady balance of payment surplus. With the Americanization of the war in Vietnam, the United States called on Japan for burden-sharing. The return of Okinawa was the top priority for Prime Minister Sato, and proving that Japan was a loyal and reliable ally was crucial to achieving this goal. But the war in Vietnam was a divisive issue in Japan. Sato thus did whatever he could in the name of burden-sharing in Southeast Asia short of direct military involvement in the war. The government hosted the first meeting of the Ministerial Conference for the Economic Development of Southeast Asia in 1966. Shortly thereafter, it pledged U.S. $30 million to Suharto's Indonesia for its economic recovery effort and provided Indonesia with one-fourth of its foreign aid from 1967 through 1970 and one-third of nonfood aid in the first half of the 1970s, all within the multilateral framework of the IGGI (Inter-Governmental Group for Indonesia). Japan also took the initiative in the creation of the Asian Development Bank, which was established in 1966 with 25 percent of its initial capital provided by the United States and another 25 percent by Japan. Japanese aid to Thailand, Cambodia, Laos, and South Vietnam also started in the late 1960s, and South Vietnam became the sixth-largest recipient of Japanese aid for the period from 1970 to 1974.[21]

Nor did burden-sharing come to an end with the "fall" of Saigon. In the wake of the Vietnamese invasion of Cambodia in 1978, Japanese aid to Thailand increased substantially in part because of its status as a frontline state, making it the third-largest recipient of Japanese aid between 1980 and 1988. More recently, Japanese aid to the Philippines rose dramatically after the 1986 revolution, not only to support the government under President Corazon Aquino, but as the timing of its aid approvals suggests, to pressure her government to agree to the retention of U.S.

---

[21] For the increase in Japanese aid to Southeast Asia as part of the bargain for the return of Okinawa, see Kei Wakaizumi's informative memoir, *Tasaku nakarishiwo shinzemu to hossu* [I want to believe there were no other ways] (Tokyo: Bungei-Shunju-sha, 1994). See Tsusho-sangyo-sho, *Keizai Kyoryoku no Genjo to Mondai-ten* [The current state and problems of economic cooperation] (Tokyo: Tsusho-sangyo-sho, various issues).

bases in the Philippines.[22] The burden-sharing ("Japan needs to make contributions appropriate to its standing in the world economy") has thus become an important and enduring component of Japan's Southeast Asia policy (as well as its aid policy) since the mid-1960s and has established Japan as a junior alliance partner with the United States in Asia and in the world.

This, however, does not mean that Japan consistently played the role as loyal, junior partner to the United States thoughout these years. There was a crisis in the early 1970s, when many assumptions on which Japan's politics of productivity was predicated were seriously questioned because of a series of "shocks." The first shock was President Nixon's Guam Doctrine in 1969 (which stated that the United States would look to its allies to take the primary burden in dealing with internal insurgencies). This was followed by the announcement of his coming visit to China in July 1971 (of which Washington informed Prime Minister Sato one hour before its official announcement); the announcement of his new economic initiatives in August 1971, which let the dollar float in international exchange and led to substantial appreciation of the yen in 1971 and 1972; the first oil crisis in late 1973; the 1973 Paris Peace Agreements, which ended U.S. military intervention in Vietnam; and finally the "fall" of the Lon Nol government in Cambodia and the Thieu government in South Vietnam in 1975.

The announcement of Nixon's visit to China undermined the most important assumption of Japan's postwar Asia policy: the closure of China. Succeeding Sato as prime minister in 1972, Kakuei Tanaka immediately seized this opportunity, overrode the opposition of MOFA officials and pro-Taiwanese LDP politicians (led by Kishi), and normalized Japan's diplomatic relationship with China. Yet all the same, that stable regional vision of Free Asia which Japan had entertained for so long was no longer stable, and with the "fall" of Saigon in 1975 and the U.S. military withdrawal from mainland Southeast Asia, it became clear that Free Asia had lost much of its meaning.

The appreciation of the yen also deprived Japan of its sense of stability in the world economy. While Nixon's decision to float the dollar in international exchange led European monetary authorities to embark on the creation of a zone of monetary stability, the Japanese government in the same years lifted its control over Japanese overseas investment and let

[22] See Juichi Inada, "ODA to Nihon Gaiko: Tai Filipin Enjo ni tsuite no Jirei Kenkyu," [ODA and Japan's diplomacy: A case study on aid to the Philippines] in *Nihon no ODA to Kokusai Chitsujo* [Japan's ODA and the international order], ed. Takeshi Igarashi (Tokyo: Nihon Kokusai Mondai Kenkyu-sho, 1990).

individual Japanese firms move into Southeast Asia. By that time, Southeast Asian countries, above all Indonesia, Malaysia, the Philippines, and Thailand had already embarked on import-substitution industrialization. Japanese investments in these countries grew enormously. To retain access to their protected markets, Japanese firms moved into manufacturing sectors such as textiles and automobile production.[23] The surge in Japanese direct investment, however, soon created its own problems. Japanese firms found it necessary to establish joint ventures with powerful Southeast Asian politicians and their mainly Chinese business allies to ensure the security of their investments, to avoid bureaucratic red tape, and even to retain access to these markets. As a result, complex transnational politico-business alliances were created, often built on networks forged in the 1950s and 1960s, but not so much by LDP politicians as by the trading companies themselves.

In the case of Indonesia, Takeo Fukuda inherited Kishi's and Kawashima's networks of "Indonesian experts," brokers, and fixers on the Japanese side, but more central were trading companies, which participated in many joint ventures as minority shareholders. On the Indonesian side Suharto, Ibnu Sutowo, and Sudjono Humardani were central, along with the largely Sino-Indonesian business cronies representing business groups such as Astra, Panin, Nyo Han Siang, Ong Seng Kheng, Salim, and The Kiam Siang. Joint ventures were established on these networks by Toyota and William Suryajaya's Astra (with the backing of Ibnu Sutowo and Sudjono Humardani); Mitsubishi and Ibnu Sutowo's Krama Yudha; the Nippon Credit Bank and Ibnu Sutowo's Gading Mas, Tri Usaha Bhakti (affiliated with Suharto and the Army Siliwangi Division in West Java), and Panin (affiliated with Ali Murtopo); and Mitsui, Aica Kogyo, Astra, and Pakarti Yoga (affiliated with Ali Murtopo).[24] Though less well researched, similar patterns obtained in Japanese joint ventures in Thailand and the Philippines (where Ferdinand Marcos and Nissho Iwai were central from the late 1960s to the mid-1980s). These "unholy" alliances of Japanese firms with powerful Southeast Asian politicians and their mainly Chinese cronies in the business community invited popular protest in 1972–74, leading to the anti-Japanese boycotts and the student revolution in Thailand in 1972–73 and a massive anti-Japanese riot in Jakarta when Tanaka

---

[23] See Kunio Igusa, "Nihon no Tonan Ajia Shinshutsu no Kozu" [The structure of Japan's advancement into Southeast Asia], in *Tonan Ajia to Nihon*, [Southeast Asia and Japan] ed. Toru Yano (Tokyo: Kobun-do, 1991), pp. 204–32.

[24] See *Ampo: Special Issue on Japanese Transnational Enterprises in Indonesia* 12.4 (1980): 34–43, and Takashi Shiraishi, *Indonesia: Kokka to Seiji* [Indonesia: Government and politics] (Tokyo: Libroport, 1991), chap. 6.

visited there in January 1974. Japan could no longer take easy access to Southeast Asian natural resources and markets for granted.

And finally, the appreciation of yen and the first oil crisis, combined with Tanaka's single-minded pursuit of high economic growth, jolted the Japanese economy and threatened the continuing dominance of the conservative coalition in Japanese politics. (Recall opposition victories in Japan's local elections in the early 1970s.) What Finance Minister Fukuda called "crazy inflation (kyoran bukka)" reached more than 30 percent at its peak in February 1974. This experience, coupled with the disappearance of kerosene, toilet paper, and even salt from store shelves in late 1973 and early 1974, had a lasting impact on the Japanese. Now "*antei* (stable, steady)" became the word for everything in this time of uncertainty. The Japanese government publicly announced price stability (*bukka antei*) as its top policy priority. The Japanese economy changed its gear from high economic growth to steady economic growth (*antei seicho*). Japanese labor opted for stable employment (*antei koyo*) in exchange for labor loyalty. And MOFA officials defined stability and peace (*antei to heiwa*) as Japan's foreign policy objective in Asia.

It was under these circumstances that Japan tested the outer limits of American hegemony in Asia and then retreated in its foreign resource policy from autonomous (that is, independent) resource development (*jishu shigen kaihatsu*) to stable supply (*antei kyokyu*). The case in point is Japan's resource diplomacy toward Indonesia, above all its 1973 oil loans and the 1974 LNG (liquid natural gas) loans to the Indonesian government, both provided interestingly outside the multilateral IGGI framework.[25]

The negotiations for the 1973 oil loans started in May 1971 and were concluded in May 1972, before the first oil crisis. The major forces in Japan for the deal were MITI led by Vice-Minister Yoshihiko Morozumi, his ally Kakuei Tanaka (then minister of finance), Soppei Nakayama (president of the Industrial Bank of Japan), Shoichi Kamiya (president of Toyota Motor Sales), and Seigen Tanaka (a fixer, especially in the oil business). As a part of the deal a new oil-importing firm was created as a joint venture between Pertamina, the Indonesian state oil company, and a group of Japanese investors, with 26 percent of capital provided by Toy-

---

[25] These two loans were special not only because they were extended to Indonesia outside the IGGI framework but also because as their names suggest the decisions were made extrabureaucratically. In the 1970s, the Japanese government provided four special loans to Indonesia, two Asahan loans in 1976 and 1978 (for the Asahan hydraulic power plant and an aluminium processing plant), and the oil and LNG loans, in addition to annual routine soft loans prosaically called the 1970 first loan, the 1970 second loan, and so on.

ota and 24 percent by seven Japanese utility companies. Foreign oil majors such as Shell and Caltex were completely left out of the deal, despite their dominant position in Japan. The new oil-importing firm also was a direct challenge to the Far East Oil Trading, till then the sole importing firm of Indonesian oil and under Kishi's control since its inception in 1960. The oil loans signified an attempt by Japan's resource autonomists to break the dominance of foreign oil majors over the Japanese oil market and Kakuei Tanaka's challenge to Kishi and his heir, Fukuda, as the head of Japan's Indonesia lobby.

The negotiations for the 1974 LNG loans started in early 1973, but were concluded in early 1974, after the first oil crisis. By then, resource autonomy was no longer important, but a stable supply of oil and natural gas was. A different transnational coalition was formed behind the deal: Mobil, Pertamina, the MITI, a Japanese trading firm (Nissho Iwai), and Japanese utilities and banks. As part of the deal, Japan provided U.S.$1.1 billion for loans, with U.S.$200 million as soft loans from the OECF and U.S.$900 million from Japanese utilities and banks, in return for the stable supply of LNG over twenty years; contracts for the construction of LNG plants went to General Dynamics and other U.S. engineering firms; Mobil was the only company for the development of natural gas fields; Pertamina became the sole exporter of LNG; and Nissho Iwai earned fees for importing LNG to Japan. The policy change took place because Japanese utilities had shifted from the resource autonomy to the stable resource supply camp. The major losers were the resource autonomists in MITI and their business and political allies, most notably Kakuei Tanaka, and the major casualty was Japan National Oil Corporation (JNOC), which leading MITI resource autonomist Morozumi had created in 1967 for funding oil exploration abroad by Japanese oil firms and which he hoped would become a Japanese oil major. The JNOC has remained since then a funding agency, and Japanese utilities and trading firms have teamed up with oil majors for the supply of oil and gas to Japan.

Japan thus tested the outer limits of U.S. hegemony in Asia and retreated. "A light hold on the Japanese jugular," as Bruce Cumings put it, remained.[26] Yet all the same Japan could no longer count solely on the United States, but had to look for a regional stability within the overall framework set by the United States. Two diplomatic initiatives Prime Min-

---

[26] Bruce Cumings, "The Origins and Development of the Northeast Asian Political Economy: Industrial Sectors, Product Cycles, and Political Consequences," in *The Political Economy of the New Asian Industrialization*, ed. Frederic C. Deyo (Ithaca: Cornell University Press, 1987), p. 63.

ister Fukuda undertook in 1977 and 1978 can be understood in this context. One was the conclusion of a treaty of peace and friendship and the start of economic cooperation with China. The other, which is more important for our discussion, was his "ASEAN diplomacy."

Since Susumu Yamakage disccusses Japan's ASEAN diplomacy in Chapter 8, we need only note two considerations that guided Fukuda's ASEAN initiative. First, there were momentous changes in international relations in Southeast Asia in the mid-1970s. All of Indochina went communist in 1975 and there were signs of rising communist insurgencies in Thailand and the Philippines. How to build a bridge between the noncommunist ASEAN countries and communist Indochina in order to prevent Southeast Asia from becoming a major arena for superpower rivalry was one major question. The second was how to establish a better and more stable relationship with the ASEAN countries or in Fukuda's words, how to create a "special" relationship with ASEAN in the wake of anti-Japanese popular protest in the early 1970s.[27] To achieve these twin objectives, Fukuda promised to double Japan's economic aid to the members of ASEAN, to provide U.S. $1 billion for ASEAN industrialization, and to keep Japan's aid to China below that to the ASEAN countries. In other words, he underlined the importance of ASEAN for Japan and attempted to promote ASEAN as a regional organization by encouraging its members to discuss what industrial project each wanted to have with Japanese funding.

Fukuda, who was responsible for the creation of Japan Foundation in 1972, also called on the ASEAN countries for the "heart to heart" dialogue with Japan and initiated a program of cultural diplomacy with them. His basic idea was that "economic cooperation" alone was no longer sufficient, that more extensive cultural exchanges and dialogues would be required to create the needed "special relationship." The Japanese government under Fukuda also advised the Vietnamese government to remain "independent" and not to join the Soviet camp, promised economic aid to Hanoi, and asked it to purchase what Vietnam needed from ASEAN countries with Japanese funding.

Fukuda's initiative for bridge building came to naught because of the Vietnamese invasion in Cambodia. (But this idea was revived in the early 1990s when Prime Minister Miyazawa promised financial support for "south to south" cooperation with ASEAN and Indochina in mind.) Fukuda's ASEAN diplomacy marked a clear shift in Japan's Southeast Asia

---

[27] For Fukuda's ASEAN diplomacy, see above all Sueo Sudo's informative dissertation, "Postwar Nanshin and the Fukuda Doctrine: Explaining Policy Changes in Japan-Southeast Asian Relations" (Ph.D. diss., Department of Political Science, University of Michigan, 1987).

policy. After his visit to the ASEAN countries in 1977, the word "ASEAN" replaced "Southeast Asia" in Japanese political parlance, and ASEAN and China emerged as two major regional units in Japan's Asia policy.

Fukuda also announced in his visit to the ASEAN countries in 1977 that Japan would not become a military power and seek to take over the U.S. role in Asian security. In the 1980s Japanese military became more closely integrated into the US security arrangements in Asia. Despite its growth in size and capabilities, therefore, the Japanese Self-Defense Forces remain dependent on and subordinate to the U.S. military in a system that is essentially of U.S. making.[28]

Legacies of all these policies and thinking—economic cooperation, burden sharing, a special relationship with the ASEAN countries, bridge building between ASEAN and Indochina, and aid as the major policy instrument—are still there. In the 1970s and the first half of the 1980s, however, all that was missing was an integrative regional vision that could replace "Free Asia" and give Japan a sense of direction for its future position in the region.

An Emerging New World

T. J. Pempel discusses the current Asian economic dynamism extensively in Chapter 1, so I need only note some important trends: (1) East and Southeast Asia, which the Japanese began to see as one region and now often call "East Asia," has emerged as the world center of economic growth; (2) Japanese investment in Asian NICs and the ASEAN countries has surged since the Plaza Accord in 1985 with Japanese manufacturing firms shifting their production bases there for the export of their manufactured goods to Japan and the third country; (3) Japan, which provided capital and intermediate goods in the past, has emerged as a leading market for manufactured goods from NICs and ASEAN countries; (4) NICs have emerged along with Japan and the United States as major investors and trade partners with ASEAN countries; (5) the intra-regional trade has become larger than the region's trade with the United States.

The current Japanese regional vision is based on this reality and its future projection: the region-wide economic dynamism with its ever expanding frontiers from Asian NICs to Thailand, Malaysia, and Indonesia, to coastal regions of China, to the Philippines and Vietnam, and perhaps in some future to Burma and beyond. If seen from Tokyo, this "flying

---

[28] See Peter J. Katzenstein and Nobuo Okawara, *Japan's National Security: Structures, Norms and Policy Responses in a Changing World* (Ithaca: Cornell University East Asia Program, 1993).

geese pattern" regional economic development means ever expanding possibilities for Japanese business at a time when the Japanese economic "bubble" has burst and Japan is experiencing the worst recession in the postwar era. It is easy, then, to see why Japan is so excited about this new Asian economic dynamism and what vision now informs its "comprehensive economic cooperation."

For Japan economic cooperation no longer means trade promotion and resources procurement as it did in the past, but the encouragement and promotion of Asian economic dynamism with Japanese direct investment, Japanese aid for structural adjustment, infrastructural and human resources development, and Japanese imports from Asian NICs and the ASEAN countries. This is the basic point about Japan's formal policy line. It is in essence the extension of its politics of productivity beyond Japanese borders onto Asia, whether one calls it East Asia or Asia-Pacific.

Another important element of Japan's formal policy line is its openness. The current Asian regional economic dynamism is market-driven and open. Access to the U.S. market is crucial to sustain this dynamism. But there are worrisome signs that the United States might become more protectionist. Although U.S. business wants to benefit from this regional economic dynamism, Washington is not in a position to provide massive aid and loans to Asia. What should Japan as the world's largest creditor do? The formal policy line says that Japan should provide funds, both official and private, to the ASEAN countries, China, and Vietnam, not only for its economic cooperation with these countries, but also to encourage U.S. and European firms to do business in this region and to maintain open regionalism. This is a new line of thought and a logical extension of Japan's burden-sharing and ASEAN-first policies: Asia, especially Southeast Asia, is to be an arena for international and multilateral economic cooperation.

One should not be too cynical about this new line of thought. The shift in Japan's aid, its most important policy instrument, is the case in point. Since the mid-1980s, Japan steadily increased the portion of general untied aid from 53.9 percent in 1984, to 85.6 percent in 1989, to 91.2 percent in 1992. The share of Japanese aid-related business U.S. and European firms obtained also increased from 9 percent in 1986 to 21 percent in 1988, though it declined to 13 percent in 1992.[29] As an outcome of

[29] In 1984, 53.9 percent of Japanese aid was general untied and 45.1 percent was LDC (Less Developed Countries)-untied, while 74.4 percent was general untied and 24.6 percent LDC-untied in 1988. Igarashi, *Nihon no ODA*, p. 204. The share of Japanese aid-related business obtained by Japanese firms declined steadily from 67 percent in 1986, to 38 percent in 1989, to 35 percent in 1992, while the LDC share increased from 24 percent in 1984 to 41 percent in 1989 to 52 percent in 1992.

President Bush's visit to Tokyo in January 1992, the Japanese and the U.S. government also started a U.S. $1 billion cooperative financing scheme for five infrastructural projects, including projects in Indonesia, the Philippines, and Thailand.[30] And both MITI officials and trading firm executives say that MITI now encourages business team-ups with U.S. firms for long-term, large-scale infrastructural projects.

This new economic cooperation policy is linked with Japan's geopolitics. According to Japanese geopolitical calculation, Japan and Southeast Asia lie between the two hegemonic powers, the United States and China. Japan's "south to south" economic cooperation policy is to encourage the expansion of ASEAN to include Vietnam and, combined with its ASEAN-first policy, is meant to make ASEAN into a counterweight to China. The thinking behind "Southeast Asia as an arena for international cooperation" is to keep the Americans and the Europeans in the region, not only to support U.S. hegemony in the region but also to offset China. The same geopolitical consideration was behind its Cambodian policy. Its real target was not Cambodia, but Vietnam, that is, to "solve" the Cambodian question, stop bleeding Vietnam, promote economic cooperation with it, and make it part of ASEAN-led Southeast Asia. Hence Japan's more recent emphasis on the ASEAN-centered security dialogue.

The formal line, however, only tells us part of the story. Given its developmental-state past in which its foreign economic policy was integral to its national objective of economic growth and industrial transformation under "Economic General Staff" MITI, it is certainly not narrow-minded to ask whether there might be a hidden agenda behind this new policy line and whether Japan is trying to steer Asian economic regionalism with its money, its technology, its corporations, and its example of success. Fallows, for instance, mentions the existence of "a kind of war room in MITI, in which bureaucrats mapped out investment plans for the rest of Asia." "Japanese firms would invest in Southeast Asia according to an agreed-on joint strategy." He continued:

> The companies making word processors, answering machines, athletic shoes, and faxes would set up shop in Malaysia. Those making furniture, die-cast molds, and toys would go to Thailand. Indonesia would get wood products factories, plastic works, and textile mills. I went to this very office in MITI . . . , at which point the officials were saying they had no coordi-

---

[30] "Japan, U.S. Cooperate on Loans," *Wall Street Journal,* March 17, 1992, A-11. Also see Satoru Oki, "Nichi Bei Kyocho Yushi Rosen wa Shosha Kino Hakki no Butai" [The Japan-United States cofinancing line is where trading companies demonstrate their functions], *Asia Market Review,* February 15, 1992, pp. 8–9.

nated plans and were shocked, just shocked, at the suggestion that they did. Nonetheless, events unfolded with a logical shape.[31]

What Fallows has in mind when he says "an agreed-on joint strategy" is MITI's New Aid Plan, an acronym for New Asian Industries Development Plan, announced by Minister of International Trade and Industry Hajime Tamura in Bangkok in 1987 and which Chalmers Johnson called "Japan's proposal for a new regional order, a new and much more prosperous version of the Greater East Asia Co-Prosperity Sphere."[32] But this argument misses an important shift in the balance of power within the conservative coalition that long defined Japan's conception of national interest. What I mean by shift is not the collapse of the LDP dominant party system and the ongoing party realignment, though this recent development is enormously important because it will most likely end the alliance of steel (and automobiles and semiconductors) and rice and lead to the inclusion of organized labor in a new ruling coalition (which has taken place to some extent since 1993). More important for our discussion is the shift in the balance of power between the state bureaucracy and big business.

Internationalization of Japanese industry and finance sharply enhanced the influence of the private sector vis-à-vis the bureaucracy and politicians in the 1980s. While bureaucrats and politicians cannot go multinational, firms are not so constrained. They can, and do, seek the least expensive capital, components, production bases, information, and government support to be found anywhere. This was made starkly clear by the surge in Japanese foreign direct investment to over $67 billion by 1990, over five times the level of 1985.[33] This threatened the state bureaucracy, above all MITI, because its power traditionally lay in its gatekeeper role.

MITI's New Aid Plan was an attempt to find a new role at a time when it had lost "an impressive armory of weapons for intervention in the economy" it once had and when many manufacturing industries had become too powerful to listen to MITI's guidance.[34] It sought to combine the re-

---

[31] Fallows, *Looking at the Sun*, p. 270.
[32] Ibid., p. 483, quoting from Chalmers Johnson's "History Restarted."
[33] Calder, *Japan's Changing Role in Asia*, pp. 26–28. Japanese direct investment in Asia also surged. It amounted to $3 billion in Korea for 1985–92 (67 percent of Japan's accumulated direct investment from 1951 to 1992); $2.8 billion in Taiwan (81 percent); $8.7 billion in Hong Kong (76 percent); $5.9 billion in Singapore (75 percent); $5.2 billion in Thailand (88 percent); $3.8 billion in Malaysia (78 percent); $6.4 billion in Indonesia (45 percent); $1.1 billion in the Philippines (57 percent); and $3.2 billion in China (97 percent).
[34] The quote is from Pempel, "Japanese Foreign Economic Policy," p. 157. The most recent evidence that Japanese manufacturing sectors have become too powerful for MITI's guidance is the U.S. attempt to negotiate directly with the automobile industry to open up the Japanese automobile market.

sources of the Japanese state—aid, technical cooperation, and measures to open Japanese markets—with private capital and technology. Its aim was to develop the economies of the NICs and new NICs in such a way that, at the very least, they would enhance the ongoing restructuring of the Japanese economy by establishing lower-cost component-making and export bases for Japan's manufacturing industries throughout East and Southeast Asia. As the *Economist* pointed out in 1989, MITI's hidden agenda was "to commit government money for the relocation of Japanese industry into lower-cost Asian countries as an inducement for private industry to serve whatever policies the bureaucracy wants to pursue." In other words it was an attempt to exploit to the full what was already happening in order to remain in command of the development: regional economic integration was (and still is) happening anyway, Japanese firms were (and still are) moving production offshore to remain competitive and to avoid protectionism and rising costs at home. MITI sought to finesse the market—"diverting some Japanese direct investment in manufacturing from America and Europe to Asia and deploying it in a way that MITI thought to be most effective for the restructuring of the Japanese economy."[35]

When Japanese firms, not only large firms but also medium and small-scale firms, began shifting their production offshore to Thailand, Malaysia, and Indonesia (but not in the Philippines, mainly because of its security situation), however, their foremost concern was investment risk. The New Aid Plan could not address this concern directly and after a few studies, it was quietly dropped. Although MITI's 1989 White Paper on Economic Aid mentioned the Eastern Seaboard Industrial Estate Project in Thailand as its major project, it was in fact started in 1983 by the Thai government, initially to be funded by the World Bank. But the Thai government turned to the Japanese government for funding when the World Bank insisted on the need for structural adjustment measures. The Japanese aid for the program started in 1983 with the funding of an engineering service for it, and the Japanese government designated it an aid project in 1985. It had started long before the New Aid Plan was conceived.[36] In 1994 I visited the MITI "war room" Fallows had visited in the late 1980s. I interviewed MITI officials at the Tokyo headquarters as well as in Jakarta and Bangkok. When I asked about the New Aid Plan, none of them knew what I was

[35] "The Yen Bloc," *Economist,* July 15, 1989.
[36] See Hitoshi Hirata's insightful essay, "Nihon no tai-ASEAN Kyoryoku (New Aid Plan oyobi AJDF) no Haikei to sono Ichi-zuke," [Japan's cooperation with ASEAN (New Aid Plan and AJDF), its background and significance] (an unpublished manuscript in my possession).

talking about. By 1994 the project had long been dead even for MITI officials.

Less disastrous a failure was the ASEAN-Japan Development Fund, which Prime Minister Yasuhiro Nakasone announced in 1987 in Bangkok. As part of the $30 billion capital recycling plan announced in 1987, the Fund was to promote the development of the private sector in the ASEAN countries with $2 billion, to help finance primarily Japanese joint ventures and joint ventures across more than one ASEAN country, and to create an investment vehicle, the Japan ASEAN Investment Corporation, for the purchase of equities and bonds in joint ventures. The Fund, especially its Japan ASEAN Investment Corporation, which addressed Japanese firms' concern for investment risk, was modestly successful in its first few years. But its major plan to provide concessional loans for promoting the private sector in the ASEAN countries did not go anywhere, because it came out of the blue for the ASEAN governments and because the plan ran into the opposition of the World Bank and the IMF, which insisted that the funds for it be lent at market rates.

Maneuvering within the Outer Limits

The failure of the New Aid Plan and the ASEAN-Japan Development Fund clearly demonstrates that the reach of the Japanese state does not extend very far beyond Japanese borders. Both current Asian economic development and the Japanese transfer of production in the region are market driven. Seen from the bureaucrats' perspective, this looks as if market forces are getting "out of control." Hence their fear of Japan's industrial hollowing out, their despair at how little power the government actually has to finesse the market, and their call for yet another transformation of Japanese economy to industrial sectors that are more technology intensive and have a higher value-added.

This, however, does not mean that the government stopped trying to be "useful" for Japanese firms going offshore in Southeast Asia. MOF is deeply interested in developing financial markets in Southeast Asia, while MITI and its subsidiary, Japan External Trade Organization (JETRO), are doing whatever they can with technical cooperation. This also explains the increasing importance of the APEC for Japan in the 1990s and its ambivalence to the EAEC proposed by Malyasian prime minister Mahathir Mohamad. Japanese firms, driven offshore by market forces, need less regulated, more uniform, and more transparent trade and investment regimes in East and Southeast Asia. If the Japanese government cannot finesse the market, it can at least try to provide what Japanese firms as well as non-Japanese firms need anyway in a multilateral, regional framework. Hence the increasing importance of the APEC. Yet Mahathir's EAEC beckons, for it might give Japan another opportunity for Japan-centered initiatives, a return match, so to speak, for the New Aid Plan and the ASEAN-Japan Development Fund.

Either way, it is important to emphasize that both the state bureaucracy and big business understand that Japanese industry and finance are too large for Japan and for Asia. They are keenly aware of the crucial importance of U.S. hegemony in Asia as well as the world over for Japan's long-term economic and security interests. It is also important to note that its politics of productivity, which has achieved social peace and prosperity in the postwar era, not only remains intact but is in fact seen as the key to maintaining future social peace in the coming industrial transformation and in rapidly aging Japan, and that the current Asian economic dynamism is understood as clear evidence of its efficaciousness in Asia. This means that as long as Asian industrialization remains dynamic and Asian politics remain stable, Japan's current strategic vision, the extension of its politics of productivity beyond Japanese borders, remains in place.[37] It is not surprising, then, that as Hisahiko Okazaki, a former MOFA "strategist," recently argued in his book, *Grand Strategy toward New Asia: Vision for Japan's Development*, many see in the current Asian economic dynamism a possibility for the first time in modern times for Japan to be Asianist and internationalist simultaneously, to expand Japan's postwar politics of productivity beyond Japan's borders, to play an important role in the creation of an open regionalism in Asia-Pacific, and yet to harmonize the future Japanese economic expansion with the maintainance of the Japan–U.S. Pacific alliance.[38]

If that projection seems too rosy, it is nonetheless important to note that this is the reasoning for the new policy line, which binds Japan both internationally and domestically. The wartime Co-Prosperity Sphere was bankrupt when it was conjured up, because the original strategic vision that led to the establishment of Manchukuo had long disintegrated. Japan's postwar strategy for trade promotion and natural resources procurement, which was so integral to the twin national objectives of economic

---

[37] Compare Ichiro Ozawa's *Nippon Kaizo Keikaku* [Plan for Japan's reform] (Tokyo: Kodansha, 1993) and The Round Table on Japan and the Asia-Pacific Region in the 21st Century, "Japan and the Asia-Pacific Region in the 21st Century: Promotion of Openness and Respect for Plurality" (unofficial translation in my possession, 1992), to see how little difference there is in their visions.

[38] Hisahiko Okazaki, *Atarashii Ajia he no Dai-Senryaku: Nippon Hatten no Vision* [Grand strategy toward New Asia: Vision for Japan's development] (Tokyo: Yomiuri Shinbun-sha, 1993).

growth and industrial transformation, has lost much of its coherence, because of its success. Yet its politics of productivity has by now turned into firm belief. If things go well, a new ruling coalition will be built on this belief, and big business and finance, which have gone multinational, will be its most important component. This means that Japan's presence in Southeast Asia will become more diffuse, less focused, less state-centered, and more network centered (keiretsus, multinational business alliances and joint ventures, transnational politico-business alliances, and so on, as Richard Doner explains in Chapter 6). Economic cooperation will remain central to Japan's Southeast Asia policy, but its aid projects will be more like its domestic public works projects, penetrated by politico-business alliances.

The problem is that Japan's comprehensive economic cooperation, which now means the extension of its politics of productivity into Southeast Asia (as well as into China), is predicated on the dubious assumption that the authoritarian developmentalism now being practiced in many countries there is fundamentally similar to the politics of productivity the Japanese conservative coalition has pursued since the 1950s. Authoritarian developmentalism is based on the coercive exclusion of labor and peasant farmers from the political process, a policy that sooner or later results in a participatory crisis. Japan's participatory crisis was solved under U.S. occupation, before the inception of its politics of productivity. South Korea, Taiwan, and perhaps Thailand have undergone this crisis more or less successfully. But this is not guarantee that other regimes will fare equally well without derailing the current economic dynamism.

The real crisis will come when the effectiveness of what Japan believes is the politics of productivity comes into serious doubt in China and Indonesia. In the prewar years, Japan turned to a disastrous course when it was confronted with the systemic crisis of the collective informal imperialism in China, because Japan's stake there made the crisis an "imperial" question. If a systemic crisis arises that makes Japan's international presence another imperial issue in this fin de siècle Asia, it will manifest as a series of local crises in the current economic dynamism (which is equated with Japan's postwar politics of productivity) that threatens its long-term social peace and safety. With its huge foreign direct investment and its region-wide production networks, Japan is more vulnerable now to local crises. To see this point, one only need to recall how unsettling the kidnapping of Mitsui chief in 1986 was for Japanese firms in the Philippines. One wonders then what repercussions there will be if the current explosive economic expansion in China's coastal regions leads to social crisis and/or if the deepening succession crisis in Indonesia leads to popular challenges to the New Order regime.

In retrospect, the cold war era might turn out to have been the best era for Japan in modern times, better even than the good prewar years from 1905 to the mid-1920s when Japan exploited the British-dominated, informal collective imperialism in China to build an empire. This might be so because of the presence of a U.S. hegemony, the inaccessibility of China (which turned out to be not very important for Japan economically when it finally opened), and the successes of the Southeast Asian states, who had staked their stability and legitimacy on authoritarian developmentalism. But that era is now passing; the Japanese state has lost its gatekeeper role; and Japanese multinationals, driven by market forces, have become deeply entangled in networks and alliances with Southeast Asian bureaucratic elites and their Chinese business associates.

History does not repeat itself, even as farce. After all, the "China problem" drove Japan to establish Manchukuo and eventually to challenge Anglo-American hegemony in Greater East Asia in the 1930s and the first half of the 1940s, because it had become Japan's imperial issue when its interests as well as the informal, collective, imperialist system in which Japan had pursued its interests in China were threatened by rising anti-imperialist Chinese nationalism. In the declining years of the twentieth century and the early next century, however, Japan may face not a "China problem," but an "Asia problem," that is, political and social crises arising from the current economic expansion in China's coastal regions and coming participatory crises for authoritarian developmentalism in Southeast Asia. If such an "Asia problem" develops that threatens the current Asian economic dynamism and Japan's vital stake in it, it is better for Japan to deal with it collectively with the United States as the senior partner rather than making it an "imperial" issue to be resolved by Japan alone.

III

REGIONAL ISSUES: ECONOMY AND CULTURE

6

Japan in East Asia: Institutions and Regional Leadership

RICHARD F. DONER

Vigorous institutions and a proactive approach to structural economic change are prominent features of Japan's political economy.[1] Private sector associations, ongoing public-private sector groups, and relatively cohesive state agencies have all been quite active in addressing collective action problems—reconciling interests of diverse economic actors—that emerge in the process of Japanese economic transformation.[2] This institutional activism reflects an acknowledgment of and a desire to guide structural economic transformation. Japanese theoretical and policy discussions of economic change are striking in their acceptance of dynamic national comparative advantage: Japan must be capable of "riding" and benefiting from shifting product cycles. But unlike the more firm-specific views of Western theorists, the Japanese approach to product cycles emphasizes transformations of leading sectors.[3] Successful transitions from one sector

[1] In addition to helpful suggestions from members of the Cornell Workshop on Japan in Asia, especially Peter Katzenstein, Takashi Shiraishi, and Bob Bullock, I am grateful for comments from Walter Mattli.

[2] See, for example, Peter J. Katzenstein, "Conclusion: Domestic Structures and Strategies of Foreign Economic Policy," *Between Power and Plenty: Foreign Economic Policies of Advanced Industrial States*, ed. Katzenstein (Madison: University of Wisconsin Press, 1978); Chalmers Johnson, "History Restarted: Japanese-American Relations at the End of the Century," in *Pacific Economic Relations in the 1990s*, ed. R. Giggott, R. Leaver, and J. Ravenhill (Boulder, Colo.: Lynne Rienner, 1993); Leonard H. Lynn and Timothy J. McKeown, *Organizing Business: Trade Associations in America and Japan* (Washington, D.C.: American Enterprise Institute, 1988); and Mark Tilton, "Informal Market Governance in Japan's Basic Materials Industries," *International Organization* 48 (Autumn 1994): 663–85.

[3] Kaname Akamatsu, "A Theory of Unbalanced Growth in the World Economy," *Weltwirt-*

to another, or from lower to higher technology niches within sectors, involve inter- and intra-industry resource shifts. Institutional linkages among affected actors can facilitate such shifts.

Studies of Japan's economic presence in East Asia commonly emphasize only the country's product cycle virtuosity. Japanese explain the country's economic relations with the region as part of a dynamic but harmonious division of labor in which Japan's neighbors enter industries or product niches no longer consistent with Japan's shifting factor endowments.[4] From this perspective, Japanese trade and, more important, foreign direct investment (FDI) constitute "a house-cleaning-and-renovating vehicle" for Japan's domestic structural changes.[5] In this chapter I explore the less-studied institutional component of this process: how do Japanese businesses and state officials use domestic-based institutions to promote a regional division of labor favorable to Japan in East Asia? For my purposes here, East Asia comprises the four Newly Industrializing Countries or NICs (Taiwan, South Korea, Singapore, and Hong Kong), four members of the Association of Southeast Asian Nations or ASEAN (Indonesia, Malaysia, the Philippines, and Thailand), and the People's Republic of China.

Answers to this question bear on two important issues: the nature of Japanese leadership, and the institutional requirements for organizing intra-industry trade and investment. Numerous scholars have noted Japan's lack of leadership in foreign affairs, pointing to the state's reactive nature, its lack of moral vision, its fragmented decision-making capacity on global issues, and its low capacity for credible international commitments.[6] Such arguments assume a vision of leadership exercised through overtly dominant behavior. But others have begun to explore the possibility of Japanese capacity for a different kind of leadership in East Asia, a "leadership from

schaftliches Archiv 86.1 (1961); Mitchell Bernard and John Ravenhill, "Beyond Product Cycles and Flying Geese: Regionalization, Hierarchy, and Industrialization of East Asia," *World Politics* 47 (January 1995): 171–209; and Raymond Vernon, "The Product Cycle Hypothesis in a New International Environment," *Oxford Bulletin of Economics and Statistics* 41 (November 1979): 255–67, discuss the Japanese approach to product cycles.

[4] See, for example, Teresa Morris-Suzuki, "Reshaping the International Division of Labor: Japanese Manufacturing Investment in South-East Asia," *Japan and the Global Economy*, ed. J. Morris (London: Routledge, 1991), and Ippei Yamazawa, "Gearing the Japanese Economy to International Harmony," *Developing Economies* 28.1 (1990): 3–12.

[5] Terutomo Ozawa, "Japan in a New Phase of Multinationalism and Industrial Upgrading: Functional Integration of Trade, Growth, and FDI," *Journal of World Trade* 25 (February 1991): 43–60.

[6] For a discussion of Japan's lack of leadership in foreign affairs, see Peter F. Cowhey, "Domestic Institutions and the Credibility of International Commitments: Japan and the United States," *International Organization* 47 (Spring 1993): 299–326, and Kent E. Calder, "Japanese Foreign Economic Policy: Explaining the Reactive State," *World Politics* 40 (July 1988): 517–41.

behind.''[7] In general terms, this scenario portrays Japan as helping to develop innovative institutional options and encouraging an ongoing process in which national interests are redefined in support of these options. Structural bargaining occurs largely in a bilateral setting, with Japan participating in but eschewing overt dominance of multilateral forums. Japan's normative understanding of the relationship between political change and economic growth bolsters its capacity for such a soft role. According to this view, Japan sympathizes with the political fragility of neighboring regimes and, rather than provoking legitimacy crises through calls for human rights, provides resources to enhance regime capacity for long-term growth.[8] All of this amounts to what one Japanese scholar terms a "coordinatorship" role in which Japan attempts "to achieve an alignment of diverse interests and to form consensus, or an appearance of it at least, among the region's countries with respect to intra-regional and global economic issues. Coordinatorship . . . will be much more in tune with Japan's domestic political culture and negotiating style. It will also be less visible than a leadership role and therefore much less likely to arouse emotional reactions from its Asian neighbors."[9]

With recent exceptions, however, we lack a concrete sense of how such leadership from behind might occur.[10] I approach the leadership issue by asking whether and how Japanese institutions help to manage changing levels and types of intra-regional economic transactions. Put somewhat differently, can the operation of Japanese institutions help to explain the absence of supranational institutions, despite increasing trade and investment within the region?

Consider the intensification of regional economic activity. Although the United States remains the single largest export market for the region, its share has been exceeded by that of the entire East Asian region.[11] Intra-Asian trade as a proportion of the region's total trade has risen from 11.8 percent in 1980 to 18.1 percent in 1992, with intra-regional exports amounting to some 30 percent of regional exports.[12] Inward foreign in-

[7] See Alan Rix, "Japan and the Region: Leading from Behind," in *The U.S.–Japan Economic Relationship in East and Southeast Asia: A Policy Framework for Asia-Pacific Economic Cooperation*, ed. Kaoru Okuizumi, Kent Calder, and Geritt Gong (Boulder, Colo.: Westview Press, 1993), and Johnson, "History Restarted."

[8] David Arase, "Japan in East Asia," in *Japan in the Posthegemonic World*, ed. Tsuneo Akaha and Frank Langdon (Boulder, Colo.: Lynne Rienner, 1993), pp. 113–33.

[9] Yanagihara, 1987, p. 418.

[10] David Arase, *Buying Power* (Boulder, Colo.: Lynne Rienner, 1995).

[11] Satoshi Ohoka, "East Asia and Japan: New Development of Regional Division of Labor" (paper prepared for BRIE–Asia Foundation Conference on Japanese Production Networks in Asia, San Francisco, 1994), p. 4.

[12] See Chapter 1 herein.

vestment for most of the region's developing countries is now dominated by funds from regional neighbors, most of whose outward investment goes to other countries in the region.[13] As T. J. Pempel shows in Chapter 1, Japan's role in this process has been critical. Japan is the largest source of cumulative investment and of aid to the region, even as the region has become Japan's largest export market, surpassing the United States in 1991.

Most critical for our purposes, this process of interdependence has involved increasing levels of intra-industry trade between Japan and the rest of the region. Driven by its foreign investment, Japan has shifted from a largely inter-sectoral emphasis on securing raw materials and exporting finished manufactured goods, to manufacture for protected local markets, and finally to investments driven by production rather than market considerations. The rest of East Asia is now producing growing quantities of ever more sophisticated manufactured goods, many of which are exported to third countries (and some to Japan itself) as part of Japanese firms' regional or global production arrangements.

Parties in such intra-industry trade necessarily invest in assets specific to their particular relationship. Because the loss of these assets would result in significant costs to one or both parties, the growth of intra-industry trade is usually assumed to require some sort of institution capable of reducing the danger that either side might fail to live up to its side of the bargain.[14] Such institutions can involve government-to-government forms of assurance ranging from bilateral agreements, to multilateral ones, such as GATT, to "minilateral"/regional preferential trading arrangements (PTAs), such as the European Union. PTAs may be especially suitable where trade involves large relation-specific investments operating, say, through user-supplier relations that cross national boundaries and are thus particularly vulnerable to opportunistic holdups by governments.

Yet despite the rapid growth of such user-supplier relations, multilateral and minilateral arrangements are weak in East Asia. The ASEAN countries have proposed an ASEAN Free Trade Area (AFTA), but this arrangement is marred by a lack of details, extensive exclusions, and the fact that intra-ASEAN trade accounts for only 20 percent of the members' trade (and a third of that percentage consists of raw materials not eligible for liberalization.[15] Moreover, Japan, ASEAN's largest trading partner, has not given

---

[13] Axel Borrmann and Rolf Jungnickel, "Foreign Investment as a Factor in Asian Pacific Integration," *Intereconomics* (November/December 1992): 282–88.

[14] Beth V. Yarbrough and Robert M. Yarbrough, *Cooperation and Governance in International Trade: The Strategic Organizational Approach* (Princeton: Princeton University Press, 1992).

[15] John Ravenhill, "Economic Cooperation in Southeast Asia: Changing Incentives," *Asian Survey* 35 (September 1995): 850–66.

the AFTA process its explicit support. There has been some progress in APEC. This eighteen-member group has adopted a set of investment norms favoring informal dispute resolution. APEC has also committed itself to free trade by 2010 for the industrialized economies and by 2020 for the developing economies. But these deadlines are "indicative," and there remain real questions about Japan's capacity and willingness to facilitate concrete trade liberalization measures. The fear is rather that Japan's leadership will be a "passive" one.[16]

One explanation for the weakness of PTAs in East Asia is the region's continued reliance on U.S. markets. A second explanation would posit an institutional lag in which state-to-state arrangements have not caught up with East Asia's very rapid expansion of intra-industry trade and investments. Third, one might point to the impact of the U.S. presence *within* the area: In Northeast Asia, U.S. hegemony and containment strategy resulted in a vertical regime under which the capitalist countries of the region communicated with one another through the United States.[17] In Southeast Asia, U.S. hegemony allowed the nations of the region to neglect their own security while also creating a fear of dependence that undermined multilateralism.[18] These arguments might predict the eventual emergence of PTAs in East Asia as the region's reliance on U.S. markets and security provisions declines. Finally, firms may opt to avoid supranational arrangements altogether by keeping all transactions "in-house" through vertical integration. Indeed, vertical integration can be understood as the private sector analogue of preferential trading arrangements.

I propose a different explanation for the absence of supranationalism, one that incorporates but goes beyond vertical integration by emphasizing Japan's institutional attributes. According to this view, Japan's private, public-private, and state-level arrangements have substituted for PTAs by helping to resolve one type of collective action dilemma known as a "coordination" problem. These are problems which can be resolved through the use of the same rules, standards, or approaches. Their critical feature is that while the parties involved may have different preferences or interests concerning the precise nature of those standards or rules, the parties have little incentive to defect from the particular solution once it is achieved. In coordination, a centralized authority is not so critical; to the extent that such an authority has a role, it is not to enforce the agreement but rather to provide incentives for all parties to achieve it and sub-

---

[16] John McBeth, and V. G. Kulkarni, "Charting the Future," *Far Eastern Economic Review*, November 24, 1994, p. 15.
[17] See Chapter 4 herein.
[18] Donald Crone, "Does Hegemony Matter? The Reorganization of the Pacific Political Economy," *World Politics* 45 (July 1993): 501–26.

sequently to provide sufficient information for its codification and smooth implementation.[19] The Japanese use of the term "coordinatorship" cited above thus shares this element of decentralized authority with the coordination dilemmas discussed here.

My argument is that Japan, through a range of its institutions, is exerting "leadership from behind" in East Asia by helping to solve coordination problems. Such problems are ubiquitous in economic regionalization as expanded trade and investment highlight inconsistencies among the practices, customs, rules, and routines governing products and transactions in different countries. Questions remain, however, whether Japan will address a more challenging set of distributive, prisoners' dilemma-type problems such as overproduction and trade imbalances. Because parties are typically tempted to abandon agreed-upon solutions in such situations, prisoners' dilemmas often require a centralized authority to enforce agreements.[20]

Given Japan's relatively recent institutional expansion into the region, a thorough test of this argument is not yet feasible. Here I can only attempt a more detailed step beyond transaction-cost approaches to the issue of Japanese leadership.[21] First, I explore the origins of Japan's institutional presence in East Asia by tracing the linkages between Japan's domestic adjustment and its activities in the rest of East Asia prior to and after the *endaka*-inspired expansion of Japanese FDI in the region. Then I examine Japan's institutional efforts to promote regional economic restructuring. Finally, I analyze potential weaknesses in the capacity of Japanese institutions to sustain the growth of intra-regional transactions.

[19] Duncan Snidal, "Coordination versus Prisoners' Dilemma: Implications for International Cooperation and Regimes," *American Political Science Review* 79 (December 1985): 923–42.

[20] Ibid. Note that coordination games actually address what Stephan Haggard terms "deep" integration more than "shallow" integration; see *Developing Nations and the Politics of Integration* (Washington, D.C.: Brookings Institution, 1995). Shallow integration refers to the loosening of cross-border restrictions on investment and trade and the granting of national treatment for firms and products. My assumption is that liberalization of this shallow type involves significant threats to entrenched economic interests, prompts affected parties to defect from agreements, and is thus politically quite difficult. Deep integration involves harmonization of "behind-the-border" policies such as (1) trade-related investment measures, (2) structural asymmetries such as differences in retail systems, and (3) national regulatory practices such as national standards, intellectual property rules, and technology policies. As Haggard argues, "deep integration would imply a reform process that is more comprehensive and thus more demanding" (p. 5). But agreements on some (not all) of the components of deep integration such as standards, rules, and business practices, are less vulnerable to constant defection than are agreements on tariff liberalization and general reconciliation of production structures necessary for a region-wide division of labor.

[21] For examples, see Peter Petri, "One Bloc, Two Blocs or None? Political Economic Factors in Pacific Trade Policy," in *The U.S.–Japan Economic Relationship*, ed. Okuizumi, Calder, and Gong, and the introduction to this book.

Domestic Adjustment, FDI, and Institutions before 1985

The yen appreciation of 1985 led to a massive outflow of Japanese foreign investment to and a significant expansion of intra-industry trade with East Asia.[22] Yet the region was important to Japan prior to the mid-1980s as a source of raw materials, as an overseas production site for firms losing their domestic competitiveness, as a way of circumventing third-country protectionism, and as a potentially large export market.

Japanese foreign investment in East Asia during the first three decades after the war focused on raw materials, textiles, and electronics. Investment during the 1950s was severely constrained by capital controls and anti-Japanese sentiment, but the government did permit early foreign investment in natural resources, especially mining (including petroleum). This sector accounted for some 49 percent of total Japanese investment in 1972 and roughly one-third of Japanese FDI in East Asia in 1977. Stimulated by the economy's shift toward heavy and chemical industries, Japanese firms invested in natural gas in Brunei, oil in Indonesia, and copper and iron ore in Malaysia and the Philippines.[23] By the early 1970s, heavy and chemical industries encountered environmental constraints as well as rising oil prices. As a result, the production of goods such as chemical fertilizers, shipbuilding, low-grade steel, synthetic fabrics, and aluminum were relocated overseas.

Overseas raw materials investments were thus "fully compatible with and supportive of" Japanese industrial upgrading at home.[24] But this investment and procurement process did not occur solely through unfettered market forces. Critical to the process was Japan's emerging Overseas Development Assistance (ODA) program and the broader system of "economic cooperation" (*keizai kyoryoku*) to which it belongs. Japan's "economic cooperation" is "a densely institutionalized network for information exchange and policy coordination among the relevant governmental and private sector actors."[25] Its purpose is to combine aid, trade

---

[22] Japanese FDI in East Asia in 1966 amounted to $500 million (compared to $731 million for the United States). By 1977, Japanese totals of $6.4 billion exceeded U.S. figures of $4.6 billion. Japanese totals continued to rise, amounting to $32.1 billion in 1988 and $59.9 billion in 1992. Dennis Encarnation, *Bringing East Asia into the U.S.–Japan Rivalry: The Regional Evolution of American and Japanese Multinationals* (Cambridge: MIT Japan Program, 1994), table 1. For further data on evolution of Japanese FDI flows, see Chapter 1 herein.
[23] Lawrence B. Krause and Sueo Sekiguchi, "Japan and the World Economy," in *Asia's New Giant: How the Japanese Economy Works*, ed. Hugh Patrick and Henry Rosovsky (Washington, D.C.: Brookings Institution, 1976); Encarnation, *Bringing East Asia into the U.S.–Japan Rivalry*, Table 4.
[24] Ozawa, "Japan in a New Phase," 1991, p. 53.
[25] Arase, *Buying Power*, chap 3. The principal state agencies involved in economic cooperation

and investment in ways that both facilitate the movement of Japanese private sector into the developing world and use the private sector to serve
Japan's national interests. Beginning in the early 1960s, the "economic
cooperation" network expanded to include newly created, specialized organizations whose functions included the provision of loans and investments (Overseas Economic Cooperation Fund, OECF), exports and
investment loans (Exim Bank), research (Institute of Developing Economies, IDE), and grant and technical cooperation (e.g., Japan International
Cooperation Agency, JICA, Japan Transport Consultants Association, and
the Agricultural Development Consultants Association). The origins of this
system lay in Japan's need to secure sources of raw material imports and
promote export markets right after the war. Expanding from war reparations in the early 1950s to yen loans later in the decade, *keizai kyoryoku*
became more formalized when a special LDP committee urged the creation of a government fund to promote Japanese resource development
projects in Southeast Asia. This led to the establishment of a bilateral plan
through which Japan would provide developing countries with equipment,
technical training, and financing in exchange for assured access to raw
materials. Specific projects were often first identified by Japanese trade
associations and then developed in coordination with various other public
as well as private sector interests. For example, in the North Sumatra Oil
Development Project, Japanese private firms and banks combined with
public sector agencies (Japan Oil Development Corporation, the OECF,
and the Exim Bank) to establish the North Sumatra Oil Development
Corp. This firm provided funds, equipment, and services to the Indonesian
national oil company in return for a guaranteed share of oil production
in North Sumatra.[26]

During the 1970s, the "economic cooperation" network helped to coordinate domestic efforts at relocating heavy and chemical industries affected by pollution constraints and higher oil prices. Government agencies
encouraged private sector cooperation in large projects and helped in the
provision of special tax exemptions, financing, and information. The network also helped to develop and support what were then considered "new
forms of investment" such as patent licensing agreements, turnkey contracts, and "lend-and-import" contracts.[27] These innovations reduced investor risk even as they facilitated access to raw material sources.

---

are the Economic Planning Agency and the ministries of International Trade and Industry,
Finance, and Foreign Affairs. The private sector has been involved both directly, through
peak and trade associations such as Keidanren and the Japan Plant Exporters' Association,
and indirectly, through various *shingikai* or deliberation councils.

[26] Ibid., p. 44.

[27] Krause and Sekiguchi, "Japan and the World Economy," p. 447; Terutomo Ozawa, "Jap-

The most striking case of such support for industrial relocation involved the Asahan project in Indonesia. Asahan involved the construction of a large dam and a hydroelectric power station, an aluminum refinery that uses the power generated, and associated infrastructural facilities.[28] Financing was arranged by Japanese official sources and commercial banks, with Indonesia contributing 10 percent. While the Indonesian government owns 41 percent of the project, management rests in the hands of a firm composed of Japanese aluminum makers and trading companies whose investments were financed by government-sponsored loans. Western firms did not participate in the project.

The project is significant in part because it is the largest aid project ever completed by Japan and supplied almost 20 percent of Japan's virgin aluminum imports by the mid-1980s.[29] By excluding Western firms, Asahan also represented an effort to expand Japanese resource autonomy, a pattern also seen in Japan's oil and LNG (liquid natural gas) loans to Indonesia during the early 1970s.[30] Finally, the Asahan formula of public sector cooperation on the Japanese side in a joint venture with foreign governments was important as an institutional innovation that (1) coordinated the interests of a large number of actors in a way that satisfied both public and private interests; (2) reduced the costs incurred by private Japanese firms in expensive projects; (3) provided support for capital-needy governments anxious to launch large projects; and (4) maintained management control in Japanese hands.

The institutional feature may help to explain a phenomenon that appears striking in comparison with Latin America—namely, the absence of outright or even threatened expropriations of large natural resource or infrastructural projects in the region. Given the importance of such projects to Japan, the known susceptibility of large investments to expropriation, and the strength of Indonesia's nationalist heritage—memories of the Japanese occupation and an ambivalence toward capitalism—Tokyo's investments would seem to have been vulnerable to opportunistic takeover by the host country. Indeed, the Indonesians charged that the project failed in terms of technology transfer, employment creation, and regional development, and that the project has been a financial disappointment

anese Multinationals and 1992," in *Multinationals and Europe 1992: Strategies for the Future*, ed. B. Burgenmeier and J. L. Mucchieli (New York: Routledge, 1991), p. 142.
[28] Terutomo Ozawa, *Multinationalism, Japanese Style: The Political Economy of Outward Dependency* (Princeton: Princeton University Press, 1979), p. 101; Arase, *Buying Power*, p. 87.
[29] Arase, *Buying Power*, p. 79.
[30] See Chapter 5 herein.

because of Japanese transfer pricing.[31] In 1988 the Indonesians imposed an embargo on the project's aluminum exports to Japan.

But the embargo was only temporary. Why? One part of the answer illustrates the importance of the project's ties to the Indonesian government. Given President Suharto's dominant political position, there was little public willingness to criticize the project, for whom the project has been a success. Second, Indonesia did not have the human resources to replace the Japanese managers of the project. And finally, the Japanese benefited from at least implicit issue linkage. The Indonesian government wanted large projects but was very cautious about financing them itself due to previous financial losses from domestic project mismanagement. The fact that Japan was its largest aid donor thus restricted Indonesia's freedom of action.[32]

By the mid-1970s, Japan had abandoned a critical component of the Asahan formula—its exclusion of Western firms. As the Japanese began to value stability of oil and natural gas supplies over resource autonomy, Tokyo came to rely on transnational corporate bargains backed up with insurance and finance by different governments.[33] But public-private sector cooperation continued to be a core component of Japanese raw material procurement efforts. Such cooperation was evident in projects involving petrochemicals in Singapore, petroleum in the Middle East, and, in the late 1970s, raw materials and intermediate goods in China. The latter effort involved a Japanese ODA program to facilitate Chinese exports of energy and steel in exchange for sales of Japanese equipment and plants. This aid took the form of OECF and ExIm Bank loans used for major infrastructure projects and joint ventures involving Japanese steelmakers.[34]

Light manufacturers became a second focus of Japanese FDI in East Asia. Starting in the mid to late 1960s, Japanese producers of textiles, electrical appliances and sundries began to encounter rising wage rates, U.S. protectionism, and the yen's rapid appreciation. In response, the government encouraged a rationalization of domestic capacity, especially in textiles.[35] These push conditions led to an outflow of textile and electronics investment to East Asia, especially to South Korea and Taiwan; however,

---

[31] Arase, *Buying Power*, p. 87.
[32] Ibid., pp. 87–90; John Bresnan, *Managing Indonesia: The Modern Political Economy* (New York: Columbia University Press, 1993), p. 192.
[33] See Chapter 5 herein.
[34] Ibid., pp. 103, 145–46; Arase, *Buying Power*, p. 77.
[35] Michael G. Plummer and Eric D. Ramstetter, "Multinational Affiliates and the Changing Division of Labor in the Asia-Pacific Region," in *Direct Foreign Investment in Asia's Developing Economies and Structural Change in the Asia-Pacific Region*, ed. Ramstetter (Boulder, Colo.: Westview Press, 1991), p. 251.

textile and electronics firms differed in their domestic industrial organization, the homogeneity of their products, and the export-sales ratios of their overseas operations. As a result, their institutional supports differed as well.

In electronics, large firms such as NEC, Matsushita, Sanyo, Hitachi, and Fujitsu led the investment flow to East Asia. Because their focus was on production of low-technology, household appliances (such as small TV sets) for protected host country markets, these investments took the form of minority joint ventures operating with considerable independence from the parent firm. Matsushita's "mini-Matsus," for example, had extensive autonomy in production organization, support services, and, most critical, distribution channels and marketing approaches.[36]

In contrast to electronics, most Japanese textile firms investing in East Asia during the 1960s were fairly small. This pattern reflected the structure of Japan's domestic textile industry, in which a multitude of small and medium-scale enterprises in weaving and finishing coexisted with large fiber producers.[37] Textiles also differed from electronics in that overseas textile operations exported a significant proportion of output to third countries through subcontracting arrangements.

These conditions posed daunting information and coordination problems for small textile firms lacking experience in foreign operations. They consequently invested in groups, usually centered on banks and trading companies (*sogo shosha*). While the former provided finance, the trading companies supplied international trade expertise and linkage capacities. Because textiles usually involved homogeneous products, the *shosha* were able to supply key inputs and manage output distribution.[38] By introducing new machinery, techniques, and Japanese technicians for ongoing training to regular clients, the *shosha* also helped coordinate local and Japan-based production units. Trading companies thus helped smaller firms to "exploit firm-specific assets and/or internalize transactions through DFI in a manner similar to larger firms in less competitive industries."[39] The trading companies were then, along with links between producers, a key mechanism for the regionalization of Japanese production.

But trading companies were not limited to serving small firms in ho-

---

[36] Dieter Ernst, "Carriers of Regionalization: The East Asian Production Networks of Japanese Electronics Firms," Working Paper 73, Berkeley Roundtable on the International Economy, 1994, pp. 13–14.
[37] Economist Intelligence Unit, "A Japanese Approach to Investment," *EIU Textile Outlook International*, March 1991, p. 36.
[38] Encarnation, *Bringing East Asia into the U.S-Japan Rivalry*, p. 20.
[39] Eric D. Ramstetter, "Regional Patterns of Japanese Multinational Activities in Japan and Asia's Developing Countries" (Department of Economics, Kansai University, 1991), p. 97.

mogeneous product markets. In textiles, as with C. Itoh's role in Teijin's initial investment in Thailand during the 1960s, the trading companies facilitated the overseas expansion of large upstream fiber firms.[40] In the automobile industry, host country industrialization strategies compelled Japanese assemblers to set up production and assembly facilities in Southeast Asia in the early 1970s. The *shosha* helped the automakers create distribution networks, to set up after-sales service facilities, and obtain local supplies.[41] Together with networks of assemblers and their affiliated auto parts suppliers, the trading companies also helped producers contend with lower-level political and economic risks, especially those, such as foreign equity limitations and local contents requirements, associated with what Charles Lipson calls "creeping expropriation."[42] By helping identify local partners, the trading companies allowed Japanese producers to operate in minority ventures with political protection. By facilitating the movement of affiliated parts suppliers to East Asia, the *shosha* and the assemblers were at least publicly able to meet local-content requirements in small, fragmented markets, without sacrificing quality or price. The capacity to meet such requirements was also enhanced by two other factors: (1) the practice of importing components from Japan through a local firm and then buying them as "locally produced parts," and (2) the ability to transfer small-batch production methods to Southeast Asia, thus lowering the costs of producing many different models. And in the case of autos, it was precisely the capacity to contend with unfamiliar markets and "creeping expropriation" that allowed the Japanese to replace the previously dominant Western producers.

The preceding discussion illustrates three central points: first, foreign investment in East Asia was often part of Japan's early domestic restructuring. Second, institutions—the ODA or "economic cooperation" network, large firms, and trading companies—played important roles in facilitating coordination among firms lacking capital or information and therefore minimizing risks involved in these investments. Third, although these institutions all exhibit network and information-sharing characteristics, their differences allowed them to address the particular coordination and risk-minimizing challenges of specific industries.

---

[40] Jeffrey S. Arpan, Mary Barry, and Tran Van Tho, "The Textile Complex in the Asia-Pacific Region: The Patterns and Textures of Competition and the Shape of Things to Come," in *Research in International Business and Finance 4:B* (Greenwich, Conn: (JAI Press, 1984), p. 144.
[41] Unless noted, the discussion of auto investments in Southeast Asia draws on Richard F. Doner, *Driving a Bargain: Auto Industrialization and Japanese Firms in Southeast Asia* (Berkeley and Los Angeles: University of California Press, 1991).
[42] Charles Lipson, *Standing Guard: Protecting Foreign Capital in the Nineteenth and Twentieth Centuries* (Berkeley and Los Angeles: University of California Press, 1985).

Supplementing these specialized arrangements were more general institutional responses to issues surrounding Japan's role in East Asia. One challenge involved host country opposition to Japan's rapidly growing economic presence in the region. Following large anti-Japanese demonstrations in Bangkok and Jakarta during the early 1970s, the Japanese formed a number of joint, public-private organizations to address criticisms of Japanese firms and business practices. Tokyo formed the Japan Overseas Enterprises Association in 1974 to "serve as a coordinator, a mediator, a consultant, and a trouble shooter for Japanese corporations expanding their operations abroad," especially in the developing countries of Asia.[43] Japan also expanded its mechanisms for technology transfer to the region. These included, for example, the Association for Overseas Technical Scholarship, an organization through which East Asian employees of Japanese affiliates were trained in Japan. By 1984, this organization had enrolled over 27,000 students. It also involved, in the case of Thailand, a Technological Promotion Association, organized by MITI and funded by Japanese firms, that succeeded in coopting some of those involved in anti-Japanese activities.[44]

Tokyo also played pivotal roles in the development of institutions designed to promote broader regional linkages. The lineage of these activities can be traced to Saburo Okita's pre–World War II efforts to establish a regional forum for economic cooperation.[45] Okita also played a central role in Japan's postwar regional initiatives. These included the creation of both functionalist organizations and groups devoted to the broader concept of regional cooperation. In 1961, under pressure from the Japanese private sector, (acting through the Japan Productivity Center), Tokyo initiated the Asian Productivity Organization (APO). Through research, conferences, study missions, and training courses held in conjunction with National Productivity Organizations, the APO is designed to strengthen member countries' institutional and technical capacities in business administration and production engineering.[46] By the mid-1960s, the APO's success, combined with Tokyo's desire to counter regional concerns about

---

[43] The organization focused on seven countries—South Korea, the Philippines, Singapore, Thailand, Malaysia, Indonesia, and Brazil. Ozawa, *Multinationalism*, pp. 194–95.
[44] Richard F. Doner, "Japanese Foreign Investment and the Creation of a Pacific Asian Region," in *Regionalism and Rivalry: Japan and the United States in Pacific Asia*, ed. Miles Kahler and Jeffrey Frankel (Chicago: University of Chicago Press, 1993), pp. 188–189n. 28. See also Arase, *Buying Power*, p. 198.
[45] Unless otherwise noted, the discussion of Japanese regional initiatives draws on Lawrence T. Woods, *Asia-Pacific Diplomacy: Nongovernmental Organizations and International Relations* (Vancouver: University of British Columbia Press, 1993).
[46] Michael Haas, *The Asian Way to Peace: A Story of Regional Cooperation* (New York: Praeger, 1989), pp. 67–69, chap. 6.

the prospect of a new Co-Prosperity Sphere, led Japan to establish additional forums through which Southeast Asian nations could make their own demands on Japan, rather than the other way around. These included functional organizations whose activities ranged from fisheries development to transport and communications.

Japan also initiated or helped to create institutions devoted to cooperation in a broader sense. After failing to achieve agreement on free trade, the Japan-initiated Pacific Trade and Development Conference (PAFTAD) helped to develop a policy-oriented research network that reportedly influenced the region's shift toward export promotion. The Pacific Basin Economic Council (PBEC) was organized at the initiative of a Japanese peak business association and became the focus of private sector efforts toward Pacific economic cooperation. The Pacific Economic Cooperation Council (PECC), initiated in the late 1970s by Japan and Australia, attempted to become a sort of Asian Trilateral Commission in which business leaders and academics could address specific issues such as industrial policies, services, and regional trade.[47]

The results of these efforts were uneven. But by providing various collective goods—contact coordination, technological support, and policy-related research and discussion—they seem to have created regional goodwill toward Japan, promoted a belief in the utility of economic openness, and convinced Japan's neighbors of the virtues of intra-regional variety in development. Together, they constituted a functionalist mechanism that encouraged and supplemented region-wide, state-to-state contacts on trade and development. State-to-state contacts eventually took the form of APEC.

In contrast to such enthusiasm for regional economic cooperation, Japan adopted a relatively indifferent position toward the region's broadest and most successful group—the Association of Southeast Asian Nations (ASEAN), established in 1967. Until the mid-1970s, Tokyo provided little institutional support for ASEAN and dealt with the member countries on a *bilateral* basis. This was largely because until 1976 ASEAN functioned as a security-oriented institution. Only when issues affecting its economic relations with several members emerged did Japan begin to deal with the group on a multilateral basis. The earliest indication of this shift occurred in 1976 when Tokyo was forced to address collective ASEAN concerns that Japan's production of synthetic rubber would undermine the natural rubber industries of member states.[48] Negotiations not only resulted in a

---

[47] Also see the introduction to this book.
[48] Arnfinn Jorgensen-Dahl, *Regional Organization and Order in South-East Asia* (New York: St. Martin's Press, 1982), pp. 146–47.

Japanese pledge to restrict synthetic rubber production and to provide technical support for research into new uses for natural rubber. They also led to the creation of an institutional forum to address Japan-ASEAN conflicts. In 1977 this was followed by a Japanese pledge of substantial financial support for ASEAN industrial projects devoted to the production of intermediate materials. But the Japanese did not embrace ASEAN as a key to economic integration. For example, until the late 1980s, they resisted an ASEAN plan for regional auto production that would have expanded scale economies but would have also undermined auto exports from Japan.

Two other features of Japan's initiatives in regional institutions merit note. One is the extensive role, in some cases the initiative, of the Japanese private sector. The other is the process through which Japan seems to have learned to operate as first among equals in a loose kind of multilateralism. Both features are illustrated in the case of the Asian Development Bank, established in 1966. Japan was the moving force behind the creation of the ADB. The original concept for the institution came from a study group of financial sector leaders and retired officials. After extensive bureaucratic maneuvering, the Japanese government proposed the Bank's creation, assuming that Tokyo, as the initiator and most powerful regional actor, would become the site of the Bank's headquarters. To Japan's surprise, under Philippine leadership, the other Asian states voted to establish the ADB headquarters in Manila. Despite Asian acceptance of a Japanese as president of the ADB, the headquarters decision made the Japanese delegation realize that other Asians "were not ready to acquiesce to Japan's self-appointed leadership role in Asia" simply on the basis of its economic accomplishments.[49] In response, Tokyo developed a leadership style within the Bank that renounced national interest criteria in the formulation of ADB policy.

Stimulated by currency shifts, expanding domestic markets, and liberalized foreign investment regimes, Japanese investment in East Asia skyrocketed in the latter half of the 1980s. Although the global proportion of Japanese FDI going to East Asia declined because of higher rates of growth for FDI to Europe and North America, the absolute levels rose sharply.[50] In addition several more specific changes occurred that, taken together, posed new challenges for Japanese firms.

---

[49] Dennis T. Yasutomo, *Japan and the Asian Development Bank* (New York: Praeger, 1983), p. 77, from which this account is drawn.
[50] See Chapter 1 herein.

Toward an Expanded, Intra-Industry Division of Labor

Recent Japanese investment into the region has resulted in a geographic expansion of integrated manufacturing activities. Japanese FDI in Asian manufacturing from 1986 to 1989 was greater than the cumulative total for the period 1951–85.[51] The sectoral emphasis of these flows has been, in order of importance, on electronics and electrical equipment, textile products, transportation equipment, petroleum and chemical products, and iron and nonferrous metals.[52] Much of this manufacturing investment went to the ASEAN states and China rather than to Korea and Taiwan, and, since the early 1990s, especially to China.[53] The Japanese shifted their export-oriented production of consumer goods and, eventually, electronic components, from the NICs to the PRC and Southeast Asia. Japanese investment in the NICs began to emphasize service industries, while the NICs contributed to this expansion of production by investing heavily in the ASEAN countries and the PRC. The NICs accounted for 70 percent of the FDI to China between 1986 and 1992 and almost 30 percent to ASEAN during the same period, compared to levels of 10 percent and 26 percent for Japan.[54] Overseas Chinese (OC) funds were a critical part of these flows. By 1992 OC investment throughout the region had risen to 10.6 percent of global investment inflows, up from 5.5 percent in 1990.[55]

Japanese FDI flows to the region, especially those to the ASEAN countries, have also become increasingly export oriented.[56] By 1990, the export-sales ratio of Japanese affiliates in East Asia was 40 percent, up from 36 percent a decade earlier and significantly higher than levels for affiliates

[51] Bernard and Ravenhill, "Beyond Product Cycles," p. 181.

[52] Takeshi Aoki, "Japanese FDI and the Forming of Networks in the Asia-Pacific Region: Experience in Malaysia and Its Implications," in *Japan's Foreign Investment*, ed. Shojiro Tokunaga (1992), p. 96.

[53] Measured by number of projects, Japanese investments in China rose from 6.9 percent of total Japanese investment in 1990 to *40.4 percent* in 1992. JETRO (Japan External Trade Organization), *JETRO White Paper on Foreign Direct Investment, 1994* (Tokyo: JETRO, 1994), p. 15.

[54] World Bank, *The East Asian Miracle: Economic Growth and Public Policy* (World Bank: Oxford University Press, 1993), p. 45; see also Chapter 9 herein. In 1990, the NICs as a group were the largest investor in every ASEAN country and China. Shujiro Urata, "Globalization and Regionalization in the Pacific-Asia Region," *Business and the Contemporary World*, Autumn, 1993, pp. 26–45.

[55] *JETRO White Paper*, p. 7.

[56] There was some movement for Japanese affiliates in Southeast Asia to produce for export in the early 1980s in response to trade frictions with the United States and export promotion policies by host countries. To promote this shift, Japan used its ODA program to launch a major petrochemical and infrastructure project in Thailand, the Eastern Seaboard Development project. Arase, *Buying Power*, p. 102. Most Japanese production in ASEAN prior to the mid-1980s, however, was for the host country market.

in the United States (8 percent) and Western Europe (4 percent).[57] But unlike the early 1980s, these exports are increasingly going to other countries within the region, including Japan. Japanese investments in East Asia have thus promoted a more self-sufficient, regional division of labor.[58]

Characterizing this division of labor is difficult because of its dynamism and because of the differences between industries. Higher capital costs and more enduring home-country advantages and firm-specific assets in autos, for example, have meant that intra-firm linkages and regional specialization are less developed in autos than in the electronics industry. Nevertheless, we can identify several basic purposes and characteristics of this system. First, although basic innovations and core component development have remained in Japan, this division of labor involves a shift away from the assembly of parts made in Japan to the actual manufacture of parts, components, and finished products in the rest of Asia. This implies a shift away from certain aspects of Japan's "full-set" industrial structure. The argument is not that Japan will abandon certain industries. It is rather that Japanese firms, because of the closing of "dirty, dangerous and difficult" operations such as casting, forging and plating, and the weakening of "technological communities" of specialized, small and medium-sized machining, will lose the capacity to implement a full set of manufacturing functions, from prototype development to mass production.[59]

The new system also entails a consolidation and expansion of existing facilities overseas, although in some cases Japanese firms will create completely new facilities. In Thailand, for example, Toyota is expanding its operations in a Thai version of "Toyota City" to incorporate and integrate a broader range of operations for particular groups of products. This is designed to reduce the duplication of functions common to the previous, haphazard structure of manufacturing facilities. Thus emphasis has shifted from linkages with the home office in Japan to cross-sourcing and sales within the region.

Third, the system aims at regional specialization by what Ohoka terms

---

[57] Urata, "Globalization," p. 42.

[58] Japanese affiliates in Europe, the United States, and Asia all sell roughly 90 percent of their products to their particular regional markets. Asian affiliates (in both the NICs and ASEAN) sell roughly 65 percent of their goods to the local market, export around 15 percent to Japan and another 10–11 percent to other Asian markets. U.S. affiliates sell 92 percent to the U.S. market. EC affiliates sell 55 percent to the local market and another 38 percent to the rest of Europe. Masaru Yoshitomi, "Building a New United States–Pacific Asia Economic Relationship for the Post-Uruguay Round Era," in *Economic Cooperation and Challenges in the Pacific* (Berkeley: Korea Institute of America, 1994), table 10.

[59] Seki Mitsuhiro, *Beyond the Full-Set Industrial Structure: Japanese Industry in the New Age of East Asia* (Tokyo: LTCB International Library Foundation, 1994), p. 39; Bernard and Ravenhill, "Beyond Product Cycles."

the "value-added differential."[60] This takes two forms. One, more horizontal, involves the production and exchange of intermediate goods and components whose value-added depends on the factor endowments and other locational advantages of the host country. Honda, for example, produces engine components in Indonesia, plastic parts in Malaysia, press parts and clutches in Thailand, and transmission parts in the Philippines.[61] The second form is more vertical and involves the production in East Asia of lower-end models of finished goods that Japanese firms used to produce at home for export.[62] Both of these entail an expansion of intra-industry trade.

It is also important to note that national factor endowments and locational advantages are not static phenomena. Manufacture of one product can constitute demand for an input and generate the skills to produce that input. For example, the concentration of consumer electronics manufacturing in the region, especially Malaysia, creates a demand for discrete transistors and certain types of integrated circuits. Given the need for just-in-time inventory practices, this creates the potential for Malaysian production of such inputs.

Finally, Japanese firms are attempting to combine an emphasis on standardized goods when possible with a capacity to satisfy particular host country market demand when necessary. The general preference of Japanese firms is to expand scale economies and reduce costs by producing and exchanging standardized parts in a sort of "world car" or "world microwave" strategy. This strategy of commonizing parts across the region is often combined with local procurement of molds and dies. But given fierce inter-firm competition and the rapid growth and sophisticated nature of East Asian markets, the capacity to address more particular demand is necessary. The degree to which such market-specific production occurs depends in part on the nature of the market and local private sector. Thus Indonesia and Thailand have been the source of specially designed all-purpose vehicles, motorcycles, and pickup trucks (Thailand is the second largest market for pickups in the world). Degree of product differentiation also varies with corporate preferences and capacities. Nissan tends to emulate GM and Ford's "world car" strategy based upon global production of common parts and designs; Honda attempts to develop models for particular regions; and Mazda commonizes main components but modifies the outer body to suit national design preferences.[63] Finally, some firms

[60] Ohoka, "East Asia and Japan."
[61] Henny Sender, "The Pragmatic Colossus," *Institutional Investor*, November 1991, pp. 119–25.
[62] Ozawa, "Japan in a New Phase."
[63] David W. Edgington, "The Globalization of Japanese Manufacturing Corporations," *Growth and Change* 24 (Winter 1993): 100; "Mazda Activities in Southeast Asia and China," *Tradescope*, July 1994, p. 20.

are attempting to combine standardization and diversification strategies by exporting products developed for specific, host-country markets.[64]

Where possible, this strategy involves the Asian region as part of a global production network. But the growth of Asian production integration suggests that the Japanese, as well as other Asians, see the utility of a self-sufficient region as insurance against broader trade conflicts and currency shifts.[65] Even within a self-contained region, however, Japanese firms confront several major tasks. First, as part of a region-wide production structure, firms must achieve export-level quality and price, thus losing the luxury of protected markets. On the other hand, firms must also be able to produce goods suited to particular markets. Second, because of intensified competition firms must reduce throughput time to bring finished goods to market more quickly. Logistics—the control of material flows from source to user—becomes a competitive asset. And third, given declining growth rates in the industrialized countries, Japanese firms must gain access to the larger East Asian markets, especially China and Vietnam.

Achieving each of these tasks entails unforeseeable costs and risks. Firms cannot control the quality, delivery, or prices of their inputs. Suppliers may invest large sums of funds in production for a particular client, only to find the latter refusing delivery. Firms needing to move goods quickly may not have access to rapid or reliable transportation facilities. Firms anxious to gain access to new markets may suffer from a shortage of information about consumer preferences, local partners, property rights, and so on. Moreover, these problems usually result from some combination of straightforward transaction costs (such as difficulties of finding partners, making agreements, and enforcing agreements), as well as deliberate opportunism. Such obstructionism may be private, in which partners refuse to comply with agreements; or it may be public, in which governments alter prices through devaluations, tariff changes, differing inflation rates, and so on. Japanese firms have established rules, standards, specifications, and the like to address such coordination problems arising from this increasingly integrated production system.

Institutional Responses

The institutions central to the development of East Asian production structures range from purely private sector arrangements to government-

---

[64] For example, Toyota plans production of a compact car in Thailand for possible export to South America and the Middle East. Nissan plans production of a pickup truck in Thailand for export to Taiwan and the Philippines.
[65] Edgington, "Globalization," p. 103.

sponsored programs involving a wide range of public and private interests. Many of these institutions are essentially extensions of home-based practices. This is consistent with the similarity between some of the challenges now encountered in the region, such as the need to combine standardization, cost minimization, quality, and product diversity, and those the Japanese have faced at home. In some cases, the Japanese have modified and/or expanded home-based practices designed to deal with new conditions. From a Japanese perspective, this combination of traditional and modified arrangements has functioned fairly well. In some cases, however, home-based institutions adopted without much modification may be ill-suited for use elsewhere in the region.

Japanese firms have replicated and diffused their home-based networks to East Asia since the mid-1980s. These networks are mechanisms of coordination among formally independent firms involving long-term collaboration based on a distribution of technological skills and production practices.[66] Although networks can link producers downstream to distributors, and producers to one another (to share technology or pool resources), our principal concern is with *supplier* networks. These are subcontracting or original equipment manufacture (OEM) linkages between final producers and providers of components, materials, parts, software, and subassemblies.

The supplier networks underlying Japan's FDI have been relatively closed to non-Japanese firms. They are either intra-*firm*, that is, linkages between affiliates and a parent company, or between affiliates owned by the same parent, or they are intra-*group*, that is, affiliates of firms that have long-standing relationships with the parent or its affiliates (Nippondenso and Toyota). The significance of such relationships is illustrated by figures for sales and procurement of Japan's East Asian affiliates: From 1986 to 1992, the percentage of intra-firm trade between Japan and Asian affiliates grew from 77 percent to 84 percent for exports and from 67 percent to 78 percent for imports of all manufactured products. The share of intra-firm trade was especially high for transport, precision, and electrical machinery. The latter industry alone contributed nearly half of the growth in overseas production by Japanese firms in Asia during the 1985–93 period,

[66] On Japan as a "network society," see Shumpei Kumon, "Japan as a Network Society," in *The Political Economy of Japan*, vol. 3, *Cultural and Social Dynamics*, ed. Shumpei Kumon and Henry Rosovsky (Stanford: Stanford University Press, 1993). For definitions of networks, see Ernst, "Carriers," and Ernst, "Network Transactions, Market Structure and Technology Diffusion—Implications for South-South Co-Operation," in *South-South Co-Operation in a Global Perspective*, ed. Lynn K. Mytelka (Paris: OECD, 1994); The following discussion draws heavily on the cited works of Dieter Ernst.

yet Japanese electronics affiliates in the region "procure hardly anything at all from extra-regional sources."[67]

These networks were established in East Asia for the same reasons that they operate in Japan. Major Japanese firms in the electronics and automotive industries have become assemblers of subassemblies and components provided by formally independent but in fact closely linked suppliers. With suppliers shouldering product development costs, networks can reduce the risks and expenses for final producers attempting to expand their range of products. Network-based suppliers can help final producers ensure continual and inexpensive access to key inputs such as core components, materials, and human resources. Such functions are especially important under conditions of volatile markets and changing technologies. And networks can accomplish these functions through a process of reciprocity and consensus building that reduces each side's incentives to break the agreement.[68]

In Japan, such functions have been important in helping Japanese firms deal with pressure for constant quality improvement as well as protectionism, demand fluctuations, and shortened product lifecycles. These conditions have spread to East Asia since the mid-1980s. When combined with the weaknesses of local suppliers, they have stimulated the growth of similar arrangements both within and across East Asian countries.

In some cases, these networks link downstream producers to upstream suppliers of raw materials and intermediate goods. Mitsubishi Petrochemical, a major supplier of polypropylene material for bumpers, has thus expanded its Asian operations in response to the growth of Japanese auto production in the region.[69] A greater number of cases involve the supply of parts and components. To illustrate the structure of the latter type, consider the operations of Japanese auto assemblers in Thailand. Each automaker typically has some forty to sixty suppliers.[70] These are divided up hierarchically into affiliates, close associates, and general vendors. The affiliate group is dominated by Japanese suppliers with long-standing ties to the assembler (for Toyota, for example, the firms are Nippondenso, NHK, Kalawis, and Arrow). The close associates and general vendors are

[67] Ernst, "Network Transactions," p. 11; Yoshitomi, "Building," pp. 29, 40.

[68] Ernst, "Network Transactions," pp. 92–94; Michael J. Smitka, *Competitive Ties: Subcontracting in the Japanese Automotive Industry* (New York: Columbia University Press, 1991); Kumon, "Japan as a Network Society."

[69] "Thailand: PP-Compounds JV Planned—Misubishi Petrochemical," *Japan Chemical Week*, May 19, 1994.

[70] Richard F. Doner and Patcharee Siroros, "Contending with Fragmented Markets: Firm and Group in the Thai Auto Parts Industry" (Department of Political Science, Emory University, 1993).

local firms with lower levels of technical capacity and linkages with the assembler.

The hierarchical nature of this structure is reflected in the level and nature of interaction between the assembler and the three groups. Affiliates are firms with whom the assembler has extensive technical exchanges and joint investments, and from whom it obtains most of its locally produced parts (Japanese assemblers in Thailand obtain around 70 percent of their locally procured parts from these affiliates). Associates are regular subcontractors who receive design specifications and limited technical assistance from the assemblers. Vendors are local suppliers with the lowest level of technical capacity and interaction with the assembler.

Supplementing this Thai-based network is an emerging intra-regional system of automotive parts exchange based on special tariff reductions and local content accreditation among the ASEAN member countries. Known as "brand-to-brand complementarity," this program allows Toyota affiliates in the region, for example, to obtain diesel engines from Thailand, transmissions from the Philippines, steering gears from Malaysia, and gas engines from Indonesia. As noted earlier, this program originated as an ASEAN proposal for parts exchange under national auspices. After years of resistance from the Japanese, it turned into a company-led arrangement.

Japanese corporate networks have used other networks in the region. In some instances these involve personal relationships dating back to World War II. This has been the case for some Japanese firms operating in Indonesia, but most recently and prominently in the northeast China province of Liaoning. At present, the heaviest area of Japanese activity is in the Liaoning provincial city of Dalian, the site of roughly half of Japan's cumulative investment in China for the 1987–91 period.[71] Once the headquarters of Japan's Imperial Army in Manchuria, Dalian was the site of a relatively peaceful Japanese occupation during the war and is considered home by many Japanese managers who grew up there, including the head of Nippon Steel Corporation and the governor of the Bank of Japan.[72] The city is geographically close to Japan and many of its citizens are still fluent in Japanese.

In the future, however, Japanese investment activity will spread into other areas of Liaoning.[73] The area around the province's capital city of Shenyang is China's leading heavy industry region as a result of Japanese

[71] Ministry of International Trade and Industry (MITI), *White Paper on International Trade—Japan (Summary)* (Tokyo: MITI, 1994); table 1–3–17. See also Emily Thornton, "1994. Opportunity Knocks," *Fair Eastern Economic Review,* December 8, 1994, p. 46.

[72] Sender, "Pragmatic Colossus," p. 124.

[73] The discussion of Japanese activity in Liaoning draws on Mitsuhiro, *Beyond the Full-Set Industrial Structure,* pp. 120–25.

industrial activities there before the war and extensive Soviet industrial assistance during the 1950s. Building on this base, the Chinese have begun to organize industrial development zones, as aggregations of fundamental technologies, and a science and technology zone, as a stimulus to high-tech innovations, an incubator for business startups and catalyst of high-tech joint ventures (with the regional university). These zones are beneficial for the Japanese in part because they incorporate numerous Chinese factories that once belonged to Japanese companies. Equally important, the zones offer agglomeration economies similar to and in some cases superior to those provided by industrial districts in Japan itself. From the Japanese perspective, such networks can constitute the repository for the fundamental technologies dying out in Japan. Shenyang, may become China's principal component in an East Asian industrial network.

Given the explosion of overseas Chinese capital noted earlier, Japanese firms might also be expected to make use of OC networks. Such was certainly the case before 1985. During the 1960s and 1970s, Japanese firms relied heavily on national ethnic Chinese groups to facilitate entrance into specific Southeast Asian markets. In textiles, the Japanese also established ties with regional Chinese networks built on the skills and financial support of Shanghai capitalists in Hong Kong. During the 1960s, Toray developed what one study termed a "new type of multinationalization": by linking up with TAL, a large Hong Kong textile converter, Toray was able to extend its operations into Taiwan, Thailand, and eventually the rest of Southeast Asia, where twenty-eight of its thirty-nine major subsidiaries are located.[74]

Japanese firms have not made extensive use of OC networks in the more recent period, at least in comparison with U.S. firms in electronics production. But they have relied on the overseas Chinese for two reasons, one of which is to maintain reliable access to certain types of low-end production. In Thailand, for example, a Taiwanese electronics firm produces low-end calculators on an OEM basis for Sharp, Casio, and Canon.[75] Even more important are linkages based on the ability of OC networks to facilitate Japanese access to new markets. This is perhaps clearest in the auto industry where Japanese assemblers have used ASEAN and Taiwanese local partners to reduce the risks and costs of moving into China and Vietnam.[76]

Despite some participation by NIC firms, non-Japanese suppliers have generally remained weak in Japanese production networks. But under con-

---

[74] Arpan, Barry, and Van Tho, "Textile Complex," p. 139. See also Louise do Rosario, "The Ties That Bind," *Far Eastern Economic Review*, September 5, 1991, p. 66.
[75] Bernard and Ravenhill, "Beyond Product Cycles," p. 186.
[76] See, e.g., Lee Siew Lian, "Malaysia: $100M Khazanah Investment in China," *Business Times* (Malaysia), June 9, 1994.

tinued pressures from currency shifts, national desires for technology transfer, and competition from U.S. and NIC firms, the Japanese have begun to upgrade the capacities of indigenous firms in Southeast Asia. Much of this effort occurs in a bilateral context between an assembler and an individual supplier. But in the Southeast Asian auto industry it has also taken a more multilateral form through the creation of supplier cooperation clubs organized by particular assemblers. Patterned after similar institutions in Japan, these clubs are designed with a dual purpose: to promote cohesion, trust, and linkages among related firms; and to help local firms improve performance in areas such as statistical process control, time and motion, and inventory reduction. To these ends, the clubs organize social activities as well as case studies, lectures, contests, and factory visits.[77]

Three features of these clubs merit special note. First, they do not necessarily tie local suppliers to a single assembler. Given the limited size of local markets, most large local suppliers belong to several different clubs, even if they produce primarily for one assembler. Second, local parts firms are ambivalent about these groups. While they recognize the benefits of membership, they are also conscious that the clubs reinforce Japanese domination and serve to exclude those not favored by the Japanese.

Finally, the clubs seem especially well suited to helping local firms conform to what Charles Sabel terms "discursive standards" such as ISO 9000. Unlike conventional standards, which specify and allow measurement of product attributes (for example, tensile strength of steel) or production processes (such as weld tests), discursive standards "establish procedures by which firms can be certified as competent to . . . make claims regarding their capability to perform as promised."[78] Under ISO 9000, a firm must be able to answer questions concerning its understanding of its customers' expectations, its capacity to deliver the designs and products it has promised, its ability to identify and correct weaknesses in performance. The more advanced Southeast Asian parts suppliers now recognize the importance of meeting ISO 9000 standards because they are often required for firms exporting to Western Europe and, more basically, because they reflect a firm's capacity to contend with more demanding and shifting markets. Meeting these standards requires ongoing information exchanges

---

[77] Smitka, *Competitive Ties*; Doner and Siroros, "Contending with Fragmented Markets."

[78] The following discussion draws on Charles F. Sabel, "Discussing Evaluation in a World of Discursive Standards: Assessing Manufacturing Technology Centers" (paper presented for the workshop on Manufacturing Modernization: Evaluation Practices, Methods, and Results, Atlanta, September 18–20, 1994), p. 15.

within and among firms with regard to the fit among a firm's technology, organization, procedures and changing environment. Such exchanges are one of the primary functions of producers' associations.[79]

The replication of private sector institutions such as suppliers' associations is reinforced to some degree by Japanese consultants and retired technicians (*ronin*). These individuals, sometimes but not always funded by governmental organizations, helped to improve shop-floor organization and production flows in Korea and Taiwan.[80] There is now evidence that they are becoming active in Southeast Asia as Indonesian, Malaysian, and Thai firms are compelled to meet export-level quality and prices and to conform to broader performance standards such as ISO 9000.[81]

In the simplest networks, a Japanese affiliate imports all necessary materials and components from Japan and subsequently exports all of its products to one country. In the more advanced networks, an affiliate obtains inputs locally from multiple and competing subcontractors while exporting to several different countries.[82] In addition to production, more complex networks require greater attention to tasks such as distribution, transportation, inventory management, marketing, and finance. At some point, these tasks exceed the supervisory capacity of a head office in Japan. They entail not only voluminous and complex transaction costs, but also new forms of uncertainty such as currency fluctuations.

In response, Japanese firms have begun to establish overseas or regional headquarters (OHQ) and international procurement offices (IPOs) in the region. These are most common in electronics, because of the advanced level of networks in that industry, and most numerous in Singapore. Singapore established an extensive incentive program in 1988 to attract such offices as part of its continuing effort to move into higher technology activities and to become the center of regional production. By 1990, the program had attracted over twenty-two major Japanese firms. Matsushita's OHQ, for example, manages twenty-two group factories and trading com-

---

[79] This is not to suggest that all such Japanese-sponsored groups are successful in promoting such exchanges. Raja Rasiah's research on the semiconductor industry in Penang implies that U.S. firms in some industries may be more successful than the Japanese because of the latters' reluctance to rely on indigenous suppliers. Personal communication from Rasiah, 1994.
[80] Bernard, "Pattern and Implications," p. 11.
[81] John Harriss, " 'Japanization': Context and Culture in the Indonesian Automotive Industry" (Development Studies Institute, London School of Economics, 1994); interviews by the author in Bangkok, summer 1994, 1995.
[82] Aoki, "Japanese FDI," p. 89; Lynne E. Guyton, "Japanese and the Transfer of Japanese Consumer Electronics Production to Malaysia" (report prepared for the United Nations Development Program, Kuala Lumpur, 1994).

panies in ASEAN; Fujikara's OHQ manages fifteen affiliated firms in Korea and ASEAN.[83] Sony has established what may be the most advanced headquarters operation thus far. Sony International of Singapore (SONIS) procures parts from around the world and has them shipped by the company's IPO to Southeast Asian factories. When the assembly process is completed, the IPO delivers the products to SONIS for shipment to Sony subsidiaries throughout the region and the world. By integrating production, sales, and distribution, SONIS can maintain just-in-time delivery, zero inventory, and point-of-sale information.

In addition to its capacity to facilitate information flows among related firms, the Sony system also can also address an important source of uncertainty—exchange rate shifts. Under a system of "account settlement without exchange," SONIS uses a system of local currency accounts that cover each others' losses. Remaining funds are used as a hedge against risk through international money markets or the Singapore futures exchange.[84]

Small and medium-sized suppliers have constituted an important component of Japanese investment flows in the last decade.[85] For these firms, as for their predecessors in the textile industry, the *sogo shosha* have been important; however, unlike their predecessors, for whom the *shosha* obtained supplies and identified buyers, small firms are often integrated into networks through which larger firms fulfill these functions. One area in which the trading companies continue to play a major role for small companies, as well as for larger ones, is logistics. While large firms may integrate various functions through global information networks, the physical distribution of their products is handled by specialists, often trading companies. Using extensive computer systems, bonded warehouses, and container shipping services, firms such as Mitsui have become integrated distribution agencies capable of managing entire freight shipping processes for firms as large as Sony.[86]

Since the mid-1980s, the Japanese government has worked with the private sector to develop expanded and sometimes novel instruments of support for Japan's economic growth in the region. These "FDI-promoting

[83] Aoki, "Japanese FDI," pp. 37–40, from which the following discussion of Sony operations is drawn.

[84] Ibid., p. 40. Ernst also describes a situation in Malaysia where the Japanese Chamber of Trade and Industry in Malaysia played an active and successful role in overturning Malaysian central bank currency restrictions designed to combat speculators. *Economist*, August 20, 1994, p. 62; cited in Ernst, "Carriers," p. 25.

[85] FDI by small and medium enterprises (SMEs) rose to its highest point in 1988 and then fell by almost two thirds (in numbers of projects) by 1991; however, the number of SME investments in manufacturing rose in the early 1990s. *JETRO White Paper*, p. 15.

[86] Aoki, "Japanese FDI," pp. 40–41.

systems" range from new legal and insurance mechanisms, to broader forms of "economic cooperation," to greater assertiveness with regard to the utility of the Japanese "model."[87]

The costs and risks of expanded production and distribution in the region go beyond problems such as currency shifts. The risks include an expanding range of problems resulting from private opportunism, such as nonpayment due to bankruptcy, as well as political risk, such as war and internal disorder. The costs involve the increasing demands on firms to move goods more quickly over greater distances. To address the growing range of risks, the Japanese government has expanded its insurance support for Japanese firms operating abroad. In 1987, MITI created a new trade insurance system to (1) protect against risks associated with prepaid manufactured imports, (2) cope with intermediary trade (in which Japanese producers, mostly small and medium-sized firms, establish facilities overseas for export to third countries, with subsequent payment back to Japan), and (3) include a broader range of commercial risks, especially for Japanese SMEs (small and medium enterprises) operating overseas. In addition, Japan participates in a multinational reinsurance system, the Multinational Investment Guarantee Agency, whose purpose is to reinsure developed country losses from investments in developing countries.

With firms placing greater emphasis on speed of time-to-market, the logistics of transport and distribution have become almost as important as production. This is especially the case within East Asia where six of the world's ten largest container ports are found, and intra-regional cargo traffic has now exceeded flows from the region to North America. As Japanese freight forwarders expanded their role in this activity, the Japanese government adopted new legislation to facilitate the development of intermodal transportation. The new laws, adopted in 1989, facilitated the growth of integrated logistics firms by eliminating barriers between various stages of distribution, such as unit-crafting, warehousing, forwarding, truck transport, shipping, and air freight.[88]

Japan has also significantly expanded its system of ODA and "economic cooperation" toward the region. According to one account, this growth began in the early 1980s when MITI, beginning to recognize the need for a shift of Japan's smaller export-oriented firms into Southeast Asia, responded favorably to Thai requests for help in developing a major petro-

---

[87] Shojiro Tokunaga,"Japan's FDI-Promoting System and Intra-Asia Networks: New Investment and Trade Systems Created by the Borderless Economy," in Tokunaga, *Japan's Foreign Investment*, especially pp. 25–28.

[88] Ibid., pp. 25–28.

chemical and infrastructure project on the Eastern Seaboard.[89] This represented a first step in Japan's shift from the promotion of Japanese exports to East Asia to support for Japanese export-oriented FDI in the region.

From MITI's perspective, that transition emerged more fully in the 1987 New Asian Industrial Development (AID) Plan. Rather than a specific spending target, the plan committed the government to promote export-oriented production in Asia as part of Japan's own industrial restructuring. This more activist approach toward regional interdependence reinforced the Japanese private sector's own initiatives toward internationalization. Indeed, as Takashi Shiraishi argues in Chapter 5, the AID Plan reflected MITI's effort to keep up with and exert some guidance over market forces. Individual firms, both large and small, had already begun to signal their intentions of expanding East Asian production following *endaka*. Through Keidanren, big business issued a collective call for a streamlining of Japanese ODA through greater coordination of aid, tax incentives, and trade and investment insurance schemes.[90]

Through grants, loans, and technical support, the AID plan aimed to foster an Asian division of labor by (1) promoting export-oriented infrastructure, (2) providing technical cooperation to develop export industries, including support for "fundamental" production capacities such as forging and casting, and (3) supplying financing for export industries.[91] The organizational mechanisms through which the plan was to be implemented range from purely public sector organizations, such as JICA (technical assistance) and the OECF (financial support), to private sector industry associations of engineering consultants, plant exporters, and groups of small firms operating with public sector support.

As originally conceived, the AID plan was supplemented by several other public-private institutions. The ASEAN-Japan Development Fund, for example, was established in 1987 to provide subsidized financing for regional industrial projects, for joint ventures in particular East Asian countries, and for local capital markets. The Japan International Development Organization was created in 1989 as a joint OECF-Keidanren venture to make equity investments in overseas ventures involving the purchase of obsolete Japanese equipment.

As Takashi Shiraishi notes in Chapter 5, the AID Plan no longer oper-

---

[89] Arase, *Buying Power*, pp. 102–3, from which the rest of this discussion on Japanese ODA is drawn, unless otherwise noted.
[90] Arase, *Buying Power*, pp. 122–29. The importance of private-sector initiatives in East Asian production also emerged in interviews conducted by Patcharee Siroros of Thammasat University with Japanese auto and electronics officials in Tokyo in January–February 1992.
[91] The following discussion draws on Arase, *Buying Power*, pp. 135–40; Tokunaga, "Japan's FDI-Promoting Systems," pp. 24–25; and Mitsuhiro, *Beyond the Full-Set Industrial Structure*.

ates as a cohesive, MITI-led program. Nor has the ASEAN-Japan Fund been able to go beyond addressing Japanese firms' concern for investment risk to provide significant concessional loans; however, many of the mixed institutional arrangements that the AID Plan both drew on and encouraged have continued to function, albeit in a less top-down manner than originally conceived. Although no thorough list of these activities yet exists, some examples illustrate their basic thrust. JETRO organized Japanese industry experts to evaluate and suggest improvements for Malaysia's press-die and precision-molding capacity.[92] In another case, a public-private group, the Japan-China Association of Economy and Trade, evaluates Chinese firms as potential OEM suppliers for Japanese firms unable to find sufficient capacity in "dirty, dangerous, and difficult" operations at home.[93] And throughout Southeast Asia JICA has undertaken extensive industry studies and offered guidance for industrial adjustment.[94]

Both the AID Plan and these more specific efforts reflect greater initiative on the part of the Japanese. Rather than simple responses to aid requests from other countries, they represent a deliberate and proactive approach to economic restructuring and cooperation. Underlying this approach is a more confident Japanese projection of its own policies and institutional practices to the rest of the world, as well as an emerging strategic vision independent of the United States. This is reflected in multilateral development banks where the Japanese have begun to insist on closing the gap between their financial contributions and their voice in policy decision. In the ADB, Tokyo has moved away from a "high-profile status and low-profile policy approach" toward "greater activism and preeminence."[95] Japan initiated capital increases that would expand its share of the ADB votes. Through bilateral actions, Tokyo softened sanctions against China after the Tiananmen Square incident and subsequently moved the bank to resume soft-window loans to the Chinese. Despite U.S. foot-dragging, Tokyo moved the ADB into reconstruction efforts in Indochina and support for the Aquino government in the Philippines. Finally, while accepting U.S. demands for more rigorous evaluation of ADB loans, for greater ADB lending to Asian private sectors, and for greater ADB attention to poverty alleviation and human rights, the Japanese have resisted across-the-board application of such criteria. They have questioned

[92] Doner, "Japanese Foreign Investment," p. 188.
[93] Mitsuhiro, *Beyond the Full-Set Industrial Structure*, p. 21.
[94] See, for example, Japan International Cooperation Agency, "A Study on Industrial Sector Development in the Kingdom of Thailand" (Bangkok, 1989). "Yen Bloc," *Economist*, July 15, 1989, pp. 5–19.
[95] Dennis Yasutomo, "The Politicization of Japan's 'Post-Cold War' Multilateral Diplomacy," in *Japan's Foreign Policy after the Cold War: Coping with Change*, ed. Gerald L. Curtis (New York: Columbia University Press, 1993), p. 26.

the utility of emphasizing private sector lending in countries still lacking strong business classes. They have resisted conditionality based on political criteria, arguing instead for the "Asian way" of consensus and policy consultation. And they have raised general doubts concerning the U.S. development strategy, in at least one case noting that Asia "is not Latin America . . . Latin America followed U.S. [development] philosophy, and it has become the world's baggage."[96]

The World Bank's 1993 study *The East Asian Miracle* has become the most visible illustration of Japan's growing confidence in its own policies and institutions. This report was the first case of the World Bank acknowledging the contribution of government industrial policy and other institutional factors to rapid economic growth in East Asia. The study's publication followed several years of increasing tension between the Bank and Japan over the value of market interventions, especially the issue of whether financial policies should be subordinated to a broader industrial strategy (the Japanese position), or whether credit should be allocated only at market or nonsubsidized rates (the World Bank position).

This dispute emerged most clearly over the ASEAN-Japan Development Fund discussed above. A senior Bank officer charged that the Fund's offer of subsidized, targeted loans could undermine financial sector development. In response, Japan's OECF criticized the World Bank's structural adjustment lending for its obsession with macroeconomic issues and its neglect of policies explicitly designed to promote leading industries of the future.[97] Japan then urged that the Bank undertake an overall study of development in East Asia. The study, financed by the Japanese and ultimately published as *The East Asian Miracle*, makes some concessions to the Japanese position by recognizing the positive consequences of government intervention in Northeast Asia. But the report "rapidly seeks to downplay intervention's significance in East Asia and to reject intervention as a viable option for other countries.[98] This view runs directly counter to the emerging Japanese position that its own strategy is of relevance for other countries.

Despite the *Miracle*'s minimizing the benefits of selective interventions, Japanese reaction to the study has been cautiously supportive. While care-

---

[96] MoF official, cited in Yasutomo, "Policization," p. 329.

[97] This account draws on Albert Fishlow and Catherine Gwin, "Overview: Lessons from the East Asian Experience," in *Miracle or Design: Lessons from the East Asian Experience*, ed. Albert Fishlow, Catherine Gwin, Stephan Haggard, Dani Rodrik and Robert Wade (Washington D.C.: Overseas Development Council, 1994), and Overseas Economic Cooperation Fund (OECF), "Issues Related to the World Bank's Approach to Structural Adjustment: A Proposal from a Major Partner," *OECF Occasional Papers*, no. 1 (October 1991).

[98] Fishlow and Gwin, "Overview," p. 5.

ful to avoid a "Japanese-style practices" position that would sabotage trade negotiations with the United States and the EC, MOF officials view the study as a first step in a process of pushing the Bank to be more "pragmatic" (that is, less dogmatically committed to purely free market policies) in its policy advice.

Japan has itself begun to promote both "pragmatic" policies and institutions that facilitate such policies. For example, the Japanese mold-and-die association has, with JICA support, encouraged Thailand's Metal Industries Development Institute to foster associations of Thai small and medium-sized metalworking firms. JICA insisted that subsequent Japanese financial support for the Thai metalworking industry be channeled through associations of mold and die firms. Japan has also begun to engage in cooperative ODA activities with Taiwan and South Korea, and is reportedly planning cooperative aid measures with Thailand in Indochina.[99] Japan's Ministry of Finance has begun to organize training seminars in Tokyo explaining to developing country officials the virtues of public-private sector coordination and various sectoral interventions.[100] And Tokyo has initiated its first full-scale program of policy guidance for another country, Vietnam. In response to a Vietnamese request, Japan will help to draw up a five-year development program covering industrial and investment, as well as monetary and fiscal policies.[101]

It is worth noting that such diffusion of Japanese policies and institutions is not new. Recent research shows that Taiwan and South Korea have actively studied and often emulated the Japanese experience on issues such as administrative development, subcontracting linkages, Overseas Development Assistance, upstream-downstream conflicts, and import substitution-export promotion linkages. Thus, for example, in the face of an exhausted domestic textile market, a Taiwan business association adopted a Japanese "Contract of Cooperation" in which cotton spinners agreed to reduce total production and collectively purchase cotton. South Korea sent teams to study Taiwan's duty drawback and export scheme, which was itself based on Japanese practices.[102] These efforts were facilitated by extensive organizational linkages among the three countries, whether in the form

---

[99] Information on JICA in Thailand based on author interviews with Thai Ministry of Industry officials, Bangkok, July 1989, July 1993; Arase, *Buying Power*, p. 146.
[100] See, for example, "MoF Watch: International Seminar," *Japan Times Weekly*, September 12–18, 1994.
[101] "The Struggle for Vietnam's Soul," *Economist*, June 24, 1995, pp. 33–34.
[102] Cheng-Tian Kuo, "Economic Regimes and Structural Performance in the World Economy: Taiwan and the Philippines"(Ph.D. diss., University of Chicago, Department of Political Science, 1990), p. 106. See also Wade, *Governing the Market: Economic Theory and the Role of Government in East Asian Industrialization* (Princeton: Princeton University Press, 1990), p. 334.

of trading companies operating in Taiwan, strong institutional ties between Keidanren and the Federation of Korean Industries, or Korean scholars' involvement in Japan's Institute for Developing Economies.[103]

But if policy and institutional diffusion are not new, some aspects of the more recent process clearly are and significantly so. First, Japan is more actively leading the process by finding its own "voice." In doing so, Japan has begun to expand what Bruce Cumings has termed its "discursive autonomy."[104] And as Takashi Shiraishi notes in Chapter 5, the provision of two-step loans will prove to be a critical area of contention. Second, Japan is focusing the diffusion process on Southeast Asia and China. And finally, Japan is linking the diffusion process to the development of a regional coordination mechanism, a sort of "Asian Brain" in which capital and technology movements are organized through a regional network of co-operating national authorities to promote a dynamic regional division of labor.[105]

Measured by the growth of the East Asian division of labor, the institutions and initiatives discussed above have been at least moderately successful. Through "economic cooperation," trading companies, supplier networks, business associations, and the like, the Japanese have helped to establish quality standards, reputations, specifications, property rights, monitoring capacities, and insurance schemes. They provide the *ex ante* incentives and assurances that facilitate intra-regional transactions. In so doing, they help to address coordination problems that, once resolved, do not require a centralized authority for enforcement.

Despite the important contributions of Japan's coordination-style leadership from behind, it is uncertain questions whether such a strategy can sustain the development of a regional division of labor and Japan's role in it. Several sets of problems merit note, some of which reflect the very nature of Japanese institutions. Despite their impressive results, some Japanese institutions may not "travel" well, because they are ill-suited to different factor markets and/or because they tend to exclude outsiders, especially non-Japanese.[106]

Competing in East Asian financial markets has traditionally not been a problem for Japanese firms overseas. More recently, however, with financial market liberalization and the intensification of competition, Japanese

---

[103] According to Chung-In Moon, IDE has been a mecca for Koreans to learn about their own country through Japanese eyes. Personal communication, September 15, 1994.

[104] See Chapter 4 herein.

[105] Arase, *Buying Power*. See also Mitsuhiro, *Beyond the Full-Set Industrial Structure,*

[106] David Friedman, "The Phantom of Paradise" (paper presented at the Social Science Research Council Workshop on Industrial Governance and Labor Flexibility in Comparative Perspective, New York, September 17–19, 1993).

financial institutions have been slow in adapting to new financial instruments. In China, Japanese banks have had problems contending with the increasing tendency of borrowers to tap capital markets rather than banks. Still strong in traditional syndicated project finance, the Japanese have competed poorly with U.S. investment banks and overseas Chinese institutions in deals using a wider range of instruments to hedge risk.[107]

The relatively closed nature of Japanese production networks has been an even greater problem, especially in the electronics industry. Japanese networks have been very slow in involving outsiders in upper management, in transferring technology to local suppliers, in procuring inputs from locally owned firms, and in forging equity linkages with local capital markets. These features are especially striking when compared with U.S. electronics firms in the region.[108] The weaknesses have limited the ability of Japanese affiliates to tap local engineers and technicians. They have hindered the firms' capacity to reduce reliance on costly Japanese components (due to the yen appreciation) by increasing purchases from locally owned firms. This is especially important, since financial problems have begun to weaken the ability of Japanese SMEs to shift operations overseas. They have also discouraged close ties between Japanese and overseas Chinese networks. For some product niches, the latter exhibit even greater flexibility and innovation than the Japanese arrangements. As a result, Japanese electronics firms have lacked the kind of alternate supply base that has helped U.S. firms to develop rapid design capability and product supply.[109]

The closed nature of Japanese institutions, combined with weaknesses indigenous to the ASEAN countries, has also contributed to more distributive problems. One has to do with trade imbalances: the lack of local procurement has caused a further deterioration in the region's trade deficits with Japan, especially in the all-important electronics industry. A second problem involves the potential for sharp regional inequalities and vulnerabilities. Having developed little significant industrial and techno-

---

[107] Jonathan Friedland and Henny Sender, "Faulty Finance," *Far Eastern Economic Review,* June 9, 1994, pp. 56–58.
[108] Ernst, "Carriers"; Dan Biers, "Japanese Investors in Asia Face Pressure to Localize," *Asian Wall Street Journal,* August 15, 1994, pp. 1, 5. Michael Borrus, "Punctuated Equilibria in Electronics: Microsystems, Standards' Competitions, and Asian Production Networks" (paper prepared for IGCC Conference, "The China Circle: Regional Consequences of Evolving Relations among the PRC, Taiwan, and Hong Kong–Macao," San Diego, Calif., 1994); Rajah Rasiah, "Competition and Governance: Work in Malaysia's Textile and Garment Industries," *Journal of Contemporary Asia* 23.1 (1993): 3–23.
[109] Borrus, "Punctuated Equilibria." Numerous Japanese firms have established research and development facilities in the region, although these facilities seem devoted more to modification to suit local markets through "design and development" than to actual research. Dennis Fred Simon, *The Emerging Technological Trajectory of the Pacific Rim* (Armonk, N.Y.: M. E. Sharpe, 1994); Ernst, "Carriers."

logical base of their own, the ASEAN countries (minus Singapore) run the risk of finding themselves incapable of depackaging or modifying foreign technology. This "black-box" problem may be exacerbated by Japanese firms (1) opting for automation in Southeast Asian plants producing parts to strict specifications and/or (2) using Taiwanese or Korean management and only Southeast Asian labor to produce goods whose designs and key components come from Japan.[110]

Finally, Japan and others in the region must confront the challenge of what might be termed regional rationalization. Successful development of regional manufacturing networks requires some degree of intra-regional specialization. Given limited domestic markets, no one country in East Asia can produce all goods, especially technologically and financially costly intermediate and capital goods. Yet all of the countries of East Asia, with the exception of Hong Kong, have pursued second-stage import substitution. Such region-wide vertical integration means inefficiency, since each country's facilities operate below full utilization, and few if any are able to achieve scale economies necessary for technological mastery.

Two problems have resulted from this duplication of production facilities: costly inputs for downstream producers, and trade conflict based on overcapacity. The input problem has already emerged in the context of AFTA negotiations: In Malaysia and Thailand, producers of final auto, electrical, and textile products complain that they cannot compete with regional imports if forced to buy costly petrochemical and steel inputs from domestic suppliers. But the latter have invested large sums of money in upstream facilities based on the assumption of a protected market. Trade tensions have also begun to emerge: Early in 1995, Singapore formally complained to the newly established World Trade Organization that Malaysia unfairly restricted imports of plastic resins from Singapore in order to protect its own, fledgling petrochemicals industry.[111]

Each of these three issues—trade imbalances, intra-regional inequalities, and overcapacity/inefficiency—involves serious adjustment costs. And in each case there is the possibility that these countries will abandon negotiated settlements. These issues are thus more akin to prisoners' dilemmas than the coordination problems I discussed earlier. Their distributional features indicate political obstacles to their resolution. Who, for example, is going to compensate those firms obliged to abandon their upstream investments? Who is going to pay off countries to forgo national integra-

[110] Morris-Suzuki, "Reshaping the International Division of Labor," pp. 139–42; and Bernard and Ravenhill, "Beyond Product Cycles," p. 186.
[111] S. Jayasankaran, "Plastic Explosive: Singapore Complaints to WTO about Malaysia," *Far Eastern Economic Review*, January 26, 1995, p. 44.

tion that impairs intra-regional specialization? Who is going to monitor and enforce agreements to end or limit upstream production? Who is going to provide the technical capacities necessary for greater equality throughout the region? Such issues have proven especially difficult in APEC, for example.[112]

These questions suggest the need for a more centralized authority. Will these challenges eventually compel Japan to lead from the front? Perhaps. As chair of the 1995 APEC meeting, Tokyo initiated a number of measures to help the group eradicate barriers to trade and investment by its stated goal of 2020. But even in this more active role, Japan seems to be adopting an indirect approach to difficult, distributional issues. First, Japan's recent approach in APEC (termed "Partners for Progress") is consciously designed to pursue free trade through financial aid and technical training for the group's poorer members. More specifically, the approach is "reminiscent of the former European Community's policy of using regional aid to compensate poorer member states for the damage suffered by their industries from the removal of import barriers in the 1992 internal market program."[113]

Second and related, Japanese support of "functional" institutions both within and across the region can help to increase the supply of critical public goods such as technology absorption capabilities and human resource development. Japan leads ASEAN, APEC and PECC working groups on these issues, with the APEC group's agenda reportedly based on MITI's efforts to develop Asian technoparks.[114] Japan also promotes regional human resource development networks through private and public-private bilateral channels. Nippon Telephone and Telegraph, for example, works with JICA in training Southeast Asians as part of a regional network of expertise and technical infrastructure. Supplementing private or mixed efforts have been Japanese government programs to train foreign students. In 1989, some 70 percent of the 30,000 foreign students in Japan were from China, Korea, and Taiwan.[115]

Third, Japan may help create or strengthen cooperative principles and

---

[112] Such concerns remain part of the "shallow" or cross-border integration agenda that encountered significant resistance at APEC's Seattle summit in 1993. In contrast, there was greater willingness to consider not only regional investment codes but "cooperation on issues of deep integration, including competition policy, product standards, and testing and monitoring procedures; environmental protection; and the establishment of a procedure for settling APEC disputes." Haggard, *Developing Nations*, p. 70.

[113] Dawkins and de Jonquieres, "Honest Broker Seeks Pacific Balance," *Financial Times*, 1995.

[114] Karen Minden, "Science and Technology Cooperation in the Pacific Rim: Bilateral and Multilateral Perspectives," in *The Emerging Technological Trajectory of the Pacific Rim*, ed. Dennis Fred Simon (Armonk, N.Y.: M. E. Sharpe, 1995), p. 320.

[115] Ibid., p. 328.

norms. In November 1994, for example, APEC adopted investment principles that allegedly reinforce a particularly East Asian approach to dispute settlement. These principles stress informal conflict resolution in which neither party necessarily "wins" or "loses" but both agree on the fairness of the settlement. Such principles certainly raise the credibility of APEC members toward foreign investment.[116] But, in light of the Singapore-Malaysia dispute noted earlier, it remains questionable whether these principles can help to prevent or resolve sticky distributional questions stemming from trade and overcapacity problems.

Fourth, Japan may be promoting a macroeconomic context that is conducive to politically difficult adjustments. Japanese FDI and ODA have provided a basis for much smoother economic transition processes in East Asia than has been the case in Latin America. The absence of sharp policy fluctuations might weaken national fears of trade liberalization and adjustment costs by providing assurances of a stable macroeconomic context in which "losers" from liberalization can move into new industries or niches.[117] There may also be a "stick" component of this process. Southeast Asian countries fear diversion of FDI to Vietnam and China. Often implicitly but sometimes explicitly, Japanese firms have used FDI to foster openness in trade and investment regimes and to encourage adjustment.[118]

Fifth, by strengthening and linking regional private interests, Japan might help to address adjustment issues in a number of ways. For example, the Japanese economic presence has bolstered the political and institutional position of export-oriented interests in the rest of the region, thus promoting cross-pressures that weaken opposition to trade liberalization.[119] Also, the promotion of linkages across East Asian private sectors, whether informally or through emerging "growth triangles" (or "natural economic territories" or "regionally industrializing cores"), may weaken the "na-

[116] Bijit K. Bora and Edward M. Graham, "Nonbinding Investment Principles in APEC," *CAPA Report*, no. 19, The Asia Foundation (January 1995).

[117] I am grateful to Stephan Haggard for bringing this point to my attention.

[118] See, for example, Ernst, "Carriers," p. 50. Traditionally, restrictions on the right to sell in the domestic market have discouraged Japanese electronics firms from operating in Indonesia despite that country's low wages (half of Thai and Malaysian rates, 4 percent of Japanese rates). Jakarta has recently begun to draw Japanese semiconductor firms by relaxing these conditions. The reform was based in part on the need for other industries to compensate for a decline in traditional high-volume exports such as plywood and textiles, but also on the concern that "why should electronics be everywhere but Indonesia." Thornton, "Opportunity Knocks."

[119] For example, in providing political protection for ethnic Chinese in Thailand subject to ethnic nationalist threats, Japanese investors strengthened Sino-Thai commercial banks. The latter institutions have combined raw material exports and domestic manufacturing in ways that allow for compensation of losers in trade liberalization.

tional" identity of powerful private interests. The resulting dense webs of interests may in turn weaken the tendency to view pooling of exclusive state sovereignties as a necessary condition for regional integration.[120]

Finally, Japan may be helping to blur already weak state-society distinctions by encouraging business associations, public-private sector dialogues, and so on. To the extent that this promotes more systematic and organized state-society interactions, the process may strengthen national capacities for public goods provision and for peak or industry-level bargains useful for economic adjustment.

It is impossible to determine whether this range of measures will sustain a "leadership from behind," or whether such an approach will have to be supplemented by a more open and explicit Japanese role, perhaps involving a series of bilateral or trilateral free trade pacts.[121] The one point on which we can be confident is that continued growth of a regional division of labor will generate dilemmas more politically taxing than the coordination problems that Japanese institutions have addressed so efficiently in the last decade.

[120] This point is inspired by Peter Katzenstein's introduction to this book.
[121] "Yen Bloc," p. 11.

7

Japan's Soft Power: Doraemon Goes Overseas

SAYA S. SHIRAISHI

At the end of the cold war some observers were asking whether we were witnessing a partial transformation in the nature of power rather than merely a shift in power. Joseph Nye, for example, coined the term "soft power" to capture the growing importance of cultural factors in world politics. Nye argues that Japan is a "one-dimensional" economic power marked by a cultural insularity that robs it of relevance for other societies.[1] Japan, as Richard Doner shows in Chapter 6, may be developing what Nye calls "co-optative" behavioral power (getting others to want what you want). But does Japan command such soft-power resources as cultural attraction, ideology, and international institutions?[2] Nye's negative answer to this question is based on bold assertions and summary judgments, not argumentation and evidence.

I contend that Japan's supposed insularity is less pronounced than Nye and others assume. In Japan artistic innovation has been transformed into

Research for this chapter was sponsored by the Daiwa Bank Foundation and the Toyota Foundation. For comments, criticisms and suggestions I thank Brett de Bary, Shiro Honda, Chimaki Kurokawa, Dolina Millar, Kyoko and Mark Selden, Fumiaki and Yasufumi Shiraishi, Oliver Wolters, the participants of the Toyota International Symposium and Cornell "Japan in Asia" workshops as well as the members of Cornell Southeast Asia Program Student Research Circle and the Cornell Japanese Animation Society. I am indebted to Peter Katzenstein and Takashi Shiraishi for their encouragement, without which this paper would not have been completed.

[1] Joseph S. Nye Jr., *Bound to Lead: The Changing Nature of American Power* (New York: Basic Books, 1990), pp. 166–69, 188.

[2] Ibid., p. 188.

a cultural production process; a set of "image" alliances that has augmented the culture industry in size and extent has provided the vehicle for Japan's popular culture to spread through Asia. I acknowledge the continued importance of Hollywood in the production of image-based culture products, but I reject the notion that contemporary Asian popular culture is solely Western and that Japan lacks values that resonate with Asian societies. Asian regionalism has its own undeniable and important contemporary popular culture.

The liveliest segments of Japan's popular culture are comic books and television animation. They are called "manga" in Japanese, and manga's current form originated in bomb-scorched cities of postwar Japan as entertainment for children. As the children grew up, manga grew with them to become the national entertainment. Today, as Japanese economic activities spread overseas, popular manga characters—both on television and in comic books—have accompanied them into most parts of the world "except the South Pole."[3]

"Do-ra-e-mo-n"—a blue cat-type robot or cat-robot—is the most popular manga character of postwar Japan.[4] He was created as a children's comic book character in 1970 by two artists, Hiroshi Fujimoto and Motoo Abiko who shared a pen-name, Fujio Fujiko, and then animated for television in 1978. The serialized paperback comic books had sold more than seventy million copies by 1989,[5] and his images are now found all over Japan on more than one thousand character commodities. Doraemon has become a virtual family member, and most children and young adults can draw Doraemon any time, any place. On February 10, 1995, three weeks after the earthquake, a movie theater in Kobe showed Doraemon cartoons, free of charge to cheer up the children of the ruined city. About four hundred children came to see Doraemon and their jolly laughter filled the two-hundred-seat theater that afternoon.[6]

Doraemon and his friend, Nobita, appeared on television in Italy, Hong Kong, China, Taiwan, Korea, Malaysia, Singapore, Indonesia, Thailand, Russia, Spain, Brazil and other Latin American countries, and the Middle

---

[3] See the informative and insightful book on children and *manga*, Usaku Fujishima, *Sengo Manga Minzoku-shi* [A folk history of postwar manga] (Tokyo: Kawai-Shuppan, 1990).

[4] Actually, Doraemon may be the most popular manga character Japan has ever created in its history. As far as the comics and animation are concerned, however, history begins in postwar Japan.

[5] These figures are for the Tento-Mushi Series alone. There are other paperbacks, some of which are produced by other artists, such as "study comics" in which Doraemon teaches mathematics and science. This diversity makes it impossible to count them all.

[6] *Nihon Keizai Shinbun*, February 11, 1995.

East in the 1980s. The comic books, including pirate editions, are also widely popular. A Vietnamese student studying in Bangkok, for example, loved Doraemon so much when he was studying in Bangkok that he translated the comic books from Thai to Vietnamese and began to sell the copies upon returning to Vietnam. Similar stories involving other Japanese comic books and animation characters abound from Asia to Europe. Doraemon is one of the most popular export items currently produced by Japan's fantasy industry.[7]

Manga has found an enthusiastic market in Asia and has also been successful to some extent in Europe. When a comic book by the artist Fumi Saimon was published in Hong Kong in October 1994, an evening newspaper published a review on the day of publication. Japanese popular culture is becoming Asian popular culture. Bestsellers become bestsellers because they have found "resonance" with large segments of the population.[8] It seems that the technological optimism expressed by some of Japan's popular cultural products has cultural relevance for other societies in Asia and beyond. For bestsellers to become bestsellers overseas, they also need to have the vehicle with which to cross the political and cultural borders.

This paper describes Doraemon and traces the postwar history of the manga industry, follows the move to television animation and the creation of new "image alliances," examines Japan's popular perception of technology, and investigates how they have gone "global."

Japan's Postwar Comics

Comic strips, comic books, cartoons, caricatures, and animation are all "manga" in Japanese. Studies on the history of manga in Japan often go back to the Edo Period, when the term "manga" was coined by the popular Ukiyo-e artist, Hokusai Katsushika (1760–1849). Some studies also point out the influence of the West, such as *Japan Punch*.[9] Recently, with the dawn of the television age, *komikkusu* (comic books) and *anime* (animation) have gained general circulation.

[7] For the pathbreaking book written on manga in English, see Frederik Schodt, *Manga, Manga: The World of Japanese Comics* (New York: Kodansha America, 1983).
[8] Elizabeth Long, *The American Dream and the Popular Novel* (Boston: Routledge & Kegan Paul, 1985), pp. 3–6.
[9] *Japan Punch* was published from 1862 to 1887 by British journalist-artist Charles Wirgman (1832–91) in Yokohama, apparently inspired by *Punch* of London. Isao Shimizu, *Manga no Rekishi* [History of manga], Iwanami Shinsho Series 172 (Tokyo: Iwanami Shoten, 1991), pp. 29–52.

"Children's manga" in post–World War II Japan flourished so well that the Showa Period (1926–89) is called the "Age of the Children's Manga," and Japan the "Manga kingdom." The numbers that prove the popularity of *Doraemon* are not that amazing when compared with other popular comic books or animations in the history of the manga industry. About 500 million comic books, 500 million monthly comic magazines, and 700 million weekly comic magazines were published in 1989.[10] The figures dwarf even *Doraemon*'s sales records. Doraemon's success is as much a result of the structural success of the manga industry as a product of his unique appeal and charm.

Postwar children's manga began with Osamu Tezuka (1928–89).[11] The older prewar cartoonist, Keizo Shimada (1900–1973), argued that Tezuka's works were not comics. He was right at the time. Tezuka's creations were so different that they caused a radical change in the postwar Japanese comics. Today, Tezuka's new comics define what manga is to the Japanese. Shimada is not right anymore.[12]

Tezuka began drawing comics during the war at a very young age. For the more than forty years since, he produced, with legendary enthusiasm and devotion, resplendent and voluminous works.[13] His manga had great appeal for the young, and he strove to make manga socially acceptable. He set up the "Production System" in which a team of assistants help the principal artist. That made speedy quantity production possible, improved job security, made possible on-site apprenticeship training, and laid the foundation for the postwar manga industry. Accounts of his warm personal support for and inspirational influence on young comic artists fill the pages of biographies of the celebrated artists of today—Fujio Fujiko, the creators of Doraemon, very much among them.

Tezuka created the first serialized television animation in Japan in 1963 and set up the character merchandising system to pay the cost. His creations, such as Mighty Atom (exported as Astro Boy) and Jungle Emperor, were the first comic and animation characters that had substantial commercial success abroad.

[10] Ibid., pp. 198–99; of the 6.08 billion books and magazines published in Japan in 1991, 38 percent were manga. "The Manga Market," in *Mangajin's Basic Japanese through Comics* (Atlanta: Mangajin, 1993), pp. 10–11.

[11] Tezuka has been called the "god [kami-sama] of manga."

[12] Fujishima, *Sengo Manga*, pp. 34–35; Shimada was known for his children's war-propaganda comic, "Boken Dankichi" [Adventurous Dankichi]. Tezuka caricatured him in his "Captain Atom" as the weather forecaster who says, "The wind will blow from east, south, west, north. The sky will be cloudy, and it will be a fine day with rain. Snow is expected." Osamu Tezuka, *Mighty Atom*, Luxury Reprint, vol. 1 (Tokyo: Kodansha, 1992), p. 137.

[13] There is Kodansha's 300 volume, *Tezuka Osamu Manga Zenshu* [The complete works of Tezuka Osamu], 1977–, and many more reprints have been published.

The team of Fujio Fujiko (Fujimoto, 1933–   ; Abiko, 1934–   ) were enticed into the world of comics by Tezuka's works, lived in Tezuka's old apartment, and were intimately influenced by Tezuka. Their first pen-name was Ashi-zuka.[14] Nobita's home address, "Tsuki-mi-dai [Moon-View-Hights], Nerima-ku, Tokyo" doubtless refers to Tezuka's residence/ animation studio in "Fuji-mi-dai [Fuji-View-Hights], Nerima-ku, Tokyo," where the *Mighty Atom* was produced.

Doraemon For Everyone

A fine sunny afternoon, a ten-year-old boy comes home. Returning to his room on the second floor of his wooden house in a residential area in Tokyo, he bursts into tears. Waiting for him in the room is Doraemon, who fully comprehends the emotional crisis of tender childhood. His round hand immediately searches his front pocket for the fantastic high-tech gadgets that will most effectively help the boy deal with the harsh reality of everyday life.

Thus begins *Doraemon*. The boy's name is Nobita Nobi. *"Nobi nobi"* ex-presses the way a young child grows up free, healthy, and happy, unre-strained in any sense.[15] That is precisely the ideal of "childhood" in contemporary Japan. This happy, innocent, gentle, and thoroughly undis-ciplined, easygoing child is, hence, doing poorly at school and is routinely bullied by the shrewder or stronger children in the neighborhood.

Nobita's great-great-grandson, who lives in the twenty-second century, knows all this, thanks to advanced technology, and sends (or, should I say "will send"?) his own toy robot, Doraemon, to be Nobita's tutor. Dorae-mon becomes a full-time, live-in, guardian-tutor-friend to Nobita and not only understands his misery but also figures out how to relieve the pain with the aid of high-tech devices from the future.

Most of the Doraemon's gadgets are portable, with no intrinsic weight, and readily expand or shrink as needed. They rarely break down and are neatly stored in, or delivered through, Doraemon's pocket. They are ap-parently manufactured with high quality control and easily transcend time, space, gravity, energy, and volume. In other words, current science and technology cannot explain what they are made of or how they are me-chanically composed or controlled.[16] Doraemon selects equipment to meet

[14] Fujishima, *Sengo Manga*, pp. 42.
[15] Nobita's father explains the meaning of the name in "The Day I Was Born," in *Doraemon*, Tento-Mushi Series, vol. 2 (Tokyo: Shogakukan, 1984), p. 56.
[16] Paul Deane argues that one of the reasons that science, scientists, and technology have received little attention in the children's books in the United States is the problem of lan-

Nobita's highly personal immediate needs and instructs him in using the gizmos, which are always simple and user-friendly—the ultimate goal of commodity designing.[17] No screwdrivers are needed to assemble the parts, and batteries are always included. There are no user's manuals.[18]

TV audiences and comic book readers must have loved these gadgets because there is now an encyclopedia dedicated to them which lists, studies, and explains over 1,100 of Doraemon's devices.[19] The best-known is the "take-copter."[20] Nobita and his friends have used it 214 times. Second in popularity is the time machine, which has appeared 97 times. The third most frequently enjoyed gadget is the Anywhere Door (68 times).[21] Nonetheless, Doraemon, himself a product of high technology, occupies the central position of the story. His endearing nature captivates young audiences. Both children's intimate friend and a family member, Doraemon represents the optimistic view of the relationship between technology and humanity.

Doraemon was first created in *Korokoro Comic*, a children's monthly magazine, and was soon compiled in paperback in the Tento-Mushi [Ladybug] Series.[22] In 1978, TV Asahi began to broadcast an animated version, and Doraemon was an instant hit. Animated features were produced, and massive merchandising of the characters followed, all of which stimulated

---

guage. In *Batteries Not Included,* for example, pseudoscientific jargon such as the robot boy "has an internal interface radio," "electrologic memory banks," "dynakinetic circuits," and so on put children off. Paul Deane, *Mirrors of American Culture: Children's Fiction Series in the Twentieth Century* (Metuchen, N.J.: Scarecrow Press, 1991), pp. 150–51.

[17] "Designing for idiots is the highest expression of the engineering art." David Noble, as quoted in Richard Ohmann, "Advertising and the New Discourse of Mass Culture," in *Politics of Letters* (Middletown, Conn.: Wesleyan University Press, 1987), p. 223.

[18] Hence, a rumor circulating among the children in Tokyo concerning Doraemon ("too good to be true") says that future manufactures are keeping records on Nobita's reactions to their products in order to prepare comprehensive user's manuals. Nobita is chosen as the monitor because he is both naive and a vigorous experimenter, who leaves no stone unturned. For these rumors, see Shizuka Kiryu and Koei Cult Club, eds., *Toshi ni Habikoru Kimyona Uwasa* [Strange rumors in big cities] (Yokohama: Koei, 1994).

[19] Setagaya Doraemon Kenkyu-Kai, *Doraemon Kenkyu Kanzen Jiten* [The complete encyclopedia of Doraemon studies] (Tokyo: Data House, 1994).

[20] A small propeller worn like a hat that enables the wearer to fly, apparently through a combination of antigravity and effective use of the wind. The direction and speed can be controlled "as wished," that is, by brain waves. The maximum speed is 80km/hour and it needs to be recharged after eight hours of continuous use. It can be unstable in strong winds. Ibid., p. 139.

[21] Nihon Doraemon To, *Nobi-ke no Shinjitsu* [The truth of the Nobi Family] (Tokyo: Wani Books, 1993), pp. 227–30.

[22] Now the two artists go separate ways. Hiroshi Fujimoto uses the pen name "Fujio F. Fujiko"; Motoo Abiko uses "Fujio Fujiko A."

further sales of comic books. Throughout the 1980s, families with young children watched Doraemon five evenings a week, from 6:45 to 7:00, just before the seven o'clock primetime news programs. On Sundays, there was often "Doraemon Land" in which four-episodes were rerun, and in summer and winter, the feature version ran in theaters during the school holidays. Records, videos, and cassette tapes were made. Doraemon images saturated commercial products such as toys, dolls, games, stickers, stationery, bags, desks and chairs, children's clothes, hats, shoes, boots, umbrellas, lunch boxes, dishes, snacks, calendars, bicycles, and entertainment facilities in playgrounds and amusement parks. Doraemon had become a part of the daily family life of the postwar generation in Japan.[23]

Manga: Visual Narration

When Tezuka's initial fifteen comic books were printed as the *Red Book Manga*, he was barely twenty years old. The reddish colored comic books were small, thin tissue-paper books published by family-managed candy wholesalers in devastated postwar Osaka. They were sold at candy stalls and night markets for ten to fifty yen. The "bubble" publishers appeared and disappeared overnight, and published, or freely reprinted, the comics drawn by nameless young comic artists.

From the outset, Tezuka created a unique narrative style and novel-like complex composition, which was soon named "story manga" or narrative comics. Tezuka was a passionate movie watcher and employed cinematic techniques—the close up, the long shot, montage, and dynamic camera angles—in irregular frames designed to create the impression of movement and build tension.[24] He has pointed out the inspiration he found in German, French, British and American movies and animations. Popular Hollywood movies are still one of the sources of inspiration for Japanese comics and animations.

Tezuka's *New Treasure Island*, published in 1947, is now acclaimed as the ancestor of postwar comics.[25] Without much advertisement, the two-hundred-page narrative comic sold a record-breaking four-hundred-thousand copies in one year. Young readers were engrossed by its freshness

---

[23] "Mothers who watched the movies when they were children are now taking their own children to see them." Akihiro Motoyama quoted in Mark Schilling, "Doraemon: Making Dreams Come True," *Japan Quarterly* vol. 20, No. 4 (1993): 406.

[24] Schodt, *Manga, Manga*, pp. 18–22; Tadao Sato, *Manga to Hyogen* [Manga and representation] (Tokyo: Hyoron-sha, 1984), p. 82.

[25] Fujishima, *Sengo Manga*, p. 30; Sato, *Manga to Hyogen*, pp. 95–96; Shimizu, *Manga no Rekishi*, pp. 176–77.

and were inspired to create and experiment with narrative comics of their own.

Fujio Fujiko wrote of the overwhelming experience they had as second-year junior high students in 1947:

> When I first opened [*New Treasure Island*], I was dazzled. Under the subtitle, "Toward the Sea of Adventure," there was a frame in which a boy with a dashing hat was driving his sports car from right to left. Its left page was divided horizontally into three frames. In the top frame, the car ran through from the surface [of the page] deep inside, passing by the sign which said "Harbor." In the second frame, the car was approaching us on the road by the sea. The third frame was the long shot of the harbor. The car was still running from right to left, about to make a sharp stop, and the boy was jumping out of the car at the moment. All the while, no word, no sound-effects. . . . Nonetheless, I heard the roar of the machine, GYAAAN!! and inhaled the dust the sports car stirred. . . .
>
> This is a mere manga printed on sheets of paper, and yet, this car is running with breakneck speed. It was just like watching a movie!![26]

A new mode of visual narrative had been introduced. Part of its aesthetic appeal lay in how it used pictorial representation to depict action. Tezuka's visual narrative techniques replaced verbal narrative techniques of earlier cartoons and comics and changed the nature of postwar Japanese comics. As Frederik Schodt put it, "In many cases the picture alone carries the story. Just as a dramatic film might opt for a minute of silence, several pages of a comic story may have no narration or dialogue."[27] This new technique requires many more frames and pages for even a momentary incident. The comic books have grown thick. At the same time, because such visual messages—the long strings of frames depicting successive passages of motion—can be fully received at a glance, it takes only a few seconds for the experienced readers to scan the frames and pages. Foreign observers prefer to use the term "browsing" to "reading" to describe the prevalent activity they encounter daily in Japan.

The picture had taken the central position. It no longer simply "illustrated" or "decorated" the voices that, in previous comics, were the primary storytellers. Picture and voice may contradict each other, or voice and sound may "illustrate" the pictorial text that "tells" the story. A playful sense of liberation from the stillness of writing and from the former

---

[26] Quoted by Sato, *Manga to Hyogen*, p. 81.
[27] Schodt, *Manga, Manga*, p. 21.

Figure 7-1. The ancestor of postwar comics. *New Treasure Island*, by Osamu Tezuka. Copyright © Tezuka Productions. Reprinted by permission.

immobility of pictures had emerged. One remarkable technical outgrowth is noted as follows:

> In recent years artists have wrought miracles of paradox: the use of sound to depict silent activities and emotions. When a ninja warrior-assassin vanishes in midair the "sound" is FU: when leaves fall off a tree the sound is HIRA HIRA; when a penis suddenly stands erect the sound is BIIN; when some one's face reddens in embarrassment the sound is PO; and the sound of no sound at all is a drawn-out SHIIN, and Yukio Kawasaki created a bit of a stir with SURON, the sound of milk being added to coffee.[28]

Voice and sound, now liberated from their narrative duties, have developed the florid functions that were to be taken up in the video game "sound novels" of the 1990s.

Tezuka used to say of the drawings in his comics: "I don't consider them

---

[28] Ibid.

Figure 7-2. A drive via motor-shoe. *Doraemon* no. 39, by Fujio F. Fujiko. Copyright © Fujiko-Shogakukan. Reprinted by permission.

pictures—I think of them as a type of hieroglyphics. . . . In reality I'm not drawing. I'm writing a story with a unique type of symbol.''[29] True to the manga's diversity, not all artists agree with Tezuka, but his statement explains how manga has advanced its techniques and increased its readers.[30]

Comic artists study one another's works and vigorously borrow one anothers' novel visions, angles, and techniques. By "quoting" and "citing" others' images, the artists acknowledge, accept, and share them as new symbols and idioms. Tezuka used to say that the distinction between imitation and creation was much more difficult to make than one might think. In reality, it is never clear.[31]

Tezuka's insight that visual narration of manga is identical with hieroglyphic prompts the following observations:

First, the visual presentations of manga are signs. A picture of a corpse, for example, is equivalent of the combination of letters, D, E, A, D, in English. The eyes, nose, mouth, arms, legs, and torso are so combined that they refer to the abstract idea of death. When combined differently, they signify something else. A single pictorial sign can convey highly complex information that would require several paragraphs of the lineal linguistic text. It can show how the body became a corpse—murdered? sickness?—and how it was discovered, by whom and where with a single frame.

Second, each graphic frame hangs in midair, suspended in space and time, if separated from the rest of the frames. Depending on their sequence—the same set of frames can recount either construction, destruction, flashbacks, or a different story.

Third, readers have to become literate in visual signs and narrations—literacy of manga—by familiarizing themselves with syntax and vocabulary. Thus visual sign narration is a kind of language. Some Japanese cannot "read" manga even if its voice portion is Japanese, while some foreigners can, to some extent, even if they do not understand Japanese.

---

[29] Ibid., p. 25.

[30] The theory—figures in manga are signs—made Tezuka's "production system" possible. His assistants learned how to draw the characters as they would have learned to draw calligraphy. It also explains how easily anyone, including non-Japanese artists, learn to draw manga characters. Most of Japan's younger generation has mastered Doraemon calligraphy. For a critical analysis of Tezuka's manga-sign theory, see Eiji Otsuka, *Sengo Manga no Hyogen Kukan: Kigo-teki Shintai no Jubaku* [The representational space of the postwar manga: A bondage of body-as-sign] (Kyoto: Hozokan, 1994); on the birth of modern manga readers, see Natsuo Sekikawa, *Chishikiteki Taishu Shokun, Kore mo Manga da* [Dear intellectual mass, this too is manga] (Tokyo: Bungei Shunju, 1991).

[31] Yet there were casualties of imitation. See the revealing biographical accounts of such stories by the chief editor of *Shonen Jump*, Shigeo Nishimura, *Saraba Waga Seishun, "Shonen Jump"* [Farewell to my youth, "Shonen Jump"] (Tokyo: Asuka shin-sha, 1994).

Fourth, children and youth become literate much more easily and thoroughly than the aged.

Fifth, the manga artists emerge from among those who have mastered the language.

The question then arises how the "unlettered" acquire literacy. It comes almost spontaneously to many children. Living and growing in society where everyone is "reading" manga doubtless makes the acquisition of literacy unproblematic for many children. The question becomes important when we ask whether and how manga—Japan's postwar popular culture—will fare overseas.

The Children's Revolt in the Ruined City

Tezuka's manga was initially categorized as "children's manga" not so much because they were simple as because they were most accepted by young, who embraced it as their medium for comprehension, expression, communication, and signification. These "children" were deeply involved in the war without having a say in it even if, as minors, they were mostly spared from actual battlefield experiences.[32] The Americans subjected more than sixty cities in Japan to indiscriminate systematic firebombings which razed over two million homes. Many of the children who survived the bombings and firetraps witnessed the death of their family members, friends and neighbors, as much as the massive and total destruction of human bodies, homes, buildings and cities. They suffered from scarcity during and after the war and, for years, the ruined cityscape was their playground. It was they who eventually undertook the economic recovery of society.

Manga grew out of the bomb-scorched, barren city, which became a liberating space for postwar Japanese literature. It was especially so for the visual narratives. The ruined black-and-white cityscape became the Original Experience and the Original Picture. It was so clear and transparent that it refused rhetorical elucidation. All the old structures of authority, moral values, and beliefs were destroyed in this space. The sight of devastation was the proof and sign of their failure and defeat. Vision had become the only relevant medium. It was evidently so for both the manga artists in their late teens and readers in their early teens, who set out to bring forth a new kind of image narration together.

Throughout the history of postwar manga, the scene of the ravaged city has been drawn with nostalgic affection countless times by numerous art-

---

[32] Some artists were in the last batch of suicide pilots in their late teens in August 1945. Fujishima, *Sengo Manga*, pp. 343–44.

ists. The city is repeatedly destroyed, resurrected, transformed into a scene of futuristic grandeur, only to be destroyed again. The ruins are depicted as signs of danger, desperation, and attack by hostile forces. They are also calls for help, comradeship, courage, love, and hope. Destruction, the struggle for survival and reconstruction, and the majestic future city can all be found in the Original Picture in a paradoxical depiction of the simultaneous experiences of despair and optimism.

Consider the account of how a robot hero, Iron Man No. 28, was conceived as a symbol of victory through technological advancement:

> [Mitsuteru Yokoyama] was influenced by three things in his youth. "One was the sight I saw when the war ended and I returned to [my home] Kobe from my rural evacuation site. Everything as far as I could see had been transformed into scorched earth and piles of rubble. . . . I was . . . stunned by the destructive power of war. Second was the V1 and V2 missiles that the German Nazis developed. I had heard that Hitler tried to use them as an ace in the hole to reverse his waning fortunes. The third influence was from the American movie *Frankenstein.*"[33]

Yokoyama's giant iron robot, inspired by the failed dream of V1 and V2 missiles, modeled after the lonely artificial man of the Hollywood movie, and painted the color of ruined city, manifested the future in its purest form.

In the early days of manga, both the readers and the artists were very young. The artists were usually published by age nineteen, by which time they had already been drawing manga for years.[34] They were often quite poor and had been less educated than most established writers in the publishing community. Yet the young adored and participated in creating this distinctly new entertainment art. The distance between producers and consumers of manga was much smaller than that for movies. Readers were creating their own manga, artists were devoted manga readers, and some editors were aspiring artists themselves.

Editors were primarily responsible for discovering artists and helping them develop their talents.[35] They worked with artists step by step from the initial stages of planning to actual drawing. They evaluated the readers' reactions and transmitted them to artists, who would adjust the stories and characters accordingly. The readers' responses were their primary guides.

[33] Quoted in Frederik L. Schodt, *Inside the Robot Kingdom: Japan, Mechatronics, and the Coming Robotopia* (Tokyo and New York: Kodansha International, 1988), pp. 78–79. Iron Man No. 28, which was exported to the United States under the name Gigantor, and Mighty Atom are the prototypes of robot imagery.
[34] Sato, *Manga to Hyogen*, pp. 96–98.
[35] Nishimura, *Saraba Waga Seishun*, pp. 78–82.

Together they—artists, editors, and readers—experimented with rebellious pictorial depiction and new techniques. Many images and themes—however scandalous they appeared at the outset—eventually became standard symbols and signs and enriched the vocabulary of the new medium. Comic magazines still come with a "reader's card" inserted.

As the children grew, manga accompanied them into their youth and then adulthood. The "children's manga" have become manga for everyone, young and old. Although the comics themselves and their themes were changing radically, the category "children's manga" endured, and the concept of childhood was continuously provoked.[36] Inside the "children's domain," taboos were thus challenged and broken.

Manga artists have shown an avid interest in human body—a visual sign of human being—its motion, destruction, and transformation, just as they have been attracted by the vision of the city—its destruction and resurrection. Sexual organs, intercourse, cannibalism, torture and killings, creatures from outer space, and parasites that deform human bodies are among the objects of their exploration. (See Figure 7-3; Kiseiju [Parasite animal] by Hitoshi Iwaaki) An American sex-education textbook was translated and printed, with its illustrations, in the "boys' " manga weekly.[37] Experiments in how far a figure may be deconstructed and still be recognizable as a lifeform, or how to signify individuality and emotional shifts with a few simple visual lines, are constantly being made. The photos of mutilated Vietnamese bodies being roped and dragged by American soldiers were printed in a weekly "boys'" manga magazine. Women's bodies chopped up by Japanese soldiers in Nanking appeared in another "boys'" manga weekly when the government still prohibited printing the facts in textbooks.[38] Sports manga that focuses on the outer limits of bodily motion is another favored subject. Many of them share the theme of empowerment of children and youth.

U.S. occupying forces effectively censored manga in its early days,[39] hence, General Douglas MacArthur and the occupying military forces missed their chance to appear in what was the steaming laboratory for the things to come. From time to time, intellectuals, "concerned" teachers, and many parents condemned the new medium categorically as something repulsive, morally corrupt, or at best, unproductive and meaningless. In

---

[36] On the birth of "children" and modern middle-class family life in Europe, see Philippe Ariès, *Centuries of Childhood: A Social History of Family Life*, trans. Robert Baldick (New York: Vintage Books, 1962).

[37] Fujishima, *Sengo Manga*, pp. 139–40.

[38] Ibid, pp. 159–60.

[39] Shimizu, *Manga no Rekishi*, p.184–85. By 1951, with the start of the Korean War and the Red Purge, all the comic magazines for adults, such as *Shinso*, which caricatured the emperor, were forced to stop publication and the "children's manga" began to thrive.

Figure 7-3. A visual experiment. *Kiseiju* [parasite-animal], by Hitoshi Iwaaki. Copyright © Iwaaki Hitoshi/Kodansha Afternoon. Reprinted by permission.

some cases piles of manga books and magazines were burnt on school grounds during the 1950s.[40]

Now, things have changed. Succeeding generations have effortlessly, if not more enthusiastically than their older brothers and sisters, accepted the medium. The manga generations are now in the majority. Fifty years since the end of World War II, the age limit of those who "understand" manga is reported to be around fifty. In 1985, Tezuka's manga were printed in a primary school Japanese language and literature textbook. Manga artists, such as Shotaro Ishinomori, are invited to advisory councils of government ministries and business groups, which are eager to absorb manga artists' multidimensional inspirations. Some textbook publishers have decided to replace traditional arts and performances, such as No, with manga as a focus for discussion on Japanese culture. In April 1995, Shogaku-tosho released a high school English textbook with an excerpt from Frederik Schodt's analysis on manga and technology in Japan. School libraries are stuffing their shelves with comic books.[41]

The Manga Industry

Comic books in Japan are typically black-and-white and inexpensive. As the Japanese began to have more money to spend for leisure, and as the number of television sets exceeded 10 million in 1962 and 15 million in 1963, publishers and movie producers were forced to restructure their industry to survive in the television age.

As the weekly television programs began to punctuate everyday life, the weekly manga magazines replaced the monthlies.[42] Nowadays each issue carries a dozen or more serialized narrative comics, and the competition is fierce. Subscriptions are unusual. The magazines are cheap, massively printed, and sold everywhere. Sales depend on the popularity of the comics they contain.[43] Series that do not generate positive reactions disappear in about ten weeks to give space to others. A popular series continue for months or years. These are later published in book form, on better quality paper. The profit in the manga business is made from books rather than weekly magazines. The books are about two hundred pages long and contain ten to fifteen episodes of a series.

---

[40] Fujishima, *Sengo Manga*, pp. 72–74.

[41] Tetsushi Kajimoto, "Cartoons making inroads in educational circles," *Japan Times*, January 11, 1995; Fujishima, *Sengo Manga* pp. 336–37.

[42] *Shonen Magazine* and *Shonen Sunday* in 1959, *Shojo Friend* in 1962, *Shonen King* and *Margaret* in 1963, *Shojo Comic* and *Shonen Jump* and *Seventeen* in 1968, and others.

[43] Three popular comics dramatically improve the sale of a weekly. One is not enough, for the readers (now the expert manga browsers) simply take a quick glance at the week's episode without bothering to purchase the magazine. *Manga Jin*, p. 12.

Yet weekly magazines are crucial in introducing new artists and their works, and selecting popular comics for paperback publication. All the ten best-selling weekly manga magazines have circulations of over one million, and *Shonen Jump* constantly sells five to six million copies each week. They have typically three or four hundred pages, and cost around 200 yen, or two dollars. Five publishers—Shueisha, Shogakukan, Kodansha, Hakusensha, and Futabasha—have an estimated 78 percent of the comics market. In 1992, manga sales totaled 540 billion yen (or over U.S. $5 billion), which was 23 percent of all the sales of books in Japan.[44]

The industry's primary concern has always been how to recruit talented artists. A manga artist must be able to do what a script writer, a director, a costume designer, a set designer, a cameraman, and an illustrator do. It takes energy, devotion, creativity and ingrained unconventionality to keep producing episodes week after week for demanding, outspoken readers.[45]

Manga is a medium for popular entertainment, comparable to American popular music. It has grown large enough to maintain its profitability. In order to multiply its revenue, however, it has undergone further institutional rearrangements.

Television Animation and Image Alliance

In 1956, NHK Terebi (Television) and TBS began broadcasting in Japan. Nihon Terebi (1957), Fuji Terebi (1959) and Terebi Asahi (1959), followed. The old American cartoon *Popeye* and many others, such as *Mighty Mouse* and *Woody Woodpecker*, went on the air after 1959. In 1957, Japan's first animation production company, Toei Doga Production was set up and started to produce animation movies for theaters. Tezuka participated in its early productions. He also studied the Walt Disney animation movies. He is said to have seen "Bambi" over eighty times and "Snow White" fifty times.[46] By 1960, the price for a black-and-white 12 inch television set was down to 50,000 yen from the initial 200,000 yen. The starting monthly salary for a primary school teacher was 13,000 yen in that year.

In 1962, Tezuka established Mushi [Beetle] Production and in January of the next year—when the number of television sets reached 15 million—*Mighty Atom* was broadcast by Nihon Terebi as the first serialized Japanese television animation. Animation is an extremely labor intensive industry.

---

44 Ibid, pp. 10–11.
45 Nishimura, *Saraba Waga Seishun*, passim.
46 Sato, *Manga to Jyogen*, p. 77; Fujishima, *Sengo Manga*, p. 120.

A half-hour animated cartoon requires forty people working full-time for forty-five days. Imported American cartoons with worldwide market cost only a little over 100,000 yen for a thirty minute program then, while it actually cost more than 1 million yen to produce thirty-minutes of animation in Japan. By 1970, it cost about four million yen, and seven to eight million yen in 1989. Meiji Confectionery Company, which sponsored *Mighty Atom*, initially paid 550,000 yen for each episode, which did not even cover the cost of production.[47]

Mushi Productions implemented several procedures to reduce the cost. For a half-hour program, only 3,000 to 4,300 pictures were used. Tezuka's "bank system" further simplified the process. Several kinds of mouth, eyes, nose and arms were prepared and, when possible, only these parts were exchanged instead of drawing entire figures anew. His "manga is hieroglyphics" theory found a practical use. While Disney used two hundred colors for its animation, Mushi Productions made do with only eighty. Tezuka wanted his products to be enjoyed by many, even if he had to sacrifice quality at the beginning. He has kept the spirit of his early *Red Book Manga* days. Tezuka's product, nevertheless, was of higher quality than the many mass-produced television animations that followed soon after. Since then Japan's animation industry has grown to be the world largest, and today Toei Doga Productions uses as many colors as it pleases.[48]

In 1993, four years after Tezuka's death, his wife wrote: "He had dreamed of creating animation ever since he was a child. The delightful sensation an artist feels when the figures he has drawn start to move is immeasurable, it is beyond anyone's imagination."[49] The delight may be shared, however, by robotics researchers. Making pictures move and making machines move are very much similar, and they are also both like having a child and seeing it walk and grow. Fittingly, the first episode of *Mighty Atom* was the thrilling creation and bringing to life of the boy-robot, Atom. Atom was a spectacular hit. The term "Atom Syndrome" was coined to summarize the phenomena. The Nielsen survey conducted in August 1964 indicated extraordinary 40.7 percent rating. Later, when Atom was exported to the United States as "Astro Boy," it also recorded over 40 percent ratings.[50]

---

[47] For the cost of TV animation, see Fujishima, *Sengo Manga*, pp. 110–23, pp. 224–49.

[48] Fujishima, *Sengo Manga*, pp. 245–48. The recent hit animation, *Heisei Tanuki-Gassen: Ponpoko* by Studio Ghibli used 502 colors and 82,289 cells for the 120 minute film.

[49] Etsuko Tezuka, "Afterwords," in *Black Jack* 1 (Tokyo: Akita Shoten, 1993), p. 288.

[50] Tezuka was very pleased to discover that a boy he met in New York City had seen Astro Boy. Fujishima, *Sengo Manga*, pp. 121–22.

After *Mighty Atom* went on the air, the sale of the comic books went up. Why? Watching television animation is distinctly easier than "reading" comic books, which requires literacy in visual signs and text. The cinematic techniques of manga encode dynamic movements, sound-effects, and characters' voices. Animating comics liberates the hitherto coded motions and sounds. Exposure to the weekly television animations appears to prepare audiences for comics' visual narration. Decoding the comics comes more easily when the reader has been familiarized with the characters' voices and motions. Having learned, readers are likely to become the awakened patrons of comic books in general, hence new members of the manga generation. Television animation trains and entices a wider population into the printed visual narration.[51] The close relation between the popularity of a television animation and the sale of its comic books is now a norm for publishers and television companies. Manga has proved to be a literary form that prospers in the television age.

Actually, television animation introduced a more affluent population to the narrative comics. Television sets were priced so high in the early days of broadcasting that the wealthy watched television more than the poor. Meanwhile, as Japan's economy developed, formerly poor children grew up to be moneyed adults. The result is that manga readership has extended upward in class and in age. The term *Komikkusu* (for comic books)[52] spread and because of its English origin, regardless of its original connotation, the new term has come to suggest a more polished image of manga along with the designation *anime* for television animation, which replaced the earlier "terebi[television] manga," and for animated features "manga eiga [movie]."

Japan's emerging consumer class has not fully adopted the entertainment and leisure habits of middle-class families in the West, and Japan's prewar middle-class entertainment and leisure practices vanished in the wake of the war, land reforms, and subsequent dramatic economic development. Some have begun to claim that manga (*komikkusu* and *anime*) is the postwar national entertainment and leisure. Thus there is much debate over whether Japanese culture should be represented abroad, and to the younger generation, by traditional theater performances such as No, now sustained by the taxpayers, who might never watch it in their lives, or by flourishing manga that accompanies the Japanese wherever they go.

---

[51] Fujishima points out TV's legitimatization effects on the Japanese audience. *Sengo Manga*, pp. 114–18.
[52] In 1966 *Comic Magazine, Sunday Comics*, and in 1968 *Big Comic, Shojo Comic* were published and the term "komikkusu" took root.

Character Merchandising

Tezuka raised money to meet the cost of animation by selling licenses to use the characters on commodities. *Mighty Atom* brought in four hundred merchandise contracts for stationery, toys, sporting goods, clothes, foods, electronic products, and many other items. Mushi Productions received three million yen for each license.[53]

In 1965, *Obaké no Q-Taro* [Our dear ghost Q-Taro] by Fujio Fujiko was made into an animated television series.[54] Children were enraptured by the endearing ghost, and Oba-Q's sponsor, Fujiya, found that its chocolate sold out, and its entire sales quickly caught up with and exceeded those of its rivals, Morinaga and Meiji.[55] The effects of the popular children's television animation on the sale of its sponsors' commodities were thus proved. The sale of comic books also exploded after Oba-Q appeared on television, and when the publisher built a new ten-story office building in Tokyo, it was promptly called the "Oba-Q building."[56]

The remarkable advantage of linking children's television cartoons, comic books, and commodities became evident. The alliance of the comics, animation, television, manufacturers, retailers, and advertisers was cemented through this experience. Schodt explains that

> the typical pattern is for a popular story first serialized in a comic magazine to be compiled into books and sold as a paperback series, then made into an animated television series, and, if still popular, finally made into an animated feature for theatrical release. . . . Animation stimulates further sales of magazines, reprints of comic paperbacks, and massive merchandising.[57]

Image is the essential component of this multi-industry alliance. The alliance produces images, evaluates them, purchases them, and sells them. As images circulate, profits are generated. The copyright, which brings in enormous profit, is now shared by the original artist, the publisher, and the television network.

In the 1970s, the oil crisis prompted a restructuring of the industries. Television stations were "rationalized" by discharging their employees,

---

[53] The practice today is to collect 3 percent of the wholesale price plus a minimum charge of 2 to 3 million yen. Highly popular characters are often more expensive. The fee was once uniformly 5 percent without a minimum charge. Fujishima, *Sengo Manga*, p. 243.
[54] "Oba-Q" first appeared in 1964 in *Shonen Sunday*.
[55] Fujishima, *Sengo Manga*, pp. 228–29.
[56] Schodt, *Manga Manga*, p. 145.
[57] Ibid., p. 146.

who set up small independent program production houses. Toei Doga followed suit, and a number of small animation studios sprouted. Mushi Productions went bankrupt in 1973.

Coordination is a key factor for an effective image alliance in this new context: numbers of small production houses; television stations with a minimum of programming staff; and numerous comic characters to choose from for animation. An advertisement agency, such as Dentsu or Hakuhodo, ordinarily initiates an animation project by courting prospective sponsors.[58] The agents propose suitable characters and stories to enhance the image of the company and its commodities. They then prescribe images to the animation producer in accordance with the sponsor's requests and negotiate with a television station for a time spot.

In most cases, the comic book characters provide the images, which the advertisers sell to the sponsors, and the sponsors sell to the consumers. There is a wide range of choices of comic characters, and they are easy to craft and engineer into certain images. Some successful characters, like Doraemon, are incredibly durable. The increased visibility of characters in daily life, in turn, makes the television program more popular and increases sales of the original comic books. The beauty of the image alliance is that each partner promotes the others. Everyone profits.

Bikkuri-Man Fever

A significant reversal of value, however, occurred when the comics industry joined the image alliance system. Now, the image, one character, one simple drawing such as Doraemon, has more value than the narrative. The image is the core of the alliance, and the comics do not necessarily monopolize image production or always occupy the principal position in the alliance. One interesting incident demonstrates this value reversal between comic narratives and character images.

In 1986, Lotte Confectionery Company's Planning Division devised a series of illustrated cards that were to be wrapped inside the packages of their new commodity—"Bikkuri-Man Chocolate." Some comic artists were enlisted to draw original "Bikkuri-Man" [Flabbergasted-Man] characters for the cards—no comic story was attached. Children, infatuated by the mysterious characters, began competing to collect all the characters of the series as if to decipher the hidden story. Lotte kept adding the number of characters and the children kept collecting them. By 1989, more than five hundred character images were created. Sales of the thirty-yen chocolate reached five billion yen (a little less than U.S. $40 million then) in

---

[58] Fujishima, *Sengo Manga*, p. 245.

one year. Forged character images were discovered to have been sold, without chocolates, to children.

The ingenious Lotte Planning Division, showing no sign of being flabbergasted, coolly arranged for their artists to make up stories for Bikkuri-Man characters. In 1988, *Korokoro Comic* began printing serialized Bikkuri-Man stories. At one point, in June 1988, Bikkuri-Man's popularity exceeded Doraemon's. That summer, the publisher released a special "Bikkuri-Man Edition" magazine, and 200,000 copies were sold out in one day. Soon, television animation was produced, and its rating exceeded 20 percent. Finally a video game was developed.[59]

In the beginning is the "image" alone. Once the image proves to be popular enough to generate profit, the image alliance takes over. Wherever a popular image appears, the alliance is there, ready to share the image and multiply the profit. Each partner helps increase the profit of the others simply by pursuing his own.

Bikkuri-Man is not an exception. "My Neighbor Totoro" was an extremely successful feature animation produced in 1987, and its characters have been shared by television networks, comic publishers, and many manufacturers. The video game, "Super Mario Brothers," has generated character merchandising and at one point a cartoon version was also created. Alliances are the machines that multiply, maximize, and squeeze profit out of any popular image.

By 1978, there were more than sixty cartoons on television each week. This meant that more than sixty image alliances were actively functioning. Mass production of animation became necessary to meet the demand. It was for the mass production that Japan's animation industry first branched out in Asia. In 1980, animation studios were set up in Seoul and Taipei, and by the middle of 1980s, 50 percent of the animations broadcast in Japan were made overseas.

Republic of Children and Robots

"Protecting mankind . . . child of science . . . everyone's friend, Mighty Atom." Thus goes the theme song for the Mighty Atom TV cartoon.[60] With the song, the popular imagery of robot as reliable friend emerged to heal postwar Japan's wounded confidence in science and technology. Atom was so popular that by 1981, over 100 million copies of various *Mighty Atom*

---

[59] For the "Bikkuri-Man" incident see ibid., pp. 272–77.
[60] Music by Tatsuo Takai, lyrics by Shuntaro Tanikawa, translated by Frederik Schodt. Schodt, *Inside the Robot Kingdom*, p. 79.

paperbacks had been sold.[61] Atom was first created by Tezuka in 1951, only six years after the atomic bombs were dropped on Japan.[62] How could "atom" become the name of a friend who protects mankind?

Czech writer, Karel Čapek, coined the word "robot" from a Czech word, *robota*, in his 1920 play, *R.U.R.* [Rossum's Universal Robots]. In the post–World War I Europe, the play created a sensation, and the metal men have appeared in novels, plays, and films. Their plots were all quite similar to the original plot, which is, in Schodt's summary, as follows: "Men mass-produce artificial slaves, or robots, to take over their work and later to wage war as well; the robots, of high intelligence, decide not to kill each other, and instead slaughter their masters, the humans."[63] In 1924, *R.U.R.* was staged in Tokyo but it did not gain popularity as it did in the West. The theme, "man make robots; robots kill man," had no resonance for the Japanese and did not take root.[64] Robots with their humanoid forms embody not only advanced technology but also its relation to humankind. When Tezuka created the robot hero Tetsuwan Atom (Mighty Atom, or Iron-Armed Atom), "robots" became what they still are to the Japanese, reliable friends of children.

In the story, Atom was made as a replacement for a son who dies in a traffic accident. His father, who was a top scientist, eventually sold Atom to a circus when he discovered that the robot would never grow up.[65] Like postwar children and youths, orphaned Atom is freed of the past and familial authority. He is born of the marriage of advanced technology and dreams of the future. This incredibly strong, atomic-powered, superrobot has the body of a young boy—he is about four and a half feet tall—and sensitive innocent eyes.

Tezuka himself had read *R.U.R.*, knew such films as *Things to Come*,[66] personally witnessed the destructive effects of the modern warfare, experienced Hiroshima in his own way, and as a medical student, had treated patients most of whom were suffering from malnutrition.[67] He originally conceived the character as a cynical parody of science and technology but, as Schodt explains it, "publishers, the public, and the times pushed him to a more romantic depiction of the future, and as is often the case his

---

[61] Fujishima, *Sengo Manga*, p. 328.

[62] Ironically, his name had to be changed to "Astro Boy" in the U.S. version.

[63] Schodt, *Inside the Robot Kingdom*, pp. 29–30.

[64] Ibid., p. 73

[65] There are several versions of episodes concerning Atom's "growth." Tezuka himself was evidently ambivalent on the subject.

[66] A British film in which the world was to be destroyed in 1949.

[67] The Japanese minister of finance had predicted that more than eight million people out of seventy million would die in the winter of 1945 from starvation. Fujishima, *Sengo Manga*, p. 11.

Figure 7-4. Atomic-powered super-robot with the body of a young boy. *Mighty Atom*, by Osamu Tezuka. Copyright © Tezuka Productions. Reprinted by permission.

character took on a life of its own. 'In the days after the war,' says Tezuka today, 'the publishers wanted me to stress a peaceful future, where Japanese science and technology were advanced and nuclear power was used for peaceful purposes.' "[68] Despite himself, Tezuka created the image of a friendly technology helping men, women, and children attain a peaceful life. It seems that Schodt is quite correct to say that whereas "the carnage wrought by technology in World War II had deepened distrust of it among many intellectuals in the West[,] in Japan it had a decidedly different effect."[69] The disastrous war between humans and technology had already happened in Japan with the atomic bombs, but in the West, the worst had "yet to happen." Tezuka created a Day After scenario in which scientific knowledge and technology would be trustworthy partners in rebuilding the land.[70] The awesome power of the atom can be a friend to a human with a pure heart. In Tezuka's story, a robot is harmful to people when it is being controlled by a man of evil intent or when it is not made with precision. Tezuka's "Principles of Robot Law" states, "Robots are created to serve mankind," and "Robots shall never injure or kill humans."[71] Robots can only fully obey their law when they are freed from their creators, men, who are prone to make mistakes. "All robots have the right to live free and equal."[72] It was a declaration of the republic of children and robots, where the future is no longer to be determined by the past, rather, it is the image and hope of the future that guides and defines the present.

"Science and technology" are intimately associated with "children," and Atom incorporated two otherwise unrelated concepts in his body. Atom has become a symbol of the confidence and hope people place in technology as the trustee of the future of their children. Technology, which once caused total devastation, was purified by this image of an innocent child, and children were conceptually empowered as those who are responsible for befriending, and advancing, science and technology.

In *Mighty Atom* young readers were treated to a feast of images, from the Manhattan-like splendor of twenty-first-century Tokyo, to glorious machines in clean spacious laboratories and honest hardworking robots in the factories. At home, there were comfortable sofas and American-style

[68] Schodt, *Inside the Robot Kingdom*, 1988, p. 76.

[69] Ibid., p. 77.

[70] Atom's story begins with the destruction of the earth and subsequent human efforts to rebuild society on a new planet, in which Atom plays a crucial role in bringing peace to the new world.

[71] For Robot Law, see Fujishima, *Sengo Manga*, pp. 293–95, and Schodt, *Inside the Robot Kingdom*, p. 77.

[72] For Robot Rights, see Hiroshi Kashiwagi, "Atomu: Sengo Nihon no Yume to Tekunologi" [Atom: Dream and technology in postwar Japan], in *Komikku Media* [Comic Media], ed. Yuki Onodera (Tokyo: NTT Shuppan, 1992), pp. 120–40.

kitchens. Bauhaus-style furniture sits in offices, and Porsche-style cars run on the streets.[73] They are both the fruits of civilization, which can easily be destroyed.

Japanese robotics researchers have grown up reading and watching Mighty Atom. The scientist Eiji Nakano wrote that "science fiction masterpieces in Japanese comics and animation . . . planted the idea of robots as friends in the minds of young Japanese and helped create the psychological conditions for the current explosion of [Industrial] robots in the Robot Kingdom [Japan]."[74] Tezuka was invited to robotics research conferences and institutions to exchange ideas. Atom stands at the crossroads of high technology and its popular perception in Japan.

Doraemon: Dream Agent of High-Tech Commodities

In January 1970, a quarter-century after World War II, nineteen years after the birth of Mighty Atom and two years after its discontinuation, Fujio Fujiko launched *Doraemon*. Doraemon also contains a nuclear reactor as his source of energy. Nobita lives in a suburban residential area, and Atom's illustrious "metropolis" has become ordinary "urban" space where the contemporary people live. Doraemon does not need to redeem the city. He comes to remedy the pain of his spoiled yet imaginative friend.

Nobita's father is a white-color *salariman* who leaves home every morning and comes back in the evenings to have dinner with his family, that is, his wife Tamako, their only son Nobita, and Doraemon. On Sundays, he usually reads newspapers or watches television. Nobita's mother stays home tending the family. They spend most of their time on the first floor, leaving Nobita's childhood world undisturbed.

Nobita's room on the second floor is connected to, and separated from, the first floor family space by the stairs.[75] The modern private family home is already set apart from the public sphere, but the child's room is further hidden inside the home. The spheres of politics, production, and transaction are invisible from Nobita's room, although Nobita's father visits them every day.

With Doraemon's "ta-ke-co-pu-ter" Nobita can fly, and using Doraemon's "Do-ko-de-mo [Anywhere] Door" he and his friends can have adventures anywhere in the world. Using the time machine parked inside Nobita's desk drawer, they can travel into the past or the future. The world

[73] Ibid., p. 126.
[74] Schodt, *Inside the Robot Kingdom*, p. 73.
[75] Concerning the second floor as a private urban space in modern Japan, see Ai Maeda, *Toshi Kukan no Nakano Bungaku* [Literature in the urban space] (Tokyo: Chikuma Shobo, 1989).

that Nobita and Doraemon explore is the world of world maps, pictures of dinosaurs and dragons, science fiction movie posters, comic books, fossil collections, and toy robots, the world of discourse that fits most comfortably inside a child's room. No newspapers allowed. The child's room is a privileged space in modern society, where the occupant can freely transcend time, space, and political boundaries.

Doraemon delivers the high-tech gadgets to Nobita who occupies this secluded space. In contemporary society where the consumers, not only the children, are separated from the site of manufacturing, transaction, and negotiation, Doraemon appears to be the ideal agent of marketing and delivery.

Advertisers target groups, point out problems and desires they may have never known they had before, and try to convince them that the purchase of a certain commodity is The Solution. Most commodities today are manufactured by strangers whom the prospective consumers have not met and will never meet. They are produced and transported in places entirely unknown to the consumers. It matters little, indeed, whether they are produced in a factory in the next town, overseas, or even in the future. In periods when lifestyles are changing so radically, such as in the late-nineteenth-century United States or in Asian countries today, goods that consumers have never heard of before are advertised. Consumers often do not know how an appliance works. The effectiveness of an advertisement relies, therefore, largely on how and by whom the commodity is introduced to the target audience.

Ohmann describes the effect of the familiar neighborly voice in advertisement commonly found in monthly magazines in 1890s America: "It is a voice *like ours*, reaching across the gap between anonymous corporation and anonymous readership, establishing in that gap a chatty, humorous, reliable, *neighborly* helper, as if to stand in place of the grandmothers and mothers who no longer live with or near the young wife or pass on to her their generational skills and wisdom" [emphasis in original].[76]

The familiar "neighbor" helps erase any uneasiness the consumer may have in purchasing a strange object. The familiar popular characters may play the role of "a chatty, humorous, reliable, neighborly helper" most effectively. Commodities in hand, they can even wait for consumers in stores.

Among them, Doraemon is a dream agent for both the manufacturer and for the consumer. He lives with Nobita, the prospective consumer and

[76] Ohmann, "Advertising," p. 155. On the discourse of magazine advertisement of the period, see pp. 152–70.

knows all Nobita's problems, dispositions, and fantasies. He may not take the place of Nobita's grandmother, but he does stand in for Nobita's great-great-grandson to pass on the "generational skills and wisdom" that will have accumulated. Although the gadgets Doraemon delivers from the future are always strange objects, Nobita is assured that they are always designed for, and manifest themselves as responses to, his personal needs. The intimate relationship between Nobita and Doraemon is converted into trust in the unfamiliar high-tech products. Doraemon selects the gadget for Nobita and frees him from the burden of searching for and updating information and from selecting suitable and affordable items. He is handier and more effective than a Sears catalogue.

Nobita: An Imaginative Consumer

Nobita is, on his side, an ideal consumer. He accepts the way the world is, despite his daily misery, and is content with his children's domain. Since nothing fundamental changes, he continues to feel miserable, which keeps him in need of Doraemon's gadgets. Thus by 1991, Doraemon had pulled out more than 1,100 items out of his pocket.

At the same time, Nobita is a vigorous and imaginative experimenter. Once his problem is solved, Nobita cheerfully experiments with each high-tech toy to find a new application not intended by its designer, manufacturer, or the supplier, Doraemon. Nobita's experiments often cause mishaps. Yet the optimistic, good-natured boy never loses his curiosity. Nobita reminds us of a young child who plays with his little toy car not only as a car, but as an airplane, as a boat or as dozens of other enchanting objects in his imaginative world. Nobita's mettle is as much a source of the comics' popularity as are its breathtakingly fresh ideas for high-tech products. In fact this playful and engaging literacy of objects that Nobita Nobi exhibits makes the entire structure of the story persuasive.[77] It is this curiosity and the free, gentle mind of a child that will eventually produce the fabulous high-tech products that Doraemon brings back from the future.

Thus Nobita brings together the elements of an affluent consumption society supported by constant advancement in technology. That is the Japan of the 1970s and 1980s as pictured in *Doraemon.*

---

[77] For the "literacy of objects," see Brian Sutton-Smith, *Toys as Culture* (New York: Garden Press, 1986).

Dawn of the Television Age in Asia

Indonesia's national broadcast company, TVRI (Televisi Republik Indonesia), started to broadcast on August 24, 1962,[78] the year Tezuka set up Mushi Productions in Tokyo. In October 1965, a state funeral for six army generals killed in an abortive coup was broadcast. President Sukarno, famed for his "baritone" voice and his radio speeches, did not attend the funeral. A speech by General Nasution made the audience cry, and General Soeharto made his first conspicuous appearance, standing silently, with his dark sunglasses, behind Nasution. The age of Sukarno the marvelous orator was about to end.

Soeharto became president in 1968, and has been known for his composed silent smile. In the mid-1970s, the government required every village to have at least one television set and requested that villagers watch the news and cultural events. Electric generators spread television to villages ahead of electrification. In 1989, there were approximately six million registered television sets, about one television set for every thirty-three persons. By 1990, TVRI's 13 regional stations, 350 transmission facilities, and 6,000 employees reached 40 percent of the land. This meant, in theory, that 70 percent of Indonesia's population was provided with national television news from Jakarta every evening at seven and nine o'clock. Soeharto's image appears at the beginning of news almost every day. His portrayals are on walls of government offices and schools throughout the archipelago.

The commercial television age began after a controversial deregulation in the late 1980s. Now, five privately run television stations have national broadcast licenses: RCTI (Rajawali Citra Televisi Indonesia), TPI (Televisi Pendidikan Indonesia), SCTV (Surya Citra Televisi), AN-Teve, and Indosiar Visual Mandiri. Thanks to satellite dishes, people in the archipelago in fact have more choices to make: TVRI, RCTI, SCTV, TPI, ANTEVE, CNNI, ESPN, STAR TV, HBO, CFI, ATVI, and DISCOVERY. The 3,500 rupiah (about $1.50) monthly television guide, *VISTA TV*, lists the programs for all the channels. A ten-foot satellite dish, with "Full Remote Control-Stereo System" is advertised at Rp. 850,000 (about $425).[79] Many second-hand dishes are also available.

Indonesian viewers are now learning how to cope with television commercials. Some intellectuals and religious groups are against television commercials that arouse unwanted desires. Television commercials started,

---

[78] At first with only thirty minutes of programming per day. See *Vista TV Special Anniversary Edition*, August 1992, for the details.

[79] *Vista TV*, May 1994, p. 58.

nevertheless, with shampoos and soaps. No alcohol. In a very short time commercials have become the norm.[80] Rich numerical data on the television industry now floods the mass media. TPI's fee for a thirty-second advertisement, for example, is reported to have been reduced from 18 million Rupiah ($9,000) to 14 million Rupiah ($7,000), and RCTI charges Rp. 17 million ($8,500) to broadcast commercials twenty-one times. It is accepted that television is a business and that popularity of the programs begets value. The programs and their target audience are noted, and audience likes and dislikes are spotlighted in the weekly and monthly surveys conducted by SRI and printed in *VISTA TV*. It is a new phenomena in the country where the intentions of the president, not that of the citizens, have been the usual object of focus for the mass media.

The second issue widely discussed concerns how much of the TV programming is produced domestically and how much is imported from abroad. In 1993, for example, RCTI broadcasted eighteen hours a day. Domestically produced programs cost about Rp. 40 million ($20,000) per hour, and they took up one third of the day (6 hours), costing the station about Rp. 240 million ($120,000) per day, Rp. 7.2 billion ($3.6 million) per month. On the other hand, the imported programs cost only Rp. 5–10 million ($2,500–5,000) per hour.

A similar situation prevailed in Japan in the 1960s, and impressive progress has been made by the domestic television production companies in both countries. With the exception of a few extremely popular imported programs, the audiences tend to prefer domestically produced programs. Over the long term, a familiar language, familiar stories, actors, landscapes, and social, political, and cultural backgrounds play a crucial role in audience preference. Program sponsors also take the nationality of the images into consideration. This is one good reason why Japan's image alliances are always on the lookout for local image producers; they feel no need to stick to Japanese characters—in many cases their nationality is already indecipherable—as long as they can participate in profit sharing and maximization. *VISTA TV*'s articles show that intellectuals and artists are constantly sought after for interviews, movie reviews, fashion or pop music information, suggestions for new programming, and so on. Indonesia is in search of its own talents and celebrity figures, who will follow their first television celebrity, President Soeharto.

The third issue often discussed focuses on television's effects on children. Usually these discussions typically end with the suggestion that mothers restrict children's viewing times or watch the programs "together" with their children. Familiar suggestions in the United States, yet a strikingly

---

[80] Television has this power of making the new seem normal through sheer repetition.

new trend for a country where the children have always accompanied their parents and neighbors everywhere and enjoyed theatrical entertainment together. The conceptual separation of the domain of childhood is progressing. The Japanese children's television animations and comics are generally regarded to be suitable and educational for children. A local Muslim leader has said that he allows his children to watch only the national news and children's animations.

Doraemon in Indonesia

American comics such as *Superman* were introduced to Indonesia in the 1950s. Affluent parents commonly bought translations of Disney picture books for their children. After television deregulation, however, Japanese cartoons and other programs were introduced with remarkable success.[81] A dominant local publisher set up the agency to import television programming from Japan.

When I visited Indonesia in 1992 and 1993, *Doraemon* had been on air since 1991 on RCTI. I found him to be a highly popular and intimately familiar figure. Once, I witnessed a friend's five-year-old son turn on the television precisely when *Doraemon* started (at 8:00 A.M. on Sunday). He watched it engrossed for half an hour (two episodes), and as soon as it was over, he switched the television off to play video games. Only *Doraemon* could compete against the games. My friend, who used to enjoy sleeping late on Sundays, now gets up at eight to watch *Doraemon* with his son. He has bought toys with *Doraemon* characters for his son's birthday. A cabinet minister also confessed that he watches *Doraemon* every Sunday, and when he cannot, he asks his wife to tape the day's episodes for him. According to a survey conducted for the week of April 24 to April 30, 1994,[82] *Doraemon* was the favorite children's program in all four areas surveyed—Jakarta, Medan, Surabaya, and Semarang.

Soon after television broadcasting of *Doraemon* began, locally drawn comic booklets appeared on the streets. The corner bookstands and hawkers sold the small, palm-size, thin (one episode each), pirated (or creative, local versions of) *Doraemon* comic books at prices even children could afford—around two to four hundred rupiah (ten to twenty cents) each. The tissue-paper booklets were drawn by teenage boys and are reminiscent of the early postwar days of Japanese manga. Japanese publishers took no

[81] Christine T. Tjandraningsih, "Japan's 'manga' oust rivals from Indonesian market," *Japan Times*, January 11, 1995.
[82] *VISTA TV*, June 1994, p. 35. It was the first survey on the "children's" television programs in Indonesia.

direct action against the pirated comics. When interviewed, they said that the domestic (Japanese) market being so large, and the pirates' businesses overseas being so minuscule, they could afford to wait and see how the situation developed. After all, that was how the narrative comics took root in postwar Japan. Their insight proved to be right. Thanks to the pirates' ingenuity and risk taking, handmade *Doraemon* comics spread and the local publishing houses decided to join the party. They struck legal deals with Japanese publishers and started to sell better quality, copyrighted Tento-Mushi Series paperback books for 3,300 rupiah (or about $1.50) through their bookstore chains. They found it in their interest to enforce the copyright against the peddlers on the streets, and the pirated editions quickly disappeared.[83]

In Indonesia, Elex Media Komputindo, a subsidiary of the largest publisher group and bookstore chain, Gramedia, publishes *Doraemon* in press runs of 40,000 for each volume. It has already translated and published more than four hundred titles of Japanese manga in last five years. The character merchandising division was created in 1994.

Copyright protection is crucial for the image alliance to maximize profit. Once the local publishers and advertisers join the alliance, they try to suppress the pirates more effectively than Japanese publishers could in order to protect their shared interest. In fact, they have requested that the Japanese publishers pay more attention to the copyright issue. *Doraemon* has helped establish an image alliance in Indonesia identical to that in Japan. *Candy Candy, Sailor Moon, Dragon Ball*, and other popular Japanese television programs are following suit. Commodities with the popular characters on them crowd the shelves in the first-generation shopping malls, which are sprouting in big cities.

TV programs, especially animated cartoons, which are popular in Japan and are therefore already supported by the image alliances, are guaranteed some degree of commercial success abroad. Their product lines accompany them on their trip abroad and help increase the characters' visibility and familiarity. Even if a character fails to gain popularity, there is an endless supply of new characters to replace it. It is the size of local consumer class—the families with TV sets who are capable and willing to spend money on their children—that determines the extent of their success. In other words, the "success" of television animations, comic books, and their character commodities attests to the presence of an emerging consumer class in the region.

Doraemon cartoons are dubbed, and the comic books are translated into

---

[83] In retrospect, the street pirates functioned both as astute market researchers and agile advertisers.

Indonesian. In the process, predictably, some mistranslations occur. On television, because the original pictorial flow is unhindered, the problem is voices. For example, when Nobita's father says to his wife, "Isn't dinner ready yet? I am hungry," in Japanese he is commanding his wife to hurry. Literally translated into Indonesian, however, the sentence is read as if a small child asking his indulgent mother, "Isn't dinner ready yet, [Mom]? I am hungry." Yet nuances appear not to matter much. The language portions are not central to the narrative. Indonesian children watch their *Dragon Ball* videos, for example, in pirated editions from Hong Kong with the Japanese voices and the Chinese subtitles.

The translation of printed manga conversation can be difficult. Utterances are short, casual, and sometimes comically crafted at the cost of grammatical precision. New words are frequently coined and quickly adopted by others. The fact that language does not necessarily determine the progression of the stories has liberated voice from logical sequence. Meaningless words can be thrown in. The translation of the manga's sound-effects that creatively illustrate the characters' activities and emotions is most arduous. Indonesian children appear to be learning quickly how to "read" manga, and many of them are routinely spotted "browsing" comic books at bookstores.

Difficulties in the U.S. Market

The difficulty of exporting the postwar comics to the U.S. market was demonstrated in the case of *Hadashi no Gen* by Keiji Nakazawa. The United States has its own history and style of comics and did not have Tezuka to stage a manga revolution. The existing distribution channels and markets for comics are not receptive to the thick, black-and-white manga comics. In spite of numerous cartoons, literacy in manga's visual narration has not taken root widely yet, and perhaps need not to. Potential manga consumers in the United States have ready access to the Hollywood movie.

Nakazawa was the victim of the atomic bomb dropped on Hiroshima. He drew his experience as an eyewitness account. A nonprofit peace group in Tokyo published an English-language edition of *Hadashi no Gen* under the title *Barefoot Gen* in the late 1970s and sent copies around the world. In the United States, a San Francisco underground publisher cut the 1,400 page narrative into several "normal" comic books, but still no one bought it. Lack of manga literacy may have been one reason; the other was the intervention by the Comics Code Authority. It considered the Day-After scenes "too graphically violent."[84] It was one thing to drop the bomb and

---

[84] For the trip of "Barefoot Gen" to the United States, see Schodt, *Manga, Manga*, p. 154.

let children go through the experience, and it was another to allow an eyewitness's visual narration to circulate.[85] Perhaps the story did not unfold "qualities of fineness and permanence," or "experiences worth reliving," which were the values presented in American literary circles for children's literature.[86] On the other hand, American adults normally do not read "children's" accounts, which was how the narrative was scripted. The line between the adult literature and the children's literature is clearer in the United States than it is in postwar Japan.

Tezuka's *Astro Boy* comics also had to be rescripted, redrawn, and colored by the Americans in order to be accepted in the United States market. In turn, American comic books—colored yet thin, which require the readers to READ each conversation of the characters—are faring no better in the Japanese market.

Japanese cartoons also have problems in the United States. They are often categorized as "animation for small children" and then censored under the broadcasting code, which is "even more stringent than the Comics Code."[87] Ironically, animation with conspicuous violence, a relatively unpopular genre in Japan,[88] has had no difficulty breaking into the United States market because they were categorized "not for children." "Children's" animation like *Doraemon* still has not been broadcast on television in the United States.[89]

The primary reason, however, that Japanese children's animations and comics have not been pushed into the U.S. market appears to be the lack of enthusiasm among Japanese agents. Tezuka compromised to get his comics accepted in the American market, and his animations were popular. The American market at that time was profitable—NBC paid 3,600,000 yen ($10,000) for each *Astro Boy* episode, while Fujiya paid 550,000 yen[90]—and Tezuka was proud to see his creature accepted by the "international" audience.

The U.S. market is mature, with its own ability to produce popular images. It is also so rich that it is possible for individual industry, such as video games, which in Japan is becoming new foci of the image alliance, to make huge profits independently of such alliances.

[85] For the censorship of children's books in the United States, see Deane, *Mirrors of American Culture*, pp. 16–29.
[86] For the "Honor List of Children's Books," see ibid., pp. 17–18.
[87] Schodt, *Manga, Manga*, 1983, p. 156.
[88] The Japanese in the United States are shocked to find violent made-in-Japan videos so available. They are hard to find in Japan.
[89] *Sailor Moon* began broadcasting in September 1995.
[90] Fujishima, *Manga, Manga*, pp. 238, 244.

Asian and European Markets

In the Asian region, economic growth has translated into the emergence of a consumer class. At the same time, the television age is dawning, which opens the gate for inexpensive animations. In the initial stage, the cartoons themselves do not have to show a profit because soon the comic books are going to follow, and so is character merchandising. The shared copyright promises eventual profit and helps promote the entire move.

The manga theme of children's empowerment finds rich soil in the developing countries. Children in the region are generally better educated than their parents, and they are expected to lead in the national march into the future. The manga's prevalent dream of a high-tech society built by the young generation also finds support and sympathy everywhere excep in the Philippines, which bans Japanese comics and TV animations from time to time because of their "violence."[91] The Chinese translation from Taiwan, however, is easily available there.

China, the largest potential market, has shown a special receptivity to Japanese cartoons and comics that encourage children to aspire to careers in science and technology. In 1980, the *Astro Boy* series became the first foreign animated television series in China. Publication of the comic books by Science Promotion Publisher accompanied, and *Doraemon* has followed. According to Mark Schilling, "In China, where a printing of 20,000 copies is considered average for a comic book, Doraemon manga have sold 900,000 copies in the past three years. The television show has become a nationwide hit, and Doraemon merchandise is sold at stores, including state stores, all over the country."[92]

In Taiwan,[93] Doraemon's images are found all over the place—on television, in comic books, on T-shirts, and even on the school bus of the "Xiao Dingdong Preschool" (Doraemon in Taiwan is Jiqi Mao Xiao Dingdong—Little Dingdong the Robot Cat). The staff at Ching Wen, a Taiwan manga publisher, speculated that *Doraemon* arrived in Taiwan seventeen or eighteen years ago both as "manga" and television animation. The term "manga" is commonly used in Taiwan. A man in his early thirties remembers that *Doraemon* was very popular from his "middle teens" and that a great variety of manga were already available on the market. In Taipei,

[91] For history and a content analysis of the comics in the Philippines written by Filipino scholars, see Motoe Terami, ed. and trans., *Filipin no Taishu Bunka* [Mass culture in the Philippines] (Tokyo: Mekon, 1992), pp. 75–129.
[92] Schilling, "Doraemon," p. 406.
[93] I would like to thank Gardner Bovingdon for collecting the materials on Doraemon in Taiwan for my research.

Doraemon cartoon show peaked in popularity around 1990. Nowadays it is only one of a vast array of cartoon shows. Many of them are backed up with comic books, videos, calendars, stationery, plastic warriors, weapons, and war machines. Evidently, the first introductory stage is long over. The image alliances are actively recreating themselves with new characters on a regular basis. TV channels 37 and 39 are devoted to programs imported from Japan. Japanese cartoons are broadcast all day, every day, not only on these channels but on others as well.

Many stationery stores carry *Doraemon* comic books as well as a great many other manga. They are new and shrink-wrapped—to prevent browsing without purchase—and usually bear the marks of the companies licensed to distribute them in Taiwan. The book rental stores rent out all varieties of manga from many different publishers, some of them still clearly illegal copies of Japanese originals and some Taiwanese imitations. A storekeeper complained that the imposition of GATT restrictions a few years ago drove the illicit manga off the market and left only the much higher priced legal manga.

Before Ching Wen and Da Ran received publishing rights, many artists of Ching Wen specialized in drawing *Doraemon*; in fact, many drew *Doraemon* for practice before moving on to other projects. "No artists draw *Doraemon* now; they all do their own comics," says a staff member. No one seems to remember exactly when Ching Wen started publishing *Doraemon*, it was "a long time ago." This most successful and visible company is housed in a small second story suite and appears to have about thirty employees: editorial staff, translators, and artists.

Other publishers also produced versions of *Doraemon*:

> Peng Li used to publish many *Doraemon* manga. According to a staff member, they stopped two to three years ago when the "copyright troubles" began. In business thirty years, they now have over fifty employees. Peng Li began publishing *Doraemon* manga about twenty years ago. They had cartoonists drawing the character, but "some of the stories" were copied, implying that some were lifted.

> Jin Wen still publishes *Doraemon* manga. They have no copyright, nor do they have cartoonists of their own. My contact there told me they have been printing *Doraemon* for at least five years, though he "wasn't too clear" on when they started. He was also "not too clear" on whether the stories were copied from Japanese comics or created by their company.

> Yang Ming continues to publish *Doraemon*, and has for at least five years. The person I spoke to there said some of the stories are copied from Japanese comics, some created by them; the same goes for the drawings.

Evidently, many artists in Taiwan today can easily create both their versions of *Doraemon* and their own comics.

The manga industry in Japan combines the manga magazine, which offers space for new stories and novice artists, and comic books, which brings in profits. Japanese publishers are trying to reproduce the system in Taiwan. Shueisha has licensed two monthly manga magazines in Taiwan to print comics of its weekly *Shonen Jump*. At the same time, they proposed that "more than 40 percent of their pages have to be reserved for the young local artists."[94] Talented artists are the most precious assets of the industry. Taiwan has already become a full member of the manga club, with its own artists, manga magazines, and paperbacks. Moreover, China and Taiwan have actively been producing and exporting the character goods to the countries in Asia including Japan.

While cartoons and comics captured their most enthusiastic market in Asia, they are doing better in Europe than in the United States. In Italy, *Candy Candy* broadcasts were followed by the publication of deluxe hardbound comic books, rescripted, redrawn, and colored by local artists. There was also the usual heavy merchandising of stationery, toys, and records with the theme songs. *Candy Candy* was so popular that after the Japanese series ended, local artist drew Italian sequels.[95]

In France, following a period of television broadcasts, young manga readers have begun to emerge over the last three years. It is even considered fashionable to buy and "read" the original Japanese versions, rather than the translated comics. These originals progress from right to left and are not cheap (about fifty franc each). A thirteen-year-old high school student who was browsing comics in a store was quoted: "I watched the television animation so I know the story. I can understand it [*Dragon Ball* by Akira Toriyama] even though it is in Japanese. The pictures are nicely drawn and have movements."[96]

The Search for Overseas Artists

In the whole structure of the image alliance, the artist who conceives and develops the original character and story still sits at the core. A talented artist, who can contrive strong characters, fresh visual devices, and witty story lines, generates and regenerates the entire system and keeps it expanding. Without talent, magazine sales drop quickly, and the rest of the

---

[94] *Takarajima Shonen* (Boy's Treasure Island) and *Netsumon Shonen TOP.*
[95] Schodt, *Manga, Manga*, pp. 156–57.
[96] "Manga, Wakamono no Kyotsu-go. Nihon Hatsu, Futsu de Bumu [Manga, lingua franca of youth. From Japan, popular in France]," *Nihon Keizai Shinbun*, November 20, 1994.

alliance dwindles. It does not really matter where the popular images and their creators come from as long as the alliance has the means to multiply and maximize profit from them. China and Taiwan are considered the most promising birthplaces for popular comic artists. Translation between Chinese and Japanese is relatively easy because the visual flow of the frame is from right to left in both. The manga market in Japan is huge and has a bottomless appetite for new visions and voices, and publishers are willing to try out foreign talents from Asia and all over the world. Local artists drawing for local markets also bring in profit for the multinational image alliances.

The video game industry, which is intimately linked with the comics and animation industries in creating characters, is also seeking exotic story lines and character images for their products. A pioneer of narrative video games (in which the player can control the story), which he calls "sound novel", confidently states, "We can enjoy more when translating from English into Japanese than from Japanese into English."[97] The artists and producers want to be fascinated and entertained themselves while entertaining others.

Kodansha has introduced manga by overseas artists in its weekly, *Shukan Morning*, and there was an "ASEAN Manga Artists Exhibition" in Tokyo in 1990. That same year, a special exhibition of the works of Osamu Tezuka was carried in the prestigious National Museum of Modern Art. Manga has gained the status of a modern national art.

Postwar Japanese comics originated as a children's medium. Its primary characteristic is pictorial storytelling, in which narrative is mainly carried by pictures with optional voice and sound. The graphic depiction of flowing movement is itself a source of entertainment. It has become a form of folklore, passed on from children to children, visually narrating scenes of destruction and devastation, resurrection and redemption. It is a forum in which children sing the themes of desperation, rebellion, optimism, and hope. As early readers have matured, manga has become popular culture for everyone, young and old.

In the Age of Television, animation helped its audience learn literacy of visual signs and narration—literacy of manga. The images on the screen also proved to be highly effective in generating popularity and profit, and image alliances were formed to multiply and maximize profit. The artists, manga publishers, animation production houses, TV companies, manufacturers, retailers, and advertisers, all join these alliances. The popular characters have marched through the screen on which Doraemon has played

[97] *Super Fami-Con*, February 10, 1995, p. 160.

a leading role because of his endearing nature and his message of optimism about technology and its relations to humanity. The series also de-
code and validate the new relations of production and consumption in
industrialized society.

When *Doraemon* went overseas, the image alliance followed and the result was multi-industrial, multinational image alliances. The penetration of
Japanese popular culture into Asia is pulled along by an insatiable local
demand. In this process, image alliances have been replicated in Asia—in
Taiwan and Hong Kong for quite some time, and increasingly throughout
Southeast Asia. In the developing countries of the region, Japan's postwar
comics, animated cartoons, and related merchandise have been welcomed
and have taken root. *Doraemon* is as much a sign of the emerging consumer
class and of new family life with television, children, and their toys as it is
a sign of optimism for the future.

In the U.S. market, Japan's animations and comics have faced more
obstacles than in Asia and other parts of the world because the United
States has its own system of popular image production and sales. Regula-
tion of children's entertainment and a lack of literacy of visual narration
have also blocked manga's entrance to the United States. The manga videos, nonetheless, have found fans among university students. To some
extent manga have been accepted in Europe and Latin America.

What is the political significance of the penetration of Japanese popular
culture in Asia? Though few would deny the importance of cultural hegemony in politics, it is notoriously difficult to pinpoint its political significance. Yet this much may be said. As Hollywood films have been
immensely important for disseminating the idea of the American way of
life in Asia as well as elsewhere, Japanese comics and television animations
are spreading Japanese ideas about childhood, war and peace, science and
technology, and the future world as well as the accessible new medium for
entertainment often without revealing their Japanese origin.

Today, for example, Disney cartoons are what parents tend to buy for
their children; Japanese comic books, animation videos, video games, and
other character merchandise are what children ask for or buy with their
own money. They are actually practicing and verifying the notion frequently found in manga that the children are capable of deciding what
they want and getting it for themselves. This notion substantiates the perception of children as the pioneers for the future world, which is closed
and alien to the older generation.

This does not necessarily mean that the hegemony of American popular
culture is being undermined or that the idea of the American way of life
has lost its luster. It is rather that a new item has been added to the
popular culture mix operating in the open market of Asia, one that may
or may not have recognizable political consequences.

IV

WHAT KIND OF ASIA?

8

Japan's National Security and Asia-Pacific's Regional Institutions in the Post–Cold War Era

SUSUMU YAMAKAGE

Talking of Asia-Pacific in the post-cold war era as if it were distinctly different from that in the cold war era is based on conventional ways of thinking and is probably influenced by Eurocentric views of international society. For instance, out of the four divided nations the cold war brought into being, two still remain in Asia. No German-style unification has ever taken place there. Asia's statesmen still see regional affairs as more or less driven by the logic of power politics. Major power relations, especially those between the United States and China, remain tense in Asia. Unlike in Europe, no states in Asia fragmented suddenly when the cold war ended; no civil wars erupted; no communist regimes fell. In short there has been no clear break in the Asia-Pacific region, especially in East Asia, between the cold war era and the post–cold war era. Indeed, there are as many sources of turmoil in the region as before.

Despite its potential instability, however, the Asia-Pacific region now leads the world in economic development, growth, and deepening interdependence. Despite the difficulty inherent in defining geographic terms, there is an emerging consensus that the membership of APEC (Asia-Pacific Economic Cooperation) delimits the Asia-Pacific region.[1] The core of

This chapter reports ongoing research on the formation of Southeast Asian and extra-regional influence, sponsored by Japan's ministry of education grant for scientific research. The author expresses his gratitude to participants in the seminars, anonymous referees, and editors.

[1] APEC was established in 1989 by Australia, Brunei, Canada, Indonesia, Japan, Korea, Malaysia, New Zealand, the Philippines, Singapore, Thailand, and the United States. China, Hong Kong and Taiwan joined simultaneously in 1991, Mexico and Papua New Guinea in

APEC is a close economic linkage of two highly interdependent subregions: North America, centered on the United States, on the one hand, and East and Southeast Asia, centered on Japan, on the other. The United States has taken initiatives to establish and widen the North American Free Trade Agreement (NAFTA); Japan has become more deeply involved in Asia through generous aid programs, trade, and investment. Transpacific interconnections have been rapidly strengthened, especially in recent years by U.S. business leaders and policy makers who have become interested in "East Asian miracles" and believe that closer economic ties with the other side of the ocean will provide crucial leverage for the rebirth of U.S. industrial competitiveness.[2]

Deepening economic interdependence in the Asia-Pacific region is often contrasted with the lack of coordination in security. The United States has been the dominant military presence since the Pacific war; however, security in the Asia-Pacific region is poorly institutionalized. Until the end of the 1980s, Sino-Soviet rivalry in Southeast Asia and the antagonism between the United States and the Soviet Union ruled out any efforts either by super powers or by nations in the region to build a framework for common security. As a result, no confidence-building regime equivalent to the Conference on Security and Cooperation in Europe (CSCE) developed. Only with the end of the cold war was it possible for regional powers to begin to seek such a framework.[3] Though traditionally reluctant to play a security role, Japan has recently taken steps, sometimes hesitant ones, to explore possible roles for Japan in a new framework.

It seems inevitable that Japan will assume some responsibility for regional (and, probably, global) security. Questions remain: what kind of power is Japan seeking, and toward what aims would Japan exercise such power? Although Japanese leaders have expressed a willingness to contribute to international and regional peace, there are ambiguities about Japan's goals. Still Japan's apparent reluctance to assume an explicit security role in Asia-Pacific does not mean that Japan has done nothing to stabilize and institutionalize a regional order.

In order to make Japan's prospective security roles clearer, I shall at-

---

1993, and Chile in 1994. As of 1995, a few more countries including India have expressed a wish to join the organization.

[2] World Bank, *The East Asian Miracle* (London: Oxford University Press, 1993).

[3] For Japanese perspectives on the regional development since the end of the cold war, see Tadashi Mio, ed. *Posuto-reisen no Indoshina* [Post-cold war Indochina] (Tokyo: Japan Institute for International Affairs, 1993); Tatsumi Okabe, ed., *Posuto-Kambojia no Tonan-ajia* [Southeast Asia after the end of the Cambodian Conflict] (Tokyo: Japan Institute for International Affairs, 1992); and Tatsumi Okabe, ed., *Posuto-reisen no Ajia-taiheiyo* [Post-cold war Asia Pacific] (Tokyo: Japan Institute for International Affairs, 1995).

tempt to delineate its attitude toward, and its involvement in, the institutionalization of regional security. Needless to say, the security policies of the United States, whether unilateral, bilateral, or multilateral, have affected and will continue to affect not only Japan's security policies but also those of the entire region. Japan's view of regional affairs has not been identical with that of the United States. In particular, the Japanese concept of comprehensive security is much broader than the more purely military view of the United States.

National Security and Regional Order

Defeat changed Japan in many ways. First of all, since the war, the Japanese have regarded Japan as a small power no matter the size or influence of its economy. A major power can, or at least can try to, change the international environment in its favor. A small power, on the other hand, must adapt itself to the international environment in order to secure peace and prosperity. For postwar Japan, adaptation has been the main theme of external relations.[4] The Japanese Diplomatic Blue Book—the year does not matter—focuses sharply on changes in the international environment, notably the relationship between major powers, and evaluates their effect on Japan. The tools and strategies suggested for adaptation are usually cooperation in international and regional organizations, and the enhancement of friendly bilateral relations. In this context, China's outlook in general and its attitude toward Japan in particular have been the most influential factors in Japan's perception of regional order.[5] Only in the last few years has Japan modified its understanding of itself as a small power and begun a public discussion of its contribution to international peace.

Second, Japan's security policy has been closely tied to U.S. global strategy. After the war, the occupation authority was essentially the United States; the San Francisco Peace Treaty was concluded under U.S. leadership, and the U.S.-Japan Mutual Security Treaty stipulated that U.S. forces would remain stationed in Japan.[6] By the same token, the United States strongly backed Japan's reentry into the international economic re-

---

[4] One might say that Japan has been reluctant to take on the management of international affairs. One cannot both adapt and manage.

[5] A systematic analysis of postwar Japan's relations with China is provided in Akihiko Tanaka, *Nicchu-kankai, 1945–1990* [Japan–China relations, 1945–1990] (Tokyo: Tokyo University Press, 1991).

[6] For more detailed discussions, see Martin E. Weinstein, *Japan's Postwar Defense Policy, 1947–1968* (New York: Columbia University Press, 1971).

gime despite the deep resentment of other allied nations, especially Britain and Australia.[7] Revised in 1960, the current mutual security treaty is more reciprocal than the old one, but the structure of Japan's dependence on U.S. forces is unchanged. Since 1970, the treaty has been automatically extended annually. Changes in the international environment have occasionally caused Japanese authorities to consider modifying Japan's relations with the United States, but close ties have been maintained, and even strengthened. Until the 1960s, Japan had no options; since the 1970s Japan has chosen to tie its policy to U.S. policy.

Third, Japan's own defense policy has been severely constrained both domestically and externally. The major, but not the sole, constraint is Article 9 of the Constitution of Japan. Since 1968 the government has committed itself to the principles of no possession, no development, and no introduction of nuclear weapons. The structure of the government is decentralized in the formulation of national defense policy. While the Defense Agency (JDA) alone is responsible for controlling the defense forces, the National Security Council (NSC), consisting of seven cabinet members chaired by the prime minister, makes all important decisions on national defense prior to decision by the full Cabinet.[8] Moreover, the JDA's bureaucracy is deeply penetrated by the ministries of Finance (MOF), Foreign Affairs (MOFA), and International Trade and Industry (MITI), which effectively limits the JDA's institutional autonomy.[9] External constraints are no less significant. Memories of Japan's wrongdoing still prevail among peoples in Korea, China, and other areas in the region, and increases in Japan's defense capabilities have caused fears that Japan might try again to project its power.[10]

Moreover, the lack of national consensus among the Japanese public has made constructive discussions on defense policy very difficult. While there has been agreement that Japan should pursue peace and stability,

[7] Tatsuo Akaneya, *Nihon no GATT Kanyu mondai: Rejimu-riron no bunseki-sikaku ni yoru jirei-kenkyu* [The Question of Japan's participation in GATT: A case study in the analytical perspective of regime theory] (Tokyo: Tokyo University Press, 1992).

[8] The Japanese NSC consists of the prime minister, the foreign minister, the finance minister, the cabinet secretary, the JDA director, the Economic Planning Agency director, and the chief public safety commissioner. The JDA was established in 1954; the National Defense Council, which consists of the prime minister, the foreign minister, the finance minister, the JDA director, and the Economic Planning Agency director was established in 1956. This council was enlarged and renamed the NSC in 1986.

[9] Peter J. Katzenstein and Nobuo Okawara. *Japan's National Security: Structures, Norms, and Policy Responses in a Changing World* (Ithaca: Cornell University Press, 1993), pp. 21–56.

[10] Raul S. Manglapus, *Japan in Southeast Asia: Collision Course* (Washington, D.C.: Carnegie Endowment for International Peace, 1976).

how to pursue that goal has led to irreconcilable controversies.[11] Even more or less mainstream conservatives differ over security policy.[12] The end of the cold war did little to resolve these differences. When they came to power, the Socialists changed their long-standing position on defense, but the discussion among conservatives remains as it was in the 1980s. Furthermore, the JDA and the defense forces are isolated from the public by the antimilitary sentiment widely shared by the Japanese.[13]

Last, and related to the foregoing, Japan's military has only the capability to defend Japanese territory against a small-scale attack. Remilitarization dates back to 1950 when occupied Japan was ordered to form a security police force to complement the occupation forces when the Korean War broke out.[14] Japan's new military, or what the Japanese call the Self-Defense Forces (SDF), was officially established in 1954. The government was not eager to build up new military forces. After its few formative years, the defense budget has never exceeded one percent of Japan's GNP except for a short period in the 1980s. The SDF, consisting of some two hundred thousand personnel, did not achieve its full planned strength until the end of the 1980s. Its weapon systems are designed and deployed according to a strict interpretation of its mission to defend Japanese territory, although since the 1980s reconaissance capability began extending far beyond Japan's borders. The SDF has no offensive weapons such as aircraft carriers, long-range missiles, or bombers. Japan's military has tried to compensate for its general weakness by being highly sophisticated. But although Japan has accepted primary responsibility for countering aggression, the defense of Japan remains dependent on U.S. global strategy.

Thus Japan's sense of security, its security policy, and its view of regional order has never been narrowly defined in military terms, but more broadly to include economics. MOFA, MITI, and MOF actively participate in security policy. More fundamentally, Japan has always been aware that economic security, and Japan's prosperity, is not automatically guaranteed even if military security is not threatened. To state this differently, economic security is

---

[11] The call for national consensus and constructive debates was made first by Shinkichi Eto, in three articles, "Nashonaru Consensasu Sairon" [Once again on national consensus], *Bessatu Ushio* (Spring 1968); "Nihon no Anzenhoshoryoku wo do takameruka" [How to enhance Japan's security capabilities], *Chuo-Koron* (May 1965); and "Increasing Japan's Security Capabilities," *Journal of Social and Political Ideas in Japan* 4 (August 1966).

[12] Mike M. Mochizuki, "Japan's Search for Strategy," *International Security* 8 (Winter, 1983/84): 152–79.

[13] Katzenstein and Okawara, *Japan's National Security*, pp. 57–65.

[14] Concerning the question of remilitarization in the context of Japanese politics, see Hideo Otake, *Saigunbi to nashonarizumu* [Remilitarization and nationalism] (Tokyo: Chuokoron-sha, 1988).

not a function of military security. Therefore, although the term "comprehensive security" was coined in the late 1970s, Japan's sense of security had been comprehensive throughout the post–World War II era.[15]

The fact that Japan's peace and prosperity depends heavily upon the United States is at the core of the U.S.-Japan alliance. Militarily, Japan's defense capability and policy is almost completely tied to the U.S. global strategy and defense industry. Economically, Japan's postwar economic growth was made possible within international economic regimes led by the United States. In the region, however, Japan's security in a broad sense may not be identical with the U.S. position. On the one hand, shifts in the Sino-U.S. relationship may have serious security consequences for Japan. On the other hand, Japan's economic interests in Asia may not result in desirable effects on the United States.

While Japan's global security is by and large guaranteed by the close relationship with the United States, Japan's regional security concerns are more Japan's own territorial defense. Sine the war Japan has had to adapt itself to regional situations largely influenced by Sino-U.S. relations and has had to manage its relations with China, Korea, Indonesia, and so on in a manner that promotes its own security. In this context, Japan's regional security policy must be seen as an attempt to promote its own security by formulating and/or stabilizing regional order without hurting seriously overall U.S.-Japan relations, either by offending the United States or by infringing on its interests.

Whether this premise still holds and to what extent Japan will influence Asia-Pacific regional order in both economic and political terms in the twenty-first century cannot be determined without knowing first how successfully or unsuccessfully Japan has pursued its own security policy and engaged itself in the formulation and institutionalization of regional order, and how strongly or weakly the U.S.-Japan alliance has influenced and/or constrained Japan's security and regional policies.

The Sea Change in the Cold War Structure and Japan's Response

The end of the cold war in the late 1980s was doubtless the most important event in the post–World War II world political economy; however, whether

---

[15] The conceptualization of comprehensive security was conducted by a group of scholars and bureaucrats under the commission of Prime Minister Ohira. See Sogo-Anzen-Hosho Kenkyu Gurupu, *Sogo-Anzen-Hosho Senryaku* [Comprehensive security strategy] (Tokyo: Okura-sho Insatsu-kyoku, 1980).

the end of the cold war was the most important event in the past half-century for Asia specifically is a legitimate question. True, like any other regions, Asia-Pacific experienced various changes accompanying the end of the worldwide cold war, but the cold war in Asia cannot be called over until the two divided states out of the four created by the cold war either reunify or normalize their relations by mutual recognition. Yet even though certain structures created by the cold war persist in Asia-Pacific, this does not mean that major power relations have remained unchanged. On the contrary, the region experienced drastic changes in power relations a quarter of a century ago that dwarf the end of the cold war in importance.

In the European theater the cold war was characterized by a struggle between two camps backed by the United States and the Soviet Union. This struggle was quite naturally seen as an East-West confrontation. Yet superpower contentions have not been bipolar in Asia-Pacific since the late 1960s. Here China was as important as either the United States or the Soviet Union. By the late 1960s the Soviet Union and China had dropped any pretense of mutual friendship. When Richard Nixon took the White House in 1969, the United States began to deal with China outside questions of ideology in order to balance Soviet power. By the same token, in 1969 President Nixon declared the Guam Doctrine, which promised that the United States would not intervene in conflicts between Asian countries (and would disengage from the Vietnam War) but would honor its commitment to allied nations. Thus, the cold war system of Asia-Pacific changed its structural characteristics around 1970. In the summer of 1971, the news that Nixon would visit China in 1972 shook the world, notably Asia, tremendously. Regional conflicts and potential threats have become varied in nature, and they have been interconnected within the region in a complicated manner. Communist forces took power in all the Indochina states in 1975, but that area remained very unstable.

The Guam Doctrine was taken very seriously in Japan. Although it promised continued commitment to Japan's security, it made clear that U.S. military presence would decline in the region. Yasuhiro Nakasone became JDA director in 1970 and launched the autonomous defense initiative (*jishu boei koso*). He had interpreted the Guam Doctrine and the president's address on U.S. foreign policy for the 1970s to mean that Japan was to become more responsible for its own defense; however, the United States sent an unmistakable message to Japan that it would incorporate Japan's defense capabilities in the U.S. global strategy. By the time Nakasone left JDA in 1971, Japan had agreed to strengthen its military alliance with the

United States.[16] Indeed, the return of Okinawa in 1972 to Japan was consistent with the firm basis of the alliance.[17] Sino-American rapprochement in the early 1970s did not alter the basic character of the U.S.-Japan alliance although it did shock the Japanese and led to Eisaku Sato's resignation. Sato's successor, Kakuei Tanaka, hastily normalized diplomatic relations with China. The U.S. government successfully persuaded the Beijing leadership that the U.S.-Japan Mutual Security Treaty also protected China from Japan.[18] Although diplomatic relations between the United States and China were not normalized until 1979, the U.S.-Japan alliance was no obstacle to the improved relationship among all three.

In response to such a new regional alignment, Japan's basic defense policy, spelled out in the Basic Principle of National Defense (*kokubo no kihon hoshin*), which the Cabinet adopted in 1957, was replaced in 1976 with the National Defense Program Outline (NDPO; *boei keikaku no taiko*), which was based on the concept of a basic defense force (*kibanteki boeiryoku koso*).[19] The NDPO called for a more capable, not a larger, defense force that would be able to conduct joint operations with the U.S. forces and was designed to convince the Japanese public of the need to upgrade Japan's defenses despite the decline in regional tension. It was at this time that the ceiling on defense spending was fixed at one percent of the GNP. This statutory ceiling on defense spending was widely regarded as a ploy to obtain public support, but in reality it provided defense authorities with additional funds to modernize their weapons systems in order to integrate Japan's defense forces with their U.S. counterparts.[20] Based on the NDPO, the Mid-Term Defense Program Estimate (*chuki boei mitsumori*) was formulated in 1978 as a plan for bulding up Japan's defenses, although the MOF kept cutting the JDA's budget.[21] In the same year, Japan and the

[16] Yoshimasa Muroyama, *Nichibei Ampo Taisei* [Japan-United States Security regime] (Tokyo: Yuhikaku, 1992), pp. 297-328.

[17] For an overall picture of the negotiation, see Akio Watanabe, *Sengo Nihon no Seiji to Gaiko* [Politics and diplomacy in postwar Japan] (Tokyo: Fukumura Shuppan, 1970). For a discussion of the most sensitive issue of nuclear weapons in Okinawa, see Kei Wakaizumi, *Tasaku nakarishi wo shinzemuto hossu* [I want to believe there were no other ways] (Tokyo: Bungeishunjusha 1994).

[18] Sadako Ogata, *Normalization with China: A Comparative Study of U.S. and Japanese Processes* (Berkeley and Los Angeles: University of California Press, 1988), pp. 33-36.

[19] For a discussion of the formulation of NDPO, see Hideo Otake. *Nihon no boei to kokunaiseiji: Detanto kara Gunkaku he* [Defense and domestic politics in Japan: From Détante to defense buildup] (Tokyo: Sanichi Shobo, 1983); Katsuya Hirose, *Kanryo to Gunjin: Bunmin Tosei no Genkai* [Bureaucrats and military men: Limits of civilian control] (Tokyo: Iwanami Shoten, 1989); and Kubo Takuya Iko-tsuitoshu kanko-kai, ed., *Iko-tsuito Kubo Takuya* [Papers in memory of Takuya Kubo] (1981).

[20] Muroyama, *Nichibei Ampo Taisei*, pp. 371-435.

[21] Katzenstein and Okawara, *Japan's National Security*, pp. 156-58.

United States agreed on the nonbinding Guidelines for U.S.-Japan Defense Cooperation, which covered three topics: (1) the prevention of aggression; (2) the possibility of armed attack on Japan; and (3) cooperation between the United States and Japan in the Far East.

While the importance of the alliance with the United States was unquestioned in the 1970s, the Japanese government showed a certain degree of independence on regional policy: note Kakuei Tanaka's resource diplomacy and hasty normalization of diplomatic relations with China; Takeo Fukuda's omnidirectional peace diplomacy (*zen-hoi heiwa gaiko*), or the so-called Fukuda Doctrine; and Masayoshi Ohira's advocacy of comprehensive national security and Pacific-Basin cooperation. All of those initiatives departed to some degree from U.S. cold war foreign policy.

In fact, Japan had been taking a semi-independent line in regional affairs since the mid 1960s. The government was very eager to establish a regional development bank. The Asian Development Bank was established in 1966 with Japan and the United States as the largest contributors.[22] (To Japan's surprise, other members wanted to locate the bank's headquarters in Manila.) The Japanese government also invited all the Southeast Asian countries other than North Vietnam to the Ministerial Conference on Economic Development in Southeast Asia (MCEDSEA), which was to be held in 1966. Because neutral countries declined to attend, the participants were all anticommunist countries, but they agreed to convene the conference every year.[23]

In the same year, the Asia Pacific Council (ASPAC) was established according to the proposal made by President Park Chung Hee of South Korea. Though the United States was regarded as the country outside the region and did not participate, the participants, including Japan, were obviously anticommunist, and many took part in the Vietnam War. ASPAC was in fact an integral part of U.S. Asia policy, namely, the containment of China and the conduct of the Vietnam War. Japan identified MCEDSEA and ASPAC as the two major vehicles for Japanese participation in regional affairs and tried to promote regional cooperation based on those organizations;[24] however, in the early 1970s, the sea change in the cold war structure destroyed the basic assumptions and motivations for such re-

[22] For a more detailed discussion, see Dennis T. Yasutomo, *Japan and the Asian Development Bank* (New York: Praeger Publishers, 1983).

[23] Indonesia attended as an observer. See Susumu Yamakage, *ASEAN: Sinboru kara Sisutemu he* [ASEAN: From symbol to system] (Tokyo: Tokyo University Press, 1991), pp. 175–76, and "Ajia-taiheiyo to Nihon" [Asia Pacific and Japan], in *Sengo-Nihon no Taigai-seisaku* [Postwar Japan's external policies], ed. Akio Watanabe (Yuhikaku, 1985), pp. 135–61.

[24] *Waga Gaiko no kinkyo* [The recent situation of our diplomacy], various editions between the mid-1960s and the early 1970s.

gional cooperation. Both MCEDSEA and ASPAC had disappeared by the mid-1970s.[25]

In the 1970s, Japan's security concern shifted from East to Southeast Asia for at least four reasons: (1) the normalization of relations with China; (2) troubled economic relations with Southeast Asian countries, especially Thailand and Indonesia; (3) the importance of Southeast Asia for energy security; and (4) the communist takeover of Indochina.[26] Japan's regional initiatives from the mid-1970s on were based on friendly relations with China and correct relations with the communist regimes of Indochina. Japan also realized the viability of the Association of Southeast Asian Nations (ASEAN) and worked to encourage peaceful coexistence between the ASEAN countries and the communist states of Indochina.[27] When Prime Minister Fukuda visited Southeast Asia in 1977, he made a policy speech in Manila, which laid out the so-called Fukuda Doctrine.[28] It contained three messages: (1) Japan would not become a militaristic power; (2) Japan would seek equal partnerships with Southeast Asian peoples based on heart-to-heart dialogue; and (3) Japan would like to contribute to peaceful coexistence between ASEAN and Indochina. Stability in Southeast Asia was not achieved, however. Hostilities between Cambodia's Pol Pot government and Vietnam were followed by the latter's invasion of Cambodia, the Sino-Vietnam border war, and prolonged civil war in Cambodia. Japan had to wait another decade for favorable circumstances.[29]

The concept of Pacific Basin cooperation was based on Japan's long-standing advocacy of economic cooperation among industrial nations surrounding the Pacific on the one hand, and on the deepening interdependence between those industrial nations and Asian developing countries on the other.[30] This concept can be regarded as part of the rise of Asia-Pacific regionalism.[31] Foreign Minister Sunao Sonoda of the Ohira

---

[25] Yamakage, "Ajia-taiheiyo to Nihon," pp. 135–61.

[26] Concerning the importance of Southeast Asia to Japan's security, see Alan Rix, "ASEAN and Japan: More than Economics," in *Understanding ASEAN*, ed. Alison Broinowski (New York: St. Martin's Press, 1982), pp. 169–95.

[27] Susumu Yamakage, "Japan and ASEAN: Are They Really Becoming Closer?" in *Aspects of ASEAN*, ed. Werner Pfennig and Mark B. M. Suh (London: Weltforum-Verlag, 1984).

[28] Sueo Sudo analyzes the politics of the formulation of the Fukuda Doctrine in Sudo, *The Fukuda Doctrine and ASEAN: New Dimensions in Japanese Foreign Policy* (Singapore: Institute of Southeast Asian Studies, 1992).

[29] As for Japan's policy concerning the Indochina conflict, see Seki Tomoda, "Nihon no Cambodia Seisaku" [Japan's Cambodia Policy], *Ajia-daigaku Ajia Kenkyujo kiyo* [Bulletin of the Asia Institute, Asia University] 19 (1992): 145–86.

[30] Sogo-Anzen-Hosho Kenkyu Gurupu, *Sogo-Anzen-Hosho Senryaku*.

[31] Mie Ohba and Susumu Yamakage, "Ajia-taiheiyo Chiiki-shugi ni okeru Juso-kozo no keisei to henyou" [The formation and transformation of a multilayered structure in the Asia Pacific region], *Kokusai Mondai* [International Problems], October 1994, pp. 2–29.

Cabinet proposed a ministerial conference to work out the idea with ASEAN leaders, but the latter responded negatively. They reportedly feared Japan's hegemony.[32] The compromise was to convene a seminar at the nongovernmental level, which led to Pacific Economic Cooperation Conference (PECC). In the end, however, Japan's initiative was not welcomed.

Japan suffered another setback in 1978 when it ran for reelection to a non-permanent seat on the United Nations Security Council. This time several Asian governments which usually voted for Japan shifted their support to Bangladesh. Japan was forced to withdraw its candidacy.

Japan's Foreign Policy during the New Cold War: Between the United States and ASEAN

The Soviet invasion of Afghanistan led to the so-called new cold war period. The administration of President Ronald Reagan proclaimed a stronger America to confront the Soviet Union, and Defense Secretary Casper Weinberger called for burden-sharing between the United States and allied nations.[33] Japan defined itself as a member of the Western Camp (*nishigawa no ichi-in*), and the Japanese government reaffirmed its alliance with the United States and initiated concrete measures for U.S.-Japan security cooperation.[34] Prime Minister Zenko Suzuki visited Washington in May 1981 to meet President Reagan and issued the joint statement on "the Alliance between the United States and Japan."[35] Suzuki also proclaimed the plan to defend sea lanes as far as one thousand nautical miles from Japan proper. The next prime minister, Yasuhiro Nakasone, eloquently emphasized closer security ties with Washington. Although he was a nationalist, Nakasone chose to strengthen the alliance with the United States and succeeded in establishing a good relationship with the Reagan administration.

Throughout the 1980s, Japan gradually increased its involvement in regional security matters. It reinforced the alliance with the United States along the lines of burden-sharing. It significantly enhanced naval and airborne capabilities for the defense of its sea lanes of communication. Japan's naval forces participated in the RIMPAC (Rim of the Pacific

---

[32] Yamakage, *ASEAN*, pp.291–92.

[33] U.S. Department of Defense, *Report on Allied Commitments to Defense Spending* (March 1981).

[34] *Nihon no Kokubo* [Japan's Defense] (1980).

[35] After returning to Japan, Suzuki denied that "alliance" described U.S.-Japan relations. This inconsistency led to Foreign Minister Masayoshi Ito's resignation, but did not damage relations between the two nations seriously.

Excercise) in 1980. Joint military exercises were held on the ground as well.[36] The U.S.-Japan Joint Operation Planning Document was drafted in 1984. As the host nation, Japan also repeatedly increased its subsidy payments to the U.S. forces in Japan under the rubric of "sympathy budget" (*omoiyari yosan*). Furthermore, the Japanese government, contrary to its voluntary prohibition of the export of arms and military technology, allowed the transfer of military (actually dual use) technology from Japan to the United States with the justification that such cooperation was integral part of the U.S.-Japan security cooperation.

The SDF's materiel base was modernized, enlarged, and improved to meet a new demand, although to stay within the provisions of the NDPO, the Japanese government postdated the buildup program to 1985. Thus, despite the zero-percent annual increase of the national budget demanded by Japan's ultra-tight fiscal policy, the defense budget grew by more than 5 percent. In fact defense spending actually exceeded the traditional one-percent-of GNP limit in the late 1980s.[37]

Japan's grand strategy was not limited to military defense narrowly defined. Official development assistance (ODA), the single most obvious lever for Japan's exercise of power, was defined as an instrument for the nation's comprehensive security. The Japanese government provided "strategic aid" to some frontline states, Thailand being the first recipient. It also extended aid to such countries as Turkey, Nicaragua, and Egypt, indicating that Japan's strategic aid was closely connected to U.S. global strategy.[38] In a word, Japan began to involve itself in security matters outside its territory. In order to compensate for a relative decline in U.S. power, the Japanese government accepted the notion of burden-sharing, and both nations enhanced their security cooperation and intensified joint military exercises. Even Japan's ODA was spent at least partly in direct support of U.S. interests.

The changes in Japan's security policy in the 1980s is quite significant; however, they had roots in the 1970s and cannot be attributed solely to the new cold war or to Nakasone's personality. In 1977, Japan decided to bear local costs for U.S. forces in Japan and in the 1980s increased its already massive host-nation support budget. The increase in joint military exercises was based on the Guidelines for U.S.-Japan Defense Cooperation

[36] See the compiled chart in Katzenstein and Okawara, *Japan's National Security*, p. 98.
[37] For a discussion of the debates among the Japanese public concerning the defense budget, see ibid., pp. 155–60.
[38] See Dennis T. Yasutomo, *The Manner of Giving: Strategic Aid and Japanese Foreign Policy* (Lexington, Mass.: D.C. Heath, 1986), and Robert M. Orr Jr., *The Emergence of Japan's Foreign Aid Power* (New York: Columbia University Press, 1990).

of 1978. Dialogues and consultations between Japanese and U.S. defense communities date back further.[39] Strategic aid became possible partly because in 1978 the Japanese government started consecutive mid-term plans to double ODA in five years or so.[40] Furthermore, economic security became an integral part of Japan's national security policy under the concept of comprehensive security proclaimed in 1979, which was further refined by Prime Minister Nakasone's private advisory group in 1984.[41]

Since Japan's proposal for Pacific Basin cooperation was rejected by its Asian neighbors, the government did not attempt to take intitiatives in regional order in the 1980s. Instead, Japan began to work more closely with ASEAN. For instance, Japan supported ASEAN's position on Indo-chinese refugee problems, on sanctions against Vietnam for invading Cambodia, and on the effort to create Cambodia's anti-Vietnamese coalition government.[42] In this way Japan and ASEAN have increasingly cooperated to institutionalize regional order both in political and economic terms.

ASEAN's Initiatives and Japan

The end of the cold war broadened Japan's security policy options. While maintaining its alliance with the United States, Japan began to search for the possibility of security policy outside the framework of the U.S.-Japan alliance. The Japanese government envisaged an international role for Japan compatible with its alliance with the United States. While firmly keeping its own security dependent upon its alliance with the United States, Japan has become more assertive on security-related issues. The Takeshita Cabinet sought to lay out political and economic roles by which Japan could promote global peace and prosperity. Prime Minister Noboru Takeshita made public the Three Pillars of Japan's International Cooperation: (1) contribution to international peace; (2) the promotion of cultural exchange for mutual understanding; and (3) the expansion of ODA. It was clear, however, that Japan's primary interests lay in Asia-Pacific, and

---

[39] Katzenstein and Okawara, *Japan's National Security*, pp. 83–99.

[40] Concerning Japan's ODA policy in the 1980s, see Takeshi Igarashi, ed., *Nihon no ODA to Kokusai-chitsujo* [Japan's ODA and the International Order] (Tokyo: Japan Institute for International Affairs, 1990).

[41] Sogo-Anzen-Hosho Kenkyu Gurupu, *Sogo-Anzen-Hosho Senryaku*; and Heiwa-mondai kenkyukai, *Kokusai-kokka Nihon no Sogo-Anzen-Hosho Seisaku* [International State Japan's Comprehensive Security Policy] (Okura-sho Insatu-kyoku, 1984).

[42] For Japan's policy vis-à-vis ASEAN, see Saburo Matsumoto, "Japan and ASEAN in the Second Decade," in *Twenty Years of ASEAN: Its Survival and Development*, ed. Tatsumi Okabe (Tokyo: Japan Institute of International Affairs, 1982), pp. 71–90.

while close relations with the United States and with China were fundamental components of Japan's foreign policy, ASEAN emerged as an almost equally important partner for Japan.

Established in 1967, ASEAN started with a framework of confidence-
building measures between its member governments. By the mid 1970s,
the original members reached a consensus on the formation of a security
community in Southeast Asia.[43] They concluded the Treaty of Amity and
Cooperation in Southeast Asia and committed themselves to the peaceful
settlement of conflicts. Other nations applied and joined in later years:
Papua New Guinea in 1989, Vietnam and Laos simultaneously in 1992,
and Cambodia in 1994. To join, these nations were required to demonstrate their recognition of ASEAN as the legitimate institution for organizing Southeast Asia by signing the Treaty of Amity and Cooperation.
Signing the treaty conferred on them observer status in ASEAN and made
them eligible for membership.[44] To date Burma has also indicated an interest in joining ASEAN. Thus, the Treaty of Amity and Cooperation, however fragile, provides the basis of mutual security in Southeast Asia.

ASEAN members are aware, however, that because regional security depends upon the actions of powers outside the region, their own commitment to peaceful settlement of conflict cannot guarantee a peaceful
Southeast Asia. They recognize the need for coordination with these external powers, and the ASEAN Post Ministerial Conference (PMC), held
immediately after ASEAN's annual ministerial meeting, has provided a
framework for such coordination since the 1980s. Attended by the foreign
ministers of Japan, the United States, Canada, Australia, New Zealand, and
Korea, as well as representatives of the European Union, the PMC has
served as the forum for external dialogue for the seven nations of
ASEAN.[45]

The PMC was formed to conduct economic dialogues with powers outside the ASEAN region, but the meetings have dealt more with political
issues than economic ones. PMC members have close trade relations with
ASEAN countries, but are essentially Western allies. The end of the cold
war allowed ASEAN to seek to enlarge PMC membership to include China
and Russia. Facing the reluctance of some of the PMC partners, however,

---

[43] Yamakage, *ASEAN.*
[44] Susumu Yamakage, "Ajia-Taiheiyo Kokusai-chitsujo keisei to ASEAN [ASEAN and the making of the Asia Pacific international order]," in *Koza Gendai-Ajia,* vol. 4, Chiiki-sisutemu to
Kokusai-kankei [Courses on contemporary Asia: The regional system and international
relations] ed. Kenichiro Hirano (Tokyo: Tokyo University Press, 1994), pp. 359–83.
[45] B. A. Hamzah, *ASEAN Relation with Dialogue Partners* (Kuala Lumpur: Selangor darul Ehsan,
Pelanduk Publications, 1989).

ASEAN decided to invite the foreign ministers of both countries to the ASEAN Ministerial Meeting (AMM) as guests.

ASEAN's search for regional security was multifold.[46] Asia-Pacific countries can be classified into four security-related categories in terms of the relationship with ASEAN. In 1993, the categories consisted of the following countries:

1 Full ASEAN members—Brunei, Indonesia, Malaysia, the Philippines, Singapore, and Thailand.
2 ASEAN observers—Papua New Guinea, Laos, and Vietnam (Laos and Vietnam became full members in 1995; Cambodia gained observer status in 1995.)
3 PMC partners—Japan, the United States, Canada, Australia, New Zealand, Korea, and the European Union.
4 AMM guests—China and Russia. (Burma, India, and North Korea will probably become AMM guests in the near future.)

While the nature of a country's association with ASEAN differs from one category to another, ASEAN's initiatives toward regional security required all categories to be involved. Influential powers like China were excluded from the PMC, and an important neighboring country like Vietnam was admitted merely as an observer; however, the newly established ASEAN Regional Forum (ARF) involved all those categories.[47] Its one-day inaugural meeting was sandwiched between the AMM and PMC meetings in Bangkok, Thailand, in July 1994. It lasted only three hours, because the Thai host intended only to create a cozy atmosphere for consultation, rather than to prepare for tough negotiation. ASEAN considered the meeting a success, and the participating governments agreed to meet annually on the occasion of AMM under the chair of AMM's host government. It was unprecedented that the foreign ministers of the United States, Russia, China, and Japan should sit at the same table to talk of security issues in Asia-Pacific. In this sense, ARF can be regarded as ASEAN's latest, and potentially most remarkable, achievement. Though the range of the agenda is still to be seen, a new concept, the ARF process, was adopted at the second meeting in Brunei. The ARF process consists of confidence building, preventive diplomacy, and approaches to conflict. The member countries agreed to focus on the first stage. A private institution, the Council for Security Cooperation in the Asia Pacific (CSCAP), is assisting in

[46] Yamakage, "Ajia-Taiheiyo Kokusai-chitsujo keisei to ASEAN."
[47] The EU was invited although it was not located in Asia-Pacific.

setting the agenda. CSCAP consists of individuals from academic, govenmental, and private sectors in ARF member countries and is in fact an assembly of security-policy-oriented think tanks in the region, which prepares recommendations for ARF members.[48] Within CSCAP, the ASEAN-CSIS (Centers for Strategic and International Studies), one of the some thirty ASEAN NGOs, plays an important role.

As mentioned above, in the 1960s Japan was preoccupied with ASPAC and MCEDSEA and did not take ASEAN seriously. The Japan-ASEAN relationship started two decades ago under ASEAN's initiative, and it was far from friendly.[49] At that time, ASEAN accused Japan of devastating the natural rubber market by exporting synthetic rubber. In 1973, ASEAN officially criticized Japan, and the following negotiations between the two sides resulted in the formation of the Japan-ASEAN Forum on Rubber. Afterward, however, ASEAN continued to express dissatisfaction with Japan's relations with ASEAN and ASEAN members. It was only in 1975 that the Japanese government began to consider ASEAN a viable and useful counterbalance to communist Indochina. Prime Minister Fukuda attended the second ASEAN Summit in 1977 and announced the Fukuda doctrine a few days later. Japan's basic goal under the Fukuda doctrine is to stabilize the region by encouraging peaceful coexistence between ASEAN and Indochina. Vietnam's invasion of Cambodia and the following Cambodian civil war made it impossible for Japan to establish close relations with both ASEAN and Vietnam, and Japan chose to support the former. At ASEAN's request, Japan suspended its ODA to Vietnam as a sanction against Vietnam's invasion of Cambodia.[50] Japan supported ASEAN's initiatives in the United Nations conference on refugees in Indochina and on United Nations resolutions on Cambodian affairs. This support led to cooperation in other areas. The PMC, established in 1979, evolved from a meeting between ASEAN foreign ministers and their Japanese counterparts in the previous year. Throughout the 1980s, the Japanese government kept expressing its full support of ASEAN.

Since the late 1970s, Japan has treated ASEAN as a very important partner in Asia-Pacific. Since 1980, when Prime Minister Zenko Suzuki chose

---

[48] As of 1996, institutions from eleven countries participate; namely, Australia, Canada, Indonesia, Japan, Malaysia, New Zealand, the Philippines, South Korea, Singapore, Thailand, and the United States. The EU is an associate member. The new membership is given on the consensus rule.

[49] Yamakage, *ASEAN*, pp. 174–78.

[50] Juichi Inada, "Tai-Etsu Enjo Toketsu wo meguru Nihon no Gaikoteki Imi" [The suspension of Japan's aid to Vietnam: Its diplomatic meaning], in *Indoshina wo meguru Kokusai-kankei* [International relations on Indochina], ed. Tadashi Mio (Tokyo: Japan Institute for International Affairs, 1988), pp. 329–52.

to make his first official visit abroad to ASEAN countries, all Japanese prime ministers, with the exceptions of Kosuke Uno and Tsutomu Hata both of whom were in office for only a couple of months, have paid visits to some, if not all, of the ASEAN countries. By doing so, Japan tried to signal how important it considered ASEAN. Japan tried not to agitate ASEAN countries with its defense build up and cooperated with ASEAN on the Cambodian problem. Some ASEAN countries like Thailand have encouraged Japan to take a greater part in security matters. Eventually, Japan, after passing the law for U.N. peacekeeping operations in 1992 with a new interpretation of its constitution, participated in United Nations peace-keeping operations in Cambodia. By the early 1990s, ASEAN leaders had begun to accept Japan's increasing political role in the region.

The end of the cold war affected ASEAN cooperation. Regional tensions between the three major powers declined, but regional conflicts and sources of threat remained. An overall reduction in tension made ASEAN member governments more frank about ASEAN's security roles, and Japan took advantage of the change. In his 1991 speech to the PMC, Foreign Minister Taro Nakayama proposed institutionalizing the PMC dialogues on security. ASEAN and U.S. reactions were lukewarm at best. Still, the idea that Nakayama had voiced was one that had already gained general support among influential security-policy-oriented think tanks in the ASEAN region. In fact, at the fourth ASEAN Summit, held in the following year, the six leaders agreed to make use of the PMC to promote regional security, which was exactly Nakayama's proposal.[51] ASEAN seems to have preferred its own initiative to Japan's. Some ASEAN officials even claimed that Japan stole ASEAN's idea.

U.S. Initiatives and APEC

Following the end of the cold war, keen attention was paid to what the regional consequences of the change in U.S. global strategy would be. The United States turned its attention to Asia-Pacific only after it had constructed the basic framework for post–cold war Europe. Visiting East Asia in 1991, Secretary of State James Baker announced active involvement in Asia-Pacific.[52] The main message was an affirmation of U.S. bilateral security commitments spreading like a transpacific "fan" from Korea in the

---

[51] Susumu Yamakage, "Chiiki-Ampo Rejimu wo Kakudai suru ASEAN" [ASEAN is expanding the regional security regime], *Sekai Shuho* [World Weekly] (8 September 1992), pp. 10–15.
[52] James A. Baker, "America in Asia: Emerging Architecture for a Pacific Community," *Foreign Affairs* 70 (Winter 1991/1992): pp. 1-18.

north to Australia in the south, with the United States as its hub. In other words, U.S. interests lay in the maintenance of bilateral alliances rather than creating any multilateral institution. Washington was not enthusiastic about the ASEAN-PMC or any new framework; however, this does not mean that U.S. policy-makers were not interested in a multilateral framework. In fact, they found APEC not only a useful economic regime, but what is more important, a potentially multifunctional entity.

APEC started in 1989 as an Australian initiative with Japanese support. In order to have the ASEAN countries participate, the nature and style of APEC was made very similar to that of ASEAN.[53] APEC was to be essentially a consultative body of diversified economic entities, just as ASEAN was. It was to be operated by consensus with minimal organizational structure, again just like ASEAN. As was true of ASEAN in its formative years, the annual ministerial meeting was to be the highest decision-making apparatus, and there was to be no central secretariat. Its membership was identical to ASEAN-PMC's (minus the EU). The venue of the ministerial meeting was to alternate annually between the ASEAN region and the outside. APEC would be a framework for consultation, not negotiation. Furthermore, the ASEAN secretary general was to attend APEC's Senior Officials Meeting. Historically, ASEAN governments had been reluctant to join any regional institution that might hamper ASEAN solidarity.[54] This time, however, they were confident that ASEAN could sustain its cohesiveness, and that APEC might be a useful framework in which ASEAN could exercise influence upon more powerful, extraregional partners.

But APEC changed quickly in directions ASEAN had not anticipated.[55] In 1991, the so-called three Chinas (the PRC, Chinese Taipei as Taiwan was called, and Hong Kong) joined simultaneously, which made ASEAN less influential, because none of them had formal ties with ASEAN. Furthermore, increasing U.S. interests in APEC led to an increasing emphasis on trade liberalization and efficient operation as topics of discussion. At APEC's fourth ministerial meeting in 1992, the U.S. government, due to host the next meeting, succeeded in making trade liberalization the main topic for 1993, and in establishing the Eminent Persons Group, chaired by an American, whose task was to make recommendations on trade.

ASEAN was about to inaugurate its own program to form a free trade area in fifteen years, and APEC was moving too fast in the same direction for some ASEAN countries. The consensus rule was key to the very char-

---

[53] Susumu Yamakage, "Ajia-taiheiyo no Rijonarizumu: ASEAN-hosiki wa Sinto site ikuka?" [Regionalism in Asia Pacific: Shall the ASEAN way spread?], *ESP*, July 1994, pp. 42–46.
[54] Susumu Yamakage, *ASEAN*, pp. 291–92.
[55] Susumu Yamakage, "Ajia-taiheiyo no Rijonarizumu," pp. 42–46.

acter of ASEAN, hence the ASEAN states refused to sacrifice the consensus rule for greater efficiency in collective decision making. To be sure, the ASEAN countries did not lose interest in APEC, nor did they want to withdraw from it. When APEC decided to set up the central secretariat, Singapore and Thailand supported the decision, and eventually the Thai government endorsed Singapore's version of the proposal; nevertheless, the ASEAN countries realized their influence in APEC would be diminished.

The Bush administration was involved in APEC, but only during the Clinton administration has the United States expressed a keen interest in it.[56] New policymakers inherited the Baker initiative and put more emphasis on APEC as a promising framework for the pursuit of U.S. interests. At the Tokyo Summit in July 1993, President Clinton announced the U.S. goal was to establish a "Pacific Community"—a community of peoples who share with each other not only common security and a common market, but, more important, common values.[57] APEC was to be the cornerstone of the prospective community, and President Clinton called for a summit meeting of the APEC countries to work toward the creation of a Pacific community.

Clinton's comprehensive proposal was to change the nature of APEC at its root. It could be said that Clinton wanted to replace the original APEC principle with his own new framework. First of all, APEC would serve as a framework to pursue trade liberalization in Asia-Pacific. Pragmatic cooperation between APEC participants based on consultation and consensus, which has been APEC's modus operandi, would eventually be replaced with more formal and binding commitments to scheduled liberalization programs.

A second implication of the Pacific community idea was a U.S. willingness to institutionalize a multilateral security framework in the region. While Washington would continue to make use of bilateral security ties, it also hoped to create a CSCE-like institution in Asia-Pacific. The United

---

[56] As for Japanese perspectives on U.S. attitudes toward APEC, see Akio Watanabe, "Bush-seiken no Shin-Sekai-chitsujo Koso to Ajia-taiheiyo Seisaku" [The Bush administration's New World Order concept and Asia Pacific policy], *Kokusai Mondai*, January, 1992, pp. 33–49; Susumu Yamakage, "Amerika-gasshukoku no Taiheiyo kyodotai-ka Koso," [The U.S. concept for a Pacific community], in Okabe, *Posuto-reisen no Ajia-taiheiyo*, pp. 79–100.

[57] President Clinton made three speeches in San Francisco, Tokyo, and Seoul. Each speech had its own characteristics. The speech in San Francisco was naturally made for an American audience, and its central theme was economic advantage for the Americans. The speech in Tokyo emphasized the economic aspects of the prospective community. The speech in Seoul focused on security issues. Human-rights issues and political value of democracy were touched upon in all three. Altogether, the three speeches comprised the concept of a Pacific community.

States seemed to accept a multilateral framework that would someday include China and probably Russia.

Third, the Clinton administration did not hesitate to press the American value system—plural democracy, free market economics, and human and civil rights. Having observed how democratization led to the rejection of communist regimes in the Soviet Union and East European countries, the United States shifted its evangelistic emphasis from anticommunism to the American value system per se. Sharing those values with the United States became the precondition to membership in a Pacific community.

A few governments welcomed the U.S. proposal of accelerated trade liberalization, but many were worried by not only the plan itself but also the manner in which the U.S. government pressed it. Given the diversified levels and structures in Asia-Pacific economies, the plan looked too ambitious and hasty. The U.S. initiative looked too pressing and straightforward compared to APEC's (and ASEAN's) usual way of doing business.

It also became obvious that APEC was not the appropriate venue for discussing security issues. The Beijing government refused to talk of security matters with the Taipei leaders present. Finally, Southeast Asian leaders were outspoken in rejecting the U.S. initiatives promoting pluralistic democracy and human and civil rights, and criticized U.S. policymakers as self-righteous and hypocritical.

Despite doubts, reluctance, and criticism of the Clinton proposal, the U.S. government took maximal advantage of hosting the fifth ministerial meeting of APEC in 1993.[58] The United States pressed to launch accelerated trade liberalization programs and to inaugurate the APEC leadership meeting. Washington failed to make APEC an instrument for security cooperation, but succeeded in strengthening its economic functions. It seemed clear that APEC was beginning to transform itself from Economic Cooperation to Economic Community. In 1994, APEC's sixth ministerial meeting and its second informal leadership meeting were held in Indonesia. There APEC participants agreed on trade and investment liberalization—by 2010 for advanced economies, and by 2020 for developing economies. This agreement was named the Bogor Declaration after the site of the meetings.

Japan was ambivalent toward the U.S. initiative on trade liberalization for several reasons.[59] First, Japan was not eager to liberalize its own trade—

---

[58] For an evaluation of APEC's Seattle meetings, see Yamakage, "Amerika-gasshukoku no Taiheiyo-kyodotai-ka Koso," pp. 79–100.

[59] A full analysis of Japan's policy toward the APEC process is to be done elsewhere. For the time being, see Susumu Yamagami, *Ajia-taiheiyo Chiiki no Jidai: APEC Setsuritsu no Keii to Tenbo* [The age of the Asia Pacific region: History of the establishment of APEC and its prospect] (Tokyo: Daiichi Hoki, 1994).

for it was obvious that Japan would have to liberalize agricultural products, politically very sensitive items, because it had already reduced the tariff level on manufactured goods. On the other hand, the government anticipated that such a scheme might forestall U.S. protectionism. Second, Japan saw economic cooperation as APEC's function and wanted to emphasize the facilitation of trade and investment liberalization rather than liberalization itself. Finally, Japan did not want choose sides in a confrontation between the United States and ASEAN. As it turned out, Japan failed to take initiative to strengthen APEC or to foster the APEC process at the Osaka meeting in 1995.

Japan's Obscure Policy on Regional Order

The end of the cold war widened the room for Japan to act on security matters internationally. Dissatisfied with the status of an "economic power," the government began to seek a political role. Japan hosted peace talks on the Middle East conflict and the Cambodian civil war. Though late, Japan participated in the Gulf War, not only by contributing 13 billion dollars, but also by sending minesweepers after the cease-fire. One of the most crucial decisions in the post–World War II Japan's foreign policy was to send Japanese military forces to foreign territory. After a lengthy debate in the Japanese Diet as well as other public forums, troops were sent to participate in U.N. forces, first in Cambodia, then in Mozambique. At the same time, Japanese leaders no longer hesitated to express interest in Japan becoming a permanent member of the United Nations Security Council.

The desire for more active security roles was revealed in the newly defined Asia-Pacific policy of the Miyazawa Cabinet. Kiichi Miyazawa's search for a new Asia-Pacific policy was in a sense the effort to shape a consistent policy vis-à-vis neighbors, for the Japanese Asia-Pacific policy seemed to have lost clarity because political and security issues were intertwined with economic concerns. His immediate predecessor, Toshiki Kaifu, had expressed Japan's willingness to play a political role in Asia, but Miyazawa wanted to draw a general design for Japan's relations with the Asia-Pacific nations. Nevertheless, it should not be concluded that the Japanese government was seized by a desire for independent activism. The Japanese government began to search for political and security roles compatible with U.S. strategy, including its policy vis-à-vis the alliance with Japan, Asian perceptions, and domestic political constraints on national defense.

The leadership knew that it was premature for Japan to take the initiative unilaterally and that it would be better for Japan to go along with the

United States. The U.S.-Japan alliance was to remain of paramount importance in the post–cold war era; however, a serious problem arose concerning the meaning of the alliance. It should be the cornerstone for Japan's national security as before, but in what sense? The cold war had ended. Although Japan had failed to settle its territorial dispute with Russia, it was hardly deniable that the Russian threat had decreased significantly. China was a potential source of trouble, but the promotion of close and friendly relations with China was one of Japan's principal goals. By no means, then, was Japan's alliance with the United States directed at China. Under these circumstances, Japan found new meaning for the U.S.-Japan alliance as a vehicle for Japan to assume political responsibilities more actively. It was necessary to maintain the U.S.-Japan alliance in order to allay misgivings about resurgent Japanese activism. In other words, the U.S.-Japan alliance is as useful in the post–cold war era as it was before because it guarantees that Japan will not threaten its Asian neighbors or the United States.

While the U.S.-Japan alliance served to relax Asian misgivings about Japan, the Miyazawa Cabinet also took more direct measures to cope with its neighbors' fears. Among foreign policy authorities, it became increasingly a shared view that misgivings about Japan's future roles were tied to Japan's reluctance to deal with questions concerning former Japanese aggression and imperialism. During his unprecedented visit to China in October 1992, the Japanese emperor apologized for the hardships Japan had imposed on the Chinese and expressed Japan's commitment to close and friendly relations with China. Prime Minister Miyazawa ordered the bureaucracy to conduct official research on the issue of "comfort women" or sex slaves for Japanese soldiers, and to prepare for belated payments of the debts Japan owes Taiwanese. These actions suggested that Japan was ready to acknowledge, if not officially apologize for, the damage and suffering that Japan had inflicted on other peoples.

In January 1993, Miyazawa made a speech on Japan's Asia-Pacific policy in Bangkok. Among the four areas in which Japan should contribute most, he put the highest priority on regional peace and stability.[60] He mentioned Japan's willingness to participate in various dialogues on security issues, including ASEAN-PMC. Also, he emphasized the U.S.-Japan alliance as a stabilizing factor in the region, and he did not forget to reiterate that

[60] The other three were the promotion of open regionalism with Japan's support of economic development; encouragement of democratization and of the pursuit for universal values such as protection of the environment; and cooperation with ASEAN on peace and prosperity in Indochina.

Japan would not become a military power.[61] By that time Japan had already received a positive response from nations in Asia-Pacific, including the United States, on Japan's active involvement in security matters, the JDA had started to communicate with other Asian defense communities, and MOFA also became more actively involved in various seminars and meetings on regional security issues.

The end of the cold war made Japan reconsider not only the meaning of the U.S.-Japan alliance, but also national defense policy. The Hosokawa Cabinet decided to abolish the National Defense Program Outline, which had worked as the most basic guideline for Japan's defense policy since it was formulated in 1976. In Feburuary 1994, Prime Minister Morihiro Hosokawa organized the Advisory Group on Defense Issues and charged it with producing a defense guideline suitable to the post–cold war era. The Advisory Group completed its assignment in less than six months; however, during that period not only Hosokawa but also his successor Hata had resigned, and the report was submitted to Prime Minister Tomiichi Murayama. It was ironic that the recommendation was handed to a Socialist prime minister, whose party used to be hostile to SDF and critical of its defense policy and its alliance with the United States.

As for Japan's defense capability, the report did not provide any explicit alternative. It said that the Japanese should part with the NDPO, but it added that the preparation of an alternative document was a question to be considered by the government; however, it recommended various reforms with special emphasis on intelligence; modernized, efficient combat units; and the flexible operations. In terms of security policy, the report adopted a position close to, if not identical with, the U.S. stance. Namely, it shared with the United States views on likely threats to peace: (1) instability in Russia or China or both, which endanger U.S.-led consolidation for global security; (2) regional conflicts; (3) the proliferation of weapons and related technology for mass destruction; and (4) the loss of governability in the poorest countries as well as in resource-rich but unstable countries. The report urged a closer alliance between the United States and Japan and the pursuit of greater interoperability in various fields. In addition to bilateral security cooperation with the United States the report also advocated participation in multilateral frameworks, especially the United Nations. In this connection, the government was urged to allow Japanese military forces to take part in peacekeeping forces. In short, Japan's defense capability was to be incorporated with both the United

---

[61] In fact, Miyazawa was impressed that the audience applauded most when he said that Japan would not become a policeman in Asia.

Nations collective security system and the U.S.-Japan alliance. Based on this premise, the report advocated an active, constructive, and comprehensive security policy. The report emphasized the importance of a domestic defense industry capable of not only producing but also developing high-tech equipment. The promotion of the defense industry may enhance U.S.-Japan security cooperation in the field of military technology, but it may also intensify friction, as the FSX case illustrates.[62]

In any case, Japan's new defense policy has yet to be seen. Because NDPO is no longer in effect, the BPND has been reactivated as the framework for defense policy. Adopted in 1957, however, it is too general to suggest new policy in the post–cold war era and is not an effective guideline. On the other hand, the above-mentioned advisory group failed to draw up a draft guideline and left it to the government to decide whether to make a new one. Morale is low among both defense authorities and the defense industry. Budget cuts are almost inevitable, and the future of military technology is unclear.

Options, Obstacles, and Opportunities

Japan's official position is that security depends on economic as well as military factors. This notion of "comprehensive security" has become more relevant in the post–cold war era than it was fifteen years ago when it was officially adopted by the Ohira Cabinet. Nevertheless, when economic factors are taken into consideration, Japan's security interests are unclear and ambiguous. Policymakers, business leaders, and intellectuals are now talking of a dilemma between "Japan in Asia" and "Japan with the United States." This dilemma does not require making a stark choice. Rather it asks for a shifting of policy emphasis in changing circumstances. In the 1980s the two policies were quite compatible. But the end of the cold war has posed the issue once more in a new context. Those who argue for the United States see a world full of conflict, even after the end of the cold war, in which Japan's comprehensive security, not to mention military security, is best protected by the close relations with the United States. The Asia-first argument is based on the perception that Japan depends excessively on the United States, either economically or politically or both.

---

[62] Concerning the FSX incident, see Ryuichi Tejima, *Nippon FSX wo ute* [Shoot down Japan's FSX] (Tokyo: Sincho-sha, 1991), and Shinji Otsuki and Masaru Honda, *Nichi-Bei Domei wo yurugasu Gijutsu-Masatsu: Nichi-Bei FSX Senso* [The technology conflict that threatens the Japan-United States alliance: The Japan-United States FSX war] (Tokyo: Rohso-sha, 1991).

There seem to be at least three reasons why the "Japan in Asia" and "Japan with the United States" policies no longer seem compatible. First is the change in Japan's external economic relations. While the United States remains an indispensable trade partner, friction seems endless, and the U.S. attitude toward Japan seems increasingly hostile.[63] On the other hand, economic relations with East and Southeast Asian countries are growing and becoming more important and more integrated, and Japan's partnership with Asia seems to be on a surer footing than ever.[64] While the importance of the U.S.–Japan alliance is taken for granted, an increasing number of responsible Japanese are attracted by the "Japan in Asia" scenario. Advocates of "Japan in Asia" believe that such a policy would put Japan in a better position to deal with the United States in trade and security negotiations.[65]

A second factor is the development of the concept of East Asian regionalism as opposed to Asia-Pacific regionalism. The idea of the East Asian Economic Group (EAEG) proposed by Malaysian prime minister Mahathir Mohamad in the end of 1991 worked as a litmus test of the Japanese public's inclination to either Asia or the United States.[66] EAEG was to consist of East Asian countries: ASEAN and other Southeast Asian countries, China, Japan, Korea, and so on, but it was not to include either the United States or Australia. China supported the proposal from the beginning. The U.S. government objected quickly because such a framework would divide Asia-Pacific. The United States was criticized for applying a double standard, because the United States was already pursuing NAFTA. The Japanese government avoided making Japan's position clear. The major obstacle was the U.S. objection, but the government was also concerned with the exclusion of Australia and New Zealand. The advocates of "Japan

---

[63] Among many arguments, the most famous is Shintaro Ishihara and Akio Morita, *No to ieru Nihon* [The Japan that can say no] (Tokyo: Kobun-sha, 1989).

[64] See, for instance, Toshio Watanabe, *Nishi-taiheiyo no Jidai: Ajia Shin-Sangyo-kokka no Seiji-Keisai-gaku* [The era of the Western Pacific: The political economies of the Asian newly industrialized states] (Tokyo: Bungei-Shunju-sha, 1989); Toshio Watanabe, Hirokazu Kajiwara, and Kimio Takanaka, *Ajia Sogo-izon no Jidai: Tenkai suru Rijonaru-nettowaku* [The era of Asian interdependence: Developing regional networks] (Tokyo: Yuhikaku, 1991); and Yashichi Ohata and Shujiro Urada, *ASEAN no Keizai Nihon no Yakuwari* [ASEAN economies and Japan's role] (Tokyo: Yuhikaku, 1992).

[65] Nobutoshi Akao, "Kosyo-Tantosha ga kataru Uruguay-Round Seiritu no Butai ura" [The behind-the-scene story of the Uruguay Round told by a negotiator], *Gaiko Forum* No.67 (April 1994): 40–48. Akao was Japan's representative at the Uruguay Round, where he presented exactly this argument.

[66] As for politics concerning the EAEG/EAEC, see Koichi Sato, "Higashi-Ajia Keizai-Kaigi Koso wo meguru Kokusai-kankei: Mahathir-Koso to Ajia-taiheiyo Kyoryoku" [International relations of the EAEC concept: Mahathir's concept and Asia-Pacific cooperation], *Gaiko-Jiho*, no. 1286 (March 1992): 4–21.

in Asia" supported the concept of EAEC and urged the government to endorse the idea.[67] More than three years have passed since Mahathir launched the idea, but nothing substantial has changed since then.[68]

The differences over political freedom and other values between the United States and some Asian countries make up the third factor. Recent controversies between Americans and Asians concerning human rights and other "universal" values seem to illustrate the widening gap between declining and frustrated Americans on the one hand and developing and increasingly self-confident Asians on the other. The Tiananmen Square massacre of 1989 triggered major controversy, but there have been many other incidents of East-West confrontation. Mahathir and Singapore's former premier Lee Kwan Yew have challenged the political culture that the Americans have insisted on introducing.[69] The Japanese feel that the two sides of the Pacific Ocean need to work on mutual understanding and collaboration.[70] They have supported the idea of democracy and human and civil rights, but they dislike the domineering manner in which the Americans attempt to impose these ideas upon Asians.[71]

This dilemma seems to be based on a misperception, however. The controversy is only meaningful within Japan and is irrelevant in an international context. In reality, Japan is not at a crossroads where it must choose between Asia and the United States. The relationship between Asian countries and the United States is not in crisis. Most of the former depend upon the latter for their military security. When U.S. bases in the Philippines closed, even Malaysia and Singapore took every measure to keep a U.S. military presence in Southeast Asia.[72] As China's advance in the South China Sea is becoming obvious, Southeast Asian governments are concerned to maintain U.S. interest in the area.[73] Furthermore, East and

---

[67] Kenichi Omae, *Ajia-jin to Nihon-jin* [Asians and Japanese] (Tokyo: Shogakukan, 1994).

[68] The idea of the EAEG did not gain the full support of the other ASEAN countries either. ASEAN agreed on Indonesia's suggestion to change the name from EAEG to EAEC (East Asian Economic Caucus) in 1992.

[69] Kim Dae-jung's article offers another view on human rights and democracy. See Kim Dae-jung, "Is Culture Destiny? The Myth of Asia's Anti-Democratic Values," *Foreign Affairs* 73 (November/December, 1994): 189–94.

[70] The question that Samuel Huntington raised on the possibility of the clash of civilizations promoted public discussions on Asian way of democracy.

[71] A typical argument can be found in Shintaro Ishihara and Malaysian prime minister Mahathir Mohamad, *No to ieru Ajia* [Asia that can say no] (Tokyo: Kobun-sha, 1994).

[72] Koichi Sato, "Posuto-Cambodia no Singapore: 'Mare-jin no taikai' ni ikiru 'Kajin Kokka' no Shinro" [Singapore after the Cambodian conflict: the path of the "Chinese" state in the sea of the Malays], in Okabe, *Posuto-Kambojia no Tonan-ajia*, pp. 222–55.

[73] Kazunori Tamaki, "Tonan-Ajia no Kaiiki-Mondai to ASEAN" [Southeast Asian maritime zone problems and ASEAN], in Okabe, *Posuto-reisen no Ajia-taiheiyo*, pp. 205–27.

Southeast Asian economies are still closely linked to U.S. capital and technology. In the near future, neither the newly industrializing economies (NIES) of Asia nor Japan can take over the role the U.S. economy currently holds.[74]

There are also some who offer an alternative to the two scenarios, arguing that Japan should act as an honest broker between Asia and the United States—taking advantage of Japan's Asian cultural tradition on the one hand and its modern experiences of westernization on the other.[75] The Japanese are supposed to know Asians better than Americans do and Americans better than Asians do. There is a vital shortcoming in this proposal. If relationships deteriorate, few governments, if any, in Asia will trust or want Japan to mediate between the United States and themselves. They believe that they can deal with Americans as well as, and probably better than, the Japanese.

In short, Japan should avoid being forced to choose between Asia and the United States. It is in Japan's interest to promote cooperative institutions that embrace both sides of the Pacific. The most promising framework is a combination of the ARF in security and APEC.

The ARF provides Japan with a promising framework in which the nation can show its commitment to regional peace. Cooperation with ASEAN has also gained more importance in Japan's foreign policy. While many Asia-Pacific countries including Japan are allied with the United States, such bilateral alignments do not provide a framework for common security in which Japan, the United States, and ASEAN can cooperate for common security with China, Russia, and others. So far, the ARF is the most appropriate framework.[76]

The Clinton administration has recognized that multilateral institutions such as the ARF may complement, but not supplant, bilateral ties which the United States has traditionally advocated. As the U.S. government became more active in institutionalizing a multilateral framework for common security, so did the Japanese government. Both goverments seem to understand the potential of ARF. ASEAN may be able to take initiatives that would fail were Japan or the United States to attempt them. Thus both governments, recognizing that it is premature to propose a better

[74] Ken Aoki, *Ajia-taiheiyo Keizai-ken no Seisei* [The evolution of the Asia Pacific economic zone] (Tokyo: Chuo Keizai Shya, 1994).

[75] Yoichi Funabashi, *Nihon no Taigai Koso: Reisen-go no bijon wo kaku* [Japan's external concept: Writing a post–cold war vision] (Tokyo: Iwanami-Shoten, 1993).

[76] Masashi Nishihara, "Ajia-taiheiyo-chiiki to Takokukan-Anzenhosho Kyoryoku no Wakugumi" [Asia Pacific region and the framework for multilateral security cooperation], *Kokusai Mondai*, October 1994, pp. 60–74.

alternative to the ARF, have encouraged ASEAN's initiatives and supported ASEAN's plan to have all the major actors in the region sit at the same table to discuss security issues.

To state the case differently, although the U.S.-Japan alliance may contribute to regional peace and stability, it is not the basis for the creation of multilateral institutions for common security. Enhancing security cooperation, from military operations to weapons development, may not enhance common security. Both Japan and the United States need to realize that the potential domain of mutual cooperation extends beyond security cooperation under the alliance. By having the United States, Japan, China, Russia, and other regional powers consult with one another on security issues, the ARF paved the way toward further facilitation for Asia-Pacific security.

The establishment of the ARF is certainly a major step, but the economically like-minded participants do not yet share a vision of common security. The ASEAN governments wanted to expand ASEAN-PMC with China, Russia, and Vietnam as new members and strengthen the PMC's functions, but some PMC partners were reluctant to invite the proposed new members.[77] Thus, ASEAN invented the ARF in order to institutionalize a consultation framework on regional security issues without involving the PMC.[78]

Needless to say, the ARF's impact will be inevitably limited. ASEAN cannot impose anything on the major powers. No ASEAN country denies its dependence on U.S. military power. China is reluctant to discuss concrete security problems such as the South China Sea dispute, and it is doubtful that such important issues as North Korean truce violations will be dealt with in the ARF at all. For Japan, however, those shortcomings do not constitute reasons to overlook the new forum. In the foreseeable future, Japan could propose intitiatives for regional peace and security only through the ARF process.

APEC is also a promising vehicle for Japan in the promotion of regional order. This is one of the few governmental institutions for regional economic cooperation with members both sides of the Pacific. Thus APEC provides Japan with an invaluable framework in which Japan can take initiatives without offending either the United States, China, or ASEAN. APEC's high interdependence, close cooperation, and managed economic friction serves not only Japan's comprehensive security but also the region's. The Asia-Pacific free trade area agreed to in 1994 will promote

[77] Vietnam was not a member of ASEAN when the ASEAN governments were trying to set up an organ dealing with security issues.

[78] Nishihara, "Ajia-taiheiyo-chiiki to Takokukan-Anzenhosho Kyoryoku no Wakugumi."

Japan's comprehensive security in economic terms, and as the host of the 1995 meeting of APEC, Japan can introduce initiatives to facilitate regional cooperation. Deepening economic interdependence may also impose self-restraint in political conflicts. In this sense, APEC might have some positive, if indirect, effect upon regional—and thus Japan's—political security.

The ARF and APEC share their core members—Japan, the United States, Australia, the ASEAN countries, China, Korea, and so on.[79] Although they have not yet agreed to create an Asia-Pacific community, powers in the region, whether major or small, are now intertwined with one another on issues both economic and security-related. The Japanese government can strengthen the foundations of these institutions in order to promote the building of a regional order. Within ARF, in addition to participating in a maritime safety project, Japan should propose regular communications between defense authorities to enhance transparency in defense capability and policy. As for APEC, it is of utmost importance for Japan to find the most effective path for furthering economic cooperation and integration on which all members can agree.

By promoting such regional cooperation, Japan will be able to cope with three major uncertainties: the viability of the U.S.-Japan alliance, China's expansionism, and the rise of protectionist regionalism and intensified economic friction. Because the cold war has ended, the United States is no longer needed to defend Japanese territory against military attack, and the termination of the mutual security treaty is not inconceivable.[80] But the alliance can contribute to regional stability; and within the framework of the ARF, the alliance will find new meaning. China's participation in both economic and security institutions must be encouraged, because it will be impossible to contain China without China's cooperation. This large and energetic nation must be incorporated into frameworks like the ARF and APEC. Finally, dynamic economic growth and aggressive exporting by Asian economies will almost inevitably intensify economic frictions among the United States, Japan, the NIE, ASEAN countries, China, and others. Under such circumstances, protectionism may gain momentum in North America. Global economic prosperity must be accompanied by global interdependence. APEC can prevent protectionism and contribute to global interdependence.

---

[79] ASEAN's new member, Vietnam, is not a member of APEC, but it will join in the near future, probably in 1996. In 1993, APEC decided not to expand its membership after Chile's accession until 1996.

[80] A former diplomat Motofumi Asai argues to enhance Japan's security without the security ties with the United States. See Motofumi Asai, *Nihon Gaiko: Hansei to Tenkan* [Japan's diplomacy: Reflections and change] (Tokyo: Iwanami-Shoten, 1989).

The end of the cold war triggered various profound changes in international society. The Asia-Pacific region is no exception. Yet this does not mean that what the cold war brought into being has disappeared. For instance, the U.S.-Soviet rivalry divided four nations; one in Europe and three in Asia. Unlike divided Germany, all of the three Asian nations experienced civil war. After the cease-fires, mutual hatred and mistrust prevailed in each of the divided nations. Even today, two remain divided: China and Korea. Whether or not peaceful unification takes place, the future of these two nations will affect the entire region.

It is often said that the post–cold war era is characterized more by economic issues than by military ones. Again, the Asia-Pacific region is no exception. The leaders of the Asia-Pacific nations are more positive about economic integration and cooperation than ever. Nevertheless, the logic of power politics still prevails in regional relations. Russian disengagement and the gradual decline of U.S. military presence have caused, as many smaller nations in the region feared, a power vacuum. China's naval advance in the South China Sea is seen as an attempt to fill this vacuum, and neighboring nations have strong misgivings. A recent military buildup in the ASEAN countries and Taiwan suggests that those leaders are still preoccupied with a military balance of power. Furthermore, North Korea's alleged development of nuclear weapons has added another factor to power politics.

The end of the cold war eased the tensions between the superpowers, but did not resolve regional security issues. While Europe has succeeded in developing a framework for common security, the Asia-Pacific region has failed to introduce so-called confidence-building measures, and the institutionalization of common security is yet to be seen. Prospects for the ARF are still unclear. It is time for Japan to convince its Asia-Pacific partners that Japan can support a viable institution for common security. Such capability is at least as important as defense capability.

It is often said that the end of the cold war fragmented economic interests and allowed regional protectionism. The EC and NAFTA are regarded as instances of this protectionism. APEC, however, explicitly rejects protectionism in favor of open regionalism. In order to pursue APEC's goal, a series of cooperative programs must be implemented. Japan has much to offer.

The end of the cold war also affected Japanese politics. In mid-1993, Prime Minister Miyazawa was forced to step down following a split of the conservative Liberal Democratic Party (LDP), which had ruled the nation for nealy four decades. Anti-LDP coalition governments led by two prime ministers, Hosokawa and Hata, were succeeded by another coalition government headed by the Socialists and managed by the LDP. All those changes took place in less than two years. Nevertheless, none of those governments altered Japan's security or Asia-Pacific policies significantly.[81]

The first anti-LDP coalition government, led by Prime Minister Hosokawa, was preoccupied with domestic political reforms during the months when the Uruguay Round of the GATT was concluded and Japan's rice market was opened and during disputes between the International Atomic Energy Agency and North Korea. Hosokawa followed his predecessor's Asia-Pacific policy, but his government did not or, more precisely, could not, do anything concrete while he was in office. As for defense policy, he directed a review of the NDPO, but he resigned before he could implement any recommended changes.

The coalition of traditional adversaries, namely, the LDP and the Socialists, has survived for more than a year, much longer than anticipated (as of September 1995). Prime Minister Tomiichi Murayama's Cabinet is currently eager to strengthen Japan's relations with Asia, while Murayama's sponsor, the LDP, is now reluctant. The fiftieth anniversary of Japan's defeat has been marked by unseemly debates concerning Japanese war guilt. Prime Minister Murayama's press speech in August on the same issue was doubtlessly better than the Diet's, but was equally unsuccessful in convincing other Asians of Japan's full recognition of wrongdoings before and during the war.

The process of political reform and the reshuffling of political parties is still under way. Political realignment will take at least a few years, and until the reshuffling is complete, the Japanese government must be based on some form of coalition, and will inevitably be weak and shaky. If a crisis occurs before Japanese politics stabilizes, the government will face serious difficulties in defining the national interest and its efficiency and leadership ability will be tested.[82] If an international crisis occurs and it fails to respond properly, the result might be disastrous not only for Japan but for the Asia-Pacific region.

Japan may acquire permanent membership in the United Nations Security Council in the near future; it may also agree to institutionalize the ARF. It may attempt to lead the APEC process. But its efficiency and leadership will be tested continuously if it tries to take charge of regional institutions in any real way. It seems unlikely that it will be able to pass such tests, at least until the process of political realignment is complete.

---

[81] What changed fundamentally were the Socialist positions that had been kept almost intact for decades.

[82] The recent earthquake in western Japan proved that the government lacks both efficiency and leadership.

9

China, Japan and the Regional Political Economy of East Asia, 1945–1995

MARK SELDEN

In this chapter I explore the postwar China-Japan relationship as a focal point for mapping the changing character of the regional political economy of East Asia and grasping its ascending global position in the final decades of the twentieth century. The latter half of this century in East Asia is a time of contrasts. On the one hand the United States reached the height of its hegemonic power and regional economic leadership; on the other, with the beginnings of regional integration in a posthegemonic order, China has begun its resurgence and East Asia has emerged as the primary zone of world accumulation, which may be indicative of the return of the historic East Asian tributary-trade system in a modern form.

Japan, China, and "Development by Invitation," 1945–1970: The Political Economy of Bipolarity

The trajectories of the Chinese and Japanese political economies and their interrelationships in the years 1945–70 were profoundly influenced by the outcomes of the Second World War and the U.S.-Soviet conflict. This U.S.-Soviet conflict, the defining feature of the postwar global system, was refracted with unique intensity in East Asia and was the basis for the deep divisions in East Asia's bifurcated political economy. It was this conflict that led to isolation of China and the creation of a Soviet bloc and the consequent conflicting approaches to development and the world economy endorsed by the two antagonistic zones that comprised the region. This bipolar Asia constituted a break from the two previous attempts at regional integration. These were a China-centered tributary-trade system whose strength and reach had waxed and waned over the preceding millennium, and the ambitious but abortive Japanese attempt in the first half of the twentieth century to overcome both Chinese primacy and Western colonial domination and create a Japan-centered Greater East Asia.

By taking this regional approach I hope to build on the pioneering research of Takeshi Hamashita, Heita Kawakatsu, and their colleagues into the historical formation of East Asia and explore its relevance to postwar regional development, particularly to the emerging regional configuration in the final years of the twentieth century.[1] The following points derive from or build on their insights into the historical evolution of the region:

1. East Asia is better conceptualized, not in terms of nations, but as a regional ensemble shaped by the articulation of a series of interconnected seas and the Asian landmass, particularly the cities and subregions of its coastal and insular areas. These great oceanic highways, extending from the Sea of Okhotsk in Northeast Asia southward along the Asian coast and through Southeast Asia all the way to the Tasman Sea in Australasia, provide important historical and contemporary transport, communication, trade, and investment channels with potential for regional unification of diverse peoples and cultures.

2. Over a millennium or more, the tributary-trade system and associated business networks served as the context within which intra-regional economic, financial, and political relations were defined on a spectrum ranging from hierarchy to competition to mutuality determined by changing power and ritual relations. For example, Japan and Vietnam not only sent tribute to China, but at various times received tribute from Okinawa and Laos.

3. Tribute missions were inextricably intertwined with private trade networks in a vast integrated silver zone and regional market. The proliferation of a Chinese merchant class throughout much of East and Southeast Asia provided a powerful regional commercializing force and was able to sustain its presence through periods of Chinese dynastic interregnum or self-imposed isolation.

In this perspective, East Asia is conceived as an integrated historical system, one equally capable of "incorporating" Western trading powers (precisely the outcome from the sixteenth century to well into the nineteenth century) as well as "being incorporated." The emergence of a Japan-dominated East Asia in the early decades of the twentieth century can

---

[1] See Chapter 3 herein.

thus be understood in part in terms of a Japanese bid to change the locus of power within the tributary-trade system. What was new in the nineteenth and twentieth centuries was the incorporation of East Asia into global regimes whose locus lay outside the region yet impinged on intra-regional as well as extra-regional relationships. The period of integration, notably China's reemergence as a regional power and the regionwide presence of overseas Chinese capital since the 1970s, suggests new variants on the regional system, one this time firmly implanted within the world economy.

U.S. Power and Japanese Postwar Development

Following the failure of Japan's abortive military-driven attempt to construct an integrated and autarkic Greater East Asia under its sway in the 1930s and 1940s, the United States emerged as the dominant regional and global power. Beginning in 1947, U.S. regional policy crystallized around two goals: the reconstruction of Japan as the economic and financial linchpin of Asia within the framework of U.S. strategic and economic supremacy and the creation of a pan-Asian structure of U.S. bases and alliances deployed to counter Soviet and Chinese regional power and prevent the spread of revolution.[2]

In September 1946 the Japanese Foreign Ministry reported the following to the U.S. Occupation authorities:

> Both from the Chinese and the Japanese viewpoints, it would be only natural that China import Japanese industrial products. . . . A similar relationship

---

[2] Akira Iriye and Bruce Cumings have argued that Japan's position throughout the twentieth century, with the brief aberration of the years 1941–45, has hinged on its acceptance of subordination to the hegemonic power (first Britain, subsequently the United States) as the price for membership in the core and a position as a regional power. See particularly Akira Iriye, *China and Japan in the Global Setting* (Cambridge: Harvard University Press, 1992); *Across the Pacific: An Inner History of American-East Asian Relations* (Cambridge: Harvard University Press, 1967); and *Power and Culture: The Japanese-American War, 1941–1945* (Cambridge: Harvard University Press, 1981). Cf. Bruce Cumings, "The End of the Seventy Years' Crisis: Trilateralism and the New World Order," in *Past As Prelude: History in the Making of a New World Order* ed. Meredith Woo-Cumings and Michael Loriaux (Boulder, Colo: Westview Press, 1993), p. 20. Their point is important in assessing Japan's rise both in the early and final decades of the twentieth century. It seems to me, however, to understate the extent to which Japan embarked on an autonomous course in Asia at odds both with the dominant global powers and with China, which was long the dominant power in East Asia, over the fifteen-year span from 1931 to 1945, with U.S.-Japan and China-Japan tensions emerging with striking clarity by the late 1930s. Of particular importance was Japan's effort to create a closed zone in East Asia under its direct control extending from Korea to Taiwan to Manchuria and North China and eventually to South China and on to Southeast Asia. In Hamashita's terms, this may be understood as Japan's effort to replace China as the center of the East Asian tributary-trade system and of regional business networks. But Japan-imposed regional autarchy also constituted a break with the historical character of the regional tributary-trade system.

can be also applied to Korea, French Indochina, and other countries in Asia [*toyo*]. The recovery of Japanese industry would contribute to the prompt industrialization and the substantial improvements of living standards of East Asian peoples. It would be most desirable, therefore, not to hold Japanese economic development in check but to promote vigorously the industrialization of Asia as a whole, including Japan. Moreover, if a poor and populous Asia succeeded in industrialization, it would provide the United States and Europe with vast markets and thus contribute greatly to the prosperity of the entire world.[3]

Beginning in 1947, the United States promoted the restoration of the Japanese economy within the parameters of its power. It encouraged the reconstitution of the zaibatsu it had earlier set out to dismantle; it fostered reindustrialization and technological advance and opened the U.S. market to Japanese exports; it commmitted U.S. forces to relieve Japan of the necessity for military spending (and to preclude autonomous actions); it encouraged the restoration of Japan's trade and financial ties with Asian nations within the U.S. orbit; and it provided economic aid and loans followed by the bonanza of procurement contracts in the Korean and Indochina wars.[4] In subsequent decades, this package was to spur the growth of Japan in concert with the East Asian NIEs within the U.S. zone of a polarized Asia.

U.S. policymakers recognized that Japan's Asian colonies and the countries in its sphere of influence had provided 35 percent of prewar Japan's raw materials and absorbed 40 percent of its exports. Restoration of these links with other Asian nations in the orbit of U.S. power would be critical to a Japanese economic recovery consistent with the U.S. attempt to isolate China.[5] The Korean War made the restoration of Japan's economic ties with Taiwan and (South) Korea, as well as with the nations of Southeast Asia, even more urgent, particularly as a means to reduce pressures for expanded economic relations with China. Japan was the dominant economic power in the U.S. zone of a polarized East Asia and the primary U.S. ally in U.S.-Soviet and U.S.-Chinese conflicts in the region.

Differences quickly emerged, however, between the United States and its allies, including not only Japan but also Britain, France, and other Eu-

---

[3] Quoted in Akio Watanabe, "Southeast Asia in U.S.-Japan Relations," in *The United States and Japan*, ed. Warren Cohen and Akira Iriye (Lexington: the University Press of Kentucky, 1989), p. 85.

[4] John Dower, "Occupied Japan and the Cold War in Asia," in *Japan in War and Peace: Selected Essays* (New York: New Press, 1993), pp. 155–207, offers a comprehensive introduction to the Occupation.

[5] William Borden, *The Pacific Alliance: United States Foreign Economic Policy and Japanese Trade Recovery, 1947–1955* (Madison: University of Wisconsin Press, 1984), p. 205.

ropean nations over China. By the mid-1950s, under pressure from its allies, the United States relaxed some of the harshest restrictions on trade with China, opening the way for Japan's emergence as China's leading trading partner in the 1960s.[6] From 1957, while the U.S. public position on China remained frozen, U.S. allies expanded trade with China, thus placing pressure on the bipolar division that emerged from World War II.

Soviet Power and China's Postwar Development

China's postwar industrial advance, like Japan's, took place within the framework of U.S.-Soviet conflict, which had divided into two zones what had been one region. The shift in China's primary economic and trade ties from the industrialized capitalist nations to the Soviet bloc in the early 1950s; the processes of collectivization, nationalization, and heavy industry-led development; and China's relative decline as a trading nation, were in part responses to the strategic politics played out in the era of the Korean War, the U.S. blockade, and the Sino-Soviet alliance.

China's rapid industrialization, which began in the 1950s, was achieved with substantial Soviet assistance and employed a variant of the Soviet model of antimarket collectivism and heavy industry-led growth. The loss of U.S. and Japanese markets, the U.S.-led blockade, the Korean War, and subsequent military tensions undermined the argument of Chinese leaders who in the late 1940s and early 1950s had sought access to U.S. capital, technology, and markets in order to reduce their dependence on the Soviet Union. This conjuncture, building on traditions associated with the anti-Japanese resistance and civil war that propelled the Party to power, strengthened Chinese proponents of anti-market, inward-looking, self-reliant strategies, which skewed and slowed but did not derail rapid industrial growth. As Edward Friedman observes of Chinese politics in the early People's Republic, "The new worldview that independence meant keeping foreigners out was expressed in the anthem of the new People's Republic: 'Arise! Refuse to be enslaved! We'll use our flesh and blood to

---

[6] Warren Cohen, "China in Japanese-American Relations," in Cohen and Iriye, *The United States and Japan*, pp. 36–60. Dulles consistently pressed to isolate China. As Cohen observes, Eisenhower astutely recognized the advantages to restoring Chinese-Japanese trade ties, notably the reduction of Chinese dependence on the Soviet Union and potential gains for the Japanese economy. He also understood the impossibility of permanently enforcing the embargo on China. This was consistent with the thinking of a semiofficial study group organized by the Council on Foreign Relations in the years 1953–55 to explore ways of dividing China from the Soviet Union. Its members included Averell Harriman, John McCloy, Dean Rusk, Arthur Dean, and Lyman Lemnitzer, several of whom publically and privately disagreed with Dulles and the China lobby. Gordon Chang, *Friends and Enemies: The United States, China, and the Soviet Union* (Stanford: Stanford University Press, 1990), pp. 102–7.

build a new Great Wall.''[7] Stated differently, this was a developmental perspective that emphasized China's vast agrarian landmass and turned its back on the sea and commerce.

Throughout the 1950s, China received from the Soviet Union and its allies generous technology transfer, training, blueprints, and limited medium-term loans. This constituted a variant on the U.S.-sponsored development-by-invitation pattern—far less lavishly funded ($300 million in medium-term Soviet loans) and at odds with the global hegemonic power—which helped lay the foundations for state-centered heavy industry. There were other important differences. Rapid industrial growth rates were accompanied by, even predicated on, stagnation in per capita incomes, particularly for China's vast rural population in the years 1950–78 as state and collective enforced high rates of accumulation and held wages down.[8]

In short, the period 1945–70 was one of rapid state-promoted industrialization throughout much of East Asia. But only in the U.S.-Japan zone, including the NIEs, did these gains translate into the beginnings of the ascent in the world economic hierarchy as measured by per capita GNP. By the end of the period, Japan had resumed its place among upper-middle-income countries and the East Asian NIEs were beginning their advance. Indeed, the consequences of these industrializing processes included growing pressures for changing the power relations and policy preferences that defined the blocs. China and Japan led the way in redefining these processes.

Thus diverse development trajectories emerged within the two antago-

[7] Edward Friedman, *National Identity and Democratic Prospects in China* (Armonk, N.Y.: M. E. Sharpe, 1995), pp. 6, 79, 100–110. Friedman juxtaposes pluralist, outward-looking, commercial and democratic strains in Chinese politics against authoritarian, militarist, and nationalist strains. He particularly associates the former with southern coastal regions and a vision of Greater China whose dynamism would deeply stamp the period of regional integration discussed below, but with a sense that other mixes are possible, including the unification of commercial and nationalist impulses. China's striving for an autarkic, self-reliant anticommercial development path was carried to its apogee with the Third Front strategy set in place in 1964 as China confronted both superpowers simultaneously. At immense cost, China relocated major industries, particularly heavy and military industries, from vulnerable coastal and Soviet border areas to remote mountain areas in China's southwest. Barry Naughton, "The Third Front: Defence Industrialization in the Chinese Interior," *China Quarterly*, December 1988, pp. 351–87.
[8] Mark Selden, *The Political Economy of Chinese Development* (Armonk, N.Y.: M. E. Sharpe, 1993), examines the social consequences of the high accumulation–low consumption strategy of China's anti-market collectivism, comparing differential consequences for city and countryside in the People's Republic. The famine years of the Great Leap Forward (the early 1960s) and the peak years of the violence of the Cultural Revolution (1966–67) were important exceptions to the pattern of industrial growth.

nistic blocs that formed in East Asia in the aftermath of World War II which were consistent with subordinate affiliations with one or the other superpower: that of Japan and most of her former colonies and dependencies in the U.S. orbit, and that of China, North Korea, and North Vietnam in the Soviet orbit. A striking feature of intra-regional relationships in the 1950s was the strength of the vertical ties—economic, political, social, and cultural—between each of the semisovereign states and its superpower, and the relative weakness of the horizontal ties among the dependent states. Or, in Giovanni Arrighi's analogy with the relationship between territorial Spain and a Genoese capitalist organization in pursuit of profit in fifteenth-century Europe, a division of labor emerged between the U.S. military and a semisovereign Japan free to specialize in the pursuit of profit.[9] Within the U.S. zone the weakness of the ties among the dependent states was in part a legacy of lingering bitterness toward Japan in her former colonies; in the Soviet zone, it was less pronounced but nevertheless present and was a legacy of the liberation wars fought in China, Korea and, Vietnam and the inner-directed developmental priorities that were among the products of protracted wars fought against technologically superior invaders.

The blocs were, however, neither completely autonomous nor frozen in their competition or character. In particular, in the 1960s Japan quickly replaced the Soviet Union as China's leading trade partner as China entered a period in which the China-Soviet conflict overshadowed the China-U.S. conflict. Moreover, certain common qualities in developmental approaches spanning the divide help clarify both the economic dynamic of the region and the speed with which the bipolar rupture could be healed once strategic conditions ripened. First, the injunctions of neoclassical economists to the contrary notwithstanding, China, Japan, and the NIEs all adopted strong state-centered approaches geared toward accelerated development, despite radically different policies defining the role of markets.[10] Second, in both zones we observe political-strategic weakness, or what Peter Katzenstein has termed the semisovereign state: divided nations, as in the case of China, Korea, and Vietnam (before 1975); nations strategically subordinated and restricted by the presence of foreign

---

[9] Giovanni Arrighi, "The Rise of East Asia and the Withering of the Interstate System," Fernand Braudel Center paper (presented at the annual meeting of the American Sociological Association, Washington, D.C., August 19–23, 1995).

[10] Among others, Chalmers Johnson, *MITI and the Japanese Miracle: The Growth of Industrial Policy, 1925–1975* (Stanford: Stanford University Press, 1982); Alice Amsden, *Asia's Next Giant: South Korea and Late Industrialization* (New York: Oxford University Press, 1989); and Robert Wade, *Governing the Market: Economic Theory and the Role of Government in East Asian Industrialization* (Princeton: Princeton University Press, 1990), have powerfully documented this point for Japan and the NIEs.

troops, as in the case of Japan, South Korea, and Taiwan; and nations dependent on others for a nuclear umbrella and advanced military technology and more generally on the dominant military presence in the region to guarantee security. Third, China, Japan, and the NIEs, in the early postwar years, all fiercely resisted foreign control of the commanding heights of their economies, particularly by sharply restricting direct foreign investment and tightly controlling trade.[11] Fourth, China, Japan, Taiwan, and Korea all carried out far-reaching agrarian reforms that broke the grip of the landlord elite, facilitated state penetration of the countryside, and stimulated agriculture. And last, Taiwan, Korea, and parts of China, as well as (briefly) Hong Kong and Singapore, shared a legacy of prewar or wartime Japanese-directed economic development, including infrastructure, education, and training.

The postwar trajectories of all of the states and regions of East Asia were shaped by U.S. and Soviet policies and conflicts. Strategic shifts and the relative weakening of the two superpowers vis-à-vis the nations of the region opened the way toward greater autonomy, regional unification, rapid integrative regional growth, and redefinition of the regional position of both superpowers. By the late 1960s, several consequences of U.S., Asian, and global policies and changing Soviet-China relations undermined the basic premises of the bipolar postwar order in Asia. Protracted wars in Korea and Indochina, together with the costs of maintaining a far-flung network of bases, undermined the strength of the dollar and the fiscal foundations of U.S. hegemony. Japan's economic resurgence, followed by that of the NIEs and, to a lesser extent, China, together with the fierce conflict between China and the Soviet Union, increased pressures to bridge the polarized economic and strategic order in Asia. The growing restiveness on the part of China and Japan with the order imposed by the United States and the Soviet Union in the early postwar years paved the way for regional transformation in the 1970s.

Japan, China, and "Development by Integration," 1970–1995: The Political Economy of East Asian Regionalism

The following global and regional events precipitated a transition in the hegemonic politics and the regional political economy of East Asia. They all occurred during or around 1970.

[11] This does not mean that Japanese state controls succeeded in every instance. The United States maintained important economic and financial levers through Japan's dependence on oil controlled by the Seven Sisters, and through the role of U.S. financial institutions in Japan. Among the NIEs, colonial Hong Kong was an exception in encouraging foreign investment in the early postwar years.

The collapse of the U.S. dollar and the end of the gold standard (1970);
The proclamation of the Nixon Doctrine, the U.S. inability to prevail on
the battlefield in Indochina (1969), the scaling back of U.S. strategic
commitments in mainland Asia, and a new approach toward China
(1970);
The end of China's Cultural Revolution, signified by the fall of Chen
Boda (1970), followed by the death of Lin Biao (1971), the rise of Zhou
Enlai and the start of China's foreign trade drive and a conservative modernization strategy (1970);
The beginning of significant Japanese overseas manufacturing investment
in Asia, particularly in the NIEs (early 1970s); and
The U.S.-China diplomatic breakthrough (1971), which transformed the
lines of global and regional power, paving the way for China's full reentry
in the United Nations and the world economy and heralding its future
market transition, its emergence as a major trading nation, and its institutional transformation.

The relative decline of U.S. and Soviet power and the end of regional
bifurcation signaled by U.S.-China rapprochement, the end of the Indochina War, and China's spiraling international trade opened the way for
the formation of an Asian regional political economy whose salient features include the growing economic integration of Japan, China, the NIEs,
the ASEAN nations, and the United States within a dynamic market and
investment region, and the emergence of overseas Chinese economic
power throughout the region. Emblematic of these changes is China's
strengthened position in both the regional and the global political economies, the redefinition of the relationships and relative positions of all
other major and minor regional actors, and an expanded regionwide role
for overseas Chinese enterprise. Regional integration, involving new hierarchies of trade, investment, and financial and technological interlocks, is
central to the emergence of East Asia as the highest growth region of the
world economy and the primary zone of world accumulation, investment,
and trade in the final decades of the twentieth century.

East Asia has sustained uniquely rapid growth and technological transformation as intra-regional trade, investment, GNP, and per capita income
have continued to soar even during periods of general stagnation in the
global economy such as the 1980s and 1990s. It is the only region in which
several nations have risen significantly within the global hierarchy of
wealth and power during the twentieth century. Over the last thirty years,
real GNP multiplied twelve times in the NIEs, eleven times in Japan, and
six times in China and the ASEAN countries. By comparison, the U.S.

Table 9-1. Real GDP Growth Rate in East Asia, 1970–1993 (%)

Country/region	70–75	75–80	80–85	85–90	91–93
Japan	4.4	4.6	3.7	4.6	1.8
China	5.7	5.8	9.9	7.3	11.5
NIEs	8.8	9.4	7.2	9.1	6.5
South Korea	9.5	7.7	8.5	10.2	6.2
Taiwan	8.9	10.6	6.7	8.7	6.4
Hong Kong	6.6	12.3	5.6	7.6	4.9
Singapore	9.4	8.5	6.1	7.9	7.5
ASEAN	6.4	7.4	3.9	6.9	6.1
Malaysia	7.1	8.6	5.1	6.9	8.3
Thailand	5.6	7.8	5.6	10.1	7.9
Philippines	5.7	6.0	−1.3	4.5	0.7
Indonesia	6.9	7.5	5.0	6.2	6.6

Source: Calculated from Sueo Kojima, "Alternative Export-Oriented Development Strategies in Greater China," *China Newsletter,* November–December 1994, p. 19.

economy expanded two and a half times and the world economy three times.[12]

In the years 1980–93 China's per capita GNP increased at the rate of 8.2 percent annually compared with 0.1 percent for all low-income countries except China and India and 2.2 percent for high-income countries. In these years, Japan's per capita GNP rose at the annual rate of 3.4 percent, Hong Kong's at 5.4 percent, but that of the United States, only 1.7 percent.[13]

Japan and China in the Era of Regional Integration

For nearly a century, with the exception of the years immediately following the Pacific War, Japan has been and is once again by most measures the economic colossus of Asia. Japan's 1991 GDP of $3.4 trillion by World Bank reckoning was nine times greater than China's $370 billion GDP and approximately twice that of the combined total of China, the four NIEs, and the five ASEAN nations.[14] This sharp imbalance in economic, finan-

---

[12] C. H. Kwan, *Economic Interdependence in the Asia-Pacific Region: Toward a Yen Bloc* (London: Routledge, 1994), p. 11.

[13] World Bank, *World Development Report 1995* (New York: Oxford University Press, 1995), pp. 162–63.

[14] World Bank, *World Development Report 1993* (New York: Oxford University Press, 1993), pp. 242–43; Shuichi Ono, "Sino-Japanese Economic Relationships: Trade, Direct Investment, and Future Strategy," *World Bank Discussion Papers, China and Mongolia Department Series* 146 (Washington, D.C.: The World Bank, 1992), p. 46. In 1993 Japan's GDP of $4.2 trillion was nearly

Table 9-2. China-Japan Trade, 1950–1993 (in millions of U.S. dollars)

Year	Chinese Imports	Chinese Exports	Total Chinese Japanese trade
1950–52	8.7	25.3	34.0
1953–57	36.0	63.1	99.1
1958–60	19.0	31.3	50.4
1961–64	67.6	77.2	144.9
1965–69	312.5	250.9	564.7
1970–74	956.0	669.4	1,625.4
1975–79	2,521.4	1,886.8	4,408.2
1980–84	5,162.7	5,214.6	10,365.2
1985–89	9,715.1	8,108.2	17,823.3
1990–93	10,986.2	15,946.7	26,932.9

Sources: Chae-Jin Lee, *China and Japan. New Economic Diplomacy*, pp. 4, 18; JETRO, *China Newsletter*, November–December, 1988, pp. 8 and 106, and JETRO, *China Newsletter*, September–October, 1993, p. 21. Based on Japanese customs clearance statistics. Some slight discrepancies in totals due to rounding.

cial, and technical power, with the consequent pronounced divergence between core and peripheral regions, differs significantly from European patterns of regional integration. Japan's trade, technology, loans, and investment have played a leading role in China's economic advance since the 1960s when that nation was on a collision course with both superpowers. Japan also played an important economic, financial, and technological role in the early stages of China's market transition in the 1970s and early 1980s. Trade patterns reveal the long-term, sustained, and rapid growth in China-Japan trade since the early 1960s as well as Japan's predominance as a trade partner through the mid-1980s.

Since the 1960s, but particularly since the U.S.-China diplomatic rapprochement in 1970, China became a significant and growing export market and outlet for Japanese capital in the form of loans and investment. In the 1980s Japan consolidated its position as China's leading trade partner, enjoying a large and growing surplus from the late 1960s until the balance stabilized in the 1980s and reversed in China's favor in the early 1990s. Japan has also been an important provider of advanced technology for China.

In the 1970s China's international economic relations diversified with its growing economic ties with the United States and European countries and, as China gained membership in the full range of international organizations, in the United Nations (1971), the International Monetary

---

ten times China's $0.43 trillion and two-thirds that of the United States, which was $6.3 trillion. *World Development Report 1995*, pp. 166–67.

Fund (1980), and the World Bank (1980), with World Trade Organization membership pending in 1995.

Significant changes have occurred in the character of Japan-China economic relations since the late 1970s when China's principal exports to Japan were raw materials (primarily oil and coal), indicative of a strategy designed to jump-start Chinese exports despite China's growing need for petroleum and other resources to fuel economic growth. From the 1980s, China's leading exports were better aligned with her comparative advantage as cloth and subsequently clothing and other labor intensive manufactures replaced raw materials. In the 1990s, China continues to provide Japan with some raw and semi-processed materials but primarily it exports growing quantities of low value-added manufactures of increasing sophistication in exchange for financing and high technology products and equipment, as in the construction of Shanghai's vast Baoshan steel complex. Exports to Japan have changed in step with the global shift in China's exports as the share of manufactures increased from 49.5 percent in 1985 to 81.8 percent by 1993.[15]

For three decades, Japan has been one of China's two most important economic partners. China, however, was only one of approximately a dozen roughly comparable trade, loan, and investment partners or recipients for Japan, all of whom lag far behind the United States in importance. Similarly, Japan has been a significant source of technology, investment, and loans for China. Japan was not only the first country to offer China bilateral aid, but with four major assistance packages involving loans totaling $10 billion (1.6 trillion yen) in the years 1979–95, it has provided more than three fourths of all China's bilateral loans. Only the World Bank, with total disbursed loans of $9.6 billion between 1983 and 1993 offered financing on a comparable scale.[16] The large capital infusions into China, whether from Japan, other nations, the World Bank, the Asian Development Bank, or private investors are a product both of the politics of integration that has emerged since the 1970s and China's changed development priorities and economic performance. While the China-Japan economic relationship continued its rapid growth, Japan became

---

[15] The share of manufactures in China's imports rose sharply in the same years from 65 to 86 percent as China invested heavily in machinery and equipment imports. Nicholas Lardy, *China in the World Economy* (Washington, D.C.: Institute for International Economics, 1994), pp. 31–32; cf. Peng Min, "An Analysis of China's Foreign Trade Efficiency and Foreign Exchange Policy," in *Studies on Economic Reforms and Development in the People's Republic of China*, ed. Hsueh Tien-tung, Sung Yun-wing, and Yu Jingxuan (New York: St. Martin's, 1993), pp. 149–52.

[16] Lardy, *China in the World Economy*, pp. 49–63; *World Development Report 1993*, tables 21–23.

less indispensable as China's international contacts multiplied and others vied for Chinese trade and investment opportunities.

China's share in Japan's global investment portfolio is modest. The bulk of Japanese investment continues to flow with ever higher concentration to the United States, and its composition has shifted to financial investments while manufactures and mining declined. The share of Japanese investment in Asia fell from 24 percent of Japan's total in the early 1970s to just 12 percent in the late 1980s, with most of this directed not to China but to the NIEs and ASEAN. As important as Asia is to Japan's economy, the overwhelming target for overseas investment remains the United States and Europe, a pattern that contrasts sharply with prewar investment concentrated overwhelmingly in Japan's Asian colonies and dependencies.

Japan's ascent as a global economic power challenging U.S. primacy and its rise as a dominant player in the regional economy is illustrated by numerous facts. Japan's foreign direct investment in the years 1986–89 increased at average annual rates exceeding 50 percent as Japan became the world's leading source of FDI, averaging more than $40 billion per year. Japan's former colonies, Taiwan and South Korea, simultaneously increased their FDI at even more rapid rates, though at far lower absolute levels.[17] By 1991 five of the top ten global firms measured by market value were Japanese, as were ten of the top twenty, led by financial institutions.[18] Such figures, highlighting individual enterprises, doubtless understate the concentrations of Japanese industrial, commercial and financial power unified through keiretsu empires and trading companies.[19]

In assessing Japan's rise and the changing character of East Asia, however, many analysts have paid insufficient attention to the continued salience of U.S. power. Not only is the United States the dominant global and regional military and political presence, but its economic and financial importance for China, Japan, and the entire region remains critical. The United States is Japan's number one trade partner by a wide margin, the most important source of a growing Japanese trade surplus, and the largest outlet for Japanese capital. For China and most of East Asia, the United States remains the critical market for exports. Not only is the United States

[17] Mitchell Bernard and John Ravenhill, "Beyond Product Cycles and Flying Geese: Regionalization, Hierarchy, and the Industrialization of East Asia," *World Politics* 47 (January 1995): 181.

[18] Philip Meeks, "Japan and Global Economic Hegemony," in *Japan in the Posthegemonic World*, ed. Tsuneo Akaha and Frank Langdon (Boulder, Colo.: Lynne Rienner, 1993), pp. 51–52.

[19] Kiyoshi Kojima and Terutomo Ozawa, *Japan's General Trading Companies: Merchants of Economic Development* (Paris: Development Centre of the Organisation for Economic Co-Operation and Development, 1984).

Table 9-3. Three Major Waves of Japan's Foreign Direct Investment by Region and Industry

	1st upsurge (1969–73)		2nd upsurge (1978–84)		3rd upsurge (1986–89)	
Subtotal (in $ million)	$ 259	100%	$49,220	100%	$170,246	100%
Region						
North America	1,870	22.6	16,070	32.6	82,028	48.2
Latin America	1,390	16.8	9,262	18.8	21,219	12.5
Asia	2,000	24.2	11,699	23.8	21,002	12.3
Middle East	448	5.4	1,448	2.9	431	0.3
Europe	1,784	21.6	5,997	12.2	33,969	20.0
Africa	193	2.3	2,284	4.6	1,905	1.1
Oceania	572	6.9	2,462	5.0	9,691	5.7
Industry						
Manufacturing	2,678	32.4	14,911	30.3	41,727	24.5
Food	134	1.6	639	1.3	2,174	1.3
Textiles	637	7.7	769	1.6	1,119	0.7
Chemicals	506	6.1	2,480	5.0	4,667	2.7
Ferrous/nonferrous	395	4.8	3,755	7.6	4,072	2.4
Machinery (nonelect.)	170	2.1	1,106	2.2	4,507	2.6
Electronic Machinery	299	3.6	2,385	4.8	10,929	6.4
Transport equipment	144	1.7	2,208	4.5	5.635	3.3
Nonmanufacturing						
Mining	2,077	25.1	5,845	11.9	3,455	2.0
Commerce	914	11.0	8,173	16.6	12,482	7.3
Finance/insurance	661	8.0	5,360	10.9	46,412	27.3
Branches	364	4.4	942	1.9	2,340	1.4
Real estate	288	3.5	294	0.6	n.a.	n.a.

Source: Terutomo Ozawa, "Foreign Direct Investment and Structural Transformation: Japan as a Recycler of Market and Industry," *Business and the Contemporary World,* Spring 1993, p. 136. Reprinted by permission.

the dominant market for the largest and most rapidly growing sector of Asian trade, manufacturing exports, but in important instances, including China, Thailand, and Singapore, the U.S. market share increased between 1980 and 1992, and in all of these instances it is a far more important market than Japan.

Attention to the U.S. economic role is helpful in clarifying the growing regional character and changing regional patterns of trade. The U.S. share in the exports of a number of Asian nations, including Hong Kong and Taiwan, dropped following the 1985 Plaza Accord, as these nations and Japan invested heavily in Chinese and ASEAN industry, which then were credited with a substantial share of Asian exports to the United States. In

Table 9-4. U.S. and Japanese Shares in East Asian Exports of Manufactured Goods

	1980		1984		1992	
	U.S.	Japan	U.S.	Japan	U.S.	Japan
China	9.0	11.0	18.9	10.8	23.7	9.7
Hong Kong	34.1	2.8	46.0	3.3	28.6	4.3
South Korea	29.0	13.3	38.6	10.1	25.1	12.8
Singapore	21.0	8.1	32.5	3.6	26.0	5.7
Taiwan	38.3	7.3	53.7	6.3	35.2	8.3
Malaysia	31.7	5.7	41.3	5.9	29.1	7.5
Thailand	17.5	7.1	29.4	6.8	31.7	16.3

Source: Mitchell Bernard and John Ravenhill, " "Beyond Product Cycles and Flying Geese. Regionalization, Hierarchy, and the Industrialization of East Asia," *World Politics* 47 (January 1995): p. 205.

a regional perspective, U.S. gains in cutting the trade deficit with Japan was the other side of the coin of the mounting U.S. deficits with China, Taiwan, and Hong Kong.

If Japanese capital now challenges the technological and financial supremacy of U.S.-based enterprises globally, the United States faces no significant military challenge—if by this we mean a nation capable of rivaling U.S. military power—and it remains an important economic partner and competitor for Japan and other East Asian nations. For most of the last fifteen years, the United States surpassed Japan as a source of direct investment funds and loans to China. In short, the United States is an important economic player in East Asia and it retains military and political primacy. For this reason, the major, if still fragile, regional grouping is the Asia Pacific Economic Council (APEC), which includes the United States, Canada, Australia, and New Zealand, Pacific Rim powers, together with the Asian nations, and Malaysian Prime Minister Mahathir Mohamad's plan for an Asian grouping that excludes non-Asian Pacific powers has languished.

China's international market transition began in the early 1970s, not, as many studies assume, in 1976 or 1978 following the death of Mao and the rise of Deng, with the surge in international trade paving the way for the transformation of collective- and state-centered economic institutions. Since that time, average annual growth rates in China's foreign trade have approached 20 percent. China's purchase of turn-key plants and equipment from the United States and Japan also began in the early 1970s. These processes of technology transfer and expanding foreign trade accelerated with the domestic market transition after 1978 as China abandoned the classic import substitution model of industrialization in favor of export-oriented development and an outward-looking coastal development strategy.[20] In the early 1980s, China dismantled the communes, reduced the scope of collective institutions, relaxed controls on the movement of one hundred million villagers, welcomed substantial foreign investment, aid, and loans, promoted domestic markets, and embarked on a national development strategy that was instrumental for regional integration. The shift from discrete economic blocs to regional integation is pehaps most clearly seen in the rapid growth in the full range of economie relations involving Taiwan and South Korea with China and Vietnam, relationships precluded by the military and political conflicts of the preceding era of bipolar confrontation. These changes, made possible by the transformation of the international strategic order, inaugurated a new stage in Chinese–Japanese–East Asian regional relations and China's emergence as an integral part of a global center of accumulation, industrialization, and trade.

East Asian Regionality in an Era of Integration

At the heart of regional formation since the 1970s has been the intensification of diverse forms of intra-regional economic exchange, including flows of trade, loans, direct and indirect investment, technology, communications, transportation, labor, and travel. We can only sample some of the most important developments here. Both Japanese enterprises and Overseas Chinese businesses have played central roles in trade-driven economic integration. Prior to the mid-1980s, foreign trade in East Asia was dominated by trans-pacific trade. Between 1986 and 1992, however, the share of Asian exports destined for other Asian countries rose from 32 to 44 percent while those destined for the United States dropped from 37 to a still hefty 24 percent.[21] In contrast to the prewar period, the strengthening of intra-regional trade ties since the 1970s, far from constituting a move toward autarky, has simultaneously strengthened both regional and global ties. Between 1978 and 1992, for example, U.S.-China trade increased thirty-fold, from $1.1 billion to $33.1 billion.[22]

Among the factors spurring intensified regionalization was the 1985 Plaza Accord an attempt to bring under control Japan's enormous trade surpluses with the United States and other nations. The accord, which strengthened not only the yen but also the currencies of Taiwan and South Korea, improved the export competitiveness of several other Asian coun-

[20] Nicholas Lardy spells out the import substitution features of China's pre-1980s trade regime in *Foreign Trade and Economic Reform in China, 1978–1990* (Cambridge: Cambridge University Press, 1992).

[21] Kwan, *Economic Interdependence*, pp. 4, 102–4.

[22] Ibid., p. 108; also see Table 9-6.

tries. It also generated a surge of Japanese, Taiwanese, South Korean, and Overseas Chinese investment in Asia that fueled intra-regional industrialization and trade as well as a shift in manufactured exports to the United States away from Japan and the NIEs and toward China and ASEAN nations. From 1985 a larger share of Japanese and NIE exports were directed to Asia, including machinery, equipment, and semi-processed goods for processing and assembly in newly opened plants.[23]

East Asian trade surged not only in absolute terms but as a percentage of world trade. While the U.S. and European shares of world trade edged up slightly between 1980 and 1992 (from 12.4 to 13.5 percent and from 38.1 to 40.0 percent), East Asia's share jumped from 14.6 percent to 22.3 percent with exports advancing from 14.4 percent to 24.0 percent. By 1992 Japan accounted for 7.7 percent, the Asian NIEs for 9.3 percent, ASEAN for 3.2 percent and China 2.1 percent of world trade. In 1993 Hong Kong became the world's eighth largest trader, China the tenth largest, and Taiwan fourteenth.[24] China has been an important source of growth over two decades during which its export dependence (exports/ GNP) rose from just two percent in 1970 to 20 percent in 1992. This is twice the level of Japan's export dependence, though far below the dependence levels of the NIEs and the ASEAN countries.[25] Since 1986, the value of U.S. exports to Asia has surpassed that of its exports to Europe. In sum, over a quarter century of spiraling East Asian trade, intra-Asian trade networks experienced the most rapid growth, the focal point of U.S. trade shifted from Europe to Asia, Japan's share of Asia's exports declined as a percentage of Asia's more diversified exports to the United States, and the U.S. balance of trade deficit with Asia spiraled despite the upward valuation of the currencies of Japan, Taiwan, and South Korea and the decline of the dollar against strong currencies.

[23] Japanese Ministry of Finance Statistics, "A Policy Framework for Asia-Pacific Economic Cooperation," in *The U.S.-Japan Economic Relationship in East and Southeast Asia: A Policy Framework for Asia-Pacific Economic Cooperation,* ed. Kaoru Okuizumi, Kent Calder, and Gerrit Gong (Boulder, Colo.: Westview Press, 1992), pp. 6–10, emphasizes the redirection of Japanese and NIE trade following the Plaza Accord. Terutomo Ozawa, "Foreign Direct Investment and Structural Transformation: Japan as a Recycler of Market and Industry," *Business and the Contemporary World,* Spring 1993, p. 142; Kwan, *Economic Interdependence,* pp. 4, 14–15, 100–101.
[24] *China News Digest,* April 21, 1994; Sueo Kojima, "Alternative Export-Oriented Development Strategies in Greater China," *China Newsletter,* November–December 1994, p. 18.
[25] Kwan, *Economic Interdependence,* pp. 10, 12, 101, 171. The 20 percent figure undoubtedly overstated China's level of export dependence because of the widely recognized understatement of China's GNP. It well represents, however, the rapid advance in export dependence. By 1991, six of the top ten container ports in the world were in East Asia, including five of the top six: Singapore, Hong Kong, Kaohsiung, Rotterdam, Pusan, Kobe, Hamburg, Los Angeles, Keelung, and New York.

Table 9-5. A Regional Breakdown of World Trade

Country/ Region	World Share (%)								
	1980	1985	1986	1987	1988	1989	1990	1991	1992
Exports									
United States	11.6	11.8	11.0	10.6	11.9	12.5	11.8	12.3	12.3
Japan	6.9	9.8	10.6	9.8	9.8	9.4	8.6	9.2	9.3
Asian NIEs	4.0	6.3	6.7	7.6	8.3	8.5	8.0	8.9	9.4
ASEAN	2.5	2.5	2.1	2.2	2.4	2.6	2.6	2.9	3.1
China	1.0	1.5	1.6	1.7	1.8	1.8	1.8	2.0	2.2
Asia-Pacific(a)	14.4	20.1	21.0	21.3	22.3	22.3	21.1	23.0	24.0
EC(b)	36.5	35.9	40.3	40.7	39.6	38.9	41.2	39.9	39.8
N. America(c)	15.2	16.8	14.4	14.8	16.3	16.6	15.7	16.0	16.0
(a)+(b)+(c)	66.1	72.8	75.7	76.8	78.2	77.8	77.9	78.9	79.8
Imports									
United States	13.2	19.1	18.8	17.4	16.7	16.4	15.1	14.3	14.7
Japan	7.3	6.9	6.2	6.2	6.8	7.0	6.9	6.7	6.2
Asian NIEs	4.5	5.7	5.7	6.4	7.6	7.9	7.8	8.7	9.3
ASEAN	2.0	2.0	1.7	1.8	2.1	2.5	2.8	3.2	3.3
China	1.0	2.2	2.1	1.8	2.0	1.9	1.6	1.8	2.0
Asia-Pacific(a)	14.8	16.8	15.7	16.2	18.5	19.3	19.1	20.3	20.8
EC(b)	39.7	35.1	37.9	39.2	39.1	38.8	41.3	40.9	40.3
N. America(c)	16.3	23.3	21.5	21.1	20.7	20.4	18.6	17.8	18.1
(a)+(b)+(c)	70.8	75.2	75.1	76.5	78.3	78.5	79.0	79.1	79.2
Total Trade									
United States	12.4	15.5	15.0	14.1	14.3	14.5	13.5	13.3	13.5
Japan	7.1	8.3	8.4	8.0	8.3	8.2	7.7	7.9	7.7
Asian NIEs	4.3	6.0	6.2	7.0	7.9	8.2	7.9	8.8	9.3
ASEAN	2.2	2.2	1.9	2.0	2.2	2.5	2.7	3.1	3.2
Chine	1.0	1.9	1.8	1.7	1.9	1.9	1.7	1.9	2.1
Asia-Pacific(a)	14.6	18.4	18.3	18.7	20.3	20.8	20.1	21.7	22.3
EC(b)	38.1	35.5	39.0	39.9	39.4	38.9	41.2	40.4	40.0
N. America(c)	15.8	20.1	18.0	18.0	18.5	18.6	17.1	16.9	17.1
(a)+(b)+(c)	68.5	74.0	75.3	76.6	78.2	78.3	78.5	79.0	79.5

Source: IMF, *International Financial Statistics*; reprinted in C. H. Kwan, *Economic Interdependence in the Asia-Pacific Region: Towards a Yen Bloc* (London: Routledge, 1994), p. 12. Reprinted by permission.

As China's market transition advanced both domestically and internationally, Japan, China's primary economic partner, in trade, aid, technology transfer, loans, and foreign investment, faced a powerful competitor, and from the late 1980s was surpassed in important respects by Hong Kong. Hong Kong emerged as a driving force in fostering regional ties and internationalization of the Chinese economy centered on rapidly growing economic linkages between coastal (particularly central and southern) China, Hong Kong, Taiwan, and Overseas Chinese capital from other parts of Asia and globally.[26]

Chinese Capital and East Asian Regionality

The growing importance of Chinese capital and business enterprise is evident within the parameters of the post-1970 rise of East Asia as a cohesive economic region. Some observors, such as David Shambaugh, project this growth into the not-too-distant future:

> It is not unimaginable or unrealistic to assume that early in the 21st century the combined Gross Domestic Product (GDP) of Greater China will surpass those of the European Community and United States; it will be the world's leading trader and in possession of the world's largest foreign exchange reserves; it will be a source of state-of-the-art high technology and scientific and medical advances; it will be the world's largest consumer; it will garrison the world's largest military establishment; and may be the pre-eminent member of the Group of Nine nations (including Russia). Greater China will also overtake Japan as the dominant regional power with Shanghai and Hong Kong the financial nexus of East Asia economic dynamism.[27]

In 1993, the combined exports and imports of China, Hong Kong, and Taiwan surpassed Japan's total trade for the first time. Between 1978 and 1992, the ratio of intra-regional exports to total exports increased from 26 to 45 percent for China, from 3 to 38 percent for Hong Kong, and from 7 to 19 percent for Taiwan.[28] In 1991 Japan's $103 billion in exports to Asia, led by exports to the NIEs followed by ASEAN and China, for the first time surpassed those to the United States, which nevertheless remained Japan's leading trade partner, while China climbed to second

---

[26] A useful introduction to the literature on Chinese enterprise and the debate over "Greater China" is the special (December 1993) issue of the *China Quarterly*; see also Wang Gungwu, *Community and Nation: China, Southeast Asia, and Australia* (Sydney: Allen & Unwin, 1992), and *China and the Chinese Overseas*, (Singapore: Times Academic Press, 1991). J. A. C. Mackie, "Overseas Chinese Entrepreneurship," *Asian-Pacific Economic Literature* 6 (May 1992): 41–64.

[27] David Shambaugh, "Introduction: The Emergence of 'Greater China,'" *China Quarterly*, December 1993, p. 653. Shambaugh defines Greater China as "the activities in, and interactions between, mainland China, Hong Kong, Macao, Taiwan, and the offshore islands, and Chinese overseas."

[28] Kojima, "Alternative Export-Oriented Development Strategies in Greater China," p. 21; Nobuo Maruyama, "New Directions in East Asian Regional Economy," *China Newsletter*, 114, January–February 1995, p. 5.

place.[29] Japan, long China's top trade partner, was surpassed by Hong Kong in 1985, and the margin of Hong Kong's advantage has grown since. Given the nature of Hong Kong's huge re-export trade (up from 20 percent of its China trade in the 1970s to 75 percent in 1992), however, figures showing Hong Kong's China trade as twice that of Japan's in the 1990s require interpretation.[30] In 1990, 53.9 percent of China's exports went to Hong Kong, but Hong Kong was the final destination for only 6.2 percent while the United States led with 25.6 percent followed by Japan with 11.5 percent. In 1994, China calculated its trade surplus with the United States at $7.5 billion, but the United States, including the value of re-exports from Hong Kong, put China's surplus at $30 billion.

By 1993 Taiwan and China were each other's fourth largest trade partner with China exporting $1.5 billion and importing $12.9 billion, a figure fueled by the flow of machinery, equipment, and partially finished goods to Taiwan-owned enterprises on the mainland.[31] China's Taiwan trade has grown rapidly since the 1980s, reaching $5.8 billion in 1991 and $8.6 billion in 1993 ($7.5 billion of the total representing Taiwan exports). For the years 1979 to 1993 Taiwan's China trade grew at annual rates of 40 percent. And this was simply the legal trade directed through Hong Kong.[32] These figures, moreover, conceal the immense and rapidly growing Overseas Chinese trade and investment emanating from other countries.

Central to the flourishing of Chinese capital and to the character of the East Asia region is the deepening of intra-regional trade and investment concentrated on the China coast, initially notably the Hong Kong–Guangdong region followed by coastal Fujian dominated by Taiwan investors, but in the mid-1990s extending vigorously to the Jiangsu-Shanghai region further north. Hong Kong, Taiwan, and Overseas Chinese capital in the 1990s

---

[29] Kwan, *Economic Interdependence*, pp. 4–10; "China Now Japan's Second Largest Trade Partner," *China Newsletter*, September–October 1993, p. 20.

[30] Robert Ash and Y. Y. Kueh, "Economic Integration within Greater China: Trade and Investment Flows Between China, Hong Kong, and Taiwan," *China Quarterly*, December 1993, pp. 710–45; Edward Chen and Anna Ho, "Southern China Growth Triangle: An Overview" in *Growth Triangles in Asia: A New Approach to Regional Economic Cooperation*, ed. Myo Thant, Min Tang, and Hiroshi Kakazu (Hong Kong: Oxford University Press, 1994), p. 15; Kwan, *Economic Interdependence*, p. 128.

[31] Kojima, "Alternative Export-Oriented Development Strategies in Greater China," p. 21. Since much Taiwan trade and investment continues to enter the mainland through Hong Kong, official figures grossly understate Taiwan data and inflate those for Hong Kong.

[32] Ibid., p. 19; Kao Charng, "Economic Interdependence Between Taiwan and Mainland China," in *The Economic Transformation of South China: Reform and Development in the Post-Mao Era*, ed. Thomas Lyons and Victor Nee (Ithaca: Cornell East Asia Series, 1994), pp. 243–48.

Table 9-6. China's Foreign Trade with Major Partners, 1976–1992 (in millions of U.S. dollars)

Year	Japan	Hong Kong	United States	Taiwan	South Korea	Soviet Union	Total
1976	3,039	1,787	317	40	-	415	13,440
1977	3,465	1,913	294	30	-	329	14,800
1978	4,824	2,533	1,145	47	-	437	20,640
1979	6,708	3,328	2,316	77	100	493	29,330
1980	9,201	4,353	4,812	321	200	492	38,140
1981	9,978	5,174	5,468	467	400	225	44,030
1982	8,761	4,977	5,196	298	300	276	41,610
1983	9,077	5,382	4,417	265	260	674	43,620
1984	12,728	8,954	6,069	553	550	1,183	53,550
1985	18,960	10,844	7,718	1,104	1,100	1,881	69,600
1986	15,509	15,395	7,877	925	1,282	2,640	73,850
1987	15,651	22,215	9,790	1,516	1,679	2,519	82,650
1988	19,335	30,242	13,532	2,717	3,100	3,258	102,790
1989	19,662	34,458	17,765	3,483	3,200	3,997	111,680
1990	18,184	41,540	20,043	4,040	3,800	4,370	115,440
1991	22,809	49,600	25,247	5,800	4,500	2,980	135,630
1992	28,902	58,050	33,146	7,400			165,610

Sources: For Hong Kong, Taiwan, Soviet Union, Xiangming Chen, "China's Growing Integration with the Asia-Pacific Economy," in *What Is in a Rim? Critical Perspectives on the Pacific Region Idea*, ed. Arif Dirlik (Boulder, Colo.: Westview Press, 1993), p. 92; for Japan and the United States, Nicholas Lardy, *Foreign Trade and Economic Relations in China, 1978–1990* (Cambridge: Cambridge University Press, 1992), p. 12; Nicholas Lardy, "Chinese Foreign Trade," *China Quarterly*, September 1992, p. 694. Nicholas Lardy, *China in the World Economy* (Washington, D.C.: Institute for International Economics, 1994). For China's total trade, *China Statistical Yearbook 1993* (Beijing: State Statistical Bureau, 1994), p. 573.

surpassed Japan as the dominant source of trade, capital, and investment in China, particularly coastal China.[33]

An important by-product of East Asia's surging trade is the concentration of foreign exchange reserves in the region. By 1992, China, Hong Kong, and Taiwan had accumulated $165 billion in foreign reserves, approaching the $180 billion combined total for the United States, Japan, and Germany that year.[34] Stated differently, China, Japan, and the NIEs in the mid-1990s control the lion's share of world currency reserves. This is a direct consequence of their enormous positive trade balances, particularly with the United States.

Terutomo Ozawa has observed that "the more geographically concen-

[33] Japan for three decades provided important financial and technological inputs into the Chinese economy, yet only a very small fraction of Japanese FDI has been directed toward China, and little of that has been in manufacturing. This contrasts sharply with Hong Kong and Taiwan, whose investment on China centers on manufacturing.

[34] Kwan, *Econonomic Interdependence*, pp. 24–25.

trated a hierarchy of economies in close proximity to each other and the greater the diversity of economic conditions in the hierarchy, the larger the economies of concatenation because of lower transaction costs. . . . The point, therefore, is that industrial dynamism in the Asian Pacific de-rives from this highly *dense* concatenation of economies along the ladder of industrialization.''[35] With the elimination of major strategic, political and ideological barriers to China's participation in the regional economy, no world area, with the possible exception of the U.S.-Mexican border, offers a comparable combination of Ozawa's two conditions for regional development: hierarchy of industrial positions and proximity that are the bases for economies of concatenation.[36]

The character of regional integration has been shaped by significant capital flows, including loans, aid, and foreign investment, concentrated in coastal China. For example, China's growing trade surplus with both

---

[35] Ozawa, "Foreign Direct Investment," pp. 138–39. Building on the work of Kaname Aka-matsu, originator in 1935 of the "flying geese model," Ozawa has become the most eloquent contemporary framer of a vocabulary highlighting the view that Japan's economic advance is the sine qua non for the advance of the entire region and the driving force that assures others that they will replicate Japan's successes. Akamatsu's metaphor for Japan's rise was first ex-tended to the East Asian NIEs by Ippei Yamazawa and subsequently by Saburo Okita and Bruce Cumings who wedded it to product-cycle theory. Ozawa recognizes one of the limits of the flying geese metaphor: its assumption that followers, while advancing, nevertheless are destined to always trail the leader. He also offers a more upbeat picture, pointing out that Japan, which was once "a follower of the Western economies," "now flies more-or-less parallel to them." Such a perspective is surely more satisfying to NIE and Chinese policymakers contemplating their own future. Yet it misses the central weakness of the flying geese meta-phor for Asia in the 1990s: Japan's regional leadership is now severely challenged from many quarters, particularly from a revived China and expansive Chinese business networks. Ozawa occasionally becomes carried away with his own rhetoric, crediting Japanese multinational investors in Asia with a "Robin Hood effect," that is "robbing the rich in (in the advanced countries' markets) and giving to the poor (in the developing countries' labor markets)" a reference to his claim that Japanese electronic producers pay "relatively high wages, higher than the average local wages" (p. 141). Whatever the industrializing effects of Japanese trade and investment in Asia, and these are discussed below, Ozawa's claim of altruism is sheer ideological obfuscation. Lynne Guyton's searching examination of Japanese electronic invest-ment in Malaysia concludes that there is no significant transfer of technology and that the dependency relationship is maintained. See her article "Japanese Technology and Technol-ogy Transfer to Malaysia," in *Capital, the State, and Late Industrialization: Comparative Perspectives on the Pacific Rim*, ed. John Borrego, Alejandro Alvarez Bejar, and K. S. Jomo (Boulder, Colo.: Westview Press, 1996). The evidence for China and the NIEs, by contrast, is that they have advanced up the technological ladder, for reasons that include the nature of overseas Chinese investment and the role of the Chinese state.

[36] Ozawa's two conditions aptly capture important bases for East Asia's regional advance in the final decades of the twentieth century, but his model is only one of several that explain high growth. The growth of the European economy, with its more articulated institutional structure, includes a high volume of trade among nations in which the hierarchy of industrial positions is far less pronounced.

Japan and the United States in the late 1980s and early 1990s was in significant part a function of the transfer of Hong Kong's export-oriented industry to Guangdong, while Japan and Taiwan engaged in similar activity on a smaller scale in Guangdong, Fujian, and elsewhere.[37] In the 1990s, moreover, China has stepped up its own already extensive investments in Hong Kong and Macao, including those in banking, real estate, and infrastructure. Indeed, not long ago FDI in Asia was limited to Japanese, North American, and European investors; in the 1990s all of the NIEs as well as Thailand and China engage in substantial intra-regional investment. In many parts of East and Southeast Asia, including China, Thailand, Malaysia and Vietnam, the NIEs, particularly Taiwan and Hong Kong, have emerged as the largest or second largest investors with Overseas Chinese investors particularly active and frequently dominating local commerce.

In the early 1990s, FDI became China's single largest source of external capital as total new foreign investment surged from $4.7 billion (implemented value) in 1991 to $11.2 billion in 1992. Hong Kong, long the leader in investment in China, accounted for 70 percent of China's FDI total, with Taiwan advancing rapidly to challenge Japan for the second position. (Taiwan's role is far greater than is apparent in these statistics since much Taiwan investment is disguised as Hong Kong investment.) By 1992, 34,200 firms employed 4.8 Chinese million workers and generated substantial export revenues. New FDI in China rose to $25.8 billion in 1993. Since the early 1990s China has been the leader among developing nations in attracting foreign investment, far ahead of Argentina, the second place in new FDI among developing countries with $6.3 billion. China's cumulative FDI in the years 1979–93 was $60 billion (implemented), with $220 billion contracted.[38]

An important factor defining China's regional position is the character of its coastal and border areas as hinterlands for investment. While Japan

---

[37] Chung Chin, "Taiwan's DFI in Mainland China: Impact on the Domestic and Host Economies," in Lyons and Nee, *Economic Transformation of South China*, p. 237, estimates that by 1991 Taiwan had shifted $1.8 billion worth of exports of labor-intensive manufactures to the United States from its own trade account as a result of $754 million invested in mainland factories. A corollary effect is the increase of Taiwan exports to the mainland, providing machinery as well as intermediate inputs for these products. Pochih Chen, "Foreign Investment in the Southern China Growth Triangle," in Thant, Tang, and Kakazu, *Growth Triangles in Asia*, pp. 73–79.

[38] Lardy, *China in the World Economy*, pp. 63–64; "Investment Roundup, 1992–93," *China Newsletter*, March–April 1994, pp. 15–17; World Bank, *World Development Report 1995*, pp. 204–5. Hong Kong figures are inflated since they conceal investments from Taiwan, Japan, and elsewhere. FDI figures for China underrepresent Taiwan investment, but some of the spiraling numbers also doubtless represent Chinese enterprises sending money abroad to bring it back in the form of "foreign investment" to take advantage of tax and other breaks offered to foreign investors.

Table 9-7. Comparison of Japanese, U.S., Hong Kong, and Taiwan Direct Investment in China, 1979–1992 (contracted value in millions of U.S. dollars)

	Japan	United States	Hong Kong	Taiwan	World
1979–83	955	781	6,490*	-	7,926
1984	203	165		-	2,874
1985	471	1,152	4,130	-	6,332
1986	210	526	1,440	-	3,330
1987	301	361	1,950	100	4,391
1988	276	384	3,470	321	6,191
1989	440	645	3,160	102	6,293
1990	457	366	3,680	461	6,986
1991	812	548	7,510	1,389	12,430
1992	1,614	1,380	40,764	5,543	57,506
1979–92	5,739	6,230	72,594	7,916	114,259

*1979–84

Sources: Figures for Japan, the United States, and the world from Susumu Yabuki, *China's New Political Economy: The Giant Awakes* (Boulder, Colo.: Westview Press, 1995), p. 172; Figures for Taiwan and Hong Kong from Chung Chin, "Taiwan's DFI in Mainland China: Impact on the Domestic and Host Economies," in *The Economic Transformation of South China: Reform and Development in the Post-Mao Era*, ed. Thomas Lyons and Victor Nee (Ithaca: Cornell East Asian Series, 1994), p. 218. Also, "Investment Roundup—1992–93," *China Newsletter*, March–April 1994, p. 16. The totals for 1979–83 and 1979–92 are from Yabuki; those for 1979–84 are from Chung.

has held back from direct investment in Chinese manufacturing, Hong Kong and Taiwan have led the way.[39] Between the early 1980s and 1991, the number of factory workers in Hong Kong fell from 900,000 to 650,000 and the share of manufacturing fell from 42 percent in 1980 to 28 percent in 1990 as the service sector expanded. By the mid-1990s, the bulk of Hong Kong manufacturing had moved across the border, leaving only the most highly skilled manufacturing, marketing, investment, and financial sectors in Hong Kong.

Primary factors for regional investors considering China include the search for disciplined, low-cost labor, competitively priced land and utilities, and locations that permit the transfer of smokestack industries. Stated differently, the complementarity of the economies of Japan, the NIEs, the

[39] I have focused on the areas adjacent to Hong Kong and Taiwan, the major magnets for foreign investment. Other smaller but significant areas include the China-Korea, China-Russia, and China-Vietnam borders, and the area centered on the Japan Sea, some of which are discussed in the Asian Development Bank study, *Growth Triangles in Asia: A New Approach to Regional Economic Cooperation*, ed. Myo Thant, Min Tang, and Hiroshi Kakazu (Oxford: Oxford University Press, 1994), and in Brantly Womack and Guangzhi Zhao, "The Many Worlds of China's Provinces: Foreign Trade and Diversification," in *China Deconstructs: Politics, Trade and Regionalism*, ed. David Goodman and Gerald Segal (London: Routledge, 1994).

ASEAN countries, and China, with Overseas Chinese capital playing a leading role, is central to processes of integration that have transformed the regional economy. The attractions of industrial relocation across the Hong Kong border can be summed up in cost-factor comparisons for different areas of Guangdong, including the capital, Guangzhou, the Shenzhen Special Export Zone, and Dongguan, a Pearl River county. For example, in 1989, wages in Shenzhen were one-seventh those of Hong Kong and the price of land was one-eighth that of Hong Kong.[40] But rising labor, land, and infrastructure costs in Guangdong have already contributed to the shift of capital toward Jiangsu and Shanghai as well as further north to Shandong, Liaoning, and other dynamic coastal regions.

During the early decades of the People's Republic, China's borders effectively barred major flows of capital, trade, and FDI or, more precisely, a vigilant state sharply restricted and controlled points of entry. As Simon Long observed, "Viewed in the starkest terms, the coastline of Fujian is the informal ceasefire line in China's civil war," an observation that could equally be applied to China's long border with the Soviet Union as well as its borders with India, Vietnam, Mongolia, and others at various times. Such factors held back many coastal and border areas in the period of polarization.[41] Beginning in the late 1970s, however, most of China's sea and land borders became points of entry for technology, goods, and capital in the form of trade, loans, and investment flowing in multiple directions through myriad formal and informal networks. While attention has focused on the high-growth coastal centers of trade and investment, China's numerous inland borders have also been the site of thriving cross-border trade and investment involving Russia, Vietnam, North Korea, Mongolia, Burma, and Uzbekistan, to name a few.[42]

Taiwan, with the largest capital reserves in the region in the 1990s, and facing mounting labor and land costs, rampant environmental destruction, and other externalities that restrict further domestic industrial development, has invested heavily in Guangdong and Fujian in China and in several ASEAN nations. Taiwan government sources list $2.96 billion in 9,098 investments in the mainland by June 1993 with a recorded $2.2 billion of

---

[40] Chen and Ho, "Southern China Growth Triangle," p. 39.

[41] Simon Long, "Regionalism in Fujian," in Goodman and Segal, *China Deconstructs*, p. 203.

[42] *The Almanac of China's Foreign Economic Relations and Trade* (Beijing, 1993) provides provincial data documenting the flourishing of cross-border and coastal trade, though offering no indication of the scale of the thriving smuggling traffic. While Hong Kong was the number one trade partner with twenty-three of China's twenty-nine provinces and three municipalities in 1990, the trend has been toward increasing diversification of trade partners. Cf. Womack and Zhao, "Many Worlds."

this total in industrial enterprises.[43] The actual total is surely many times larger.

Since the 1980s, the export boom in China's coastal areas has been spurred by both Chinese and foreign investment and capital inputs. Guangdong's share of China's foreign trade grew from 6.6 to 23 percent in the years 1979 to 1991 as exports increased sixfold in value. Fujian's share grew from 0.9 to 3 percent, driven by a twelvefold increase in exports.[44]

Substantial portions of China's export boom in the 1980s and 1990s are directly attributable to the injection of foreign capital and investment or the activities of foreign corporations. Between 1980 and 1985, the share of China's total exports produced by firms with foreign investment increased from 1 to 12.5 percent and by 1993, with investments of more than $25 billion, they accounted for 27.5 percent of China's total exports. At the same time, by 1993, China's imports of machinery and transportation equipment rose to nearly 90 percent of the value of imports, much of it directed to foreign-funded enterprises. Substantial and growing portions of China's imports and exports, 17 and 18 percent by 1991, took the form of industrial processing of goods and raw materials provided by foreign enterprises. In sum, in sharp contrast to the early stages of import-substituting growth in Japan, South Korea, and Taiwan, high levels of foreign investment and injection of loans and capital have been instrumental in fueling China's export drive since the 1970s.[45]

Throughout the 1970s and 1980s, the amount of aid and loan capital consistently surpassed direct investment in fueling the rapid growth of Chinese local enterprises that have transformed the most dynamic coastal and some inland regions. This takes many forms, ranging from substantial loans provided by international lending agencies, particularly the World Bank and the Asian Development Bank, to government loans and aid provided by and coordinated by Japan, the United States, and Hong Kong, to commercial bank loans.

---

[43] Chung Chin, "Taiwan's DFI in Mainland China," pp. 215–42; Masao Hirano, "Recent Trends in Investment and Operations of Foreign Affiliates," *China Newsletter*, May–June 1993, pp. 2–3; Kozue Hiraiwa, "Foreign Investment in the PRC, 1990–91," *China Newsletter*, January–February 1992, pp. 11–14; Susumu Kohari, "Chinese–South Korean Economic Relations—An Update," *China Newsletter*, March–April, 1992, pp. 13–18; Hideo Ohashi, "The Economic Development of Fujian Province," *China Newsletter*, November–December 1992, pp. 8–19.
[44] Pochih Chen, "Foreign Investment in the Southern China Growth Triangle," p. 89; Wang Jun, "Expansion of the Southern China Growth Triangle, in Thant, Tang, and Kakazu, *Growth Triangles in Asia*, p. 157.
[45] Lardy, *China in the World Economy*, pp. 71–72, 108, 112–13.

For the decade 1979–89, China's foreign loans, totaling $78.6 billion, amounted to twice the contracted total of FDI ($37.3 billion) and four times the implemented value of $18.4 billion.[46] Hong Kong alone provided loans directly or as a syndicate center amounting to $9.4 billion. By the late 1980s, Hong Kong was responsible for providing or syndicating one-fourth of all loans to China and more than half the commercial loans.[47]

Loans and foreign investment have concentrated heavily in what the Asian Development Bank calls the Southern China Growth Triangle, particularly in Guangdong's Pearl River delta and in coastal Fujian, the zones that have experienced the most rapid trade expansion and the areas in which ancestral ties among overseas Chinese are strongest.

Japan was among the first to provide both loans and FDI to China in the mid-1980s. Nevertheless, despite substantial trade and loans, Japanese investors have held back from direct investment in China. By 1990 Japan had invested $2.5 billion in 691 projects; however, only 17 percent of this investment was in manufacturing, far below the 38 percent of Japanese investment in Asia as a whole.[48] Hong Kong and other sources of Chinese capital far surpass Japan's FDI in China as Japanese investors prefer to foster trade relations or provide loans and technology in selected areas such as steel and oil, but not cutting-edge technology in microelectronics or biotechnology. In FY 1990, for example, 72.9 percent of Japan's FDI was in North America and Europe. Of the 12.4 percent in Asia, the largest amounts were invested in the NIEs and ASEAN. These patterns have held to the mid-1990s.

In the 1980s and 1990s, China's reintegration in the East Asian regional political economy as a major recipient of capital and FDI and an industrializing nation carrying out institutional transformations conducive to further integration, has been pivotal in the restructuring of a regional economy intertwined with other nodes in the global economy.[49]

---

[46] Table 9-7 and Y. Y. Kueh, "Foreign Investment and Economic Change in China," *China Quarterly*, September 1992, pp. 682–83.

[47] Chen and Ho, "Southern China Growth Triangle," p. 55.

[48] Jian-An Chen, "Japanese Firms with Direct Investments in China and Their Local Management," in *Japan's Foreign Investment and Asian Economic Interdependence: Production, Trade, and Financial Systems*, ed. Shojiro Tokunaga (Tokyo: University of Tokyo Press, 1992), pp. 258–61.

[49] China's economic achievements, including institutional restructuring, are particularly striking when contrasted with the chaos and general collapse experienced by formerly communist Eastern and Central European nations. Cf. Mark Selden, "Pathways from Collectivization: Socialist and Post-Socialist Agrarian Alternatives in Russia and China," *Review* 17.4 (1994): 423–49.

Contradictory Dimensions of East Asian Regional Experience

How are we to comprehend the disjuncture between high growth rates sustained over several decades and China's low per capita income? Measured by the World Bank in terms of per capita GNP, China remains among the world's poorer nations. Indeed, after decades of per capita income stagnation, despite rising levels in the 1980s, the income gap between China and the industrial nations has continued to widen. These conundrums have important political implications, for example in U.S.-China sparring over whether China is a developing country in the context of her contested application to join the World Trade Organization.

Over the last fifteen years, rapid economic growth has been accompanied by substantial increases in food consumption, home building, and consumer purchases, ranging from television sets, bicycles, and sewing machines in the 1970s and 1980s, to washing machines, motorcycles, and refrigerators in the 1990s, all indicative of rising per capita incomes for a significant sector of China's population. Income and consumption gains have been widely if unequally experienced in all regions of China and by diverse social classes and ethnic groups. China has simultaneously made significant strides in reducing poverty.[50] The gains have been greatest in but are by no means limited to the coastal areas where advances in per capita income and consumption have been highest. A large disjuncture continues to exist, however, between low per capita income and high and sustained growth; between dynamic and stagnant regions; and between city and countryside, despite substantial rural gains.[51]

For all its explosive economic expansion, China's per capita GNP in 1991, by World Bank reckoning, was $370, narrowly edging India's $330 despite China's much higher growth rates over several decades. By comparison, Taiwan's 1991 per capita GNP was $8,815, Hong Kong's $13,430, and Japan's $26,930. Official figures indicate that China's richest province, Guangdong, had a per capita income of $527 while Shanghai municipality had $1,203 and Shenzhen City, China's richest, $2,306.[52] Part of the explanation for low per capita income figures (measured in U.S. dollares) is the declining value of China's overvalued currency, whose exchange rate dropped from 1.5 yuan per U.S. dollar in 1980 to 4.8 yuan per dollar in 1990 and 8 yuan per dollar in 1995.

---

[50] Zhu Ling and Jiang Zhongyi, *Yigong daizhen yu huanjie pinkun* [Public works and poverty alleviation in China] (Shanghai: Sanlien Shudian, 1994).
[51] For a discussion, see Mark Selden, *The Political Economy of Chinese Development* (Armonk, N.Y.: M. E. Sharpe, 1993).
[52] World Bank, *World Development Report 1993*, pp. 238–39; Ash and Kueh, "Economic Integration within Greater China," p. 744.

Some recent estimates, however, have suggested much higher incomes. A controversial 1993 IMF report concluded that China's economy was four times larger than previous estimates indicated. Other measures, particularly calculations based on purchasing power parity indexes, which evaluate such factors as life expectancy, food consumption, and infant mortality, yield 1992–93 per capita income estimates between $1,000 and $2,598, that is, three to seven times higher than World Bank calculations based on conventional measurement techniques. Nicholas Lardy's exhaustive analysis of the methodologies of more than a dozen studies involving purchasing power parity indexes cogently concludes that China's 1990 per capita income was approximately equivalent to $1,100, placing it in the ranks of lower middle income countries. This figure, three times the World Bank estimate, yields an aggregate Gross National Product of $1.25 trillion, ranking China above Germany as the world's third largest economy though less than a third the size of Japan.[53]

Like the NIEs, China experienced rapid industrialization from the 1950s onward; unlike them, however, in the 1960s and 1970s, China failed to advance in the world economic hierarchy as measured by the most widely used indicators of per capita GNP and GDP. In fact, by these measures, the gap between China and the richest nations significantly widened as a product of the striking disjuncture between high growth rates and extraordinary levels of accumulation on the one hand and low per capita income on the other that was characteristic of China throughout the collective era. Giovanni Arrighi rightly notes that industrialization alone is no guarantee of membership in the elite club of the rich, or what he calls the "organic core" of the world economy.[54] Nevertheless, industrialization set the stage beginning in the 1950s for China's subsequent rise by permitting advance along the scale of value added and labor productivity and by creating opportunities that subsequently bore fruit in a period of greater market openness and capital induction.

The literature on Chinese and East Asian development is littered with triumphalist flourishes. This chapter has also recorded significant regional economic achievements in terms of accumulation, investment, industrialization, trade, and per capita incomes. The sharpest critics of Chinese,

[53] Lardy, *China in the World Economy*, pp. 14–18. I have discussed issues of measurement including purchasing power parity comparisons in Jim Matson and Mark Selden, "Poverty and Inequality in China and India," *Economic and Political Weekly*, April 4, 1992, pp. 701–2.
[54] Giovanni Arrighi, "The Rise of East Asia: World-Systemic and Regional Aspects" (paper prepared for the conference "L'economia mondiale in transformazione," Fondazione Instituto Gramsci, Universia di Roma, October 6–8, 1994); Giovanni Arrighi and Jessica Drangel, "The Stratification of the World-Economy: An Exploration of the Semiperipheral Zone," *Review* 10.1 (1974): 9–74.

NIE, and ASEAN development point out, among other things, however, that these and other poor nations remain locked in positions of subordination to U.S. and Japanese capital, their high speed industrialization concealing the fact that the rich nations and the multinationals hold the reins of technological mastery and super profits. Critics rightly perceive the continued salience of hierarchies structuring the international political and economic order. And they note the high environmental costs associated with breakneck rates of industrial growth—an area in which China has led the world over the last fifteen years.

Bruce Cumings, in Chapter 4 in this volume, introduces an important qualification to the "flying geese-product cycle" development model he earlier pioneered; specifically, he now emphasizes the dominant role of "the real lead goose or the ceiling above which the regional formation does not fly." For Cumings, that "real lead goose"—in East Asia and globally— at least since the 1920s and down to the present, has been the United States.

Despite Japan's impressive technological gains, he rightly argues that (1) viewed comprehensively, that is, in terms that include strategic and political power, natural resources, cultural reach, and so forth, Japan is far from able to challenge U.S. hegemony; and (2) regional interpenetration and interdependence is far more likely in the short to medium run than autarky and the formation of antagonistic blocs or U.S.-Japan armed conflict. I challenge, however, an unexamined assumption concerning the flying geese–product cycle analysis that runs through his work over the last decade: that the result of FDI and regional economic growth throughout contemporary East Asia is a replay of the cycle of industrialization and system advance that Japan and the NIEs successively experienced.[55]

Bernard and Ravenhill have documented the fact that FDI-driven industrialization in the ASEAN countries differs in essential respects from the NIE model. Strong states, such as Taiwan and South Korea, pursued import-substituting industrialization and technological advance while sharply restricting FDI in the early decades of their industrialization as did Japan earlier. By contrast, rapid industrialization and trade expansion in contemporary Thailand, Malaysia, and Vietnam is driven by multinational corporations primarily through FDI. It takes place independent of industrial foundations in these nations, produces little or no transfer of technology, provides few if any backward linkages or trade benefits to local

---

[55] See Bruce Cumings, "The Origins and Development of the Northeast Asian Political Economy: Industrial Sector, Product Cycles, and Political Consequences," *International Organization* 38 (Winter 1984), and Chapter 4 in this volume. The critique that follows builds in part on Bernard and Ravenhill, "Beyond Product Cycles and Flying Geese," pp. 171–209.

enterprises, and the exports and imports generated by the investments are largely confined to the subsidiaries of multinationals.

A telling case in point is Malaysia's booming electronic industry, more than 90 percent of whose labor intensive production is foreign owned with nine Japanese electronic giants taking the lead in investments, which form part of regional networks for products whose final markets are the United States and Europe. These are trade-creating enterprises in the dual sense of inducing imports of semi-finished products and equipment and exporting the assembled products. But the trade, like the technology, remains almost entirely within the purview of the keiretsu network.

In the absence of effective state leadership, Malaysia is not building an electronic industry but is providing a portion of the labor that drives global electronic firms for whom Malaysia provides, at present, a source of cheap labor, land and utilities, tax advantages, and a means to circumvent import restrictions, for example, on Japanese imports into the United States and Europe.[56]

This suggests a basic flaw in the flying geese and product-cycle market with respect to much multinational investment in ASEAN manufacturing. Rather than technology transfer and the building of manufacturing industries with backward and forward linkages, these nations provide a convenient link in a keiretsu chain in which technological advance, marketing savvy, and high profits are all controlled from abroad. Finally, the multinational enterprises retain control over the manufacture and exports of the product rather than transferring that control elsewhere as the product cycle posits. In short, the pattern suggests new forms of dependent development that defy premises of the flying geese–product cycle paradigm. Yet I don't seek to replace this paradigm with a simplistic dependency model. In this chapter I have tried rather to grasp those situations and strategies that have permitted some nations, including Japan, the NIEs, and China, to advance even while considering the price of development.

This suggests a deeper flaw in the flying geese model. No single goose shows the way in contemporary East Asia. In the 1990s, in varying ways, China, Japan, and the United States each exhibit substantial strengths and potentials for shaping the future of Asian: the United States remains the dominant military-political power and the major market for exports; Japan is a financial and technological colossus as well as an important market; and China, the historic center of the region, is gaining strength as a result

---

[56] Guyton, "Japanese Technology and Technology Transfer to Malaysia," and her dissertation "The Organisation of Japanese Foreign Direct Investment in Southeast Asia: Implications for Regional Economic Development" (Ph.D. diss., Cambridge University, Department of Economics, 1995). See also Walden Bello and Stephanie Rosenfeld, *Dragons in Distress: Asia's Miracle Economies in Crisis* (San Francisco: Institute for Food and Development Policy, 1990).

of the imminent recovery of Hong Kong and Macao, its far-reaching economic integration of Taiwan, and advantages associated with the network of Overseas Chinese enterprise. The metaphor of a single pacesetter obscures the complex dynamics of the East Asia region in the era of integration.[57]

Further consideration of China's situation permits us to clarify the industrial outcomes in Malaysia and other ASEAN nations with developmental aspirations in the 1990s. Particularly important have been the role of the state and China's greater industrial strength, including the existence of its own heavy industrial foundations, a relatively comprehensive if inefficient complement of industries including electronics and its own (limited) research infrastructure. The direct reach and strength of the Chinese state has diminished to be sure in recent years with privatization of industry and agriculture, the surge of private and international capital into positions of strength in leading sectors, and the fiscal crisis of the state. It nevertheless retains substantial regulatory and organizational powers. While sharing certain features of the regionally integrated patterns described above for the Malayan electronic industry, China's prospects for achieving comprehensive industrialization and greater coordination of industries seem brighter, and the resources and technology of Overseas Chinese investors appear likely to play pivotal roles in the process.

Economic dynamism and the advance of East Asia should not blind us, as it has many economists, to the deep divisions and formidable problems that flow from China's growth trajectory and institutional choices. A short list of these would include the large rift between city and countryside, the twin problems of official corruption and soaring inflation (the combination that toppled the Guomindang in the years 1945–49 and that energized the democratic movement of 1989), horrendous environmental destruction and pollution of air and water, large zones of stagnation beyond the pale of the dynamic coastal and industrializing areas, a ruling communist party shorn of its ideology and confronting problems of legitimation even as it continues attempts to monopolize political power, the persistence of the mentality of control associated with *hukou* and *danwei* systems, and multiple ethnic and regional challenges to national unity. These constitute important elements of the dark side that is omitted from

---

[57] Giovanni Arrighi's striking formulation for the present division of wealth and power—"the United States in control of most of the guns, Japan and the Overseas Chinese in control of most of the money, and the PRC in control of most of the labor"—seems to me to understate important dimensions of Chinese strength, particularly in light of the integration of China, Hong Kong, and Taiwan, as well as the investment and trade interlocks of all of the above and Overseas Chinese capital. "The Rise of East Asia and the Withering of the Interstate System."

the celebratory literature of "economic miracles" that continues to cloak the subject of East Asian development in satin raiment.

Toward the Twenty-first Century

Since the 1960s, the U.S. decline as a hegemonic power has coincided with the rapid advance of an integrated East Asian economy with Japan and China at its center. In contrast with Europe, and even with North America in the NAFTA era, Asian economic integration has been little noted because it has occurred in a region with few formal political, security, and economic institutions. Informal networks have played indispensable roles. These networks, particularly those centering on China, involving the Chinese diaspora and cutting across borders in ways indicative of the growth of a cohesive regional economy, suggest resonances with Asia's historic tributary trade system and its associated business networks. The historic tension between the political-ritual concerns of imperial power in Beijing and the drive for autonomy and profit of other states and of business interests continues in the late twentieth century. Nevertheless, certain differences are equally significant. The integration of recent decades has taken place within a milieu framed by U.S. security, political, and economic initiatives, both multilateral and bilateral; and U.S.-centered security arrangements from bases to bombers continue to undergird regional cohesion just as international financial institutions fuel its growth. The political economy of the region in the era of integration cannot, in short, be encompassed by the geographical area designated as Asia but must be located within larger Pacific and global perspectives that have no regional precedent, while noting China's growing strength. Beijing's economic and technological weaknesses prevent it from defining or dominating the region at this time.

In contrast with Japan's attempts to build an autarkic regional bloc in the 1930s, and the bifurcated bloc structure of the 1950s and 1960s, the United States, while plagued with a host of problems associated with its declining global position and mounting social antagonisms at home, continues to play a vital regional role as a major trade partner, investor, and military guarantor for Asia. The evidence suggests that Japan, China, and many other Asian nations wish this significant U.S. presence to continue, not only because their prosperity hinges on the ability to tap the unrivaled richness of the U.S. market, but also as a check on a potential rival seeking to achieve regional hegemony. Nevertheless, in the 1990s, the most dynamic forces for regional change center in China, notably coastal China, in Chinese diaspora enterprise, and in Japan.

Three powerful dynamic forces, complementary and contentious, shape the region in the 1990s, each with unique strengths and resources: the United States, Japan, and China. The United States remains the dominant strategic and political presence globally and in East Asia. It is also the world's largest market and investment outlet as well as a source of capital and advanced technology. Japan and Japanese enterprises dominate the most lucrative sectors of the regional economy, but they face growing competition, particularly from Chinese interests, including those of China and the Chinese diaspora. Arrighi (and Braudel) have observed, in their analyses of half a millennium of historical hegemonies, that financial power tends to assume decisive importance in periods of hegemonic transition like the late twentieth century.[58] The explosive growth of its financial power brought Japan to the very pinnacle of world finance in the late 1980s and early 1990s as measured by the size of her commercial banks, foreign investments, and loans. In 1985 Japanese banks surpassed the share of international assets held by U.S. banks. By 1990 Japan held 36 percent of international assets while the U.S. share fell to just 12 percent. Although Japan's position subsequently weakened with the collapse of the "bubble economy in the early 1990s," in early 1995 the world's eight largest banks (and eleven of the top sixteen), were Japanese.[59] Similarly, Japan's total foreign investment of $67 billion in 1989 and $57 billion in 1990 easily surpassed that of the United States with a 1989 total of $41 billion, and they continued to grow in the early 1990s by approximately $15 billion annually.[60] Through large trading companies and financial institutions linked as keiretsu, Japanese firms dominate much of East Asia's intra- and inter-regional trade and compete vigorously at the highest levels of the global economy. Japan has accumulated enormous trade surpluses that make possible that nation's financial and investment power and the rise of the yen.

For all the strengths of the United States and Japan, the 1990s have been most notable for the regional surge of China, strengthened by the imminent recovery of Hong Kong and Macao and growing if fragile Taiwan-China links. In the 1990s China for the first time in this century can begin to challenge Japan's regional economic and political supremacy in East Asia. The growing strength of China pivots on powerful links with

---

[58] Giovanni Arighi, *The Long Twentieth Century: Money, Power, and the Origins of Our Times* (London: Verso, 1995), pp. 335–38.

[59] *Der Spiegel* 14, 1995, p. 122. Peter Katzenstein called this article to my attention.

[60] Guyton, "The Organisation of Japanese Direct Investment in Southeast Asia," p. 3; Phillip Das, *The Yen Appreciation and the International Economy* (London: Macmillan, 1993), p. 73; Alvin So and Stephen Chiu, *East Asia and the World Economy* (Beverly Hills: Sage, in press), mspp. 10–13; *Japan Statistical Yearbook 1995* (Tokyo: Statistical Bureau, Management and Coordinating Agency, 1994), p. 428.

Hong Kong, Macao, Taiwan, and diaspora Chinese capital—and the increasing regional presence of all of the above with their capacity for informal local, regional, and global networking. This resurgence of the Chinese nation and Chinese regional and global enterprise is at the heart of the political-strategic realignment of Asia in which, for the first time in the twentieth century, the United States finds itself in conflict with both China and Japan, and in which China-Japan tensions, and tensions between China and many parts of East and Southeast Asia, have risen sharply.

Conclusion: Regions in World Politics: Japan and Asia—Germany in Europe

PETER J. KATZENSTEIN AND
TAKASHI SHIRAISHI

Asian regionalism is a specific manifestation of a general phenomenon in world politics. The peace process in the Middle East, for example, is fueled largely by regional pressures, not by the intervention of major powers. The Russian project of reconstructing a sphere of influence in the "near abroad" of the Commonwealth of Independent States (CIS) is also driven by regional political factors. In Latin America a substantial decrease in political tensions and military expenditures is preparing the ground for sharp increases in regional economic cooperation. Finally, in Europe German unification has had a substantial effect on simultaneous moves toward both a deepening and a broadening of European integration.[1]

In this concluding chapter we explore the character of Asian regionalism in contemporary world politics by reviewing several of the book's empirical chapters from a perspective that stresses the interaction between global and regional processes. Then we draw out the implications of this book's central argument for Japan's position between the Sinocentric and the American world as well as for the swings between a maritime and a continental politics in Asia. We contrast Japan's and Germany's involve-

For comments and suggestions on previous drafts we thank Bruce Cumings, Richard Doner, Victor Koschmann, Andrew MacIntyre, and an anonymous reviewer for Cornell University Press.
[1] Unlike others, we are not interested here in analyzing the interactions between Japan and Asia on the one hand and Germany and Europe on the other. See, for example, Loukas Tsoukalis and Maureen White, eds., *Japan and Western Europe: Conflict and Cooperation* (New York: St. Martin's Press, 1982), and Gordon Daniels and Reinhard Drifte, eds., *Europe and Japan: Changing Relationships since 1945* (Woodchurch, Kent: Paul Norbury Publications, 1986).

ment in regional and global affairs since 1945, underlining the specificity of the present by contrasting it with the unsuccessful attempt of Japan and Germany to break in the interwar years with military means the international Anglo-American hegemony. Finally, we turn the analysis back to the role the United States continues to play in global and regional politics.

Globalization and Regionalism

Asian regionalism reflects a general trend in world politics that can be traced from Russia's "near abroad" to the Caribbean and Latin America, from the Baltic to sub-Saharan Africa, and of course in each of the three main economic regions: Asia, Europe, and North America.[2] Globalization

[2] For examples of regional analyses focusing on Asia, see U.S. International Trade Commission, *East Asia: Regional Economic Integration and the Implications for the United States* (Washington, D.C.: USITC Publication 2621, May 1993); Peter A. Gourevitch, ed., "The Pacific Region: Challenges to Policy and Theory," *Annals of the American Academy of Political and Social Science* 505 (September 1989); Richard Higgott, Richard Leaver, and John Ravenhill, eds., *Pacific Economic Relations in the 1990s: Cooperation or Conflict?* (Boulder, Colo.: Lynn Rienner, 1993); Kenichi Ohmae, *The End of the Nation State: The Rise of Regional Economies* (New York: Free Press, 1995); Stephan Haggard, *Developing Nations and the Politics of Global Integration* (Washington, D.C.: Brookings Institution, 1995); T. Keisei Tanahashi, *Asian Alternative for Regional Cooperation: A Quest of Asian Strategy for Globalization* (Bangkok: Institute of Asian Studies, Chulalongkorn University, IAS Monographs no. 048, 1992); and Soogil Young, "East Asia as a Regional Force for Globalism," in *Regional Integration and the Global Trading System*, ed. Kym Anderson and Richard Blackhurst (New York: St. Martin's Press, 1993), pp. 126–43. For the analysis of other regions, see Charles Oman, *Globalisation and Regionalisation: The Challenge for Developing Countries* (Paris: OECD, Development Centre, 1994); Organization for Economic Co-Operation and Development, Development Centre, *Documents: South-South Co-Operation in a Global Perspective* (Paris: OECD, 1994); Anderson and Blackhurst, *Regional Integration*; Vinod K. Aggarwal, "Comparing Regional Cooperation Efforts in the Asia-Pacific and North America," in *Pacific Cooperation: Building Economic and Security Regimes in the Asia-Pacific Region*, ed. Andrew Mack and John Ravenhill (Boulder, Colo.: Westview Press, 1995), pp. 40–65; Muthiah Alagappa, "Regionalism and Security: A Conceptual Investigation," in Mack and Ravenhill, *Pacific Cooperation*, pp. 152–79; *Asia-Pacific and the Americas: Reconciling Regional and Global Economic Interests* (La Jolla, Calif.: Institute of the Americas, University of California, San Diego, 1994); Carl Kaysen, Robert A. Pastor, and Laura W. Reed, eds., *Collective Responses to Regional Problems: The Case of Latin America and the Caribbean* (Cambridge, Mass.: Committee on International Security Studies, American Academy of Arts and Sciences, 1994); Ole Waever, "Region, Subregion, and Proto-region: Security Dynamics in Northern Europe in the 1980s and 1990s," Centre for Peace and Conflict Research, Working Papers 21/1990, Copenhagen,t Denmark; Miles Kahler, *Regional Futures and Transatlantic Economic Relations* (New York: Council of Foreign Relations Press, 1995); Iver B. Neumann, *Regions in International Relations Theory: The Case for a Region-Building Approach* (Oslo: Norwegian Institute of International Affairs, No.162, November 1992); Peter H. Smith, ed., *The Challenge of Integration: Europe and the Americas* (New Brunswick, N.J.: Transaction Publishers, 1993); Mario Carranza, "Regional Security and Economic Integration in Latin America and Southeast Asia: A Comparative Study" (paper prepared for the thirty-fourth annual meeting of the International Studies

and regionalism are not antithetical. Globalization is not an irreversible process, as some liberal economists insist, sweeping away the residues of resistance, be they national or regional. And with the end of the cold war the world is not breaking up into rival economic blocs as some neomercantilists have argued. Instead, globalization and regionalism are complementary processes. They occur simultaneously and feed on each other, thus leading to growing tensions between economic regionalism and economic multilateralism.[3]

Asian regionalism in an era of global processes is not new. Once we discard our unilinear and teleological view of modernization, we can see that regions are one important site where the contending forces of global integration and local autonomy meet. The conflict is not for or against the forces of globalism. It is rather about the terms of integration, and those terms are shaped by power relations, market exchanges, and contested identities of individuals and collectivities. In the past, evasion, resistance, and renewal have all been part of the processes that have made regionalism an important arena of world politics. In the words of Charles Bright and Michael Geyer, "Global integration and local autonomy were not alternative trajectories or possibilities, but parallel and mutually interactive processes. . . . Any interpretation of world history in the twentieth century ought to begin with a decisive emphasis on regionalism in global politics."[4]

Association, Acapulco, Mexico, March 23–27, 1994), and "Geo-Economic Regionalism in a Post-Sovereign World: The Future of ASEAN and the European Union" (paper prepared to the thirty-sixth annual meeting of the International Studies Association, Chicago, Ill., February 21–25, 1995); James Brooke, "In Latin America, a Free Trade Rush," *New York Times*, June 13, 1994, D4–D5; Sylvia Ostry and Richard R. Nelson, *Techno-Nationalism and Techno-Globalism: Conflict and Cooperation* (Washington, D.C.: Brookings Institution, 1995), pp. 20–26; and Daniels and Drifte, *Europe and Japan*.

[3] Robert Gilpin, "Economic Change and the Challenge of Uncertainty," in *East Asia in Transition: Toward a New Regional Order*, ed. Robert S. Ross (Armonk, N.Y.: M. E. Sharpe, 1995), pp. 16–18. For empirical evidence supporting this view see, for example, Kym Anderson and Hegge Norheim, "History, Geography, and Regional Economic Integration," in Anderson and Blackhurst, *Regional Integration*, pp. 45–46.

[4] Charles Bright and Michael Geyer, "For a Unified History of the World in the Twentieth Century," *Radical History Review* 39 (September 1987): 71. See also *Globalization and Regionalization: Implications and Options for the Asian NIE's* (Honolulu: East-West Center, Office of Program Development, 1994); James H. Mittelman, "Rethinking 'The New Regionalism' in the Context of Globalization," in *The New Regionalism and the International System: Implications for Development and Security*, ed. Bjorn Hettne (forthcoming); Jeffrey Hart and Aseem Prakash, "Globalization and Regionalization: Conceptual Issues and Reflections" (paper prepared for the annual meeting of the International Studies Association, Chicago, February 22–26, 1995); Anderson and Blackhurst, *Regional Integration*; Organization for Economic Co-Operation and Development, Trade Directorate, "Study on Regional Integration" (November 25, 1993); David Lake, "Regional Relations: A Systems Approach" (Political Science Department, Uni-

Global and regional factors are closely intertwined. This is very evident in the area of political economy. The increasing globalization and deregulation of markets describes an erosion of national economic control that industrial states in the North seek to compensate for through regional integration schemes. These differ in form. As Peter Katzenstein argues in the Introduction, regional integration can occur de jure (as in Europe) or de facto (as in Asia). And it occurs also in subregional groupings within and between states, as for example in Southeast Asia and along the South China coast. Economic regionalism thus is not only an attempt to increase economic growth or to achieve other economic objectives, but also an effort to regain some measure of political control over processes of economic globalization that have curtailed national policy instruments.[5] The economic effects of de facto or de jure regionalism can either help or hinder market competition and liberalization. By and large, the existing evidence points to the prevalence of trade creation and open forms of regionalism in the 1980s and 1990s.[6]

As a response to globalization, regional integration is attractive for a number of economic reasons. First, neighborhood effects encourage intensive trade and investment relations. Second, economic regionalization processes often do not require the reciprocity that GATT and its successor, the World Trade Organization (WTO), insist on.[7] Furthermore, the inefficacy the global GATT regime demonstrated in the 1980s and 1990s in addressing important economic issues acted as an additional impetus for regionalization. Third, at the regional level efficiency and competitiveness

---

versity of California, San Diego, 1995); Miles Kahler, *International Institutions and the Political Economy of Integration* (Washington, D.C.: Brookings Institution, 1995). Philip C. Cerny, "Globalization and Collective Action," *International Organization* 49 (Autumn 1995): 595–625. Michael Zürn, "Zum Verhältnis von Globalisierung, politischer Integration und politischer Fragmentierung" (University of Bremen, Bremen, Germany). Lothar Brock and Mathias Albert, "Entgrenzung der Staatenwelt: Zur Analyse weltgesellschaftlicher Entwicklungstendenzen," *Zeitschrift für Internationale Beziehungen* 2 (December 1995): 259–85. Beate Kohler-Koch, "Politische Unverträglichkeit von Globalisierung" (Political Science Department, University of Mannheim, 1995). The Group of Lisbon, *Limits to Competition* (Cambridge: MIT Press, 1995).

[5] Oman, *Globalisation and Regionalisation*, pp. 11, 35; Helen Milner, "Industries, Governments, and the Creation of Regional Trade Blocs" (paper prepared for the conference "Political Economy of Regionalism," Columbia University, March 24–25, 1995).

[6] Barry Eichengreen and Jeffrey A. Frankel, "Economic Regionalism: Evidence from Two 20th-Century Episodes" (paper prepared for the conference "Globalization and Regionalization: Implications and Options for the Asian NIEs," Hawaii Imin International Conference Center, August 15–17, 1994); Oman, *Globalisation and Regionalisation*, pp. 24, 81; Milner, "Regional Trade Blocs," p. 5.

[7] Gary Hufbauer and Anup Malani, "The World Trade Regime: GATT, Regional Cooperation, Bilateral Confrontation" (paper prepared for the Conference on Adjustment of Policies, Organizations and Firms to Global Competition, San Diego, Calif., October 2–3, 1992), p. 12.

are often strengthened through internationalized forms of deregulation, thus weakening directly the attraction of traditional, global approaches to liberalization while strengthening them indirectly.[8] In addition, the effects of regional economies of scale and savings in transportation costs can create dynamic effects that also accelerate economic growth.[9]

Furthermore, geographic proximity and the functional interdependencies and transborder externalities that it creates have favorable implications for regional economic growth. Geographic concentration of production is increasingly driven by the emergence of technology complexes and networks of innovation and production that offer essential advantages for regional agglomeration.[10] Technological development paths are contingent upon the actions of and interactions between developers, producers, and users who hold different positions and make different choices in the national and the global economy. Technological innovation thus is a discontinuous process establishing different trajectories in different parts of the world; the trajectories can cluster both nationally and regionally.[11] The supply base of a national economy—the parts, components, subsystems, materials, and equipment technologies, as well as the interrelation among the firms that make all of these available to world markets—can also cluster regionally.[12]

In the specific case of Asia, intra-regional trade has grown faster in the 1980s than extra-regional trade. Japan's trade with Asia doubled in the

---

[8] Richard Cooper has argued that optimal global or regional areas of economic jurisdiction have yet to be found for the provision of public goods such as economies of scale, stabilization policies, and externalities. See Richard N. Cooper, "Worldwide versus Regional Integration: Is There an Optimum Size of the Integration Area," in *Economic Integration: Worldwide, Regional, Sectoral*, ed. Fritz Machlup (London: Macmillan, 1976), p. 49.

[9] Detlev Lorenz, "Trends towards Regionalism in the World Economy: A Contribution to a New International Economic Order," *Intereconomics* 24 (March/April 1989): 64–70; "Regionale Entwicklungslinien in der Weltwirtschaft—Tendenzen zur Bildung von regionalen Wachstumspolen?" in *Perspektiven der weltwirtschaftlichen Entwicklung und ihre Konsequenzen für die Bundesrepublik Deutschland*, ed. Erhard Katzenbach and Otto G. Mayer (Hamburg: Verlag Weltarchiv, 1990), pp. 11–31; and "Regionalisation versus Regionalism—Problems of Change in the World Economy," *Intereconomics* (January/February 1991): 3–10.

[10] Detlev Lorenz, "Economic Geography and the Political Economy of Regionalization: The Example of Western Europe," *American Economic Review* 82 (May 1992): 84–87; Paul Krugman, *Geography and Trade* (Cambridge: MIT Press, 1991).

[11] Michael Borrus, "The Regional Architecture of Global Electronics: Trajectories, Linkages, and Access to Technology" (The Berkeley Roundtable on the International Economy, [BRIE], University of California, Berkeley, 1992), p. 2.

[12] John Zysman, "National Roots of a 'Global' Economy" (BRIE, University of California, Berkeley, November 1994); Michael Borrus and John Zysman, "Industrial Competitiveness and American National Security," in *The Highest Stakes: the Economic Foundations of the Next Security System*, ed. Wayne Sandholtz et al. (New York: Oxford University Press, 1992), pp. 7–52.

1980s. Between 1985 and 1993 Asia's trade deficit with Japan skyrocketed from $9.3 billion to $54.2 billion. At the same time Asia's trade surplus with the United States and Europe increased from $28 billion to $70 billion. Between 1985 and 1994 Asian countries ran a cumulative trade deficit of $390 billion with Japan, which they offset with a cumulative trade surplus of $370 billion with the United States.[13] The triangular trade pattern that these statistics chart so graphically reflect the growth of the new regional production alliances that Japan built in the 1980s and 1990s. The appreciation of the yen since 1985 has accelerated the relocation of Japanese production abroad. Japanese multinationals tripled their foreign output between 1985 and 1994 to 9 percent of total output, and by 1994 had captured over 25 percent of the Japanese import market.[14]

As a consequence of these developments Japan has established itself as the undisputed leader in Asia in terms of technology, capital goods, and economic aid. For Walter Hatch and Kozo Yamamura, Asia's growing dependence on Japanese technology is not a temporary phenomenon but "a structural condition that arises out of the complementary relationship between Japanese developmentalism and Asian 'pseudo-developmentalism.'"[15] In the words of Chung Moon Jong, son of Hyundai's founder and a member of the South Korean National Assembly, "It's not a matter of choice in Asia. That's a very hard fact to recognize. In terms of money and technology, the Japanese have already conquered Asia."[16] By design or inadvertently, the creation of structural economic dependencies in Asia is extending the life of Japan's embattled political economy, which is encountering increasingly vexing political limits to its further economic growth in the international political economy.

But it would be a mistake to focus only on the intra-Asian part of the story. For Japan and Asia are both also structurally dependent on the outside world, specifically the U.S. market.[17] Although the Japanese market has absorbed an increasing share of Asian products, in 1989 the United

---

[13] Walter Hatch and Kozo Yamamura, *Asia in Japan's Embrace: Building a Regional Production Alliance* (Cambridge: Cambridge University Press, 1996) p. 175; Michael Williams, "One Plus for Japan Isn't So for Trading Partners," *Wall Street Journal*, September 12, 1995, A22.

[14] Williams, "One Plus for Japan."

[15] Hatch and Yamamura, *Asia in Japan's Embrace*, p. 78.

[16] *Washington Post National Weekly Edition*, 26 February–4 March 1990, p. 8; quoted in Hatch and Yamamura, "Asia in Japan's Embrace," p. 40.

[17] For a very rich empirical analysis that traces both sets of structural dependencies, see Kozo Kato, "Uneven Interdependence: International Placement, Domestic Institutions, and Development Cooperation Policy in Japan and Germany" (Government Department, Cornell University, 1995), esp. chap. 3.

States took almost twice as much of Asia's exports ($94 billion) as Japan did ($56 billion).[18] And there exists no compelling statistical evidence that, since the early 1980s, an Asian economic bloc is forming.[19] Along all dimensions Asian ties with the rest of the world have grown. In the near future continued dependence of the Northeast Asian and Southeast Asian economies on the U.S. market militates against a relatively closed Asian economic bloc. Indeed, multinational corporations are likely to serve as powerful wedges to keep the economic doors of this region open.[20] Asian regionalism is thus marked by two intersecting developments: Japanese economic penetration of Asian supplier networks through a system of producer alliances on the one hand, and the emergence of a pan-Pacific trading region that includes both Asia and North America on the other. We can analyze this structure in the language of emerging production alliances more adequately than in the language of economic blocs.

In chapters 1, 6 and 9, T. J. Pempel, Richard Doner, and Mark Selden show the many connections between global and regional economic processes in Asia. Pempel gives a wide range of economic and social data illustrating the dynamic impact Asia has on the global economy and describes Japan's path as marked by a "transpacific torii" establishing simultaneous links to both Asia and the global system. Richard Doner's analysis uncovers some of the institutional attributes of public and private actors in Japan that help illuminate how Japan plays its role of regional coordinator and demonstrates how, because it occurs "from behind," Japan's style of leadership is mostly invisible.[21] Japan leads from behind not

---

[18] Vinod K. Aggarwal, "Building International Institutions in Asia-Pacific," *Asian Survey* 32 (November 1993): 1038; Stephen Haggard, "Thinking about Regionalism: The Politics of Multilateralism in Asia and the Americas" (paper delivered at the annual meeting of the American Political Science Association, New York, September 1–4, 1994), pp. 22–24; Michael Borrus and John Zysman, "Industrial Competitiveness," pp. 7–52.

[19] Different studies with different results are reported in Jeffrey A. Frankel and Miles Kahler, eds., *Regionalism and Rivalry: Japan and the United States in Pacific Asia* (Chicago: University of Chicago Press, 1993). See also Jeffrey A. Frankel, with Shang-Jin Wei and Ernesto Stein, "APEC and Regional Trading Arrangements in the Pacific," *Working Papers on Asia Pacific Economic Cooperation* 94–1 (Washington, D.C.: Institute for International Economics, 1994).

[20] Office of Technology Assessment, U.S. Congress, *Multinationals and the National Interest: Playing by Different Rules*, OTA-ITE-569 (Washington, D.C.: U.S. Government Printing Office, September 1993); Office of Technology Assessment, U.S. Congress, *Multinationals and the U.S. Technology Base*, OTA-ITE-612 (Washington, D.C.: U.S. Government Printing Office, September 1994).

[21] See Alan Rix, "Japan and the Region: Leading from Behind," in Higgott, Leaver, and Ravenhill, *Pacific Economic Relationships*, pp. 62–82. For other works along these lines see Marco Orru, Nicole Woolsey Biggart, and Gary G. Hamilton, "Organizational Isomorphism in East Asia," in *The New Institutionalism in Organizational Analysis*, ed. Walter W. Powell and Paul J. DiMaggio (Chicago: University of Chicago Press, 1991), pp. 361–89, and Giovanni Ar-

only in Asia but also in its relations with the United States, as well as globally.[22] And Mark Selden documents the great dynamism that China's economic growth has given Asia in the last decade and shows how this dynamism is beginning to have noticeable effects on world politics more generally.

The connection between global and regional politics is also evident in questions of national security. With the end of the cold war, the bipolar structure of international politics has vanished, laying bare processes that have important consequences for world politics. For example, most policymakers and analysts now agree that regional conflicts have replaced the global confrontation of two superpowers during the cold war. The implications of this change for the militaries of the major states remain unresolved. But the growing importance of regional conflicts has shifted attention to some extent away from military hardware to cultural factors as determinants of state interest that national security studies had all but discarded during the cold war.[23] These cultural factors are pulling in different directions, toward subnational, ethnic sentiments and different types of nationalism on the one hand and toward international and global standards of norm-observant state behavior on the other. In brief, on questions of state security, regionalism and globalism are processes that are closely intertwined.

Susumu Yamakage illustrates in Chapter 8 such connections by focusing his analysis on Asia-Pacific's regional security order and Japan's national security policy. He argues that Japan's hesitation in unilaterally articulating an explicit role for itself in the maintenance of Asian regional security has proven to be quite compatible with a number of Japanese initiatives in support of the institutionalization of a regional order in Asia. These initiatives have focused on both Japan's links to the regional activities of multilateral global institutions such as the World Bank (WB) or the International Monetary Fund (IMF) and its bilateral links to the United States

---

righi, Satoshi Ikeda, and Alex Irwan, "The Rise of East Asia: One Miracle or Many?" in *Pacific-Asia and the Future of the World-System*, ed. Ravi Arvind Palat (Westport, Conn: Greenwood Press, 1993), pp. 41–66.

[22] Peter J. Katzenstein and Yutaka Tsujinaka, " 'Bullying,' 'Buying' and 'Binding': U.S.-Japanese Transnational Relations and Domestic Structures," in *Bringing Transnational Relations Back In: Non-State Actors, Domestic Structures, and International Institutions*, ed. Thomas Risse-Kappen (Cambridge: Cambridge University Press, 1995), pp. 79–111.

[23] Peter J. Katzenstein, ed., *The Culture of National Security: Norms and Identity in World Politics* (New York: Columbia University Press, 1996); Peter B. Evans, "Regional Perspectives and the Transformation of Security Studies" (Sociology Department, University of California, Berkeley, SSRC/IPS Fellowship Program, September 1994). See also the project on security communities that Emanuel Adler (Hebrew University) and Michael Barnett (University of Wisconsin) are jointly organizing.

as the remaining global power. Japanese policymakers have worked consistently to connect these global political links with Japan's political contacts in Asian regional organizations such as ASEAN or APEC. Yamakage argues that Japanese security policy and Asia's evolving regional order derive not from a misplaced choice between a policy favoring the "United States first" or "Asia first" but from the intimate connections between Asian regionalism and globalism.

Global and regional politics are also closely linked in the sphere of culture. World regions are arenas for the cultural politics that emanate from the nations and states that constitute these regions. And they have discernible effects on the global system of which they are a part. Regions, Karl Deutsch reminds us, are the products of history, culture, and political economy that evolve over time. "It is the multiplicity of common cultural elements and links of horizontal and vertical communication and potential understanding that makes a region, somewhat as on a smaller but more intensive scale such links often including language, religion or way of life, can make a people."[24] Regions relate to one another in multiple ways that are far more complicated than the "clashes of civilization" that Samuel Huntington has analyzed.[25]

Victor Koschmann and Saya Shiraishi deal with such cultural processes in Chapters 2 and 7. In his analysis of the ambivalent legacy of Asianism Koschmann shows the close connections that in the twentieth century have linked different conceptions of Asia to the West. Conceiving of identities in relational terms, Koschmann argues, it is impossible to think of the one without thinking of the other. Without the West there is no East and vice-versa.

Saya Shiraishi focuses not on an elite culture sustained by intellectual discourse but on a mass culture carried by "image alliances." Japanese manga offer a form of visual narration that have created a dynamic cultural print and electronic product that has made deep inroads into several Asian societies. Chapter 7 belies the ethnocentric notion that Japan lacks cultural values and products that other societies can embrace freely. Shiraishi documents in Chapter 7 a remarkable degree of cultural innovation and pro-

---

[24] Karl W. Deutsch, "On Nationalism, World Regions and the Nature of the West," in *Mobilization, Center-Periphery Structures, and Nation Building: A Volume in Commemoration of Stein Rokkan*, ed. Per Torsvik (Bergen: Universitetsforlaget, 1981), pp. 51–93.
[25] Samuel P. Huntington, "The Clash of Civilizations?" *Foreign Affairs* 72 (Summer 1993): 22–49. For a nuanced view of the relationships between different civilizations, see Donald Puchala, "International Encounters of Another Kind" (paper prepared for the annual meeting of the International Studies Association, Washington, D.C., March 30–April 2, 1994). Puchala's preliminary historical inventory of possibilities includes, besides clashes, also absorption, hybridization, hegemony, rejection and resurgence, obliteration and genocide, isolation and suspicion, and cross-fertilization.

vides a detailed examination of the dynamics that have put capitalist expansion in the service of the creation of a mass market for manga in Asia. In addition she documents the more limited spread of manga into U.S. and European markets.[26] As is true of the other empirical chapters in this book, regionalization and globalization appear here as interrelated processes that cannot be analyzed in isolation.

Japan between Different Worlds

The crossroads at which Japan finds itself at the end of the twentieth century is marked by two world empires with very different political logics of suzerainty and sovereignty. Takeshi Hamashita and Bruce Cumings analyze in Chapters 3 and 4 the differences between the Sinocentric world and the American empire. At the end of the twentieth century the Sinocentric world, in Hamashita's analysis, is not a hierarchical structure of domination but a trading network. Its outer limit is economic not military. By contrast, the American empire in Cumings's analysis has a hierarchical structure of domination. Although the American empire has, by and large, facilitated a liberal international economy, its outer limit is military not economic. While the Sinocentric world is regional, the American empire is global. Takashi Shiraishi investigates in Chapter 5 how Japan is buying time while exploring the generous space for movement that the American empire has offered for advancement in the international hierarchies of power, wealth, and status. And, as Mark Selden documents in Chapter 9, Japan is beginning to engage tentatively since the mid-1970s the reappearance of an economically dynamic Sinocentric world in Asia.

These two international orders are producing different cultures. China's influence runs deep in Northeast Asia because its language provides the conceptual basis on which political possibilities are imagined and trade-offs are discussed. In Southeast Asia, by way of contrast, European cultural influences are strong, particularly at the elite level. Compared to the long tradition of the Sinocentric world, the "thin" global culture created by the United States is of very recent origin both in Southeast Asia and in

---

[26] On a humorous note, see Dave Barry, "Let's Defend Barbie against All Foreign Invaders," *Ithaca Journal*, March 29, 1995, 10B, which identifies a different "clash of civilizations" at the level of mass culture. Japan's Sailor Moon is seeking to make inroads into the market for the all-American Barbie. According to Barry, Sailor-Moon is a "licensed-cartoon-character merchandising concept" in the style of the vastly popular and profitable Power Rangers. For a more serious journalistic analysis, see Andrew Pollack, "Japan, a Superpower among Superheroes," *New York Times*, September 17, 1995, 32, and " 'Morphing' into the Toy World's Top Ranks," *New York Times*, March 12, 1995, sec. 3, pp. 1, 6.

Japan. Yet it can be politically consequential as it triggers different regional, national, and local processes while becoming indigenous. In the area of culture Japan thus also sits between worlds.

The centripetal and centrifugal pulls of these international orders have had a direct bearing on each other. The movement of the Sinocentric world from integration to fragmentation was accelerated, some argue brought about, by Western imperialism. The reintegration of this world through its economic network structures, through its cultural ties, and through politics is deeply affected by the integration of the international system and of Asia that has occurred on Anglo-American terms, first under the auspices of the British empire and since 1945 increasingly under the auspices of the American empire.

To understand the long-term historical significance of these two international systems for Japan's position in Asia, it is useful to recall Takeshi Hamashita's notion of Asia. He talks about maritime Asia, a series of seas extending from Northeast Asia to East and Southeast Asia, encompassing countries and regions, trading centers and subcenters, located along the Asian periphery.

It is important not to think of maritime Asia as non-Chinese Asia or inland Asia as China. The Kombaung dynastic state in upper Burma and the Mataram in central Java were as inland, inward-looking, and peasant-based as the Ch'ing, while the coastal regions of Southern China in the late Ch'ing and the KMT periods were as maritime, outward-looking, and trade-based as Bangkok in the same years. The fault line between Asia's maritime and inland zones shifted back and forth historically. Sun Yat-sen, for instance, mobilized manpower and money for his revolutionary cause from among Chinese in the coastal regions of Southern China and Southeast Asia when these regions were under British rule; Communist China pushed the fault line back to the Taiwan Strait, Hong Kong, and Macao.

Historically, China managed its trade with maritime zones through the tributary system. It did so not because it wanted to translate its attraction as a market into political and cultural hegemony. Rather China sought to prevent private trade, carried out for example by "Japanese pirates" (who were more Chinese than Japanese) in the Ming period, from upsetting the internal imperial order in China. Yet China's riches were beyond any doubt and its civilizational pull was enormous, especially on countries in its proximity. Chinese hegemony thus was felt unevenly—it was economic, political, and cultural in nearby countries such as Korea, Japan, and Vietnam, and narrowly economic in areas more safely removed from the Middle Kingdom, such as Siam and the Malay world.

In the course of the nineteenth century Britain's informal empire in East and Southeast Asia was built in this maritime region. British naval power colonized Asian seas. Reversing the outflow of silver bullion, opium provided the British with the means necessary to tap China's wealth. Opium also proved very useful to coopt "respectable" Chinese in British Malaya into the British trading networks and to exploit Chinese labor in the development of plantations and mines. A major institution of the British empire was the treaty port system. The most-favored-nation clause in the treaties the Western powers concluded with China underwrote the collective nature of that empire. The treaty port system took shape in the first half of the nineteenth century with the opening of a string of commercially and militarily strategic ports stretching from Penang and Singapore to Hong Kong, Amoy, and Shanghai. Britain expanded this network in the second half of the nineteenth century with the opening of new treaty ports along the Yangtze river and on the Yellow Sea coast, and with the construction of railways into China's interior. From this vantage point Karl Marx was correct when he argued that imperialism was progressive in Asia because it shook up the Asiatic mode of production. British imperialism brought Asia's dynamic maritime world deep into China's interior, thus undermining the traditional social fabric on which China's dynastic states had been built.

Although Japan had long been on the periphery of the Sinocentric world, Chinese dynastic rhythms affected it strongly. Hideyoshi Toyotomi was tempted to "conquer" China and make Japan the Middle Kingdom in the waning years of the Ming in the late sixteenth century. Tokugawa Japan "closed" the country when the Ch'ing rose, creating, not entirely unsuccessfully, its own managed trade regime both between Japan and the Sinocentric world and between Japan and its "barbarian" trading partners to the South.[27]

The creation of a British-led Westphalian international system in maritime Asia and the crisis of the traditional Sinocentric world formed the historical context for Japan's entry into the modern world. These historical circumstances created an emergency situation, but they also offered an excellent opportunity, as Takeshi Hamashita points out in Chapter 3, for Japan to become equal with China and to survive as a modern nation. Japan played a double game in Asia. It forced a treaty on Korea, stipulating Korean independence and thus ending Korea's existence as one of China's vassal states. Furthermore, Japan implemented the first industrial revolution in Asia. This not only made the country rich and strong, it also broke

---

[27] Hideyoshi's power was based on a coalition of western daimyos and partly on his control over maritime trade. Tokugawa Japan was based on a coalition of eastern daimyos which was more agrarian in nature. Tokugawa Japan turned "inward" because of the fear that an expansion in its maritime trade, especially with the rising Ch'ing, might complicate its domestic power base.

the economic and political dominance of Chinese trading networks. Japan's victory in the Sino-Japanese War demonstrated its success, as Japan's imperialism began in earnest with its full entry into the British-led treaty port system after 1895.

Still, this success was not without cost. It created a profound crisis of collective identity. Unequal treaties were imposed in the last years of the Tokugawa era, Japanese elites reasoned, because the Japanese polity was not sufficiently civilized for European powers to trust its judicial system. Japan wanted to be equal, not only with China but also with the Western powers. It craved recognition by Western states as an authentically modern nation. In order to do so, as Victor Koschmann argues in Chapter 2, the Japanese had to come to terms with their location in Asia and their reputedly Asian character, at least in the eyes of the West. Fukuzawa argued, Koschmann reminds us, that Japan could be a modern state only at the expense of its Asian identity. From this perspective, external expansion was part of being a healthy nation state, the vehicle of civilization and the vanguard of universal human progress. Japan's formal equality with the West was seen as a symbol of modernity, while its anti-Asian racism signified the rejection of the premodern.

Modernism and Asianism thus powerfully informed Japan's role in Asia. Military security was a paramount concern for Japanese elites. Japanese industrialization started with heavy industry. Military Keynesianism, supported by foreign loans, was crucial in Japan's industrialization. The war machine built with massive military spending was crucial for Japanese imperialism. After the Sino-Japanese War, Japan entered China's treaty port system. And it acquired its first colony, Taiwan, as a springboard for a southward move. After winning the Russo-Japanese War, Japan colonized Korea in 1911 and began to project its power into Manchuria. But these two moves met different fates. Japan was stopped in the South. Anglo-Chinese business coalitions in British-led maritime Asia were simply too strong for Japanese business to penetrate, as was illustrated in the 1910s by the bankruptcy of the Kanan Bank (South China Bank), a subsidiary of the Bank of Taiwan.

Japan's continental move in Northeast Asia met with less resistance, at least initially. With Russia out of the way, Japan defined its interests on the mainland as different in kind from those which informed the treaty port system in China. In China, south of the Great Wall, Japanese policy rested, for the sake of trade and investment opportunities, on an acquiescence to Anglo-American ground rules. In Korea and Manchuria, on the other hand, Japan aimed at establishing a military and political foothold that would meet its defense requirements, while also giving Japanese economic interests an advantage over all competitors. The rise of anti-imperialist

Chinese nationalism in the 1920s, however, threatened Japanese interests. When Chinese nationalist forces attacked the treaty port system, informal imperialism in China fell into a systemic crisis. In the face of Chinese nationalism Britain showed a willingness to accept the slow demise of the system. Japan, however, had a great deal more to lose. A widespread consensus about the "special" character of the relationship between Japan and China made the fate of the treaty system "an imperial issue" for the Japanese in a way it had not been for the British.[28]

The Manchurian Incident in 1931 and the creation of the puppet state Manchukuo the following year marked a new phase of Japanese imperialism. Its thrust was continental; and drawing lessons from both Europe's experience with total war and Soviet-style heavy industrialization in the 1920s, Japan embarked on converting Japan, Korea, and Manchukuo into an autarchic regional empire industrially strong enough to wage total war. The creation of Manchukuo was also a Japanese "answer" to rising Chinese nationalism. As Victor Koschmann argues, Japanese imperialist discourse conceptualized China not as a state but as a civilization. This notion of China formed a basic assumption for Japan's China policy: China by nature is disunified. Japan thus ignored Chinese nationalism and assumed that if China could survive the modern world at all, it could do so only with Japanese assistance. Manchukuo was presented as an experiment to create a utopian unity of five different peoples (Japanese, Chinese, Manchus, Koreans, and Mongols). Japan's Pan-Asianism was thus based on a reinterpretation of the Sinocentric world. Japan occupied its center; and the principle of suzerainty was couched in the language of the "kingly way" (odo) as opposed to "imperialist" hegemony.[29]

But Manchukuo turned out to be extremely costly for Japan, involving a huge transfer of financial resources and human capital to Manchuria without any commensurate payoff. It also made Japan the target of antiimperialist nationalism in China. Unable to break Chinese resistance, Japan was drawn into a wider, far more costly war in China south of the Great Wall. Manchukuo set in motion a process that ended in the collapse of the informal empire in China and led Japan into direct conflict with the U.S. Open Door Policy. As Takashi Shiraishi argues in Chapter 5, the Greater East Asia Co-Prosperity Sphere was conjured up in a moment of desperation when the Japanese empire was confronted with the bank-

[28] Peter Duus, "Introduction/Japan's Informal Empire in China, 1895–1937: An Overview," in *The Japanese Informal Empire in China, 1895–1937*, ed. Peter Duus, Ramon H. Myers, and Mark R. Peattie (Princeton: Princeton University Press, 1989), pp. xi–xxix; W. G. Beasley, *Japanese Imperialism, 1894–1945* (New York: Oxford University Press, 1987).

[29] Shin'ichi Yamamuro, *Kimera: Manshukoku no Shozo* [Chimera: A portrait of Manchukuo] (Tokyo: Chuo-Koron-sha, 1993).

ruptcy of its original strategic vision. Nothing demonstrates this point more clearly than Japan's schizophrenic strategic move from continental to maritime Asia, caused not by any real strategic vision but by an opportunistic bureaucratic deal between the army and the navy.

If prewar Japanese imperialism in Asia was schizophrenic—going both continental and maritime, aspiring simultaneously to be a modern state "on a par" with Western powers and to be "the middle" of the Sinocentric world—there was no room for schizophrenia after 1945. The Asia to which Japan returned was maritime and under U.S. hegemony. With the onset of the cold war in the late 1940s, this informal American empire was geared to the containment of communism, which by the mid-1950s had pushed back the perimeter of continental Asia to the border separating North from South Korea, the Taiwan Strait, Hong Kong, Macao, and the demarcation line between North and South Vietnam. America's informal empire was built not on treaty ports but on a string of bases from which the United States projected its military power to contain communist, continental Asia. In contrast to Britain's informal empire whose interests were primarily commercial, Bruce Cumings argues in Chapter 4, the outer limit of U.S. hegemony was military, not economic; however, within these limits the United States encouraged Japan and other noncommunist Asian states to develop trade relations among themselves and with the United States, with its huge market and with its enormous financial, technological, and ideological hegemony.

Japan benefited from its privileged position in the informal empire. Cumings points out, U.S. policy in Asia worked as a double containment against both Asian communism and Japanese militarism. Asia under U.S. hegemony provided the regional framework within which Japan pursued trade promotion and resource procurement. The United States's large military purchases in Japan and Asia as well as its military aid to other noncommunist Asian states functioned as a form of international military Keynesianism, which helped transform Japan's war economy into a civilian economy.

Postwar Japan shared in the American conception of Asia: "Free Asia," which included Japan, South Korea, Taiwan, and most significantly, the new regional concept of Southeast Asia (*Tonan Ajia*). Southeast Asia was conceptually more sharply defined than the prewar and wartime *Nanyo* or *Nanpo*, which often signified not only the area now called Southeast Asia but also Taiwan and South China. Japan's economic cooperation with South Korea, Taiwan, and Southeast Asia was the only politics postwar Japan understood in Asia. China remained important, but not for economic and political reasons. Given Japan's cultural identity and history, China was simply impossible to ignore. With the containment of China,

Japan simply did not have the choice, as it did in the prewar era, to make a major move on the Asian continent. Instead Japan implanted itself firmly in maritime Asia. Japan's new Asianism was to play the role of "leader of Asia," while moving safely in the orbit of the United States.

With the end of the cold war and China and Vietnam joining the region's dynamic economic development, Asia is no longer divided. With Overseas Chinese, Hong Kong, Taiwanese, Korean, and other capital driving the current regional economic dynamism along with Japanese direct foreign investment and the transplanting of its production system, as Richard Doner argues in Chapter 6, the current market-driven Asian regionalism cannot be understood in terms of a model that focuses on only one economic and technological leader, such as the "flying geese model." Overseas Chinese business networks are also important for the current surge of Asian regionalism.[30] Current economic developments in China's coastal regions result from the penetration of an economically dynamic maritime Asia back into China, as Mark Selden discusses in Chapter 9. The Asia to which Japan is "re-Asianizing" is maritime; it is not continental Asia, the traditional core of the Sinocentric world. "Re-Asianization" signifies Japan's search for accommodation between the two traditional international systems in Asia.

In a broad historical perspective, what is the current and future position of Japan in Asia? In retrospect, there is little doubt that U.S. hegemony and the cold war were of great benefit to Japan. Furthermore, China was closed in the 1950s and 1960s and remained economically marginal even after it opened up in the 1970s. And throughout maritime Asia, from South Korea to Southeast Asia, Asian governments staked their stability and legitimacy successfully on authoritarian developmentalism. Based on their own historical experience Japanese elites misunderstood this process as a politics of productivity fundamentally similar to Japan's postwar experience. They latched onto what in fact was an authoritarian developmentalism and sought to promote growth through "economic cooperation" to their own advantage, thus creating or expanding a triangular structure of foreign trade that links Asia, Japan, and the United

---

[30] For convenience's sake we use the term "overseas Chinese" business networks to describe complex business arrangements knitted together by ethnic Chinese living outside the People's Republic. But this does not mean that there exists a community of overseas Chinese stretching from China's coastal regions, Taiwan, and Hong Kong to Southeast Asia. Sino-Indonesians, for instance are as Indonesian as any *pribumi* Indonesian, and most of their business activities take place in Indonesia in politico-business alliances with Indonesian officials or foreign firms. But since Southeast Asian business tycoons of Chinese descent as well as Hong Kong and Taiwanese capitalists are major investors in China's coastal regions, in this sense "Greater China" can be usefully understood as being driven by "overseas Chinese" business networks.

States. Outside Asia, observers often note the tension that exists between global forces pushing for free trade and democracy and a region that tends to celebrate authoritarianism and managed trade. But this is not the view of Japanese leaders. They prefer instead to see contemporary Asian regionalism as a bridge to globalism and an arena for international cooperation. Japan's position in Asia thus is still understood best in the language of economics, in how Japan and other Asian states conceive of their short- and long-term interests.

As long as maritime Asia remains under U.S. hegemony, it is unlikely that Japan will challenge the United States directly. Though realists and liberals in Japan differ significantly on why things went wrong before the war, both have drawn the same lesson about the folly of Japan's imperial challenge to the Anglo-American international system in Asia. But there is a quiet fear spreading in Japan and elsewhere in Asia about the passing of an era, the slow but steady decline of U.S. hegemony and the reemergence of a hegemonic China. Meanwhile, as Richard Doner and Saya Shiraishi show in Chapters 6 and 7, Japan is expanding its influence and power by transplanting Japanese business networks and, more recently, internationalizing some of its popular culture. In short, Japan is seeking to create a larger room for maneuver between the two international systems in the maritime zone of Asia, which historically has been open to the outside world.

Asian and European Regionalism after World War II

A comparison with Germany and Europe may help us understand better how and why Japan is moving the way it does in Asia. That movement expresses the terms, often institutionalized differently, by which regional and global factors interact.

Allied Occupation of Japan and Germany

Allied occupation had profound effects on the evolution of Japan's and Germany's positions in Asia and Europe. Compared to the division and dismemberment of Germany by the victorious Allies, the U.S. occupation of Japan was less far-reaching. Japan emerged from the war with its central institutions substantially intact, its four main islands undivided, and its economy poised for growth once the Korean War made Japan an indispensable armory for the United States in Asia.

In 1945 Japan was placed under U.S. occupation. U.S. occupation policy was predicated on the assumption that Japan had been hijacked by militarists, and that a healthy process of modernization would start anew once Japan's social structure and political institutions had been reformed. The U.S. occupation authorities thus restored a conservative, internationalist political establishment to power and worked through the Japanese state to implement reforms.

The official policy focused on "three Ds:" demilitarization, democratization, and decartelization. The policy of demilitarization was highly successful, both in the short term and in the long. Japanese militarism became a thing of the past. The U.S. occupation dismantled the military machine. Although Self-Defense Forces (SDF) were created in its place, their constitutionality remained suspect. Under Japan's "peace" constitution and given postwar Japan's strong pacifism, the public distrusted and resisted any sign of "remilitarization." And throughout the postwar era a conservative political establishment remained strongly committed to the principle of civilian control over the military. Under the Japan-U.S. security treaty, Japan has relied heavily on the United States for its national security. Japan's military has thus become deeply penetrated by both international and domestic forces. It is now closely integrated into the US security arrangement in Asia and dependent on and subordinate to the U.S. military in a system essentially of U.S. making. The SDF are also penetrated institutionally by civilian bureaucratic forces with the Ministry of Finance (MOF), the Ministry of International Trade and Industry (MITI), the Ministry of Foreign Affairs (MOFA), and high-ranking police officials in strategic positions in the defense establishment.[31]

The policy of decartelization, in contrast, was much less successful. Apart from the military officer corps, the purge of "militarists" and "ultranationalists" conducted under the Occupation had a relatively small impact on the long-term composition of the Japanese elites in the public and private sectors. With the exception of the Home Ministry, in the civilian bureaucracy the purge was negligible. And with their former bureaucratic rivals, the military and the Home Ministry, out of the way, economic bureaucracies such as the MOF and MITI gained power under the postwar politics of productivity. Similarly, the purge disrupted only marginally the private sector. The holding companies of the zaibatsu were abolished. But with a highly concentrated banking structure left intact, the old zaibatsus reorganized around their banks in what turned out to be an even more effective business arrangement.

Japan's postwar economy also inherited as a legacy of the war years, in the words of John Dower, "tens of thousands of small and medium-sized

---

[31] Peter J. Katzenstein and Nobuo Okawara, *Japan's National Security: Structures, Norms, and Policy Responses in a Changing World* (Ithaca: Cornell University East Asia Program, 1993).

enterprises flourishing as sub-contractors and independent entities."[32] During the war, small entrepreneurs generally responded with strong support for the militarist government. In the process they developed effective networks of political and bureaucratic patronage. In the postwar era, they constituted the foundation for Japan's postwar high economic growth, and LDP politicians successfully cultivated their support.[33]

Finally, the policy of democratization was successful in institutionalizing electoral politics, the protection of human rights and civil liberties, and the relegation of the emperor to the status of a "symbol" of the State and of the unity of the people. Land reform under the U.S. occupation dismantled the power structure in the countryside. If postwar West Germany saw the rise of Christian and social democracy, it was productivity democracy that emerged in postwar Japan. Its economic growth achieved social peace and prosperity under the conservative coalition of the civilian bureaucracy, business and finance, and the LDP. Over time, however, this productivity democracy transformed itself into a brokered democracy and money politics led to deepening corruption.[34] The collapse of the LDP rule in 1993 was due largely to the public's rejection of money politics; and the public demonstrated its deep distrust in the entire system of brokered democracy once again in the 1995 election of two comedians as governors of Tokyo and Osaka.

In 1945 Allied occupation of Germany aimed at a far-reaching change in the country's social structure and political institutions.[35] Roosevelt's liberal and Stalin's Marxist analysis of the roots of the Nazi regime were consonant. The social and psychological failings of German society and the Germans were the prime causes of the triumphant totalitarianism of the Nazi regime. As the cold war began to drive the victorious Allies apart, imperceptibly in 1945, visibly in 1946–47, and decisively in 1948, the Soviet Union in the East and the United States, as well as Britain and France, in the West went about the business of remaking Germany and the Germans.

The economic and political position of the German aristocracy was, for all intents and purposes, eliminated by Soviet policy and the division of

---

[32] John Dower, "The Useful War," in *Japan, War and Peace: Selected Essays* (New York: New Press, 1993), p. 18.

[33] Ibid. See also Kent E. Calder, *Crisis and Compensation: Public Policy and Political Stability in Japan, 1949–1986* (Princeton: Princeton University Preess, 1988), pp. 312–48.

[34] Shin'ichi Kitaoka, *Kokusai-ka Jidai no Seiji Shido* [Political leadership in the age of internationalization] (Tokyo: Chuo-Koron-sha, 1990), especially chap. 6, "Hokatsu Seito no Gorika: 70-nendai no Jiminto" [Rationalizing the catch-all party: The LDP in the 1970s]).

[35] John Montgomery, *Forced to Be Free: The Artificial Revolution in Germany and Japan* (Chicago: University of Chicago Press, 1957); Charles Maier, "The United States and the German Political Economy, 1945–49" (Lehrmann Institute, New York, January 1976).

the country. Furthermore through a series of far-reaching reforms, including in the education system as a key institution of Germany's traditional social stratification, the communist government in East Berlin, under Soviet tutelage, effected a substantial change in East German social structure. The Western allies were less drastic in dealing with the structure of German society. But defeat and the division of the country meant that after 1949 the traditional centers of German politics, the military and the aristocracy, did not play a political role in West Germany either. Furthermore, the Nazi regime had delegitimated the extreme Right; and the communist Left was held politically in check by the barbed wire with which it had encircled itself in the East. The political effects of the occupation in West Germany, if for different reasons, thus were no less dramatic than in the eastern part of the country.

The official policy of the Western Allies worked in the same direction, although with results that were less clear. That policy focused on "four Ds" of reeducation: demilitarization, denazification, decartelization, and democratization. The first of these four policies was an unmitigated success, both in the short and in the long term. German militarism became a thing of the past. Over time Germany's military emerged more fully internationalized than the military of virtually any other major state; and German society shed its traditional reverence for the military as a special state institution. Instead, the military has become a normal institution, tamed by the democratizing influence of conscription and the leveling influence of professionalization.

Denazification and decartelization were, at best, mixed successes. The Nuremberg trial and speedy prosecution of a small number of the top leaders of the Nazi regime gave way to the slow processing of millions of Germans who had been implicated in the regime as ordinary Nazis. They resented deeply a victor's justice that persecuted the "little" fishes while leaving many of the "big" ones unharmed. The reeducation policies of the occupation did little to change the composition of German elites in the bureaucracy, business, the professions, sciences, and the arts. Similarly, decartelization, though moderately successful in some industries such as chemicals, by and large did little to change the basic structure of the German economy. By the mid-1950s German business leaders and politicians had rolled back or adapted the structural reforms that the Allies had introduced to fit either traditional patterns or the requirements of Germany's economic miracle in a liberalizing international economy.

Finally, by all conventional measures the policies of the Western Allies were spectacularly successful in institutionalizing electoral competition, the protection of civil liberties, and the rule of law. The process of democratization was formalistic in the 1950s when a "without-me" generation, disillusioned by the excesses and horrors of the Nazi regime, shunned political involvement. But from the mid-1960s on generational and political change brought an invigoration of political participation that saw a flourishing of local and social-movement politics in the 1970s and 1980s to complement vigorous electoral competition at the federal level. In brief, Allied occupation had a profound and lasting effect on German politics.

Japan's and Germany's Position in the American Empire

The U.S. grand strategy of containment centered on securing both Germany and Japan, and thus Western Europe and much of Asia, from communist inroads. Until the late 1950s Europe held center stage as the cold war divided Germany and the continent and provided in Berlin a possible flashpoint threatening to ignite World War III. Between the early 1960s and the mid-1970s it was the U.S. escalation of and defeat in the Vietnam War that was most important. Since the late 1970s the United States has used its reduced influence to remain engaged both in Asia (focusing on Japan and the People's Republic of China) and in Europe (with particular attention to the framework for Western security).

Japan's position in the American empire was one of geostrategic strength, which gave the postwar conservative coalition useful political leverage. While cold war divisions were played out in German livingrooms, Korea, not Japan, was (and still remains) divided. Japan as "the workshop of Asia" and the logistical base for the U.S. military, was a bystander in a cold war fought elsewhere. Furthermore, Japan's conservative coalition welcomed the double containment of Asian communism and Japanese militarism.

The organization of Japanese defense reflected these realities. The U.S.-Japan security treaty formed, and still forms, the foundation for Japanese defense. Japan's security is guaranteed by the U.S. nuclear umbrella in exchange for granting the U.S. permission to operate military bases in Japan. Japan's SDF were created under the occupation. But Prime Minister Shigeru Yoshida successfully resisted in the early 1950s a military buildup insisted on by Secretary of State John Foster Dulles. The "Yoshida line" held that Japan should not play any military role in Asia, and that national defense expenditure should be kept to a minimum. This line was kept well into the 1970s. And in the mid-1990s the SDF still do not play a significant regional security role in Asia.

Dependence on U.S. protection, however, meant that Japan remained a semi-sovereign state. Its defense forces are fully integrated into the U.S. military. Loosely speaking, the United States became part of Japan's ruling conservative coalition in the form of the politics of *gaiatsu* (external pressure). In the 1970s and 1980s, the United States compelled Japan to link economics and politics with security. When Japan redefined its strategic posture in 1976, the military component of defense became important for the first time. U.S. pressure and Japanese interest in continued access to U.S. markets made this concession to the United States a foregone conclusion; however, Japan's idea of "comprehensive security" underscored the point that a substantial military buildup was not in the cards. There was no real inclination to make Japan into a "normal" state. This continues to be the case two decades later in the mid-1990s.

At the same time, Japan benefited enormously from the liberalization of the international economy that the United States brought about in the 1950s and 1960s and the ready access Japan had to U.S. markets. Political and economic cooperation with the United States provided the basis for Japan's economic growth at a time when Japan had lost its former empire and was cut off from the China market.

"The workshop of Asia" was a second, fundamental cornerstone defining Japan's position in the American empire. To prevent Japan from being enticed to explore Chinese markets, as Bruce Cumings argues in Chapter 4, the United States encouraged economic cooperation between Japan and other noncommunist Asian states and promoted the development of triangular trade relations in Asia-Pacific. Since it promised economic growth, Japan embraced this U.S. initiative wholeheartedly.[36] Triangular trade relations, combined with Japan's increasingly transnational product cycle and industrial transformation, drove Asian regionalism. Japanese economic interests were, and continue to be, served best by linking Asian regionalism with globalism.

The prima facie case for the growing importance of regional forces in Asia is strong also for the security issues that Susumu Yamakage analyzes in Chapter 8. In this instance as well, the case for an open rather than a closed form of regionalism is compelling. Militarily Asia is unlikely to become a self-contained region.

In sum, throughout the postwar years, Japan's position in the American empire has been firmly located in Asia, linking globalism with regionalism. There is no incentive for Japan to depart from this system, let alone "to go continental" and to be sucked into the Chinese orbit. Furthermore,

---

[36] William S. Borden, *The Pacific Alliance: U.S. Foreign Economic Policy and Japanese Trade Recovery, 1947–1955* (Madison: University of Wisconsin Press, 1984); Michael Schaller, *The American Occupation of Japan: The Origins of the Cold War in Asia* (New York: Oxford University Press, 1985); Andrew J. Rotter, *The Path to Vietnam: Origins of the American Commitment to Southeast Asia* (Ithaca: Cornell University Press, 1987); Sayuri Shimizu, "Creating People of Plenty: The United States and Japan's Economic Alternatives, 1953–1958" (Ph.D. diss., Cornell University, 1991).

this position has become institutionalized in Japan's defense organization, political institutions, and business arrangements. Admittedly, over time Asia has come to carry increasing weight in Japan's foreign policy. And the process of Japan's "re-Asianization" will proceed, given the increasing importance of Asian regionalism in political, economic, and cultural terms. But only major crises in international and domestic politics will put the notion in doubt that Japan should maintain its "special" relations with the United States and its Asian partners.

Germany's position in the American empire was one of geostrategic weakness masking political strength.[37] The weakness was self-evident in a country divided at the outset of the cold war and transformed by a conflict between the two superpowers. Hundreds of foreign bases on German territory, thousands of nuclear warheads poised to strike German targets, and hundreds of thousands of foreign soldiers represented two military alliances that had the express purpose of defending themselves against each other while observing tacitly the dictum: if you hold down your Germans, we will hold down ours.

The harsh realities of geography and military strategy were reflected in the organization of West Germany's defense. Chancellor Konrad Adenauer maneuvered the Federal Republic back into international life by linking its rearmament to the regaining of sovereignty. But the West German military remained under NATO command in times of both peace and war. De jure and de facto West Germany thus remained a semi-sovereign state.

At the same time West Germany benefited immensely from the liberalization of the international economy that the United States brought about in the 1950s and 1960s through successive rounds of tariff cutting and gradual moves to the free convertibility of currencies. A liberal international economy was essential for a divided country that relied on a strategy of export-led growth to pay for the import of foodstuffs no longer available from traditional sources in the eastern half of the country and which the cold war had cut off from its trading partners in Central and Eastern Europe.

European integration through the European Economic Community (EEC) and its successor organizations was the second, essential cornerstone defining Germany's position in the American empire. Since the United States was an active champion of European integration, West Germany embraced a deep rapprochement with France as the cornerstone of

---

[37] Charles S. Maier, "The Politics of Productivity: Foundations of American International Economic Policy after World War II," in *Between Power and Plenty: Foreign Economic Policies of Advanced Industrial States*, ed. Peter J. Katzenstein (Madison: The University of Wisconsin Press, 1978), pp. 23–50; David P. Calleo, *Beyond American Hegemony: The Future of the Western Alliance* (New York: Basic Books, 1987).

its active and consistent support of European integration. It did so without succumbing to the Gaullist temptation of seeking security and markets in a Europe stretching "from the Ural mountains to the Atlantic." During the cold war the vital security interests of the Federal Republic and the exposed position of Berlin would have made a policy designed to distance the United States from Europe plain folly. And West German economic interests were served best not by a privileged access to European markets but by free access to global markets.

West Germany's position in the American empire before 1989 and Germany's position since 1990 have created powerful incentives for the country's continuing inability to choose between the United States and Europe. And that inability became unwillingness as international constraints became internalized in German domestic politics. Over time, and especially since the achievement of unification in 1990, the relative weight of the European element in German foreign policy has undoubtedly increased. But only large-scale upheavals in international and domestic politics could uproot the notion, collectively held by the German political class, that Germany must maintain good relations with both the United States and its major European partners, especially France.

As integral parts of the informal American empire Japan and Germany occupy different positions. "The Atlantic Alliance paradigm and the American Century," writes James Kurth, "entered into their historic moment through the Pacific War. The Pacific Basin paradigm and the Pacific Century will enter into their historical moment only if the Pacific Basin remains pacific."[38] Notwithstanding their differences in social and political coalitions, domestic institutions, and political strategies, both Germany and Japan are drawn powerfully to their respective regions without sacrificing their simultaneously intensifying links to the global system. This offers strong testimony to the enduring effects that the United States has exercised on these two polities both directly as an occupying power and indirectly as a hegemonic state.

The Regional Positions of Japan and Germany in Asia and Europe

Influenced by their different experiences under Allied occupations and different positions in the American empire, Japan's and Germany's position in Asia and Europe also differ. A relative equality in state power and

---

[38] James R. Kurth, "The Pacific Basin versus the Atlantic Alliance: Two Paradigms of International Relations," *Annals of the American Academy of Political and Social Science* 505 (September 1989): 45.

strong collective norms of democracy in Europe have facilitated an institutionalized integration process that has embedded Germany firmly in Europe. Sharp differences in relative state power and the absence of region-wide political norms have worked against a far-reaching institutionalization of Asian regional integration and thus left Japan more isolated politically.

The distribution of power in the international system is a good starting point for seeking to understand the distinctiveness of Japan's and Germany's positions in the two regions.[39] In 1990 German GDP amounted to only one-quarter of the GDP of the EC while Japanese GDP came to about three-quarters of the combined GDP of the EAEC members.[40] Germany accounted for 20 percent of the exports from its European trade partners in 1990, a slight increase from 19 percent in 1970. The corresponding figures for Japan were 14 percent in 1990, a 2 percent decrease since 1970.[41] Since the Treaty of Rome determined in 1957 that trade was one of three policy sectors to be governed by supranational decision-making in Brussels, the higher German figures indicate a far-reaching institutional integration of Germany with Europe in this important policy sector. Furthermore, compared to the stability of the European balance of power, the dynamic growth of Japanese power, compared to that of other states in the region, has led to rapid changes in the Asian balance. As a percentage of the EC's GDP Germany's declined from 27 to 25 percent between 1970 and 1990; Japan's GDP, as a share of the EAEC's, increased from 57 to 73 percent. And compared to Asia European economic equality is striking. The per capita GDP of the wealthier states in the EC exceeded the income in the poorer states by a factor of three in both 1970 and 1990; in the EAEC the corresponding figures increased from nine to twenty-nine. Finally, in Europe France has been able to hold its own against Germany in intra-EC trade during the last three decades while losing some ground to Germany in extra-EC trade; Japan's followers have not done as well in East Asia.[42]

Furthermore, a number of economic background conditions, not investigated further here, have also worked for closer ties between Germany and Europe than exist between Japan and Asia. For example, extra-

[39] Aggarwal, "Building International Institutions in Asia-Pacific," pp. 1029–42; Haggard, "Thinking about Regionalism," pp. 39–40.
[40] Joseph M. Grieco, "Variation in Regional Economic Institutions in Western Europe, East Asia and the Americas: Magnitude and Sources" (Political Science Department, Duke University, 1994), pp. 20–22 and table 2.
[41] Ibid., pp. 22–24 and table 3.
[42] Ibid., pp. 30–36 and tables 7–9.

regional Asian trade, especially with the United States, is a much larger percentage of total trade than is true of Europe.[43] And along a number of different economic dimensions Asian regionalism is marked by conditions of asymmetric dependence that contrast with the conditions of symmetric interdependence characteristic of European regionalism.[44]

Norms of collective identity are a second major factor that also work for closer ties between Germany and Europe than exist between Japan and Asia. According to a Carnegie Endowment Study Group, in contrast to the democracies in Western Europe, Asian polities continue to represent a wide political spectrum "from Communism to Confucianism, from constitutional monarchies to military dictatorships, from personalized rule to bureaucratic governance, from democratically elected governments to single-party rule."[45] Between 1975 and 1986 Asian states that subsequently joined the EAEC and APEC did not experience any significant progress in overall democratization. This is in striking contrast to the democratization processes in Spain, Portugal, and Greece and the southern enlargement of the EC during the same decade.[46] Furthermore, in the 1990s the Central European states seeking admission to the EU during the next round of enlargement have made spectacular progress toward the institutionalization of democracy; no comparable developments have been reported from the People's Republic of China, North Korea, Vietnam, and Indonesia. And social crises have deepened in the Philippines despite a political transition to the form, if not the substance, of democracy. When the colonels staged a coup d'etat in 1967, Greece withdrew from the Council of Europe to avoid inevitable suspension. The enthusiasm for Asia's market-driven process of integration in the 1990s does not permit this kind of politics.

European integration was built around a German-French rapproche-

---

[43] Per Magnus Wijkman and Eva Sundkvist Lindstroem, "Pacific Basin Integration as a Step towards Freer Trade," in *Towards Freer Trade between Nations*, ed. John Nieuwenhuysen (Melbourne: Oxford University Press, 1989), pp. 152–60.

[44] Alan Siaroff, "Interdependence versus Asymmetry? A Comparison of the European and Asia-Pacific Economic Regions" (paper presented at the ISA-West meetings, Seattle, October 14–15, 1994). This generalization is based on seven empirical indicators: total population, GDP per capita, total GDP, stock of foreign investment, hosting of multinational corporations, total external assets or debts, and research and development spending.

[45] Carnegie Endowment Study Group, *Defining a Pacific Community* (New York: Carnegie Endowment for International Peace, 1994), p. 14.

[46] Grieco, "Variation in Regional Economic Institutions," pp. 28–30 and table 6; Kiichi Fujiwara, "Governmental Parties: Political Parties and the State in North- and Southeast Asia" (paper prepared for the International Political Science Association [IPSA] Roundtable, Kyoto, March 26–27, 1994). For a related discussion looking at the data for the Americas and East Asia, see Haggard, "Thinking about Regionalism," pp. 40–66.

ment that has no equivalent in Asia. To date Japan has proven unable to achieve a deeper reconciliation with its neighbors, especially China. The strength of democratic institutions, relative equality in size, and relative political homogeneity, organized around a model of the continental welfare state, have facilitated formal institutional integration in Europe. Conversely, the same factors have worked against such integration in Asia.

Power and norms both point to a distinctive Asian form of regional integration which is network-like and inclusive rather than formal and exclusive as in Europe. That difference, analyzed by Katzenstein in the Introduction, positions Germany and Japan differently in the two regions. Germany is institutionally more deeply embedded in Europe than Japan is in Asia.

Changing Trading States

Under the tutelage of the American empire, the protection it offered, and the markets it opened, Japan and Germany have emerged as highly successful trading states.[47] Exploiting the advantages of adversity rather than the disadvantages of dominance Japan and Germany have prospered in international markets. They embody institutional logics that differ from the liberal version of capitalism typified by the United States and Britain. Power in both states is held firmly by social forces and political coalitions that favor international strategies over nationalist ones and which are deeply committed to the commercial and welfare mission these two states pursue. This commonality notwithstanding, Japan and Germany embody different institutional logics of capitalism. Although they embrace market competition, the terms by which players enter markets, the rules of competition, and the social purposes that competition is to serve, all reflect different norms embodied in different institutions and organizational routines. These differences help explain the pattern of cooperation and conflict between the United States and the former Axis powers now competing in a liberalizing international economy.

Japan's political economy is brokered by conservative interests in a manner that supports markets while controlling "excessive" competition and promoting a pro-business conception of the national interest. Although it was transformed from a war to a civilian economy in the postwar era, the

---

[47] Richard Rosecrance, *The Rise of the Trading State: Commerce and Conquest in the Modern World* (New York: Basic Books, 1986); Jeffrey E. Garten, *A Cold Peace: America, Japan, Germany, and the Struggle for Supremacy* (New York: Random House, Times Books, 1992); Jeffrey T. Bergner, *The New Superpowers: Germany, Japan, the U.S., and the New World Order* (New York: St. Martin's Press, 1991).

Japanese economy inherited many of the institutions that had evolved during the "fifteen years" war.[48]

The institutional and "human capital" foundations for Japan's postwar economic growth were laid in "the second industrial revolution" that took place during the war years. As John Dower cogently argues, when much of the world was struggling to recover from the Depression in the 1930s, Japanese annual GNP growth averaged 5 percent. The expansionary pressures of the wartime economy also brought about fundamental changes in the interweaving of industrial and financial capital (a highly concentrated banking structure), in the character of the small-firm sector of the economy (the emergence of tens of thousands of small and medium-sized enterprises), and in labor-management relations (two central pillars of the Japanese employment system, "life time" employment and wages pegged to seniority for skilled and semiskilled employees). The same can also be said about Japan's planning bureaucracy and the relationship between its banking sector, business enterprises, and the state. Japan's total war also trained millions of skilled workers. And it established numerous technologically sophisticated industries.[49]

Under the auspices of a politically conservative coalition in the postwar period, this system was transformed into an economic growth machine. It consisted of the state bureaucracy, business and finance, and the LDP to the political exclusion of the left and organized labor. Japan's national interest, defined in conservative terms favoring business, focused on macrolevel economic growth as the central political goal to which virtually all other policies were subordinated. Foreign economic policies were integral to this overall strategy. International glory was domesticated and quantified in economic statistics. From the 1950s to the 1970s MITI as the key mover pursued the twin goals of economic growth and transformation. Japan's commercial policy rested on an export strategy that demanded reasonably free access to world markets. Its foreign exchange rate policy hinged on a fixed and undervalued exchange rate for the yen. Foreign capital, foreign managerial control, and "overly competitive" imports were kept out of Japan. Foreign technology was actively sought out and successfully ac-

---

[48] Dower, "Useful War"; Chalmers Johnson, *MITI and the Japanese Miracle* (Stanford, Calif.: Stanford University Press, 1982); T. J. Pempel, "Japanese Foreign Economic Policy: The Domestic Bases for International Behavior," in Katzenstein, *Between Power and Plenty*, pp. 139–90; Thomas Ehrlich Reifer, "The Japanese Phoenix and the Transformation of East Asia: World Economy, Geopolitics, and Asian Regionalism in the Long Twentieth Century" (paper submitted to the thirty-sixth annual meeting of the International Studies Association Conference, Chicago, February 21–25, 1995).

[49] Dower, "Useful War."

quired. And domestic capital was kept within national boundaries, thus avoiding an adverse impact on the balance of payments.[50]

In the 1970s and 1980s, the Japanese economy shifted gear from high to steady economic growth. It adapted to the various shocks of the international economy, above all the two oil shocks, the move to flexible exchange rates, the appreciation of the yen, and fundamental changes in technology and new production regimes. In this process, Japan emerged as a regional growth center, "recycling" its lower-value and labor-intensive industries and trade surplus across Asia through direct foreign investment and aid while it moved up into higher value-added industries through domestic restructuring.

The transnationalization of industry led to a change in Japan's approach to economic cooperation in Asia, away from export promotion and resource procurement to the extension of its politics of productivity beyond national borders. Equally important, it led to an important shift in the balance of power within the conservative coalition, specifically the decline of MITI as the "Economic General Staff" acting in favor of big business. Although the collapse of the LDP rule in 1993 was not directly related to this power shift, in the 1990s Japan's party system finds itself in a long and painful process of reorganization, and the Japanese economy is experiencing its worst recession of the postwar era. Since the politics of productivity has become an article of faith for most Japanese, a new ruling coalition may eventually be built once again around this idea, with big business and finance once again as major components.

Germany's political economy is quasi-corporatist.[51] If the Germans learned any lesson from the disasters that the Nazi regime had wrought, it was to limit the state's role in the economy. In the neoliberal order of the Freiburg school, implemented by the very embodiment of Germany's economic miracle in the 1950s, Economics Minister Ludwig Erhard, it was the "social market economy," not the state, that provided the institutional framework for organizing a capitalism that was both prosperous and humane. The twin achievements of Germany's economic ascendance after 1945—one of the world's foremost export economies and one of the world's leading welfare states—are a consequence of that institutional blueprint.

It is marked by the presence of regulatory norms as a defining aspect of Germany's legalistic culture. These norms connect multiple, segmented,

---

[50] Pempel, "Japanese Foreign Economic Policy," pp. 164–66.
[51] Peter J. Katzenstein, *Policy and Politics in West Germany: The Growth of a Semisovereign State* (Philadelphia: Temple University Press, 1987).

and otherwise loosely linked sets of policies. Through a wide array of parapublic institutions the state is present in many of these policies either as an arena or as an actor. Producer groups and unions are centralized, but less so than in the smaller corporatist states in Northern and Western Europe.[52] Compared to the small states, German state agencies and regulatory rules structure competition either directly or indirectly. Electoral competition among mass political parties and social-movement politics assure that the purpose and instrumentality of the market economy are brought together with the political requirements of the welfare state.

Throughout the 1970s and 1980s Germany adjusted to the various shocks of the international economy in an incremental and gradual fashion: neither the two oil shocks of 1973 and 1979, nor the move to flexible exchange rates and the appreciation of the deutschmark, nor the appearance of low-cost Asian competitors in world markets, nor changes in technology and new production regimes transformed the basic institutional logic of Germany's quasi-corporatist economy; all of them, individually and jointly, led rather to continuous and incremental adaptation.[53] The same was true of the institutional underpinning of German democracy. A stable bloc system of three major political parties alternated power between the forces of center-right and center-left. Reinforced by the constitutional rules organizing electoral power, the logic of coalition government has held German politics to a centrist course throughout the last four decades. A small liberal party, in power with one or the other of the two main parties, always leaned against the wind, pulling its major partner toward the center of the political spectrum. Furthermore, Germany's federal system gave the opposition in the Bundestag, and often the majority party in the Bundesrat, concurrent power in the passing of major legislation.

German unification did not upset the norms and rules of these political arrangements. Germany did not write itself a new constitution. West German institutions and practices were exported wholesale to East Germany. The spectrum of political parties broadened further. It encompassed the successor party of the East German communists as a postcommunist, regionally based party of protest; it enhanced further the political attraction of the Greens as an increasingly responsible party eager to exercise power; and it accommodated small, though growing, nationalist and neoconservative and neo-Nazi forces organizing in autonomous parties or seeking influence in established ones. The privatization of the East

---

[52] Peter J. Katzenstein, *Small States in World Markets: Industrial Policy in Europe* (Ithaca: Cornell University Press, 1985).

[53] Peter J. Katzenstein, ed., *Industry and Politics in Western Germany: Toward the Third Republic* (Ithaca: Cornell University Press, 1989).

German economy, brought about in record time and at record costs, has increased both the regional diversity of the German economy and the involvement of the government in some East German industries and firms, but it has not changed the basic tenets of the social market economy for one simple reason: the productive capacity of the East Germany amounted to considerably less than 10 percent of the West German economy. It is likely that in objective economic terms unification will be accomplished in another decade or two, while Germany will remain politically divided in terms of culture and collective identity for a longer period. But despite political discussions about a supposedly new "middle" or "rim" position, which flared up briefly right after unification, Germany's deep entanglement in and commitment to processes of regional European integration which remain open to a liberal international order has, if anything, grown in the 1990s. This commitment to an open regionalism Germany shares with Japan.

Asian and European Regionalism Compared

The institutional logic that informs Japan's brokered political economy and Germany's social market economy was influenced greatly by the occupation policies of the victorious Allies. It has evolved in an international order defined by the United States. But half a century after the end of World War II it is the institutional effects of the Japanese and German incarnations of capitalism that should merit our primary attention. In the 1990s the most important effects of Japanese and German power in Asia and Europe, and on the world at large, are not gauged adequately by statistics measuring economic might or military prowess. We learn little from the fact that in aggregate terms Japan and Germany are the second and third largest economies in the world, far behind the United States, or that the gap separating them from the United States in military terms is much greater than in economic terms. The magnitude of the Allied victory in 1945 is measured not only in the ascendance of the productive capacities of the former Axis powers but also in the different social purposes and instrumentalities of power with which they seek to shape developments in Asia and Europe and the international milieu more generally.[54]

Japan and Germany engage Asia and Europe differently. Asia's network-style of market integration has made it possible for Japan through eco-

[54] Ian Buruma, "The Pax Axis," *New York Review of Books*, April 25, 1991, pp. 25–28, 38–39; and Hans W. Maull, "Germany and Japan: The New Civilian Powers," *Foreign Affairs* 69 (Winter 1990/91): 91–106, and "Germany and Japan: The Powers to Watch?" (paper prepared for the IPSA Congress, Berlin, August 20–25, 1994).

nomic instrumentalities such as trade, investment, resource diplomacy, and aid to lead "from behind." Richard Doner describes in Chapter 6 how this process works. Mark Selden's analysis in Chapter 9 offers data that point to the existence of Chinese networks that also further Asia's regional integration through market mechanisms. By contrast Germany's deep entanglement in the European Union leads it to play a game of shifting coalitions in Brussels in order to avoid choosing between the United States and Europe. Germany consistently seeks to position itself between Britain and France with their different approaches to European integration. Germany thus wants to both broaden EU membership and deepen the scope and breadth of European integration. Analogously, Japan is interested in furthering market integration in Asia, and in accelerating numerous security dialogues while maintaining its security arrangements with and market access to the United States.[55]

This strategy shapes the economic and political interests that Germany and Japan pursue in Europe and Asia. Japan's relative economic position is best served by "shallow" rules with the WTO as the anchor of the international trade system and marked by the absence of intrusive regional arrangements. The close connection between Japan's commercial diplomacy and corporate strategies is well suited to circumvent entry barriers to and operational obstacles in foreign markets through informal, bilateral channels. Japan does not need deeper trade integration in order to establish market access for Japanese producers.[56] Germany does. Its foreign economic policy is liberal and rule-oriented. And in Germany government and business do not coordinate their strategies as closely as is typical of Japan. More important, intrusive regional arrangements have been a prime political objective of successive German governments. The strong political commitment to the creation of an integrated European polity takes precedence over narrow economic calculations. There is no better illustration of this than the apparent willingness of the German government to sacrifice the unilateral influence Germany exercises over the monetary policies of all European states through the European Monetary System (EMS) on the altar of a to-be-constructed European Monetary Union (EMU).[57]

---

[55] Mike M. Mochizuki, "Japan as an Asia-Pacific Power," in Ross, *East Asia in Transition*, pp. 144–48.

[56] We adapt here Cowhey's analysis of the United States and Japan to a comparison of Japan and Germany. See Cowhey, "Pacific Trade Relations," pp. 2, 10–12 (cited by manuscript pages; Cowhey's essay is forthcoming in Gourevitch, Inoguchi, and Purrington, *US-Japan Relations and International Institutions after the Cold War*).

[57] It is worth noting that the preferences of the government appear to diverge considerably from those of the German public and important segments of German industry and finance.

Allied occupation and the informal empire of the United States have created powerful pressures favoring an open regionalism. But differences in their structural positions in Asia and Europe and differences in the institutional forms of their trading states make Japan and Germany engage Asian and European regional integration on different terms. But whether regional leadership occurs "from behind" in markets or through changing coalitions in political institutions, in one important respect Japan and Germany are remarkably similar. In the regions that affect their political fortunes profoundly, they lead with a light hand.

Historical Alternatives to Leadership with a Light Hand in Open Regions

This was not true in the 1930s and 1940s when Japan and Germany succumbed to the temptation of constructing relatively closed, continental regional orders through brutal wars of aggression. A brief historical comparison is useful for two reasons. It highlights both dramatic changes in how Japan and Germany exercise their power in Asia and Europe while also pointing to some important continuities.

Japan and the Co-Prosperity Sphere

When the empire was in crisis both domestically and internationally, Japanese militarists took over power from the conservative establishment in the 1930s. Compared to Hitler's horrifying vision for a New Order in Europe, however, Hideki Tojo was a bureaucrat without grandiose plans. In fact, long before Tojo came to power, Chinese nationalist resistance had rendered inoperative the original strategy informing the establishment of Manchukuo as part of an autarchic empire that was industrially strong enough to wage total war. The Co-Prosperity Sphere was a phantom conjured up to seek a way out of the mess in which Japan found itself in China. Going to war against the Allies and occupying Southeast Asia was a risky gamble for Tojo at a time when Nazi Germany appeared to be winning the war in Europe. Similarly, the ideology of "Asia for Asians" was almost an afterthought to hide Japan's imperialist opportunism at a time when even Japanese militarists admitted failure in Manchuko's utopian political experiment as a plausible answer to anti-imperialist Chinese nationalism.

Even in the early days of the Greater East Asian war, as Victor Kosch-

---

Whether the German government will prevail politically at home and abroad remains uncertain.

mann argues in Chapter 2, the Co-Prosperity Sphere was thus envisioned as a collection of motley entities: "the leading country" (Japan and its colonies, Korea and Taiwan), "independent countries" (Republic of China [Nanking], Manchukuo, and Thailand), "independent protectorates" (Burma, the Philippines, Java), "directly administered areas" (Malaya), and "colonies" under the sovereignty of outside powers (French Indochina). But the situation was different in China and Southeast Asia. Though Japan managed to pacify Manchuria, south of the Great Wall in China it could control only "points and lines" and never succeeded in defeating Chinese nationalist forces. The puppet Nanking government never enjoyed popular legitimacy. The KMT currency circulated side by side with the Japanese military currency even in areas under Japanese control. And the Japanese rule of terror did not break Chinese resistance.[58]

Japanese rule in Southeast Asia was less ruthless. After all, it was not Southeast Asians but the Americans, British, Dutch, and pro-KMT and pro-communist Chinese who were Japan's enemies. As the second (and in the Philippines, the third) colonial power, Japan had to show that it was better than the Western colonial powers it replaced. Japan thus gave nominal independence to Burma and the Philippines, and the promise of full independence for Indonesia was cut short only by surrender.

Inadvertently, Japan destroyed three major pillars on which colonial Southeast Asia was built. Its swift victory in the early days of the war destroyed the myth of white supremacy, except perhaps in the Philippines. Second, because of the loss of their European and American markets, the export economies that colonial capitalism had built also collapsed. Finally, because of rampant corruption, the forceful conscription of labor and "comfort women," and the forced delivery of rice and other resources, the states Japan relied on for war mobilization also lost whatever legitimacy they had once had.[59]

By the time Japan surrendered, Southeast Asia was in a revolutionary situation, and the time of Japanese occupation marked a watershed in the transition from colonial rule to decolonization. This has contributed greatly to the ambiguity with which postwar Japanese historiography treats Japan's war in and occupation of Southeast Asia. While even Japanese conservatives are defensive about Japan's colonialism in Korea and its war in China, it can be argued with some plausibility, as conservatives often

---

[58] Hideo Kobayashi, *Dai Toa Kyoei Ken no Keisei to Hokai* [The formation and collapse of the Greater East Asia Co-Prosperity Sphere] (Tokyo: Ochanomizu Shobo, 1975).

[59] Benedict Anderson, "Japan, The Light of Asia," in *Southeast Asia in World War II*, ed. Josef Silverstein (New Haven: Yale Southeast Asia Program, 1966).

do, that Japan achieved its war objective in Southeast Asia: Asia for Asians. This historiographical ambiguity was further strengthened by the personal wartime connections that were revived once Japanese returned to the region in the 1950s and early 1960s. Japan's decision to send its first PKO troops to Cambodia must be understood within this ambiguous historical legacy.

The envisioned political economy of the Co-Prosperity Sphere was shaped by the historical experiences of Japan's attempt to build an empire in the early decades of the twentieth century. Japan's regional empire evolved gradually from the mid-1890s to the early 1940s. With the acquisition of Taiwan, Japan introduced an import substitution policy for sugar to improve its balance of payment. The Japanese government placed high import duties on foreign sugar while encouraging sugar production in Taiwan. In Korea, the Japanese government boosted rice production to provide cheaper food for Japanese workers. After the annexation of Manchuria, Japan tried to integrate its empire within a tighter international division of labor that allowed for a significant industrialization of its colonies, especially in Korea and Manchuria. Bringing industry to labor and raw materials, the Japanese government relocated industries and developed the infrastructure in communications, transportation, and hydropower generation. Within this geographically contiguous empire, Japan's second industrialization in the 1930s followed a product-cycle model. In the envisioned political economy of the Co-Prosperity Sphere, Southeast Asia, as the latest addition to the empire, was assigned the role of primary producer (oil, rubber, iron ore, and rice) to the imperial core and semiperiphery—Japan, Korea, and Manchukuo.[60] Although this imperial vision was not achieved in the war years, it was reinvented in the postwar era with the foreign investment of Japanese business, not the military might of the Japanese state, acting as a powerful engine in Asia—placed under U.S. hegemony.

Germany and the New Order

Nazi Germany was a movement regime in search of new frontiers. Its objectives were limitless. In the political conjoining of the demands for "living space" (*Lebensraum*) in the East and reinforced by the doctrine of

---

[60] Bruce Cumings, "The Origins and Development of the Northeast Asian Political Economy: Industrial Sectors, Product Cycles, and Political Consequences," in *The Political Economy of the New Asian Industrialism*, ed. Frederic C. Deyo (Ithaca: Cornell University Press, 1987), pp. 44–83; Reifer, "The Japanese Phoenix."

racial purity, Nazi Germany created a horrifying vision for a New Order in Europe.[61] Hitler was an extraordinary politician who violated and transformed all political boundaries to accomplish his megalomaniac plans. The anticapitalist and antimodern elements that were part of the racial doctrines that informed the foreign policy of the Third Reich were directed against a liberal imperialism deemed inauthentic and inferior. The purification of the German people from harmful influences—and the slave labor, incarceration, and eventual mass murder of political opponents, social "deviants," ethnic minorities, and Jews—all served the purpose of establishing a race that would dominate for a millennium.

Nazi Germany's revolutionary objectives were matched by a strategy of unlimited aggression that started in 1936 in the Rhineland and ended with a two-front war fought to the bitter end. While war with France and Russia for continental domination was in Hitler's mind inevitable, he hoped for a political accommodation with Britain and the United States, whose national interest, in the face of Soviet communism, he hoped would dictate peaceful acceptance of shifts in the continental balance of power rather than the waging of a global war. Yet Hitler misjudged fundamentally British and U.S. politics.

For the Nazis German domination in the East was to be a creative act of destructive colonization: wars of ethnic cleansing, population resettlements of vast tracts of land, annexation (of western Poland), the establishment of apartheid regimes (for example, in central Poland), a rule of terror instituted by a close cooperation of the army, the police, and the courts, and genocide. This policy aimed at reversing the dispersal of seven million ethnic Germans in Eastern Europe, and another seven to ten million in the Soviet Union, the result of many centuries, dating back to the Teutonic Knights, of Habsburg rule and the informal economic, social, and political processes through which German influence had spread. Hitler's plan was to attack Germany's national question at its roots: the political division of a people whose collective identity was believed to be built around ties of blood. The needs of Germany's war economy soon collided with these plans. But their limited implementation in Poland and the brutality with which the German armies fought their eastern campaigns both point in the direction of a policy so irrational that it turned large numbers of people who had welcomed invading German troops into sullen subjects and dogged resistance fighters. Hitler was trapped not only by the geographic vastness of the Soviet Union and the harshness of its winters. He was trapped also by his own murderous ideology.

---

[61] Konrad H. Jarausch, "From Second to Third Reich: The Problem of Continuity in German Foreign Policy," *Central European History* 12 (March 1979): 68–82.

In Western Europe Nazi Germany followed a less murderous policy, inherited from two long-standing, and conflicting, conceptions of how Germany should organize the European economy.[62] One conception, associated with the name of Gustav Stresemann (chancellor and foreign minister of the Weimar Republic), saw Germany as an important part of an informally organized zone of economic influence, intimately linked to the larger international economy. The second conception, associated with Erich Ludendorff (in charge of Germany's military strategy in the latter years of World War I and subsequently a leader of reactionary political movements), placed Germany at the center of an autarchic European bloc, protectionist in its external orientation and hierarchical in its internal organization. During the first part of the twentieth century, in fluid political and economic contexts, the balance shifted, after 1933 decisively so, from the first to the second conception. The cartelized structure of the modern segments of German industry, an uncompetitive agricultural sector in the East, and the exclusionary features of German culture, as well as the changing character of the international economy, all worked in that direction.

The bilateral trade arrangements that Germany fashioned to tie the Eastern European economies firmly to itself expressed a commitment to the principle of bilateralism. It had the effect of creating a system of economic dependence and asymmetric vulnerabilities in the relations between Germany and its smaller neighbors. And these relationships were reinforced by bilateral monetary clearing arrangements.[63] Bilateral ties were trade diverting, not trade creating. And in the 1930s they facilitated the breaking up of the international financial system into different currency blocs. Hence Barry Eichengreen and Jeffrey Frankel conclude that "commercial and financial policies between the wars were driven in the most direct possible sense by international politics."[64]

For Western Europe political economists in Nazi Germany developed ideas for a European Common Market to be organized around Germany. In the 1930s such plans were embraced by many business leaders in Western Europe who were afraid of the economic dislocations and social instabilities that an American economic juggernaut threatened to bring about

---

[62] Robert Edwin Herzstein, *When Nazi Dreams Come True: The Third Reich's Internal Struggle over the Future of Europe after a German Victory: A Look at the Nazi Mentality, 1939–45* (London: Abacus, 1982), pp. 103–28; Volker Berghahn, "German Big Business and the Quest for a European Economic Empire in the Twentieth Century," in *German Big Business and Europe in the Twentieth Century*, ed. Berghahn, Reinhard Neebe, and Jeffrey J. Anderson (Providence, R.I.: Brown University, 1993), pp. 1–38.

[63] John Gerard Ruggie, "Multilateralism: The Anatomy of an Institution," *International Organization* 46 (Summer 1993): 568–69; Albert O. Hirschman, *National Power and the Structure of Foreign Trade* (1945; reprint, Berkeley and Los Angeles: University of California Press, 1980).

[64] Eichengreen and Frankel, "Economic Regionalism," p. 47.

with its new concept of Fordist mass production. And in the 1940s these plans were implemented under extraordinary wartime conditions in the credit and balance of payments structure through which Germany linked Northern and Western Europe to itself as the most efficient means of extracting production capacities essential for its war effort.

An architect by profession, Hitler had plans for Europe as grandiose as the urban renewal plans for Berlin that he was planning to implement in the 1950s. A Europe of 400 million, led by 80 million Germans, would eventually make its bid for global leadership. The rubble to which Berlin, Germany, and Europe were reduced by May 1945 thus contained an idea that was reinvented in the late 1940s and 1950s by an international coalition of Christian Democrats who found themselves in power in France, Germany, and Italy. Shorn of the ideas of a "great regional economy" and the hierarchical international division of labor imposed directly through political means, the idea of a European common market was relaunched under U.S. tutelage. And this regional scheme was closely linked to the multilateral institutions through which the United States succeeded in reorganizing the international relations of the capitalist world after 1945.

In looking to the past we can marvel at the difference between Asian and European regionalism now and then. Japan and Germany were trapped by the allure of subjugating regional empires which they intended to rule directly. Racism and militarism blinded elites in both countries to what was a realistic option then and now: the efficacy, power, and appeal of the indirect rule of trading states serving liberal ends. Japan's and Germany's late conversion to this Anglo-American cause has implanted in the regional politics of Asia and Europe material interests and principles of rule that are likely to prove more enduring than the receding U.S. influence.

The United States as a Regional Power in Asia and Europe

The difference between a bipolar world and a world of regions is symbolized by the bottom row of keys of a touch-tone telephone. The pound sign symbolizes the cold war order divided between East and West, North and South. The asterisk points to the multiple regional overlaps in a global system.[65] In Asia and Europe political interests and ideologies are well entrenched in institutions that defend internationalist against nationalist programs and which value maritime over continental policy options. Yet

---

[65] Donald K. Emmerson, "Organizing the Rim: Asia Pacific Regionalism," *Current History* 93 (December 1994): 435.

Japan in Asia and Germany in Europe are confronting political agendas that are likely to pose the same historic choice in new contexts.

In Asia the questions that now loom large are the social and political consequences of current economic developments.[66] With Japanese firms, driven by market forces, moving their production offshore and transnationalizing their business networks in Asia, Japan fears the social and political instabilities that may derail Asia's current economic dynamism and jeopardize Japanese business operations. With its transition to a socialist market economy and the incorporation of its coastal regions into an economically dynamic maritime Asia, China's success in unleashing productive forces has both eroded the social fabric and undermined the social basis and political legitimacy of a corrupt communist regime.

In Southeast Asia, authoritarian developmentalism, whether in the form of military regimes, civilian one-party systems, or competitive democracies, is likely eventually to confront a participatory crisis if successful economic development continues. South Korea, Taiwan, and perhaps Thailand have fared quite well in coping with this crisis. But with the problem of political succession looming increasingly large, Indonesia may well experience a serious participatory crisis in the near future. If such a crisis were to occur in a time of economic downturn, this could give rise to a long-dormant populism. In brief, political instability in China or Indonesia could threaten an evolving Asian regionalism.

In the case of Germany and Europe the political choice is likely to revolve not so much around issues of economic productivity as questions of collective identity. With huge markets in Western Europe and the United States and with the prospect for risk and high profits in the economies in Central and Eastern Europe that are now making the transition from socialism to capitalism, Germany fears political instability above all. But while Germany looks east, France and Spain look south, to Africa, where they see large populations of potential migrants seeking to escape from poverty and the fervor of Islamic fundamentalism. The EU's eastern enlargement could conceivably pose a challenge to the international and maritime orientation that Europe has maintained since the 1950s. Alternatively, political enlargement toward the east and south might reinforce the transformation of the EU to a global economic institution with a membership, including associate members, of close to one hundred states. How to make a policy of European enlargement compatible with a policy of deepening

---

[66] See also Gerald L. Curtis, ed., *The United States, Japan, and Asia* (New York: W. W. Norton, 1994), and Chalmers Johnson, *Japan: Who Governs?* (New York: W. W. Norton, 1995), pp. 235–63, 281–95. For an earlier decade with a different political and analytical orientation, see Donald C. Hellmann, ed., *China and Japan: A New Balance of Power* (Lexington, Mass.: D. C. Heath, 1976).

the integration process in Europe's core, to which the German government is also fully committed, will be a major challenge for Germany and Europe in the next decade.

In different terms the choices that confront Japan in Asia and Germany in Europe also confront the United States. As a multicultural society and postmodern state, and the remaining military superpower, the United States may eventually emerge as a hub for the spokes of a world of regions. This role does not convey political superpower status. For military power is not readily transformed into many other kinds of power. And U.S. political power has declined too much to be able to dictate political outcomes in different regions of the world. But the distinctiveness of the United States lies in its role as a power involved in several world regions, including Asia and Europe.

The strong support for unilateralism in the Republican party and the U.S. Congress expresses the frustration that, despite its military superiority, the United States can no longer dictate regional political and economic developments. The multilateral impulse in U.S. foreign policy derives from an administration that sees itself entangled through global processes that it no longer controls but to which it must react. While the ebb and flow between unilateralism and multilateralism in U.S. politics is likely to change over time, neither is likely to prevail fully.

Whatever the balance between the two, U.S. foreign policy encounters different structural conditions in its relations with Europe and Asia. The economic links between the United States and Europe, for example, have evolved symmetrically, and NATO's multilateral security arrangements are supported, at least for some time, by the sunk costs of past institution-building. The links between the United States and Asia-Pacific, by contrast, are marked by economic asymmetries and the absence of multilateral security arrangements. But how the United States will, in the end, respond to regionally different structural and institutional incentives on economic and security issues will be shaped decisively by U.S. domestic politics.

Plans for the formation of "mega-regions" point to one possible solution to the problem of translating the distinctive position of the U.S. in a world of regions into political leverage. Regionalism can be a building bloc for a U.S. foreign policy intent on adapting a liberal, multilateral international economic order to changing circumstances.[67] One example would be an Asia-Pacific that institutionalizes further the links between parts of

---

[67] James H. Mittelman, "U.S. Policy on Regionalism: A Strategy for Recapturing Hegemony" (paper prepared for the Second Workshop on the New Regionalism sponsored by the United Nations University World Institute of Development Economics Research, Jerusalem, April 9–11, 1995).

Asia, the United States, and other NAFTA members as well as parts of Central and Latin America.[68] Increasing talks of a new transatlantic treaty system that reformulates the economic, military, and political links between the United States and Europe might become a second example.[69] Such initiatives would constitute, in U.S. eyes, a further evolution in the policy of "enlargement" as the latest installment of a long-standing idealist strain in American foreign policy that seeks to bring the American way of life—business opportunities, democracy, and the individual pursuit of happiness—to all regions and countries of the world.[70]

The battles between the political forces of unilateralism and multilateralism now being fought in the United States are, in different regional and national contexts, also being fought worldwide.[71] They illustrate that regionalism can also be a stumbling bloc for globalization. We have argued in this book that in the case of Asia regionalism is likely to be "open," and Japanese leadership is likely to be "soft." Although this regionalism differs from the regionalism of the 1930s, it is still an important manifestation of a political diversity that resists globalization through the political articulation of distinctive collective identities and divergent political interests. At the end of the twentieth century some choose to describe this process in Spenglerian terms as the decline of the West. We view it instead, in a world of regions, as the arrival of a truly global politics.

[68] President Clinton's call for the creation of a multilateral Pacific Community at the Tokyo summit in July 1993 replaced earlier U.S. calls for the establishment of a bilateral global partnership between the United States and Japan; however, the United States continues to oppose any regional organization in Asia from which it would be excluded. See also Richard J. Ellings, ed., "Americans Speak to APEC: Building a New Order with Asia," *NBR Analysis* 4 (November 1993).

[69] Nathaniel C. Nash, "Is a Trans-Atlantic Pact Coming Down the Pike?" *New York Times*, April 15, 1995, p. 32.

[70] Gebhard Schweigler, "Die USA zwischen Atlantik und Pazifik," *SWP-S401* (Stiftung Wissenschaft und Politik, Forschungsinstitut für Internationale Politik und Sicherheit, Ebenhausen, Germany, October 1994).

[71] Bright and Geyer, "For a Unified History of the World."

Index